WINNER OF

The 1990 Barondess/Lincoln Award

The 1990 Abraham Lincoln Association Award of
Achievement

The 1990 Lincoln Group of New York Award of
Achievement

Abraham Lincoln delivers his second inaugural address from the east portico of the United States Capitol on March 4, 1865. This was the only occasion on which Lincoln was photographed delivering a speech. It is probably the work of noted Washington camera artist Alexander Gardner. When Lincoln was introduced, journalist Noah Brooks reported, "a great burst of applause shook the air," and then the sun broke through overcast skies, flooding "the spectacle with glory and light."

(Photograph: Library of Congress)

LINCOLN ON DEMOCRACY

*His Own Words,
with Essays by
America's Foremost Historians*

❊

Edited and Introduced by
MARIO M. CUOMO
and
Harold Holzer

A Cornelia & Michael Bessie Book
An Imprint of HarperCollins*Publishers*

A hardcover edition of this book was published in 1990 by HarperCollins Publishers.

First HarperPerennial edition published 1991.

The Library of Congress has catalogued the hardcover edition as follows:

Lincoln, Abraham, 1809-1865.
   Lincoln on democracy / edited and introduced by Mario M. Cuomo and Harold Holzer; with essays by Gabor S. Boritt . . . [et al,].—1st ed.
     p.   cm.
   "A Cornelia & Michaèl Bessie book."
   ISBN 0-06-039126-X
   1. Lincoln, Abraham, 1809-1865—Views on democracy.   2. Democracy.
I. Cuomo, Mario Matthew.   II. Holzer, Harold.   III. Boritt, G. S.,
1940- .   IV. Title.
E457.92   1990
973.7'092—dc20   89-46504

ISBN 0-06-098700-6 (pbk.)

To the People of Poland,
for inviting Lincoln abroad

Why should there not be a patient confidence in the ultimate justice of the people? Is there any better, or equal, hope in the world?

Abraham Lincoln
First Inaugural Address
March 4, 1861

Contents

➤➤➤ I ⫷⫷⫷
"THE PEOPLE'S BUSINESS"
Lincoln and the American Dream

1832–1852

≫ II ≪
"All We Have Ever Held Sacred"
Lincoln and Slavery
1854–1857

≫≫ IV ≪≪
"RIGHT MAKES MIGHT"
Lincoln and the Race for President
1859–1860

>>> V <<<
"HOUR OF TRIAL"
Lincoln and Union
1861

→>> VI <<←
"FOREVER FREE"
Lincoln and Liberty

1862–1863

→»» VII «←
"FOR US THE LIVING"
Lincoln and Democracy
1863–1865

Preface

BY MARIO M. CUOMO

In July of 1989—months before democracy blossomed in the capitals of Eastern Europe—the seed for this book on democracy was planted halfway around the world, in the capital of New York State.

I had the privilege of welcoming to Albany a delegation of leading educators from Poland, a nation with a long history of yearning and fighting for liberty, but at the time, only the briefest experience enjoying liberty itself.

They were members of the Teachers' Section of Poland's Solidarity Union, the heroic coalition of working people that had been advocating democratization in the face of rigid, historic repression. They had come to the United States on a tour sponsored by the "Democracy Project," a global exchange program organized by American teachers to foster understanding and opportunity among teaching professionals here and overseas. The American hosts had invited me to greet their Polish colleagues, and I was delighted to accept, hardly realizing that their visit would inspire this volume.

When they arrived in July, I proudly guided the delegation through our recently restored and refurbished "official" governor's office. This is an ornate chamber in the capitol building known as the "Red Room," where many of my predecessors, including Theodore Roosevelt, Franklin D. Roosevelt, and Thomas E. Dewey, all enjoyed working, but which I use only for ceremonial purposes, preferring to work in smaller quarters next door. The Red Room, with its gleaming wood paneling, stately chandeliers, formal drapery, and gilt molding, is an architectural marvel. And it is more. It is a reminder of all that was accomplished by those who came before us, and of our obligation to preserve what they left us and to build upon it for the benefit of those who will come after us.

What better room to display to our Polish visitors, I thought, than a chamber where so much of our own history has taken place, where democratically elected chief executives have administered one of the greatest states in the Union. The Poles seemed to share my enthusiasm for these surroundings. But our visitors had something more on their minds than the highlights of our capitol. There is no shortage of graceful public architecture or lavish interior design in Warsaw. What *had* long been missing there was the guarantee of freedom, not its trappings; the privilege of self-government, not monuments in its honor. What had been lacking there, in those dark days before Poland and her neighbors in Czechoslovakia, Hungary, and East Germany so dramatically threw off the stifling yoke of longtime oppression, was the personal experience of democracy, and with it a meaningful, inspiring credo of freedom and self-determination that could be relied on to illuminate democratization in the future.

Speaking through translators, the Polish teachers asked whether I might help them begin building an archive of great thoughts and writings on democracy, by telling them which American writings on the subject had meant the most to me in my life and career, and might provide similar guidance for them.

I did not need to reflect on the question. My choice of a source was immediate and unequivocal: Abraham Lincoln.

I enjoy joking with people today that I've always admired Lincoln because he's reassuring to politicians like me. He was himself a big, homely-looking politician from a poor family who started off by losing a few elections, yet in the end succeeded brilliantly. Of course, my fascination with Lincoln goes far deeper, and has ever since I can remember. Lincoln was the president who argued that government has a responsibility "to do for the people what . . . they can not . . . do at all, or do so well, for themselves." I have quoted those lines many times to support my own belief that government today is no less obligated. I said so most recently at Gettysburg, on the 126th anniversary of the Gettysburg Address.

For me Lincoln's writing—his unique ability to craft arguments of raw power and breathtaking beauty, to argue with the seamless logic of a great lawyer and the large heart of a great humanitarian—is among the best produced by any American, ever.

I have read Lincoln's words over and over from the volumes of his *Collected Works*. I am always taken by the humor, the pathos, the determination, the compassion that resonate in those words. And by the great ideas.

Above all, the theme that courses through so many letters, speeches, and fragments, the great addresses and the simple greetings alike, is the unyielding commitment to the principles of our Declaration of Independence, what he calls the "sheet anchor" of our democracy. Lincoln talked about the Declaration as a stump campaigner, during the debates with Stephen Douglas, and again as president at Gettysburg. All people were created equal. All people had the right to enjoy the fruits of their own labor. All people shared the right to advance as far as their talents could take them. America, Lincoln believed, was a great society because it promised to "clear a path for all," to provide opportunity for anyone with skill and ambition. When the institution of slavery blocked that road, it was Lincoln who cleared the path. Some have since argued that he did it too slowly, or too halfheartedly, or too imprecisely. But the fact remains that it was he who did it. He saved our democracy. He improved our democracy. And he characterized our democracy in timeless words of inspiration for the benefit of all the generations of Americans who have followed.

Lincoln has been an inspiration to me and to others for as long as his words have been heard or read. He was a man of principle and purpose, who not only forged in war America's new birth of freedom but hallowed it in words as well—unforgettable words that his mind sharpened into steel and his heart softened into an embrace. Words he spoke in Illinois and Washington and Gettysburg . . . calling for the highest sacrifices Americans could make to preserve their unique experiment in government, a system Lincoln believed was "the last best, hope of earth." Lincoln brought the American people to their feet, cheering, crying, and laughing, an unforgettable reminder of the indomitability of the human spirit.

Lincoln was a model of active presidential leadership in crisis. He fought actively to maintain our system of majority rule, then broke the chains that bound four million Americans to slavery, and finally showed us the way to expanding democratic rights.

His presidency was a crucial turning point in the evolution of democracy here, and remains an example to people everywhere who aspire to exercise the full measure of their own freedom.

And so I thought, when my Polish guests asked for my advice on which expressions on democracy were worth reading, that surely Lincoln could now provide such guidance for countries too long denied the basic rights and freedoms Lincoln fought here to preserve. Surely the brilliance of his prose could withstand translation into a foreign tongue. Surely the logic of his arguments would transcend the decades and the distance, as well.

"Do Polish students study Lincoln's words today?" I asked the Polish teachers.

"No," they told me, because Lincoln's words were simply not available in Poland—not since World War II, when freedom went into retreat there. When the Russians marched in, Lincoln went out; not surprising, since his passion for liberty was not suited for coexistence with tyranny. The teachers reported that not a single volume of Lincoln's words in Polish existed in their country. That seemed a tragedy that startled and saddened me, but also a challenge that could be overcome.

Without anything more than a quick, powerful impulse, I promised on the spot to use whatever influences I had, or could produce, to see that Lincoln's words on democracy were promptly translated into Polish and delivered to Poland for the fullest possible use of the Polish people. The teachers instantly greeted the idea with tremendous enthusiasm. Why not bring the volumes over yourself? they asked. I said I would be pleased to consider doing so. And the visit ended.

My promise was, indeed, the product of the moment. But even as the idea flashed into my mind and spilled out in unrehearsed conversation, there was good reason to believe that the promise could be kept. For one thing, New York State has an International Partnership Program, which we created specifically to establish cultural and economic links to foreign nations. With an already established record of outreach to Italy, Israel, Africa, and Spain, we found Lincoln a perfect way to launch a relationship with the reemerging nations of Eastern Europe.

For another thing, I am fortunate in that the professionals in the world of Lincoln scholarship are not strangers to me, and I knew I would be able at least to ask for their help. Harold Holzer, for example, who later became the co-editor of this volume, has worked with me since 1984, and I have known him since 1977. When I was preparing to deliver a speech on Lincoln in Springfield, Illinois, on February 12, 1985, Holzer introduced me to several historians who came to Albany expressly to share their vast knowledge of the subject, and their infectious enthusiasm for it. When they published my remarks in a scholarly journal the following year, I felt, if not one of them, at least one who had been generously received by them, and it made me quite proud.

On the other hand, the promise proved easier to make than to keep. Frankly, I had thought that all we needed to do was select the best existing treasury of Lincoln's expressions on democracy and have it translated. Then I learned something that surprised me even more than the revelation that no such volume existed in Poland. No such volume existed here! Lincoln's unique prose on the subjects of freedom, self-government, and equality had never before been assembled together in English, either.

As it turned out, what might have dampened our enthusiasm for the Polish project instead heightened our enthusiasm for an English-language edition to be published in the United States. Even with Lincoln's *Collected Works* on so many library shelves, the need for access to Lincoln's thoughts on democracy had never been met. *The Collected Works* boasts a 378-page index, but not once does it mention the term "democracy."

And that is how and why this book was born. It is an American book inspired by the Polish people, just as it will be a Polish book devoted to an American—an American who belongs to another time and place, but whose devotion to democracy offers a sublime and universal diplomacy in transcendent prose.

On November 17, 1989, I had the further pleasure of formally announcing the "Lincoln on Democracy" project at an event honoring the chairman of the Solidarity Union, Lech Walesa, during his first visit to the United States. I told this extraordinary freedom fighter: "As you shake off four decades of doctrinaire rigidity, working to open the windows of liberty in every library and schoolroom in Poland—letting the sun shine in on minds too long denied the birthright of free expression—we want to help." *Lincoln on Democracy,* I suggested, constituted "a tangible way to link your struggle for freedom with our historic respect for liberty and democracy." The Polish edition, we proposed, might be only the first of many. Future translations might include Hungarian, Czech, German—even Russian and Chinese—books for every nation where there is a yearning for democracy, a need for the guidance of historical truth, and the absence until now of available materials.

"This makes me feel even more warm," Mr. Walesa said in his reply. "But I don't know if you will be able to keep pace with the other languages, because the line is forming already."

Lincoln's words belong to everyone in that line.

Lincoln brought forth a "new birth of freedom" for America, as he put it at Gettysburg. But it was not just for America that he struggled. It was to save democracy for the world. He knew that by preserving *our* Union, he would guarantee "the civil and religious liberties of mankind in many countries and through many ages."

Early in his presidency, Abraham Lincoln reminded a foreign visitor that Americans "cherish especial sentiments" for "those who, like themselves, have founded their institutions on the principle of the equal rights of men."

We cherish the same sentiments for the new spirit in Poland and all of Eastern Europe. It is our hope that *Lincoln on Democracy* not only will be tangible proof of that affection but will be of genuine and lasting benefit to future generations there, and here as well—an inspiration to further progress on the road to freedom in Eastern Europe, and for us in America an inspiration to renew faith in our own values. No one expressed or exemplified those values better than Abraham Lincoln.

Albany, New York
February 12, 1990

-≫≫ ≪≪-

Introduction

BY HAROLD HOLZER

The Civil War had been over for twenty years, five postwar presidents had come and gone, and one of them had fallen victim to another assassin's bullet by the time poet Walt Whitman looked back, took the measure of history, and pronounced Abraham Lincoln still "the grandest figure yet, on all the crowded canvas of the Nineteenth Century." So he surely seemed to the vast majority of his countrymen, after leading the convulsive struggle to save the Union and destroy slavery.

To Whitman, whose own life and work seemed to one contemporary "imbued with the spirit of democracy," the explanation for Lincoln's unwavering appeal was obvious. He had been "Dear to Democracy, to the very last!" Still, Whitman wondered: "Who knows what the future may decide?"

In fact, the future has not substantially revised Whitman's generous appraisal. For more than a century and a quarter, Lincoln's enduring spirit has animated the American experience. The sobriquets attached to him in life and the tributes that greeted his death have all been fixed in our nomenclature so firmly for so long that they nearly constitute biography. To many, Lincoln is still Honest Abe, Father Abraham, the Great Emancipator, the Martyr of Liberty. His rise from log cabin to White House, from prairie lawyer to master statesman, justifiably remains the most famous and inspiring of all the validations of American opportunity. His face alone, homely yet intrinsically noble—"so awful ugly it becomes beautiful," in Whitman's words—remains indelibly inscribed on the national consciousness, whether one pictures it gazing down from the lofty heights of Mount Rushmore or staring out from

the ubiquitous copper penny. In an increasingly diverse culture, it is a
palpable emblem of our common aspirations, itself an icon of democracy.

Inevitably, the real Lincoln has also become a victim of the irrevers-
ible passage of time. His life has entered the firm embrace of legend.
The real man in large part has been subsumed by the prolonged leaven-
ing of folklore, history, and counter-history. No longer a figure of bright
memory but one of the flickering past, he is partially, perhaps permanently veiled by distance and myth.

Even so, Lincoln may be said to hold his firmest grip on the American imagination by continuing to suggest in vivid and universal terms
the boundless possibilities of a free society. It was not surprising that
one newspaper of his day found him "as American in his fibre as the
granite foundations of our Appalachian range," noting that "the very
noblest impulses, peculiarities and aspirations of our whole people
. . . were more collectively and vividly reproduced in his genial and yet
unswerving nature than in that of any other public man of whom our
chronicles bear record." In short, he was "as indiginous to our soil as
the cranberry crop." To paraphrase Lincoln's own best-known words,
he himself was of, by, and for the people—suggesting both an ideal and
an idea, as historian Earl Schenck Miers expressed it. In both his time
and ours, moreover, Lincoln's America seemed the one place in the
world where a Lincoln was possible; America alone offered the hope,
as Lincoln would tell a regiment of soldiers at the White House, that
"any one of your children may look to come here as my father's child
has." Nowhere else, he suggested, was "presented a government of so
much liberty and equality. To the humblest and poorest amongst us are
held out the highest privileges and positions." By himself attaining the
highest positions, Lincoln convincingly authenticated democratic government itself, government ruled by ballots, he would emphasize, not
bullets.

Lincoln learned the limits and possibilities of American democracy
firsthand, early on, and from the political grass roots up. In the words
of one of his old Illinois law colleagues, he was never "exempt from
bearing his full share of the burden" in the hurly-burly of nineteenth-
century campaigns. As a young man, he served as an election day teller
in one local contest for judge, and as a clerk in village elections for
constable and sheriff, personally recording and tallying votes at rustic

polling places set up inside neighbors' log cabins. In the presidential election of 1840, he got paid $19 to deliver election returns on horseback from a nearby county to the state capital; four years later, he performed the same service, but for $1.40 less. He was alert to potential abuses of democracy, too; once he seized a poll book he believed contained evidence of fraud.

Lincoln also enjoyed the drama of political life. In his day, politics were also grand entertainment. In isolated western towns like Springfield, Illinois, to which he moved at the midway point in his life, the daily tedium was relieved only by the occasional visiting camp show, the state fair, the arrival of a guest orator, a revival meeting, or the perennial fever of local, county, state, and national politics. Townspeople thronged Fourth of July picnics, flagpole raisings, campaign barbecues, stem-winder speeches, and torchlight parades. They stood patiently and listened attentively through marathon debates. Lincoln was present, year in and year out, as both an observer and a participant in this ferment that combined ideas and spectacle. Twenty years before he engaged Stephen A. Douglas in the celebrated senatorial debates of 1858, for example, Lincoln looked on as young Douglas debated an early foe so venomously that his rival grabbed the "Little Giant" in his arms and threatened to thrash him. Douglas did not bother to ask for equal time to reply. He simply bit his opponent on the thumb.

Lincoln's own debates with Douglas would be more dignified, of course, but no less exciting for eyewitnesses. One 1858 encounter featured, according to an eyewitness, martial music, and even floats "profusely decorated with flags and bunting—and filled with young girls—in a number representing every state in the Union." Throughout the campaign, the candidates addressed crowds as large as fifteen thousand—some spectators traveling considerable distances, arriving on horseback, on foot, in covered wagons, and on the railroads, swarming into unshaded fields under blistering summer sun for the sheer pleasure of basking in the spectacle of the heated oratory. And onlookers participated as well, interrupting the debaters with hearty applause, roars of laughter, and occasional catcalls.

This was Lincoln's arena of democracy, and he thrived in it. But beyond its drama, he reveled in its substance. He meticulously researched speeches (for he publicly admitted that he was prone to say "foolish things" when he spoke extemporaneously; once as president, he appeared in a doorway to tell an eager crowd only that it was important in his position "that I should not say foolish things," to which a voice in the audience shot back, "If you can help it."). As a young politician he carefully printed petitions, wrote election notices, drafted and offered legislative bills and resolutions, chaired legislative committees, and twice ran unsuccessfully for speaker of Illinois's lower house.

Nurtured by all this hands-on experience, and honing a gift for precise, powerful writing that elevated him above his contemporaries, Lincoln emerged from the frenzied environment of debates, meetings, lawmaking, and stump oratory as a spellbinding oracle of democratic ideals. No doubt it is difficult for citizens in today's often drab, mindless era of fifteen-second sound bites, glib advertising slogans, and political inarticulation to imagine a time when nearly all politicians could speak coherently in long, complex, compelling sentences; could cultivate serious ideas, argue and debate, convince and convert; could actually write incisive, evocative prose. America's nineteenth-century political culture in fact demanded that its leaders come equipped with both a loud voice and an agile pen, and Lincoln had both. He worked so hard to be heard to the outskirts of his vast audiences, for example, that an eleven-year-old boy who pushed his way to the front of one such crowd remembered gazing up at Lincoln and being doused with "falling mist upon my brow" which, he sympathetically explained, "any speaker will emit addressing an outdoor audience." The boy was forced to keep his red bandanna handkerchief at the ready whenever Lincoln "leaned directly toward me." And yet what Lincoln said seemed so gripping, "I had no thought of changing my position till the last word was said. . . . I had been baptized that day . . . into the faith of him who spoke." As historian Arthur M. Schlesinger, Jr., has pointed out, Lincoln would go on to become "not only our greatest president, but the greatest writer among our presidents."

In all, over the course of more than thirty years in public life, Lincoln composed more than a million known words. He did almost all of his writing himself. Even as president, he employed neither speechwriters nor ghostwriters to place words in his mouth or thoughts in his head. The rare note drafted by a secretary for his signature, the occasional diplomatic letter or Thanksgiving proclamation written at the State Department, were very much the exceptions, not the rule. In his day, in and of itself such creativity was not unusual. What set Lincoln apart from other politicians was not that he crafted his own arguments but that he did so brilliantly and memorably, in resonant words that enriched the political dialogue of his age. Despite almost no formal education, this son of a farmer who could manage little more in the way of writing than to "bunglingly sign his own name" helped forge a new American political idiom, liberating it from the grandiloquent verbiage and ripe classical allusions then common to such oratory, and instead achieving, particularly after 1854, a simple grace, an assurance, a lively wit, an unshakable logic, and at times a soaring beauty. Even his earliest speeches, recalled his longtime law partner, William H. Herndon, were "cool—calm, earnest—sincere, clear." And they were punctuated by dramatic ideas, not dramatic gestures. Eulogizing his hero, Henry Clay, in 1852, Lincoln recalled an eloquence that "did not consist of . . . elegant arrangement of words and sentences; but rather of that deeply earnest and impassioned tone, and manner, which can proceed only from great sincerity and a thorough conviction . . . of the justice and importance of his cause." Taking up Clay's mantle, Lincoln eschewed bombast in favor of sober straightforwardness—although his talent was such that "elegant arrangement of words" was also inevitable. A newspaperman from the town of Galena in northwestern Illinois was particularly impressed with Lincoln's forthright manner. After hearing him speak for the first time, he filed this report in the local newspaper, the *Daily Advertiser:*

> His voice is clear, sonorous and pleasant and he enunciated with distinctness and emphasis. His style of address is earnest, not . . . bombastic, but animated without being furious and impresses one with the fact that he is speaking what he believes. His manner is neither fanciful nor rhetorical but logical. His thoughts are strong thoughts and are strongly jointed together. He is a clear reasoner and has the faculty of making himself clearly understood. He does not leave a vague impression that he has said something worth hearing; the hearer remembers what that something is. The sledge hammer effect of his speech results from the . . . force of the argument of the logician, not the fierce gestures and loud rantings of the demagogue.

Herndon, too, noticed that Lincoln the orator "never beat the air—never sawed space with his hands—never gestured at all"—unless, that is, "he was defending liberty." Then, Herndon remembered, Lincoln would extend his arms as if to "embrace the spirit of that which he so dearly loved."

Walt Whitman was not alone among the authors of his day who saw in Lincoln something unique. Harriet Beecher Stowe, whose own writing had helped awaken the nation to the corrosive evil of slavery, maintained that some of Lincoln's words were "worthy to be inscribed in letters of gold." In Mrs. Stowe's opinion, Lincoln's sincere appeals "to the simple human heart and head" evidenced "a greater power in writing than the most artful devices of rhetoric." Ralph Waldo Emerson believed Lincoln did "more for America than any other American man." Nathaniel Hawthorne, no admirer of his politically, reluctantly conceded after an interview with the President that he would as soon "have Uncle Abe for a ruler as any man." The leading historian of the day, George Bancroft, earmarked the Gettysburg Address for an honored place in an album of *Autograph Leaves of Our Country's Authors.* And to the great novelist Leo Tolstoy, Lincoln "aspired to be divine— and he was." George Washington seemed to the Russian author an ideal American much as Napoleon seemed an ideal Frenchman; but Lincoln "was a humanitarian as broad as the whole world."

Somehow, the critic Edmund Wilson seemed astonished years later to find in Lincoln's prose no evidence of the "folksy and jocular countryman" whom he had pictured "swapping yarns at the village store." Lincoln the writer, instead, seemed "intent, self-controlled, strong in intellect, tenacious of purpose." Added Wilson: "Alone among American presidents, it is possible to imagine Lincoln, grown up in a different milieu, becoming a distinguished writer of a not merely political kind."

Of course, Lincoln's writing was nearly all of a "political kind." And running like a silver thread through the fabric of his public utterances and private letters was the core sentiment that had made admirers of Whitman and others: democracy was dear to *him.* Lincoln not only defended democracy in war, he defined it in words. He was a politician, not a philosopher, but he knew that "whoever moulds public sentiment, goes deeper than he who enacts statutes, or pronounces judicial decisions." Accordingly, in logical and lyrical phrases that still echo in the vocabulary of our literature—"malice toward none," "a house divided," "a new birth of freedom," to name but a few—he vividly extolled the virtues and exposed the vulnerabilities of the American experiment. Lincoln's rhetoric consecrated in high relief the crucible of civil war, and gave majesty to the ethic of majority rule, "the only true sovereign," as Lincoln expressed it, "of a free people." Law partner Herndon, for one, was not surprised by Lincoln's emergence as a spokesman for democracy. On the subjects of "justice, right, liberty, the Government, the Constitution, and the Union," Herndon predicted, "you may all stand aside; he will rule then, and no man can move him—no set of men can do it." Neither could a rebellion. Adding both new urgency and an international vision to the original ideas in the Declaration of Independence—equality and inalienable rights—Lincoln used words as powerfully as he used arms to fight for both the preservation of American democracy and, by purging it of slavery, its purification as well. It must be saved, he insisted, even as it faced what he called its "hour of trial," not only for ourselves but for people everywhere. For America's Declaration of Independence, he believed, offered "liberty, not alone to the people of this country, but hope to the world for all future time," hope that *"all* should have an equal chance."

Most foreign governments, Lincoln pointed out, had been based "on the denial of equal rights of men." Ours, on the other hand, began "by *affirming* those rights"—by giving *"all* a chance." But if it was true that "no man is good enough to govern another man, without that other's consent," how could it be justified that Negro slaves enjoyed no such rights? "When the white man governs himself that is self-government," Lincoln insisted in 1854. "But when he governs himself, and also governs another man . . . that is despotism." In three sentences which he jotted down on a plain piece of paper a few years later, he summarized this philosophy at its purest, most basic level: "As I would not be a *slave,* so I would not be a *master.* This expresses my idea of democracy. Whatever differs from this, to the extent of the difference, is no democracy."

It was the inherent despotism in slavery, Lincoln came to believe, that undermined the promise of American democracy and its potential inspiration for the rest of the world—precious little of which could be called democratic in Lincoln's day. As the Lincoln-era Massachusetts congressman George Boutwell explained it years later, "with the curse of slavery in America there was no hope for republican institutions in other countries. In the presence of slavery, the Declaration of Independence had lost its power; practically, it had become a lie." Slavery,

Lincoln worried in 1854, "enables the enemies of free institutions, with plausibility, to taunt us as hypocrites." Lincoln urged Americans to return to the original idea of their government: "Universal Freedom." Accordingly, inequality was unacceptable, Lincoln declared on another occasion, whether "of the British aristocratic sort or the domestic slavery sort." As he expressed it at the final Lincoln-Douglas debate in 1858, there were "two principles that have stood face to face from the beginning of time, and will ever continue to struggle. The one is the common right of humanity; and the other, the divine right of kings." To Lincoln, the latter represented "the same spirit that says, 'You work and toil and earn bread, and I'll eat it.' No matter in what shape it comes, whether from the mouth of a king . . . or from one race of men . . . enslaving another race, it is the same tyrannical principle." In Lincoln's words, the retrograde institution of slavery was a "danger to liberty itself."

Lincoln was not prepared to let democracy and liberty die of hypocrisy. Americans, he believed, had not only the opportunity but the responsibility to champion democracy everywhere by defending democracy here. Appropriately, when Hungarian freedom fighter Lajos Kossuth began an American tour in 1852, Lincoln was one of several prominent men from his hometown to sign a resolution of support for "the cause of civil and religious liberty" in Europe—not only in Hungary but also in Ireland, Germany, and France. On another occasion, affixing his name to a resolution endorsing a Polish-American engineer for a military commission, Lincoln placed himself in sympathy with the Poles' "bold but unfortunate attempt to regain their national independence." Later, Lincoln extended to the Mexican liberator Benito Juárez, destined soon for temporary exile, his hopes for the "liberty of . . . your government, and its people." As president, Lincoln could ill afford to give more than encouragement to democratic struggles in other countries, faced as he was with the dissolution of his own. He would instead let American democracy speak for itself; Lincoln came to represent not just words but democracy functioning under siege, or as historian Mark E. Neely, Jr., has put it, democracy in action. Under Lincoln the Civil War became a "People's contest" to "maintain the capacity of man for self government." If "our enemies succeed," he warned, "every form of human right is endangered." But if "all lovers of liberty everywhere" joined in sympathy, he predicted, "we shall not only have saved the Union; but we shall have so saved it, as to make, and to keep it, forever worthy of the saving . . . so saved it that the succeeding millions of free happy people, the world over, shall rise up, and call us blessed, to the latest generations."

Inevitably, the people's contest began exerting an ironic impact on the people's government it was meant to preserve. As the war progressed, testing the limits of acceptable dissent in the midst of constitutional crisis, exposing raw, unprecedented tensions between democratic rights and national survival, Lincoln found himself cleaving to the "necessity" of saving the country first, in order to preserve democracy in the future. "Must a government . . . be too *strong* for the liberties of its own people, or too *weak* to maintain its own existence?" he challenged those who questioned his assumption of executive authority. By law, Lincoln would point out, "life *and* limb must be protected; yet often a limb must be amputated to save a life; but a life," he added, "is never wisely given to save a limb." It was possible, Lincoln warned, to save the Constitution and yet lose the nation. Lincoln was prepared to do all within his power—and, some charged, beyond it—to fight "the attempt to overthrow this government, which was built upon the foundation of human rights."

Confident in the ultimate justice of the people, but aware that perfect liberty was a perpetual challenge, he was comfortable with what historians have called the limits of the possible. "In relation to the principle that all men are created equal," he said in 1858, "let it be as nearly reached as we can." What was just and what was attainable was, for much of Lincoln's presidency, separated by the wide chasm of necessity. Most ironic of all, perhaps, there were even those Americans who would see a threat to liberty in Lincoln's greatest effort to extend liberty, the Emancipation Proclamation. Some Americans would hail the Proclamation as a second Declaration of Independence. But in New York City, Maria Lydig, the wife of a local judge, angrily greeted its announcement by noting in her diary: "We are under a worse despotism than they have in France or Russia. There is no law but the despotic will of Abe Lincoln." As the selections in this treasury demonstrate, Lincoln probed all these vexing issues with an unwavering "firmness in the right," with persuasiveness, statesmanship, common sense, vision, and a mastery of the language that at times approached poetry.

He reached his rhetorical zenith at Gettysburg, a Pennsylvania village of bullet-scarred stone houses where thousands had given their lives in one of the bloodiest battles ever fought anywhere on earth. A year earlier, Lincoln had called on his fellow countrymen to "disenthrall ourselves"—to "think anew, and act anew"—in order to "save our country." He had challenged Americans to "rise with the occasion." For Lincoln, that occasion was Gettysburg. Here he searched eloquently for a rationale for the enormous sacrifice, and found it in the promise of democracy. But, as he reminded his audience, the Declaration of Independence, and its guarantees of liberty and equality, still represented only a "proposition" in the eyes of the world. In "testing" whether America could survive, the Union would decide for the entire world "whether . . . any nation so conceived and so dedicated, can long endure." Government of, by, and for the people had to be rescued here to remain viable elsewhere.

Seventeen months later, the "new birth of freedom" was painfully accomplished, with Lincoln its final, and most widely mourned, casualty. Looking on incredulously as the entire city of New York cloaked itself in funeral black, British newspaper correspondent Edwin L. Godkin expressed astonishment at the universal outpouring of grief. Deaths of European leaders, he pointed out, elicited little more there than polite mourning in "the court circles," and among "those who would like to belong to it." In New York in that spring of 1865, every "little huxter or cobbler" was decorating his door with black muslin, every laborer was wearing crape on his arm or a mourning rosette on his collar. "Whatever be the faults of democratic institutions," he reported, "they at least make the meanest of the people feel themselves a part of the nation, entitled to share in its sorrows and its joys as much as its proudest and highest." No dead king, he admitted, "had ever half as many tears shed over his bier as have fallen on Abraham Lincoln's—the Illinois attorney, the ex-rail-splitter, the ex-flatboatman."

Among the tributes that began pouring into Washington after Lincoln's death were the condolences of the very monarchs whose rule the President had so vigorously questioned. To be sure, some of these expressions were obligatory and perfunctory, like the letter from Tsarist Russia acknowledging that Lincoln had restored the Union and with it, "that concord which is the source of its power and of its prosperity." More heartfelt was the message from the Polish members of the Prussian chamber of deputies—Poland itself had for a time disappeared from the world map—lauding Lincoln as "a victim, a martyr, of the great cause" of liberty. And from Italy, Giuseppe Garibaldi eulogized Lincoln as the "heir of the aspirations of Christ and of John Brown," predicting he "would pass to posterity" with a fame "more enviable than any crown or any human treasure."

Even in totalitarian France, liberals undertook to mint a memorial medal in Lincoln's honor. Although the government of Napoleon III tried to bar the tribute, official France surprisingly conceded that "Mr. Lincoln . . . passed through the most afflicting trials that could befall a government founded on liberty." Eventually, the medal was struck in Switzerland in defiance of the French government wishes, funded by public donations from Lincoln's French admirers. Transmitting a finished medal—whose inscription proclaimed that Lincoln had "Saved the Republic/Without Veiling the Statue of Liberty"—the liberals, who included novelist Victor Hugo, advised Mrs. Lincoln: "If France had the freedom enjoyed by republican America, not thousands, but millions among us would have been counted as admirers."

While the Civil War raged, there had been little support for Lincoln from the British government, either. The rebellion had interrupted the cotton trade, plunging English mills into idleness and leaving workers unemployed. Nonetheless, workingmen from South London would now send a touching letter to Lincoln's widow, assuring her that the "hero martyr of liberty and right" had been considered "one of themselves, fighting the battle of freedom for all lands." Similar, if more muted expressions of grief and appreciation arrived from Parliament. And Queen Victoria herself, still very much in mourning for her own husband, wrote a touching condolence letter to Mrs. Lincoln. Observed the English dramatist Tom Taylor—who had written the play Lincoln was watching when he was assassinated—"The Old World and The New, from sea to sea,/Utter one voice of sympathy and shame!" for "this rail-splitter, a true-born king of men."

Considering this phenomenon, Walt Whitman was astounded by the "spectacle of all the kings and queens and emperors of the earth" now "sending tributes of condolence and sorrow in memory of one raised through the commonest average of life." The man who had died for democracy now seemed in retrospect to have lived for it as well, for both American and world liberty, and his personal and political example had become a potent, perhaps even frightening symbol of democracy's possibilities to working people and royal courts alike.

Nearly a century later, the American composer Aaron Copland

would recall an incident that confirmed the enduring strength of that symbol. In the 1950s Copland traveled to Venezuela to conduct a performance of his *Lincoln Portrait*, an orchestral piece in which a narrator speaks Lincoln's most famous words against a background of inspirational music. "To everybody's surprise," Copland told a newspaper reporter, "the reigning dictator, who had rarely dared to be seen in public, arrived at the last possible moment," joining six thousand spectators jammed into an outdoor stadium. The narrator that evening was the fiery Venezuelan actress Juana Sujo. When she spoke the final words of the piece—"government of the people, by the people—*por el pueblo y para el pueblo*—shall not perish from the earth"—the audience responded by jumping to its feet and shouting and cheering so vociferously that even Copland was unable to hear the end of the piece.

"It was not long after that the dictator was deposed and fled from the country," Copland remembered. "I was later told by an American foreign service officer that the *Lincoln Portrait* was credited with having inspired the first public demonstration against him. That, in effect, it had started a revolution."

As the Copland recollection so vividly suggests—as the Solidarity Teachers' enthusiasm for this book confirms—Lincoln's written legacy continues to transcend both time and place, holding relevance for today as well as tomorrow. *"Writing,"* as Lincoln understood, ". . . is the great invention of the world . . . very great in enabling us to converse with the dead, the absent, and the unborn, at all distances of time and space." As this anthology reminds us, Lincoln's writings on democracy continue to vivify this promise. And the promise, just as Lincoln understood early and well, extends not just to Americans but to people everywhere thirsting for what he aptly described in a temperance address as the "sorrow quenching draughts of perfect liberty." What Lincoln said once of the nation's founders might as easily be said today of his own rich and hitherto uncollected speeches and writings on democracy. He "grasped not only the whole race of men then living," but "reached forward and seized upon the farthest posterity." He "erected a beacon to guide" his "children and . . . children's children, and the countless myriads who should inhabit the earth in other ages."

No American president, no American writer was ever more "Dear to democracy."

⇶ ⪻

A Note on the Lincoln Texts . . .

With but a handful of exceptions, all the 140 Lincoln texts presented on the following pages—speeches, letters, remarks, greetings, replies, drafts, and fragments—come from texts published in *The Collected Works of Abraham Lincoln,* eight volumes issued by Rutgers University Press (1953–1955) and ably edited by a team headed by Roy P. Basler, who died while *Lincoln on Democracy* was in preparation. We are grateful to the Press for granting us permission to adapt these definitive versions.

When relevant to the theme of democracy, we present the full texts of speeches and letters. In other cases, we present appropriate extracts—especially of some of the very lengthy pre-presidential addresses. We identify each such selection as "from a speech" or "from a letter," and to indicate missing sections of text, use a series of dots. Ellipses are avoided whenever possible—except for those cases in which an extract begins in the middle of a paragraph. Excerpting can be a difficult task, and in the case of a writer as cogent as Lincoln, a presumptuous one. All our consulting scholars, together with the editors, have tried to ensure that the texts flow naturally, while focusing on the issues of liberty, equality, and self-determination.

Whenever possible, Basler's texts followed Lincoln's own manuscript copies of his letters and speeches. But none of Lincoln's pre-presidential addresses survive in his own hand. Typically, such manuscripts would be taken to newspaper offices to be set in type for the next day's editions, and then simply thrown away. In such cases we are compelled to rely on these newspaper reprints.

In still other instances—principally Lincoln's impromptu remarks as president-elect and president—no handwritten texts may ever have existed. Here, on-the-scene newspaper correspondents transcribed the words, often peppering them with parenthetical indications of crowd reaction, thus providing us rare and evocative glimpses into the way in which audiences of his own day received Lincoln's spoken words. We preserve these inserted cheers and applause intact.

Finally, there is the special case of the Lincoln-Douglas Debates, every syllable of which was duly reported in the press of the day. Later, when Lincoln decided to assemble these reprints in a scrapbook, and submit it for publication as a book, the question arose as to which newspaper reprints to use. By mutual consent, Douglas's side of the debate was taken from the pro-Democratic Chicago *Times,* and Lincoln's from the pro-Republican Chicago *Press & Tribune.* Scholars have called into question the absolute reliability of these accounts, and a glimpse at the opposition *Democratic* version of Lincoln's words, or the *Republican* version of Douglas's, confirms that the friendly newspapers did provide some friendly editing to the candidate of their choice. Nonetheless, these are the only records we have, and like Lincoln and Basler before us, we have relied exclusively on the *Press & Tribune*'s accounts of Lincoln's performance in the debates.

Basler decided—and we have followed suit—to simplify some of Lincoln's curious punctuation, but to retain his individualistic spelling, even when archaic or simply incorrect. For example, Lincoln ended many sentences with a long dash instead of a period, and he sometimes used two periods after initials or abbreviations. We have reverted to the standard period to make the texts easier to read. On the other hand, while Lincoln was an overindulgent friend of commas, we have not endeavored to correct his generous use of them. And while he employed capitalization with haphazard inconsistency, we have not imposed uniformity. Likewise, Lincoln's nonuniform spelling (he spelled the same word in different ways at different times), as well as his devotion to archaic or simply personalized spellings—"criticise," "labour," "burthen," "defence," "indorsements," "contemn," and "verry," to name but a few—has been retained here, without the use of the warning sign *sic,* except in the most egregious cases, where readers might be confused without such clarification. However, in cases where crumbling manuscripts are missing an occasional word, or where period newspaper transcriptions omit key words, we have adopted Basler's generally accepted use of bracketed inserts.

Since Basler's volumes first appeared, further scholarship inevitably revealed a few errors in *The Collected Works,* and we have adopted these corrections where appropriate. For example, Basler published a period newspaper copy of the famous House Divided speech, and until historians George B. Forgie and Don E. Fehrenbacher examined it closely twenty years later, no one seemed to realize that an entire paragraph had been transposed to a later portion of the text, rendering several intervening paragraphs all but unintelligble. We have used Dr. Fehrenbacher's revised text for the House Divided speech printed here.

Text selection was not the only problem the editors confronted. Ever since collections of Lincoln writings have appeared—and the first appeared last century—editors have been properly reluctant to insert bracketed, explanatory notes within Lincoln's texts. *The Collected Works* presented all such explanations in tiny footnotes below each selection. We have chosen—prudently and sparingly, we hope—to present some crucial information within the body of Lincoln's own writings. This was not an easy decision, but after much thought it was determined that most American and surely all foreign readers might not otherwise be able to identify many of the issues and people Lincoln sometimes cited rather breezily in many speeches and letters. A footnote solution was rejected as too unwieldy, and end notes were ruled out for the same reason. So we endeavored to identify, as briefly as possible, contemporaries to whom Lincoln referred only by last name (sometimes only by first name!), as well as the more obscure issues he occasionally mentioned. Such an approach seemed especially justified for those writings of which we present only excerpts. As often as possible, we presented our explanations in introductory annotations, so as to avoid interruptions of the texts themselves. But sometimes we judged the insertion of bracketed information unavoidable, even vital.

What is remarkable is how little such explanation and introduction Lincoln's writings seem to require, even a century and a quarter after his last words were written. Though they focus almost exclusively on the issues confronting mid-nineteenth-century America, they feature expressions of the heart and mind that transcend their place and time. The editors' task, as a result, has been happily limited. Lincoln still speaks directly to us, and requires very little help to do so effectively and meaningfully.

. . . And the Introductory Essays

Each of the seven chronologically arranged sections of Lincoln materials that follows is preceded by an introductory essay by a different Lincoln scholar. Each essayist is a widely recognized and respected historian, and of course each brings his own sensibilities to the period he covers. Thus, the introductions reflect varying, although not incompatible interpretations of the Civil War and Lincoln himself.

The editors believe that such diversity is an asset to this anthology. The study of Abraham Lincoln, after all, much like democracy itself, is not fixed: it is a dynamic process of examination, interpretation, and analysis. When the best historians in the field are asked to contemplate the subject of Lincoln on democracy, and focus their attention on specific periods of Lincoln's career, the results are bound to differ, intrigue, and provoke. At least we hope so.

➵ ⋙ ⋘

"NOT MUCH OF ME"

Lincoln's "Autobiography," Age 50

[DECEMBER 20, 1859]

Abraham Lincoln wrote this "little sketch" of his first fifty years just five months before his nomination to the presidency. He composed it as a research tool for a newspaper feature designed to introduce the still largely unknown western politician to the East. "There is not much of it," Lincoln apologized in a cover letter, "for the reason, I suppose, that there is not much of me." Predictably, it was sumptuously embellished when adapted by the Chester County (Pennsylvania) Times *on February 11, 1860, even though Lincoln wanted something "modest" that did not "go beyond the materials." The article was widely reprinted in other pro-Republican organs. But it is the original Lincoln text that remains a principal source of our knowledge about the guardedly private public figure his own law partner complained was "the most shut-mouthed man I knew." In truth, the sketch rarely travels beyond perfunctory facts toward the realm of insight, and it ends with the vaguest of personal descriptions of the face that would soon become the most recognizable in America. Although he authored more than a million words altogether, Lincoln would produce nothing further about himself except for a slightly longer account of his early days written in 1860 as the basis of a campaign biography. Even though democracy could claim no more convincing validation than his own rise, Lincoln the writer hardly ever illuminated Lincoln the man. Where Lincoln is concerned, history comes no closer to autobiography than this.*

I was born Feb. 12, 1809, in Hardin County, Kentucky. My parents were both born in Virginia, of undistinguished families—second families, perhaps I should say. My mother, who died in my tenth year, was of a family of the name of Hanks, some of whom now reside in Adams, and others in Macon counties, Illinois. My paternal grandfather, Abraham Lincoln, emigrated from Rockingham County, Virginia, to Kentucky, about 1781 or 2, where, a year or two later, he was killed by indians, not in battle, but by stealth, when he was laboring to open a farm in the forest. His ancestors, who were quakers, went to Virginia from Berks County, Pennsylvania. An effort to identify them with the New-England family of the same name ended in nothing more definite, than a similarity of Christian names in both families, such as Enoch, Levi, Mordecai, Solomon, Abraham, and the like.

My father, at the death of his father, was but six years of age; and he grew up, litterally without education. He removed from Kentucky to what is now Spencer county, Indiana, in my eighth year. We reached our new home about the time the State came in the Union. It was a wild region, with many bears and other wild animals still in the woods. There I grew up. There were some schools, so called; but no qualification was ever required of a teacher, beyond *"readin, writin, and cipherin,"* to the Rule of Three. If a straggler supposed to understand latin, happened to sojourn in the neighborhood, he was looked upon as a wizzard. There was absolutely nothing to excite ambition for education. Of course when I came of age I did not know much. Still somehow, I could read, write, and cipher to the Rule of Three; but that was all. I have not been to school since. The little advance I now have upon this store of education, I have picked up from time to time under the pressure of necessity.

I was raised to farm work, which I continued till I was twenty two. At twenty one I came to Illinois, and passed the first year in Illinois—Macon county. Then I got to New-Salem, (at that time in Sangamon, now in Menard county[)], where I remained a year as a sort of Clerk in a store. Then came the Black-Hawk war; and I was elected a Captain of Volunteers—a success which gave me more pleasure than any I have had since. I went the campaign, was elated, ran for the Legislature the same year (1832) and was beaten—the only time I have been beaten by the people. The next, and three succeeding biennial elections, I was elected to the Legislature. I was not a candidate afterwards. During this Legislative period I had studied law, and removed to Springfield to practice it. In 1846 I was once elected to the lower House of Congress. Was not a candidate for re-election. From 1849 to 1854, both inclusive, practiced law more assiduously than ever before. Always a whig in politics, and generally on the whig electoral tickets, making active canvasses. I was losing interest in politics, when the repeal of the Missouri Compromise aroused me again. What I have done since then is pretty well known.

If any personal description of me is thought desirable, it may be said,

I am, in height, six feet, four inches, nearly; lean in flesh, weighing, on an average, one hundred and eighty pounds; dark complexion, with coarse black hair, and grey eyes—no other marks or brands recollected. Yours very truly

A. LINCOLN

⟫ I ⟪

"THE PEOPLE'S BUSINESS"
Lincoln and the American Dream
1832–1852

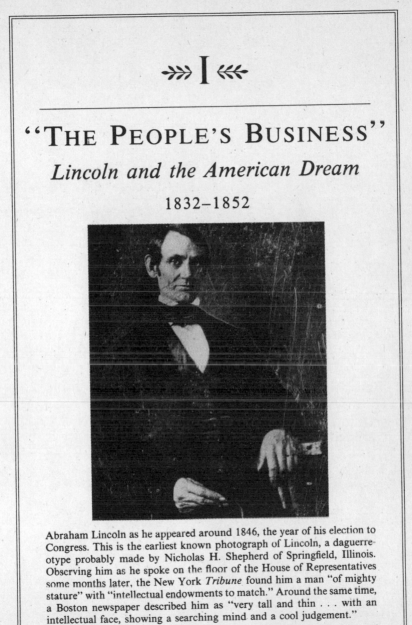

Abraham Lincoln as he appeared around 1846, the year of his election to Congress. This is the earliest known photograph of Lincoln, a daguerreotype probably made by Nicholas H. Shepherd of Springfield, Illinois. Observing him as he spoke on the floor of the House of Representatives some months later, the New York *Tribune* found him a man "of mighty stature" with "intellectual endowments to match." Around the same time, a Boston newspaper described him as "very tall and thin . . . with an intellectual face, showing a searching mind and a cool judgement."

(Photograph: Library of Congress)

Introduction

BY GABOR S. BORITT

It was planting time in the Kentucky valley where the Lincoln clan made its home. Children had to learn work very young. Little Abraham was starting his lessons, walking behind his father, dropping pumpkin seeds into the hills made by Thomas Lincoln's crude hoe. Two seeds into every second corn hill, in every second row. Then the Sabbath came and with it a great cloudburst up on the hills above them. It did not rain in their valley, but the water came swirling down from the hills, washing away corn, pumpkin, and topsoil. The *reward of their labors* was lost. This was the earliest memory, earliest pain the grown man Lincoln could recall. Nearly half a century later he told another Kentuckian, abolitionist Cassius Clay: "I always thought the man who made the corn should eat the corn."

Much happened to the United States during that half century, from the time of the cloudburst on the Knob Creek farm during the presidency of James Madison to the time of Lincoln. But amid it all, clearly the chief business for this strange and beautiful people called Americans was to rise up and grow, as James M. McPherson explained in his *Battle Cry of Freedom.* And grow the Americans did, as never before or since in their history. In the twentieth century much of this phenomenon is called economic development.

The territory of the United States quadrupled between 1803 and 1853. The thin strip of states along the Atlantic coast grew to a great land that stretched to the Pacific. The population of the country moved westward, more than quadrupled, and, incidentally, grew more diverse. The gross national product, to use another modern term, expanded almost seven times. Countryfolk, like Lincoln, moved to urban places at a fast pace. The majority, who stayed on the land, in turn increasingly entered a market economy. The rise in living standards surpassed imagination—and also the levels in much of the world.

Yet even as the average income of Americans went up tremendously, the real wages of workers may have gone up only half as much. A price paid for better life under capitalism was greater inequality. That the environment needed protection was quite beyond the culture's ken. Indians lost outright in this brave new world, most blacks endured as slaves, and modern eyes judge the place women had in society as sadly unequal. Violence erupted periodically, taking fuel from class, ethnic, and finally sectional tensions. And yet an ever-growing number of European immigrants testified that America provided rich opportunities for those whom Lincoln called "the many poor." Or, as he put it in 1838, America was "the fairest portion of the earth." It also had "a degree of political freedom," he added four years later, "far exceeding" that of other nations. Nearly all understood that the two elements were related and that the contrast to much of old Europe was stark.

The political worlds of the United States revolved around issues generated by growing pains. Some historians, like Richard Hofstadter, saw the party systems of Lincoln's adult lifetime—Democrats versus Whigs and later Republicans—in terms of consensus, arguing that Americans, their many battles notwithstanding, held fundamental matters largely in common. Other scholars, led by J. G. A. Pocock and Gordon Wood, saw sharply competing values in America, which they called republicanism and liberalism. (The first emphasized the commonweal at the expense of individual pursuits. The second argued that the common good was best reached through the efforts of individuals seeking their own good.) Still other historians, often of older schools, understood matters in terms of sectional, class, or ethnocultural divisions.

If we ignore certain idiosyncratic alignments, it might be better not to conceive of the sharp political wars of those antebellum decades, in which battles about economic issues were paramount, as between the haves and have-nots, as Marx diagnosed them for Romanticism's *Alle Menschen*" (All Mankind). The conflict then can be visualized as mostly between haves who wanted to have a little more and other haves who wanted much more and, without fully recognizing the fact, were willing to change the American way of life, indeed the ways of millennia, in order to get it. The former were the diligent and the persevering, yet a large majority of them fit poorly into the developing world and so were often past-directed; the latter were the intrepid and the enterprising individualists, the "adventurers in quest of advancement," as James Fenimore Cooper indicted them, together with capitalism, in *Home as Found.* One group tended to oppose public power, the other to support it. One tended to see matters in local terms, the other in national and at times even international ones. Many a heart pulled both ways; at moments, perhaps, Lincoln's did too. All the same, he sided with the second group and led it to victory as president.

That he opted for the Whig (and later Republican) vision over that of the Democrats is not surprising. He was born to "the most humble walks of life"; but he would rise. And if America would reach unmatched growth during his lifetime, Lincoln's personal growth would be even greater: from the illiteracy of his parents to the Gettysburg Address and the second inaugural, from the log cabin to the White House. So he became a Whig.

The fundamental requirement of economic development was to create what historian George Rogers Taylor called a "transportation revolution." The nation had to build good roads, canals, railroads; dredge rivers and harbors; invent the steamboat, the telegraph, and much more; in short, make great "internal improvements," as Americans spoke of it. These went hand in hand with the creation of credit and a sound currency through banks, however much people misunderstood and suspected them. In a related policy, tariff protection was to encourage native industries. Taxes, however hateful, would also be needed and had to be made just. Forging ahead thus, changing the nation, letting and making it grow, also required education and a temperate society, whether in terms of abstaining from toxic substances like alcohol or extremist politics that some feared might even lead to dictators and degenerate into mob violence or war. Finally, concomitant to it all there had to be political liberty. Marxists describe this world view as bourgeois.

And so we may begin to understand the words of the young Lincoln before slavery came to dominate politics. He started public life by proposing the improvement of river roads in his home county and by supporting local education, and ended in the White House signing legislation to build the Pacific railroad and to establish the foundations for publicly supported universities. He fought for the creation and continued existence of the state bank in early Illinois, while also demanding centralized banking for the entire country. In the presidency he played a crucial part in pushing Congress to adopt a national banking system. He supported the tariff as another national policy that would help development, however rudimentarily he and his age understood this modern concept. He read and used the writings of the best American economists though his own language had to be aimed at a dominantly farming constituency. In the White House he helped make protectionism an American cornerstone that lasted too long into the next century.

Lincoln also learned to use fiscal policy, painful as that was. Americans, born as a nation with antitax slogans on their lips, may have disliked having the government reach into their pocketbooks more than most other folks did. But in the face of great public outcry, Lincoln demanded taxes in young Illinois to save its failing internal improvement system. All along he groped in the direction of what we call progressive taxation. In the White House he signed such legislation into law.

Whig and later Republican policies did not always benefit the people. Lincoln championed most forcefully his state's internal improvement system but it went utterly bankrupt. Though he liked equality, some got richer much faster than others. Creating a more prosperous new world also caused dislocations and suffering. And yet, few could doubt that Lincoln's heart was with the people. He seemed to have manure on his boots even when it was not there. He groped to lead America, as best he knew how, toward a world in which all could aspire to a full, good, and ever-increasing *reward of their labors,* so that they might have the opportunity to rise in life. In this world many would rise individually, and nearly all would rise collectively, even if also less rapidly.

Political liberty went in tandem with the right to rise. Lincoln often spoke his finest words on liberty's behalf, even if in the early part of his public life, while absorbed with economics, Lincoln did not devote the bulk of his energies to that cause. For, on the whole, his youthful exaggerations notwithstanding, liberty seemed safe at home. He de-

nounced as a "tyrant" the "slavery" of alcohol, and decried mob law
with equal strength. Against violence he preached "reverence for the
laws." He wished to elevate such emotions to "the *political religion* of
the nation."

Though he took patriotic pride in the American experiment and *"the
capability of a people to govern themselves,"* sometimes in words that
to latter-day ears could even sound shrill, he opposed the Mexican War.
President James K. Polk, who started that war, he compared to kings
of old Europe, and chastised him with the fervor of an Old Testament
prophet: "The blood of this war, like the blood of Abel, is crying to
Heaven against him." Yet not many years later, in a different context
and a calmer mood, he added: "The presidency . . . is no bed of roses."

Looking abroad, toward countries where much less liberty existed,
Lincoln thought people should "rise up." The idea of self-government
he hoped would thus "liberate the world." He seemed to believe, all too
optimistically, that liberty and nationalism would go comfortably hand
in hand. So Lincoln admired the Poles who rose against the Russians,
the Greeks who defied the Turks, and the South Americans who over-
threw Spanish rule. He sympathized with Irish aspirations against the
British. And the European revolutions of 1848 captured his special
attention. He applauded the Germans and the French who rose against
their native "yoke of despotism." In Congress, he voted for economic
concessions for the latter to "afford some aid to the spirit of liberty."
When the most persistent of those '48 struggles, that of the Hungarians,
at last was defeated through the combined might of Austria and Russia,
Lincoln helped organize a protest meeting in his small hometown and
authored resolutions against the "despot" tsar. He was profoundly
patriotic, but one suspects that he really spoke about himself when
describing his early political hero, Kentucky's Senator Henry Clay, as
a man who "loved his country partly because it was his own country,
but mostly because it was a free country."

One liberty he did not stand up for was that of the African-American.
Nor was this a somewhat abstract question about a faraway land, but
a very real one right at home. He stayed silent not because of a weak
sense of justice, or a strong sense of racism, but because he learned to
practice the art of the possible. In fact, early in his career, in the Illinois
legislature, he inveighed against slavery as "founded on both injustice
and bad policy." But he could persuade only five colleagues, out of

eighty-two, to vote with him, and only one to dare explain the dissenting votes. (One is reminded of the Lincoln who in 1834 voted for tax privileges for new settlers in a minority of six, against forty-one nays, and who in 1836 called for women's suffrage in a matter-of-fact way, though the United States would not give the vote to women until 1920.) It took some years for Lincoln to learn to speak up for what was attainable. But the pragmatism that he thus acquired, and the idealism that he continued to keep, grew and combined into one of his great strengths.

Perhaps the most poignant private letter Lincoln penned on a public issue during this silent period dealt in part with slavery. In 1841, he recounted a recent riverboat trip he had taken in Kentucky. Lincoln focused on a dozen slaves who were also on board:

> They were chained six and six together. A small iron clevis was around the left wrist of each, and this fastened to the main chain by a shorter one at a convenient distance from, the others; so that the negroes were strung together precisely like so many fish upon a trot-line. In this condition they were being separated forever from the scenes of their childhood, their friends, their fathers and mothers, and brothers and sisters, and many of them, from their wives and children, and going into perpetual slavery. . . .

Yet the point of the heartrending tale was that these poor people acted happy, played the fiddle, danced, cracked jokes. "How true it is that 'God tempers the wind to the shorn lamb,' or in other words, that He renders the worst of human conditions tolerable, while He permits the best, to be nothing better than tolerable."

When nothing effective could be done about even a great misery, Lincoln would do nothing. He would wait for a better day. Nearly fourteen years passed before he would admit, openly or perhaps even to himself, how miserable that sight of human beings chained like "fish upon a trot-line" had made him. By then Lincoln knew he could act with a chance of success. And he would act. He began on the long road toward an America where blacks, too, would receive the *reward of their labors,* where they, too, might run in "the race of life." Americans are still walking that road and running that race.

→>> <<←

"NO WEALTHY ... RELATIONS TO RECOMMEND ME"

From a Message to the People of Sangamo County

[MARCH 9, 1832]

This campaign statement—one of Lincoln's first—was published in his local newspaper, and possibly also as a handbill for distribution to voters. His focus on economic matters reflects his early belief that opportunity was an essential element of democracy. Lincoln lost the ensuing election for representative in the Illinois general assembly, his first race for public office.

To the People of Sangamo County

FELLOW-CITIZENS: Having become a candidate for the honorable office of one of your representatives in the next General Assembly of this state, in accordance with an established custom, and the principles of true republicanism, it becomes my duty to make known to you—the people whom I propose to represent—my sentiments with regard to local affairs.

Time and experience have verified to a demonstration, the public utility of internal improvements. That the poorest and most thinly populated countries would be greatly benefitted by the opening of good roads, and in the clearing of navigable streams within their limits, is what no person will deny. But yet it is folly to undertake works of this or any other kind, without first knowing that we are able to finish them—as half finished work generally proves to be labor lost. There cannot justly be any objection to having rail roads and canals, any more than to other good things, provided they cost nothing. The only objection is to paying for them; and the objection to paying arises from the want of ability to pay.

   . . . .

Upon the subject of education, not presuming to dictate any plan or system respecting it, I can only say that I view it as the most important subject which we as a people can be engaged in. That every man may receive at least, a moderate education, and thereby be enabled to read the histories of his own and other countries, by which he may duly appreciate the value of our free institutions, appears to be an object of vital importance, even on this account alone, to say nothing of the advantages and satisfaction to be derived from all being able to read the scriptures and other works, both of a religious and moral nature, for themselves. For my part, I desire to see the time when education, and by its means, morality, sobriety, enterprise and industry, shall become much more general than at present, and should be gratified to have it in my power to contribute something to the advancement of any measure which might have a tendency to accelerate the happy period.

. . . .

But, Fellow-Citizens, I shall conclude. Considering the great degree of modesty which should always attend youth, it is probable I have already been more presuming than becomes me. However, upon the subjects of which I have treated, I have spoken as I thought. I may be wrong in regard to any or all of them; but holding it a sound maxim, that it is better to be only sometimes right, than at all times wrong, so soon as I discover my opinions to be erroneous, I shall be ready to renounce them.

Every man is said to have his peculiar ambition. Whether it be true or not, I can say for one that I have no other so great as that of being truly esteemed of my fellow men, by rendering myself worthy of their esteem. How far I shall succeed in gratifying this ambition, is yet to be developed. I am young and unknown to many of you. I was born and have ever remained in the most humble walks of life. I have no wealthy or popular relations to recommend me. My case is thrown exclusively upon the independent voters of this county, and if elected they will have conferred a favor upon me, for which I shall be unremitting in my labors to compensate. But if the good people in their wisdom shall see fit to keep me in the background, I have been too familiar with disappointments to be very much chagrined. Your friend and fellow-citizen,

A. LINCOLN.

"I SHALL BE GOVERNED BY THEIR WILL"

Announcement in the Sangamo Journal

[JUNE 13, 1836]

Lincoln won a seat in the Illinois legislature on his second try, in 1834. As a candidate for another term he wrote this letter setting out his platform for reelection. His interest in internal improvements was standard Whig Party policy of the day. So was his belief in the "doctrine of instructions," the obligation of elected representatives to vote the will of their constituents. Lincoln finished first among seventeen candidates in the August 1 election, but while his choice for president, Hugh L. White, did well locally, he was defeated in both the state and the nation by Martin Van Buren.

New Salem, June 13, 1836.

To the Editor of the Journal:

In your paper of last Saturday, I see a communication over the signature of "Many Voters," in which the candidates who are announced in the Journal, are called upon to "show their hands." Agreed. Here's mine!

I go for all sharing the privileges of the government, who assist in bearing its burthens. Consequently I go for admitting all whites to the right of suffrage, who pay taxes or bear arms, (by no means excluding females.)

If elected, I shall consider the whole people of Sangamon my constituents, as well those that oppose, as those that support me.

While acting as their representative, I shall be governed by their will, on all subjects upon which I have the means of knowing what their will is; and upon all others, I shall do what my own judgment teaches me will best advance their interests. Whether elected or not, I go for distributing the proceeds of the sales of the public lands to the several states, to enable our state, in common with others, to dig canals and construct rail roads, without borrowing money and paying interest on it.

If alive on the first Monday in November, I shall vote for Hugh L. White for President. Very respectfully,

A. LINCOLN.

"THE PEOPLE KNOW THEIR RIGHTS"
From a Speech to the Illinois Legislature
[JANUARY 11, 1837]

Whig Representative Lincoln backed the charter of the Illinois State Bank, and remained its steadfast supporter even when it came dangerously close to insolvency. Here he defends its management, with what historian Gabor S. Boritt has pointed out was rather "overblown oratory" for a legislative debate on the banking issue.

Singular indeed that the people should be writhing under oppression and injury, and yet not one among them to be found, to raise the voice of complaint. If the Bank be inflicting injury upon the people, why is it, that not a single petition is presented to this body on the subject? If the Bank really be a grievance, why is it, that no one of the real people is found to ask redress of it? The truth is, no such oppression exists. If it did, our table would groan with memorials and petitions, and we would not be permitted to rest day or night, till we had put it down. The people know their rights; and they are never slow to assert and maintain them, when they are invaded.

. . . .

I am opposed to encouraging that lawless and mobocratic spirit, whether in relation to the bank or any thing else, which is already abroad in the land; and is spreading with rapid and fearful impetuosity, to the ultimate overthrow of every institution, or even moral principle, in which persons and property have hitherto found security.

But supposing we had the authority, I would ask what good can result from the examination? Can we declare the Bank unconstitutional, and compel it to cease operations? Can we compel it to desist from the abuses of its power, provided we find such abuses to exist? Can we repair the injuries which it may have done to individuals? Most certainly we can do none of these things. Why then shall we spend the public money in such employment? O, say the examiners, we can injure the credit of the Bank, if nothing else. Please tell me, gentlemen, who will suffer most by that? You cannot injure, to any extent, the Stockholders. They are men of wealth—of large capital; and consequently, beyond the power of fortune, or even the shafts of malice. But by injuring the credit of the Bank, you will depreciate the value of its paper in the hands of the honest and unsuspecting farmer and mechanic, and that is all you can do. But suppose you could effect your whole purpose; suppose you could wipe the Bank from existence, which is the grand *ultimatum* of the project, what would be the consequence? Why, sir, we should spend several thousand dollars of the public treasure in the operation, annihilate the currency of the State; render valueless in the hands of our people that reward of their former labors. . . .

"INJUSTICE AND BAD POLICY"

Protest in the Illinois Legislature on Slavery

[MARCH 3, 1837]

Lincoln's earliest recorded statement on slavery includes a mild rebuke of abolitionists, but was actually intended as a measured response to a far tougher attack on abolitionism by Democrats. Earlier, the House had considered a resolution strongly condemning abolitionism and asserting that the Constitution had sanctified slavery; seventy-seven voted for the measure, and Lincoln was one of only six who opposed it. Even as a candidate for president more than twenty-three years after he wrote this protest, Lincoln was still describing the slavery position it expressed as "the same that it is now."

The following protest was presented to the House, which was read and ordered to be spread on the journals, to wit:

"Resolutions upon the subject of domestic slavery having passed both branches of the General Assembly at its present session, the undersigned hereby protest against the passage of the same.

They believe that the institution of slavery is founded on both injustice and bad policy; but that the promulgation of abolition doctrines tends rather to increase than to abate its evils.

They believe that the Congress of the United States has no power, under the constitution, to interfere with the institution of slavery in the different States.

They believe that the Congress of the United States has the power, under the constitution, to abolish slavery in the District of Columbia; but that that power ought not to be exercised unless at the request of the people of said District.

The difference between these opinions and those contained in the said resolutions, is their reason for entering this protest."

DAN STONE,
A. LINCOLN,
Representatives from the county of Sangamon.

"THE *POLITICAL RELIGION* OF THE NATION"

Address Before the Young Men's Lyceum of Springfield, Illinois

[JANUARY 27, 1838]

One of the most intensely analyzed of Lincoln's speeches, the Lyceum address was a response both to recent lynchings in the South and to the 1837 murder of the Illinois abolitionist editor, Elijah P. Lovejoy. It contains Lincoln's most impassioned plea against mob violence. But historians have focused on it chiefly for its seemingly prophetic warning against the rise of a future tyrant—a "towering genius"—who might seek glory for himself even "at the expense of emancipating slaves, or enslaving freemen." Edmund Wilson, among others, has seen in it a chilling prediction of Lincoln's own future. Novelist Gore Vidal apparently felt it justified a remark uttered by one of the characters in his novel, Lincoln: "From the beginning, he knew that he was the first man in the country." Some modern scholars have dismissed such analyses as unsubstantiable. But psychohistorian Charles B. Strozier insists the speech was not only "chillingly prophetic" but oedipal in its references to the Founding Fathers, suggesting that the "towering genius" Lincoln warned against represented his own "unacknowledged (or unconscious) wishes to better them." Don E. Fehrenbacher has noted that stylistically, the speech boasts both "decorated oratory" and "the lean, muscular eloquence" that characterized Lincoln's mature work; but most of the address was windy, turgid, and as Lincoln's future law partner put it, "highly sophomoric." The speech, delivered in a Springfield church, as historian Thomas Schwartz only recently discovered, was reprinted in full in the local newspaper.

As a subject for the remarks of the evening, *the perpetuation of our political institutions,* is selected.

In the great journal of things happening under the sun, we, the American People, find our account running, under date of the nineteenth century of the Christian era. We find ourselves in the peaceful possession, of the fairest portion of the earth, as regards extent of territory, fertility of soil, and salubrity of climate. We find ourselves under the government of a system of political institutions, conducing more essentially to the ends of civil and religious liberty, than any of which the history of former times tells us. We, when mounting the stage of existence, found ourselves the legal inheritors of these fundamental blessings. We toiled not in the acquirement or establishment of them— they are a legacy bequeathed us, by a *once* hardy, brave, and patriotic, but *now* lamented and departed race of ancestors. Their's was the *task* (and nobly they performed it) to possess themselves, and through themselves, us, of this goodly land; and to uprear upon its hills and its valleys, a political edifice of liberty and equal rights; 'tis ours only, to transmit these, the former, unprofaned by the foot of an invader; the latter, undecayed by the lapse of time and untorn by usurpation, to the latest generation that fate shall permit the world to know. This task of gratitude to our fathers, justice to ourselves, duty to posterity, and love for our species in general, all imperatively require us faithfully to perform.

How, then, shall we perform it? At what point shall we expect the approach of danger? By what means shall we fortify against it? Shall we expect some transatlantic military giant, to step the Ocean, and crush us at a blow? Never! All the armies of Europe, Asia and Africa combined, with all the treasure of the earth (our own excepted) in their military chest; with a Buonaparte for a commander, could not by force, take a drink from the Ohio, or make a track on the Blue Ridge, in a trial of a thousand years.

At what point then is the approach of danger to be expected? I answer, if it ever reach us, it must spring up amongst us. It cannot come from abroad. If destruction be our lot, we must ourselves be its author and finisher. As a nation of freemen, we must live through all time, or die by suicide.

I hope I am over wary; but if I am not, there is, even now, something of ill-omen, amongst us. I mean the increasing disregard for law which pervades the country; the growing disposition to substitute the wild and furious passions, in lieu of the sober judgment of Courts; and the worse than savage mobs, for the executive ministers of justice. This disposition is awfully fearful in any community; and that it now exists in ours, though grating to our feelings to admit, it would be a violation of truth, and an insult to our intelligence, to deny. Accounts of outrages committed by mobs, form the every-day news of the times. They have pervaded the country, from New England to Louisiana;—they are neither peculiar to the eternal snows of the former, nor the burning suns of the latter;—they are not the creature of climate—neither are they confined to the slaveholding, or the non-slaveholding States. Alike, they spring up among the pleasure hunting masters of Southern slaves, and the order loving citizens of the land of steady habits. Whatever, then, their cause may be, it is common to the whole country.

It would be tedious, as well as useless, to recount the horrors of all of them. Those happening in the State of Mississippi, and at St. Louis, are, perhaps, the most dangerous in example and revolting to humanity. In the Mississippi case, they first commenced by hanging the regular gamblers: a set of men, certainly not following for a livelihood, a very useful, or very honest occupation; but one which, so far from being forbidden by the laws, was actually licensed by an act of the Legislature, passed but a single year before. Next, negroes, suspected of conspiring to raise an insurrection, were caught up and hanged in all parts of the State: then, white men, supposed to be leagued with the negroes; and finally, strangers, from neighboring States, going thither on business, were, in many instances, subjected to the same fate. Thus went on this process of hanging, from gamblers to negroes, from negroes to white citizens, and from these to strangers; till, dead men were seen literally dangling from the boughs of trees upon every road side; and in numbers almost sufficient, to rival the native Spanish moss of the country, as a drapery of the forest.

Turn, then, to that horror-striking scene at St. Louis. A single victim was only sacrificed there. His story is very short; and is, perhaps, the most highly tragic, of anything of its length, that has ever been witnessed in real life. A mulatto man, by the name of McIntosh, was seized in the street, dragged to the suburbs of the city, chained to a tree, and actually burned to death; and all within a single hour from the time he had been a freeman, attending to his own business, and at peace with the world.

Such are the effects of mob law; and such are the scenes, becoming more and more frequent in this land so lately famed for love of law and order; and the stories of which, have even now grown too familiar, to attract any thing more, than an idle remark.

But you are, perhaps, ready to ask, "What has this to do with the perpetuation of our political institutions?" I answer, it has much to do with it. Its direct consequences are, comparatively speaking, but a small evil; and much of its danger consists, in the proneness of our minds, to regard its direct, as its only consequences. Abstractly considered, the hanging of the gamblers at Vicksburg, was of but little consequence. They constitute a portion of population, that is worse than useless in any community; and their death, if no pernicious example be set by it, is never matter of reasonable regret with any one. If they were annually swept, from the stage of existence, by the plague or small pox, honest men would, perhaps, be much profited, by the operation. Similar too, is the correct reasoning, in regard to the burning of the negro at St. Louis. He had forfeited his life, by the perpetration of an outrageous murder, upon one of the most worthy and respectable citizens of the city; and had he not died as he did, he must have died by the sentence of the law, in a very short time afterwards. As to him alone, it was as well the way it was, as it could otherwise have been. But the example in either case, was fearful. When men take it in their heads to day, to hang gamblers, or burn murderers, they should recollect, that, in the confusion usually attending such transactions, they will be as likely to hang or burn some one, who is neither a gambler nor a murderer as one who is; and that, acting upon the example they set, the mob of to-morrow, may, and probably will, hang or burn some of them by the very same mistake. And not only so; the innocent, those who have ever set their faces against violations of law in every shape, alike with the guilty, fall victims to the ravages of mob law; and thus it goes on, step by step, till all the walls erected for the defence of the persons and property of individuals, are trodden down, and disregarded. But all this even, is not the full extent of the evil. By such examples, by instances of the perpetrators of such acts going unpunished, the lawless in spirit, are encouraged to become lawless in practice; and having been used to no restraint, but dread of punishment, they thus become, absolutely unrestrained. Having ever regarded Government as their deadliest bane, they make a jubilee of the suspension of its operations; and pray for nothing so much, as its total annihilation. While, on the other hand, good men, men who love tranquility, who desire to abide by the laws, and enjoy their benefits, who would gladly spill their blood in the defence of their country; seeing their property destroyed; their families insulted, and their lives endangered; their persons injured; and seeing nothing in prospect that forebodes a change for the better; become tired of, and disgusted with, a Government that offers them no protection; and are not much averse to a change in which they imagine they have nothing to lose. Thus, then, by the operation of this mobocratic spirit, which all must admit, is now abroad in the land, the strongest bulwark of any Government, and particularly of those constituted like ours, may effectually be broken down and destroyed—I mean the *attachment* of the People. Whenever this effect shall be produced among us; whenever the vicious portion of population shall be permitted to gather in bands of hundreds and thousands, and burn churches, ravage and rob provision stores, throw printing presses into rivers, shoot editors, and hang and burn obnoxious persons at pleasure, and with impunity; depend on it, this Government cannot last. By such things, the feelings of the best citizens will become more or less alienated from it; and thus it will be left without friends, or with too few, and those few too weak, to make their friendship effectual. At such a time and under such circumstances, men of sufficient talent and ambition will not be wanting to seize the opportunity, strike the blow, and overturn that fair fabric, which for the last half century, has been the fondest hope, of the lovers of freedom, throughout the world.

I know the American People are *much* attached to their Government;—I know they would suffer *much* for its sake;—I know they would endure evils long and patiently, before they would ever think of exchanging it for another. Yet, notwithstanding all this, if the laws be continually despised and disregarded, if their rights to be secure in their persons and property, are held by no better tenure than the caprice of a mob, the alienation of their affections from the Government is the natural consequence; and to that, sooner or later, it must come.

Here then, is one point at which danger may be expected.

The question recurs, "how shall we fortify against it?" The answer is simple. Let every American, every lover of liberty, every well wisher to his posterity, swear by the blood of the Revolution, never to violate in the least particular, the laws of the country; and never to tolerate their violation by others. As the patriots of seventy-six did to the support of the Declaration of Independence, so to the support of the Constitution and Laws, let every American pledge his life, his property, and his sacred honor;—let every man remember that to violate the law, is to trample on the blood of his father, and to tear the character of his own, and his children's liberty. Let reverence for the laws, be breathed by every American mother, to the lisping babe, that prattles on her lap—let it be taught in schools, in seminaries, and in colleges;—let it be written in Primmers, spelling books, and in Almanacs;—let it be preached from the pulpit, proclaimed in legislative halls, and enforced in courts of justice. And, in short, let it become the *political religion* of the nation; and let the old and the young, the rich and the poor, the grave and the gay, of all sexes and tongues, and colors and conditions, sacrifice unceasingly upon its altars.

While ever a state of feeling, such as this, shall universally, or even, very generally prevail throughout the nation, vain will be every effort, and fruitless every attempt, to subvert our national freedom.

When I so pressingly urge a strict observance of all the laws, let me not be understood as saying there are no bad laws, nor that grievances may not arise, for the redress of which, no legal provisions have been made. I mean to say no such thing. But I do mean to say, that, although bad laws, if they exist, should be repealed as soon as possible, still while they continue in force, for the sake of example, they should be religiously observed. So also in unprovided cases. If such arise, let proper legal provisions be made for them with the least possible delay; but, till then, let them, if not too intolerable, be borne with.

There is no grievance that is a fit object of redress by mob law. In any case that arises, as for instance, the promulgation of abolitionism, one of two positions is necessarily true; that is, the thing is right within itself, and therefore deserves the protection of all law and all good citizens; or, it is wrong, and therefore proper to be prohibited by legal enactments; and in neither case, is the interposition of mob law, either necessary, justifiable, or excusable.

But, it may be asked, why suppose danger to our political institutions? Have we not preserved them for more than fifty years? And why may we not for fifty times as long?

We hope there is *no sufficient* reason. We hope all dangers may be overcome; but to conclude that no danger may ever arise, would itself be extremely dangerous. There are now, and will hereafter be, many causes, dangerous in their tendency, which have not existed heretofore; and which are not too insignificant to merit attention. That our government should have been maintained in its original form from its establishment until now, is not much to be wondered at. It had many props to support it through that period, which now are decayed, and crumbled away. Through that period, it was felt by all, to be an undecided experiment; now, it is understood to be a successful one. Then, all that sought celebrity and fame, and distinction, expected to find them in the success of that experiment. Their *all* was staked upon it:—their destiny was *inseparably* linked with it. Their ambition aspired to display before an admiring world, a practical demonstration of the truth of a proposition, which had hitherto been considered, at best no better, than problematical; namely, *the capability of a people to govern themselves.* If they succeeded, they were to be immortalized; their names were to be transferred to counties and cities, and rivers and mountains; and to be revered and sung, and toasted through all time. If they failed, they were to be called knaves and fools, and fanatics for a fleeting hour; then to sink and be forgotten. They succeeded. The experiment is successful; and thousands have won their deathless names in making it so. But the game is caught; and I believe it is true, that with the catching, end the pleasures of the chase. This field of glory is harvested, and the crop is already appropriated. But new reapers will arise, and *they,* too, will seek a field. It is to deny, what the history of the world tells us is true, to suppose that men of ambition and talents will not continue to spring up amongst us. And, when they do, they will as naturally seek the gratification of their ruling passion, as others have *so* done before them. The question then, is, can that gratification be found in supporting and maintaining an edifice that has been erected by others? Most certainly it cannot. Many great and good men sufficiently qualified for any task they should undertake, may ever be found, whose ambition would aspire to nothing beyond a seat in Congress, a gubernatorial or a presidential chair; *but such belong not to the family of the lion, or the tribe of the eagle.* What! think you these places would satisfy an Alexander, a Caesar, or a Napoleon? Never! Towering genius disdains a beaten path. It seeks regions hitherto unexplored. It sees *no distinction* in adding story to story, upon the monuments of fame, erected to the memory of others. It *denies* that it is glory enough to serve under any chief. It *scorns* to tread in the footsteps of *any* predecessor, however illustrious. It thirsts and burns for distinction; and, if possible, it will have it, whether at the expense of emancipating slaves, or enslaving freemen. Is it unreasonable then to expect, that some man possessed of the loftiest genius, coupled with ambition sufficient to push it to its utmost stretch, will at some time, spring up among us? And when such a one does, it will require the people to be united with each other, attached to the government and laws, and generally intelligent, to successfully frustrate his designs.

Distinction will be his paramount object, and although he would as willingly, perhaps more so, acquire it by doing good as harm; yet, that opportunity being past, and nothing left to be done in the way of building up, he would set boldly to the task of pulling down.

Here then, is a probable case, highly dangerous, and such a one as could not have well existed heretofore.

Another reason which *once was;* but which, to the same extent, is *now no more,* has done much in maintaining our institutions thus far. I mean the powerful influence which the interesting scenes of the revolution had upon the *passions* of the people as distinguished from their judgment. By this influence, the jealousy, envy, and avarice, incident to our nature, and so common to a state of peace, prosperity, and conscious strength, were, for the time, in a great measure smothered and rendered inactive; while the deep rooted principles of *hate,* and the powerful motive of *revenge,* instead of being turned against each other, were directed exclusively against the British nation. And thus, from the force of circumstances, the basest principles of our nature, were either made to lie dormant, or to become the active agents in the advancement of the noblest of cause—that of establishing and maintaining civil and religious liberty.

But this state of feeling *must fade, is fading, has faded,* with the circumstances that produced it.

I do not mean to say, that the scenes of the revolution *are now* or *ever will be* entirely forgotten; but that like every thing else, they must fade upon the memory of the world, and grow more and more dim by the lapse of time. In history, we hope, they will be read of, and recounted, so long as the bible shall be read;—but even granting that they will, their influence *cannot be* what it heretofore has been. Even then, they *cannot be* so universally known, nor so vividly felt, as they were by the generation just gone to rest. At the close of that struggle, nearly every adult male had been a participator in some of its scenes. The consequence was, that of those scenes, in the form of a husband, a father, a son or a brother, *a living history was* to be found in every family—a history bearing the indubitable testimonies of its own authenticity, in the limbs mangled, in the scars of wounds received, in the midst of the very scenes related—a history, too, that could be read and understood alike by all, the wise and the ignorant, the learned and the unlearned. But *those* histories are gone. They *can* be read no more forever. They *were* a fortress of strength; but, what invading foeman could *never do,* the silent artillery of time *has done;* the levelling of its walls. They are gone. They *were* a forest of giant oaks; but the all-resistless hurricane has swept over them, and left only, here and there, a lonely trunk, despoiled of its verdure, shorn of its foliage; unshading and unshaded, to murmur in a few more gentle breezes, and to combat with its mutilated limbs, a few more ruder storms, then to sink, and be no more.

They *were* the pillars of the temple of liberty; and now, that they have crumbled away, that temple must fall, unless we, their descendants, supply their places with other pillars, hewn from the solid quarry of sober reason. Passion has helped us; but can do so no more. It will in future be our enemy. Reason, cold, calculating, unimpassioned reason, must furnish all the materials for our future support and defence. Let those materials be moulded into *general intelligence, sound morality* and, in particular, a *reverence for the constitution and laws:* and, that we improved to the last; that we remained free to the last; that we revered his name to the last; that, during his long sleep, we permitted no hostile foot to pass over or desecrate his resting place; shall be that which to learn the last trump [Judgement Day, from First Corinthians—eds.] shall awaken our WASHINGTON.

Upon these let the proud fabric of freedom rest, as the rock of its basis; and as truly as has been said of the only greater institution, *"the gates of hell shall not prevail against it* [from the Book of Matthew—eds.]."

"THE WEALTHY CAN NOT *JUSTLY* COMPLAIN"

Letter to William S. Wait

[MARCH 2, 1839]

Lincoln's letter to an influential Democrat from a neighboring Illinois county defended increased taxation, pointing out breezily that even if the wealthy objected to such a policy, there weren't enough of them to vote it down.

Mr. William S. Wait: Vandalia, March 2. 1839

Sir:

Your favour of yesterday was handed me by Mr. Dale. In relation to the Revenue law, I think there is something [to] be feared from the argument you suggest, though I hope the danger is not as great as you apprehend. The passage of a Revenue law at this session, is *right* within itself; and I never despair of sustaining myself before the people upon any measure that will stand a full investigation. I presume I hardly need enter into an argument to prove to *you,* that our old revenue system, raising, as it did, all the state revenue from non-resident lands, and those lands rapidly *decreasing,* by passing into the hands of resident owners, whiles the wants of the Treasury were *increasing* with the increase of population, could not longer continue to answer the purpose of it's creation. That proposition is little less than self-evident. The only question is as to sustaining the change before the people. I believe it can be sustained, because it does not increase the tax upon the *"many poor"* but upon the *"wealthy few"* by taxing the land that is worth $50 or $100 per acre, in proportion to its value, insted of, as heretofore, no more than that which was worth but $5 per acre. This valuable land, as is well known, belongs, not to the poor, but to the wealthy citizen.

On the other hand, the wealthy can not *justly* complain, because the change is equitable within itself, and also a *sine qua non* to a compliance with the Constitution. If, however, the wealthy should, regardless of the justness of the complaint, as men often are, when interest is involved in the question, complain of the change, it is still to be remembered, that *they* are not sufficiently numerous to carry the elections. Verry Respectfully

A. LINCOLN

"MANY FREE COUNTRIES HAVE LOST THEIR LIBERTY"

From a Speech on the Subtreasury, Springfield, Illinois

[DECEMBER 26, 1839]

A local pro-Whig newspaper published the full text of this attack on the Democrats' scheme for replacing the national bank, praising it as "a speech which no man can answer." It was later reprinted in pamphlet form for the 1840 election campaign. The speech tied together the ideas of sound banking and political liberty, with Lincoln invoking "the sacred name of Democracy" against "a system for benefitting the few at the expense of the many."

We do not pretend, that a National Bank can establish and maintain a sound and uniform state of currency in the country, in *spite* of the National Government; but we do say, that it has established and maintained such a currency, and can do so again, by the *aid* of that Government; and we further say, that no duty is more imperative on that Government, than the duty it owes the people, of furnishing them a sound and uniform currency.

. . . .

Many free countries have lost their liberty; and *ours may* lose hers; but if she shall, be it my proudest plume, not that I was the *last* to desert, but that I *never* deserted her. I know that the great volcano at

Washington, aroused and directed by the evil spirit that reigns there, is belching forth the lava of political corruption, in a current broad and deep, which is sweeping with frightful velocity over the whole length and breadth of the land, bidding fair to leave unscathed no green spot or living thing, while on its bosom are riding like demons on the waves of Hell, the imps of that evil spirit, and fiendishly taunting all those who dare resist its destroying course, with the hopelessness of their effort; and knowing this, I cannot deny that all may be swept away. Broken by it, I, too, may be; bow to it I never will. The *probability* that we may fall in the struggle *ought not* to deter us from the support of a cause we believe to be just; it *shall not* deter me. If ever I feel the soul within me elevate and expand to those dimensions not wholly unworthy of its Almighty Architect, it is when I contemplate the cause of my country, deserted by all the world beside, and I standing up boldly and alone and hurling defiance at her victorious oppressors. Here, without contemplating consequences, before High Heaven, and in the face of the world, I swear eternal fidelity to the just cause, as I deem it, of the land of my life, my liberty and my love. And who, that thinks with me, will not fearlessly adopt the oath that I take. Let none faulter, who thinks he is right, and we may succeed. But, if after all, we shall fail, be it so. We still shall have the proud consolation of saying to our consciences, and to the departed shade of our country's freedom, that the cause approved of our judgment, and adored of our hearts, in disaster, in chains, in torture, in death, we NEVER faultered in defending.

" 'GOD TEMPERS THE WIND' "

From a Letter to Mary Speed

[SEPTEMBER 27, 1841]

Mary Speed was the half sister of Lincoln's closest friend, Joshua Speed. Judging from the playful tone with which this letter began, Mary and Lincoln became friendly as well during his long 1841 visit to "Farming-

ton," the Speed family plantation outside Louisville, Kentucky. Lincoln abruptly changed tone here to describe a haunting firsthand look at slavery.

Miss Mary Speed,   Bloomington, Illinois,
Louisville, Ky.   Sept. 27th. 1841

My Friend:

Having resolved to write to some of your mother's family, and not having the express permission of any one of them [to] do so, I have had some little difficulty in determining on which to inflict the task of reading what I now feel must be a most dull and silly letter; but when I remembered that you and I were something of cronies while I was at Farmington, and that, while there, I once was under the necessity of shutting you up in a room to prevent your committing an assault and battery upon me, I instantly decided that you should be the devoted one.

I assume that you have not heard from Joshua & myself since we left, because I think it doubtful whether he has written.

You remember there was some uneasiness about Joshua's health when we left. That little indisposition of his turned out to be nothing serious; and it was pretty nearly forgotten when we reached Springfield. We got on board the Steam Boat Lebanon, in the locks of the Canal about 12. o'clock. M. of the day we left, and reached St. Louis the next monday at 8 P.M. Nothing of interest happened during the passage, except the vexatious delays occasioned by the sand bars be thought interesting. By the way, a fine example was presented on board the boat for contemplating the effect of *condition* upon human happiness. A gentleman had purchased twelve negroes in different parts of Kentucky and was taking them to a farm in the South. They were chained six and six together. A small iron clevis [a manacle—eds.] was around the left wrist of each, and this fastened to the main chain by a shorter one at a convenient distance from, the others; so that the negroes were strung together precisely like so many fish upon a trot-line [a long fishing line with a series of hooks attached—eds.]. In this condition they were being separated forever from the scenes of their childhood, their friends, their fathers and mothers, and brothers and sisters, and many of them, from their wives and children, and going into perpetual slavery where the lash of the master is proverbially more ruthless and unrelenting than any other where; and yet amid all these distressing circumstances, as we would think them, they were the most cheerful and apparantly happy creatures on board. One, whose offence for which he had been sold was an over-fondness for his wife, played the fiddle almost continually; and the others danced, sung, cracked jokes, and played various games with cards from day to day. How true it is that "God tempers the wind to the shorn lamb," or in other words, that He renders the worst of human conditions tolerable, while He permits the best, to be nothing better than tolerable. . . . Your sincere friend

A. LINCOLN

"THE SORROW QUENCHING DRAUGHTS OF PERFECT LIBERTY"

From an Address Before Springfield's Washington Temperance Society

[FEBRUARY 22, 1842]

In this address, which he delivered on George Washington's 110th birthday, Lincoln did not condemn drinkers, but suggested that they sip only the nectar of liberty. The speech was published in the local press. The conclusion, presented here, eloquently stated Lincoln's reverence for Washington, the founders, and the system of government they perfected. Lincoln himself was an abstainer. "I hate the stuff," he told his law partner.

If the relative grandeur of revolutions shall be estimated by the great amount of human misery they alleviate, and the small amount they inflict, then, indeed, will this be the grandest the world shall ever have seen. Of our political revolution of '76 we all are justly proud. It has given us a degree of political freedom, far exceeding that of any other of the nations of the earth. In it the world has found a solution of the long mooted problem, as to the capability of man to govern himself. In it was the germ which was vegetated, and still is to grow and expand into the universal liberty of mankind.

But with all these glorious results, past, present, and to come, it had its evils too. It breathed forth famine, swam in blood and rode on fire; and long, long after, the orphan's cry, and the widow's wail, continued to break the sad silence that ensued. These were the price, the inevitable price, paid for the blessings it bought.

Turn now, to the temperance revolution. In *it,* we shall find a stronger bondage broken; a viler slavery, manumitted; a greater tyrant deposed. In *it,* more of want supplied, more disease healed, more sorrow assuaged. By *it* no orphans starving, no widows weeping. By *it,* none wounded in feeling, none injured in interest. Even the dram-maker and dram seller, will have glided into other occupations *so* gradually, as never to have felt the shock of change; and will stand ready to join all others in the universal song of gladness.

And what a noble ally this, to the cause of political freedom. With such an aid, its march cannot fail to be on and on, till every son of earth shall drink in rich fruition, the sorrow quenching draughts of perfect liberty. Happy day, when, all appetites controlled, all passions subdued, all matters subjected, *mind,* all conquering *mind,* shall live and move the monarch of the world. Glorious consummation! Hail fall of Fury! Reign of Reason, all hail!

And when the victory shall be complete—when there shall be neither a slave nor a drunkard on the earth—how proud the title of that *Land,* which may truly claim to be the birth-place and the cradle of both those revolutions, that shall have ended in that victory. How nobly distinguished that People, who shall have planted, and nurtured to maturity, both the political and moral freedom of their species.

This is the one hundred and tenth anniversary of the birth-day of Washington. We are met to celebrate this day. Washington is the mightiest name of earth—*long since* mightiest in the cause of civil liberty; *still* mightiest in moral reformation. On that name, an eulogy is expected. It cannot be. To add brightness to the sun, or glory to the name of Washington, is alike impossible. Let none attempt it. In solemn

awe pronounce the name, and in its naked deathless splendor, leave it
shining on.

"BY THE *FRUIT* THE TREE IS TO BE KNOWN"

Letter to Williamson Durley

[OCTOBER 3, 1845]

Lincoln's letter to a fellow Illinois Whig blamed the Liberty men, members of a small antislavery political party, for the defeat for president of his political hero, Henry Clay. But it also presented one of Lincoln's most persuasive early arguments against the extension of slavery.

Springfield, Octr. 3. 1845

Friend Durley:

When I saw you at home, it was agreed that I should write to you
and your brother Madison. Until I then saw you, I was not aware of
your being what is generally called an abolitionist, or, as you call
yourself, a Liberty-man; though I well knew there were many such in
your county. I was glad to hear you say that you intend to attempt to
bring about, at the next election in Putnam [County—eds.], a union of
the whigs proper, and such of the liberty men, as are whigs in principle
on all questions save only that of slavery. So far as I can perceive, by
such union, neither party need yield any thing, on *the* point in difference between them. If the whig abolitionists of New York had voted
with us last fall, Mr. Clay would now be president, whig principles in
the ascendent, and Texas not annexed; whereas by the division, all that
either had at stake in the contest, was lost. And, indeed, it was extremely probable, beforehand, that such would be the result. As I

always understood, the Liberty-men deprecated the annexation of Texas extremely; and, this being so, why they should refuse to so cast their votes as to prevent it, even to me, seemed wonderful. What was their process of reasoning, I can only judge from what a single one of them told me. It was this: "We are not to do *evil* that *good* may come." This general, proposition is doubtless correct; but did it apply? If by your votes you could have prevented the *extention, &c.* of slavery, would it not have been *good* and not *evil* so to have used your votes, even though it involved the casting of them for a slaveholder? By the *fruit* the tree is to be known. An *evil* tree can not bring forth *good* fruit. If the fruit of electing Mr. Clay would have been to prevent the extension of slavery, could the act of electing have been *evil?*

But I will not argue farther. I perhaps ought to say that individually I never was much interested in the Texas question. I never could see much good to come of annexation; inasmuch, as they were already a free republican people on our own model; on the other hand, I never could very clearly see how the annexation would augment the evil of slavery. It always seemed to me that slaves would be taken there in about equal numbers, with or without annexation. And if more *were* taken because of annexation, still there would be just so many the fewer left, where they were taken from. It is possibly true, to some extent, that with annexation, some slaves may be sent to Texas and continued in slavery, that otherwise might have been liberated. To whatever extent this may be true, I think annexation an evil. I hold it to be a paramount duty of us in the free states, due to the Union of the states, and perhaps to liberty itself (paradox though it may seem) to let the slavery of the other states alone; while, on the other hand, I hold it to be equally clear, that we should never knowingly lend ourselves directly or indirectly, to prevent that slavery from dying a natural death—to find new places for it to live in, when it can no longer exist in the old. Of course I am not now considering what would be our duty, in cases of insurrection among the slaves.

To recur to the Texas question, I understand the Liberty men to have viewed annexation as a much greater evil than I ever did; and I, would like to convince you if I could, that they could have prevented it, without violation of principle, if they had chosen.

I intend this letter for you and Madison together; and if you and he

or either shall think fit to drop me a line, I shall be pleased. Yours with
respect

A. LINCOLN

"USELESS LABOUR IS . . .
THE SAME AS IDLENESS"

Fragments on Labor and the Tariff Issue

[DECEMBER 1847?]

*Lincoln was a doctrinaire Whig on the tariff issue. He believed that
protection would spur the young nation's economic growth, and that
encouraging opportunity would validate and perpetuate the American
experiment in democracy. In these extensive fragments he equated tariffs
with the perpetuation of "useful labour" as necessary ingredients to maintain prosperity.*

In the early days of the world, the Almighty said to the first of our
race "In the sweat of thy face shalt thou eat bread"; and since then, if
we except the *light* and the *air* of heaven, no good thing has been, or
can be enjoyed by us, without having first cost labour. And, inasmuch
[as] most good things are produced by labour, it follows that [all] such
things of right belong to those whose labour has produced them. But
it has so happened in all ages of the world, that *some* have laboured,
and *others* have, without labour, enjoyed a large proportion of the
fruits. This is wrong, and should not continue. To [secure] to each
labourer the whole product of his labour, or as nearly as possible, is a
most worthy object of any good government. But then the question
arises, how can a government best, effect this? In our own country, in
it's present condition, will the protective principle *advance* or *retard*
this object? Upon this subject, the habits of our whole species fall into

three great classes—*useful* labour, *useless* labour and *idleness.* Of these the first only is meritorious; and to it all the products of labour rightfully belong; but the two latter, while they exist, are heavy pensioners upon the first, robbing it of a large portion of it's just rights. The only remedy for this is to, as far as possible, drive *useless* labour and *idleness* out of existence.

.   .   .   .

If at any time all *labour* should cease, and all existing provisions be equally divided among the people, at the end of a single year there could scarcely be one human being left alive—all would have perished by want of subsistence.

So again, if upon such division, all that *sort* of labour, which produces provisions, should cease, and each individual should take up so much of his share as he could, and carry it continually around his habitation, although in this carrying, the amount of labour going on might be as great as ever, so long as it could last, at the end of the year the result would be precisely the same—that is, none would be left living.

The first of these propositions shows, that universal *idleness* would speedily result in universal ruin; and the second shows, that *useless labour* is, in this respect, the same as idleness.

I submit, then, whether it does not follow, that *partial* idleness, and partial *useless labour*, would, in the proportion of their extent, in like manner result, in partial ruin—whether, if *all* should subsist upon the labour that *one half* should perform, it would not result in very scanty allowance to the whole.

Believing that these propositions, and the [conclusions] I draw from them can not be successfully controverted, I, for the present, assume their correctness, and proceed to try to show, that the abandonment of the protective [tariff—eds.] policy by the American Government, must result in the increase of both useless labour, and idleness; and so, in pro[por]tion, must produce want and ruin among our people.

"THE *RIGHT* TO RISE UP"

From a Speech in the U.S. House of Representatives on the Mexican War

[JANUARY 12, 1848]

Along with his fellow Whigs in Congress, Lincoln opposed the Mexican War, arguing it was "unnecessarily and unconstitutionally commenced by the President." The war was waged over control of the huge province of Texas, and Democrats who supported it cited Manifest Destiny to justify their claims to the additional territory. Lincoln hoped his vocal opposition would "distinguish" him in the House, but it had a greater impact at home, where local prowar Democrats mercilessly attacked him. Still, there is no truth to the story that his antiwar stand doomed his chances for reelection to Congress. Nomination for a Whig successor had already been decided under a planned system of rotation. The month after giving this speech, Lincoln said it "condensed all I could" on the war issue. It was later published as a pamphlet, and Lincoln urged several friends to read it.

Mr. Chairman:

Some, if not all the gentlemen on, the other side of the House, who have addressed the committee within the last two days, have spoken rather complainingly, if I have rightly understood them, of the vote given a week or ten days ago, declaring that the war with Mexico was unnecessarily and unconstitutionally commenced by the President. I admit that such a vote should not be given, in mere party wantonness, and that the one given, is justly censurable, if it have no other, or better foundation. I am one of those who joined in that vote; and I did so under my best impression of the *truth* of the case. How I got this impression, and how it may possibly be removed, I will now try to show. When the war began, it was my opinion that all those who, because of knowing too *little,* or because of knowing too *much,* could not conscientiously approve the conduct of the President, in the beginning of it, should, nevertheless, as good citizens and patriots, remain silent on that point, at least till the war should be ended. Some leading democrats, including Ex President Van Buren, have taken this same view, as I understand them; and I adhered to it, and acted upon it, until since I took my seat here; and I think I should still adhere to it, were it not that the President and his friends will not allow it to be so.

. . . .

. . . I carefully examined the President's messages, to ascertain what he himself had said and proved upon the point. The result of this examination was to make the impression, that taking for true, all the President states as facts, he falls far short of proving his justification; and that the President would have gone farther with his proof, if it had not been for the small matter, that the *truth* would not permit him.

. . . .

Any people anywhere, being inclined and having the power, have the *right* to rise up, and shake off the existing government, and form a new one that suits them better. This is a most valuable,—a most sacred right—a right, which we hope and believe, is to liberate the world. Nor is this right confined to cases in which the whole people of an existing government, may choose to exercise it. Any portion of such people that *can, may* revolutionize, and make their *own,* of so much of the teritory as they inhabit. More than this, a *majority* of any portion of such people may revolutionize, putting down a *minority,* intermingled with, or near about them, who may oppose their movement. Such minority, was precisely the case, of the tories of our own revolution. It is a quality of revolutions not to go by *old* lines, or *old* laws; but to break up both, and make new ones. As to the country now in question, we bought it of France in 1803, and sold it to Spain in 1819, according to the President's statements. After this, all Mexico, including Texas, revolutionized against Spain; and still later, Texas revolutionized against Mexico. In my view, just so far as she carried her revolution, by obtaining the *actual,* willing or unwilling, submission of the people, *so far,* the country was hers, and no farther. Now sir, for the purpose of obtaining the very best evidence, as to whether Texas had actually carried her revolution, to the place where the hostilities of the present war commenced, let the President answer the interrogatories, I proposed, as before mentioned, or some other similar ones. Let him answer, fully, fairly, and candidly. Let him answer with *facts,* and not with arguments. Let him remember he sits where Washington sat, and so remembering, let him answer, as Washington would answer. As a nation *should* not, and the Almighty *will* not, be evaded, so let him attempt no envasion—no equivocation.

"NO ONE MAN SHOULD HOLD THE POWER"
Letter to William H. Herndon
[FEBRUARY 15, 1848]

Herndon, Lincoln's junior law partner and later his biographer, gratuitously took credit for warning Lincoln that his opposition to the Mexican War meant "political suicide." In truth, most fellow Whigs supported Lincoln's antiwar stand. In this letter, he continued to assail President James K. Polk's assumption of war-making powers. Answering Herndon's concerns about his political future, Lincoln earlier argued that he had felt "compelled to speak" on the war issue. As president himself, Lincoln would assume unprecedented executive powers.

Washington, Feb. 15. 1848

Dear William:

Your letter of the 29th. Jany. was received last night. Being exclusively a constitutional argument, I wish to submit some reflections upon it in the same spirit of kindness that I know actuates you. Let me first state what I understand to be your position. It is, that if it shall become *necessary, to repel invasion,* the President may, without violation of the Constitution, cross the line, and *invade* the territory of another country; and that whether such *necessity* exists in any given case, the President is to be the *sole* judge.

Before going further, consider well whether this is, or is not your position. If it is, it is a position that neither the President himself, nor any friend of his, so far as I know, has ever taken. Their only positions are first, that the soil was *ours* where hostilities commenced, and second, that whether it was rightfully *ours* or not, *Congress had annexed it,* and the President, for that reason was bound to defend it, both of which are as clearly proved to be false in fact, as you can prove that your house is not mine. That soil was not ours; and Congress did not annex or attempt to annex it. But to return to your position: Allow the President to invade a neighboring nation, whenever *he* shall deem it necessary to repel an invasion, and you allow him to do so, *whenever he may choose to say* he deems it necessary for such purpose—and you allow him to make war at pleasure. Study to see if you can fix *any limit* to his power in this respect, after you have given him so much as you propose. If, to-day, he should choose to say he thinks it necessary to invade Canada, to prevent the British from invading us, how could you stop him? You may say to him, "I see no probability of the British invading us" but he will say to you "be silent; I see it, if you dont."

The provision of the Constitution giving the war-making power to Congress, was dictated, as I understand it, by the following reasons. Kings had always been involving and impoverishing their people in wars, pretending generally, if not always, that the good of the people was the object. This, our Convention understood to be the most oppressive of all Kingly oppressions; and they resolved to so frame the Constitution that *no one man* should hold the power of bringing this oppression upon us. But your view destroys the whole matter, and places our President where kings have always stood. Write soon again. Yours truly,

A LINCOLN

"THERE ARE FEW THINGS
WHOLLY EVIL, OR *WHOLLY* GOOD"

*From a Speech in the U.S. House of Representatives on
Internal Improvements*

[JUNE 20, 1848]

*Continuing his defense of internal improvements, Lincoln used both logic
and humor to deflate the argument that public projects were objectionable
because they might not benefit all sections of the country equally. He
claimed that such opposition represented a policy of " 'Do nothing at all,
lest you do something wrong.' "*

At an early day of this session the president sent us what may
properly be called an internal improvement veto message. The late
democratic convention which sat at Baltimore, and which nominated
Gen: Cass for the presidency, adopted a set of resolutions, now called
the democratic platform, among which is one in these words:

"That the constitution does not confer upon the general government
the power to commence, and carry on a general system of internal
improvements . . ."

The just conclusion from all this is, that if the nation refuse to make
improvements, of the more general kind, because their benefits may be
somewhat local, a state may, for the same reason, refuse to make an
improvement of a local kind, because it's benefits may be somewhat
general. A state may well say to the nation "If you will do nothing for
me, I will do nothing for you." Thus it is seen, that if this argument
of "inequality" is sufficient any where,—it is sufficient every where; and
puts an end to improvements altogether. I hope and believe, that if both
the nation and the states would, in good faith, in their respective
spheres, do what they could in the way of improvements, what of
inequality might be produced in one place, might be compensated in
another, and that the sum of the whole might not be very unequal.

But suppose, after all, there should be some degree of inequality.

Inequality is certainly never to be embraced for it's own sake; but is every good thing to be discarded, which may be inseparably connected with some degree of it? If so, we must discard all government. This capitol is built at the public expense, for the public benefit but does any one doubt that it is of some peculiar local advantage to the property holders, and business people of Washington? Shall we remove it for this reason? and if so, where shall we set it down, and be free from the difficulty? To make sure of our object, shall we locate it nowhere? and have congress hereafter to hold it's sessions, as the loafer lodged "in spots about"? I make no special allusion to the present president when I say there are few stronger cases in this in this [*sic*] world, of "burthen to the many, and benefit to the few"—of "inequality"—than the presidency itself is by some thought to be. An honest laborer digs coal at about seventy cents a day, while the president digs abstractions at about seventy dollars a day. The *coal* is clearly worth more than the *abstractions,* and yet what a monstrous inequality in the prices! Does the president, for this reason, propose to abolish the presidency? He *does* not, and he *ought* not. The true rule, in determining to embrace, or reject any thing, is not whether it have *any* evil in it; but whether it have more of evil, than of good. There are few things *wholly* evil, or *wholly* good. Almost every thing, especially of governmental policy, is an inseparable compound of the two; so that our best judgment of the preponderance between them is continually demanded. On this principle the president, his friends, and the world generally, act on most subjects. Why not apply it, then, upon this question? Why, as to improvements, magnify the *evil,* and stoutly refuse to see any *good* in them . . . ?

"LEAVING THE PEOPLE'S BUSINESS IN THEIR HANDS"

From a Speech in the U.S. House of Representatives on the Presidential Question

[JULY 27, 1848]

Whigs believed a president should avoid the veto whenever possible, and in this speech before Congress, Lincoln voiced the party view. During his own presidency, Lincoln would veto only six bills, as compared with his successor, Andrew Johnson, who rejected twenty-eight, most of which vetoes were overridden.

My friend from Indiana [Caleb B. Smith, his future secretary of the interior—eds.] has aptly asked "Are you willing to trust the people?" Some of you answered, substantially "We are willing to trust the trust the [sic] people; but the President is as much the representative of the people as Congress." In a certain sense, and to a certain extent, he is the representative of the people. He is elected by them, as well as congress is. But can he, in the nature [of] things, know the wants of the people, as well as three hundred other men, coming from all the various localities of the nation? If so, where is the propriety of having a congress? That the constitution gives the President a negative on legislation, all know; but that this negative should be so combined with platforms, and other appliances, as to enable him, and, in fact, almost compel him, to take the whole of legislation into his own hands, is what we object to, is what Gen: [Zachary] Taylor objects to, and is what constitutes the broad distinction between you and us. To thus transfer legislation, is clearly to take it from those who understand, with minuteness, the interests of the people, and give it to one who does not, and can not so well understand it.

. . . .

One word more, and I shall have done with this branch of the subject. You democrats, and your candidate [presidential nominee Lewis

Cass—eds.], in the main are in favor of laying down, in advance, a platform—a set of party positions, as a unit; and then of enforcing the people, by every sort of appliance, to ratify them, however unpalatable some of them may be. We, and our candidate, are in favor of making Presidential elections, and the legislation of the country, distinct matters; so that the people can elect whom they please, and afterwards, legislate just as they please, without any hindrance, save only so much as may guard against infractions of the constitution, undue haste, and want of consideration. The difference between us, is clear as noonday. That we are right, we can not doubt. We hold the true republican position. In leaving the people's business in their hands, we can not be wrong. We are willing, and even anxious, to go to the people, on this issue.

"GO TO WORK, 'TOOTH AND NAILS' "

Letter to His Stepbrother

[DECEMBER 24, 1848]

Lincoln believed from the beginning of his political career in full opportunity. But while he believed "every poor man should have a chance," he was less than patient with poor men who lacked ambition—including his own stepbrother, who was thirty-seven when Lincoln wrote this letter. Lincoln urged him to end his life of idleness, offering to match every dollar he earned. "I am always for the man who wishes to work," Lincoln continued to believe as president. But John D. Johnston did not wish to work. He died in California in 1854, leaving an estate worth only $55.90.

Dear Johnston:

Your request for eighty dollars, I do not think it best, to comply with now. At the various times when I have helped you a little, you have said to me "We can get along very well now" but in a very short time I find you in the same difficulty again. Now this can only happen by some defect in your *conduct*. What that defect is, I think I know. You are not *lazy,* and still you *are* an *idler.* I doubt whether since I saw you, you have done a good whole day's work, in any one day. You do not very much dislike to work; and still you do not work much, merely because it does not seem to you that you could get much for it. This habit of uselessly wasting time, is the whole difficulty; and it is vastly important to you, and still more so to your children that you should break this habit. It is more important to them, because they have longer to live, and can keep out of an idle habit before they are in it; easier than they can get out after they are in.

You are now in need of some ready money; and what I propose is, that you shall go to work, "tooth and nails" for some body who will give you money [for] it. Let father and your boys take charge of things at home—prepare for a crop, and make the crop; and you go to work for the best money wages, or in discharge of any debt you owe, that you can get. And to secure you a fair reward for your labor, I now promise you, that for every dollar you will, between this and the first of next May, get for your own labor, either in money, or in your own indebtedness, I will then give you one other dollar. By this, if you hire yourself at ten dolla[rs] a month, from me you will get ten more, making twenty dollars a month for your work. In this, I do not mean you shall go off to St. Louis, or the lead mines, or the gold mines, in Calif[ornia,] but I mean for you to go at it for the best wages you can get close to home [in] Coles county. Now if you will do this, you will soon be out of debt, and what is better, you will have a habit that will keep you from getting in debt again. But if I should now clear you out, next year you will be just as deep in as ever. You say you would almost give your place in Heaven for $70 or $80. Then you value your place in Heaven very cheaply for I am sure you can with the offer I make you get the seventy or eighty dollars for four or five months work. You say if I furnish you the money you will deed me the land, and, if you dont pay the money back, you will deliver possession. Nonsense! If you cant now live *with* the land, how will you then live without it? You have always been [kind] to me, and I do not now mean to be unkind to you. On the contrary, if you will but follow my advice, you will find it worth more than eight times eighty dollars to you. Affectionately Your brother

A. LINCOLN

"VALUABLE TO HIS ADOPTED COUNTRY"

Resolution and Letter on Napoleon Koscialowski

[FEBRUARY 20, 1850]

Koscialowski had served as an engineer and architect at the Illinois state capitol. Lincoln was one of twenty-two to sign the following resolution supporting the Polish national for a military commission. He also wrote a letter of reference for Koscialowski to carry to Washington. There is no record of whether he ever won his commission.

To the Honorable, The Secretary of War, of the United States.

Sir:

The undersigned, citizens of the State of Illinois, beg leave to recommend to your consideration the name of *Napoleon Koscialowski,* for the appointment of *Major,* should there be a disposable post of that rank, in one of the Regiments to be raised for the protection of the U.S. frontier. We make this recommendation more earnestly, because we believe that your Department cannot possibly make a better appointment. Mr. Koscialowski is a native of Poland, and has been bred and has served as a soldier. He entered a military school at Warsaw at the age of sixteen, and having graduated then served three years in the Body-Guard of the Emperor of Russia. He quitted that corps and joined his national banner in the year 1830, when the Poles made their bold but unfortunate attempt to regain their national independence. After several years' imprisonment, consequent upon the failure of the revolt, he with some others succeeded in making his escape to this country, and became a citizen of the U.S. in 1834. In 1846, when War was declared against Mexico, he volunteered and having raised a company in St Louis, was elected captain and served as such until discharged. He then volunteered again for the Term of During the War, and commanded a company on the Western frontier until Peace was concluded and he was discharged. In the course of this service, he has necessarily acquired much experience in this kind of warfare to which the frontier Regiments are destined—and we think, and so respectfully represent, that this experience added to his education in a regular Military Academy, peculiarly fits him for the station to which we recommend him. As an accomplished civil engineer, also, we are the more confident that his services will be valuable to his adopted country. Mr. Koscialowski is a resident of Jacksonville, Illinois.

. . . .

Springfield, Illinois.
Hon: Secretary of War— Feb: 20 1850

Sir:

Capt. Koscialowski, who will present you this letter, is an applicant for an appointment of Major in the new Regiments proposed to be raised by congress. I have already placed my name, among others, to a general recommendation of him for that appointment; but I now desire to say, a little more specifically, that I shall be much gratified if he shall be successful in his application. He is every way a gentleman, a great favorite with his acquaintances here, and, (as I understand, without any capacity for deciding myself,) has a military education, fitting him peculiarly for the position he seeks. Your Obt. Servt.

A. LINCOLN

"RESOLVE TO BE HONEST"

Notes for a Law Lecture

[JULY I, 1850?]

As a lawyer, Lincoln specialized in persuading juries—a skill he also used to persuade audiences at political meetings and debates. There is disagreement over the date of this revealing advice on how to practice law; some scholars contend it was written after 1850. Nor is there any evidence that Lincoln gave a finished lecture on this topic, even though his notes contained the admonition: "Leave nothing for to-morrow which can be done to-day."

I am not an accomplished lawyer. I find quite as much material for a lecture in those points wherein I have failed, as in those wherein I have been moderately successful. The leading rule for the lawyer, as for the man, of every other calling, is *diligence.* Leave nothing for to-morrow which can be done to-day. Never let your correspondence fall behind. Whatever piece of business you have in hand, before stopping, do all the labor pertaining to it which can *then* be done. When you bring a common-law suit, if you have the facts for doing so, write the declaration at once. If a law point be involved, examine the books, and note the authority you rely on upon the declaration itself, where you are sure to find it when wanted. The same of defenses and pleas. In business not likely to be litigated,—ordinary collection cases, foreclosures, partitions, and the like,—make all examinations of titles, and note them, and even draft orders and decrees in advance. This course has a tripple advantage; it avoids omissions and neglect, *saves* your labor, when once done, performs the labor out of court when you *have* leisure, rather than in court when you have not. Extemporaneous speaking should be practiced and cultivated. It is the lawyer's avenue to the public. However able and faithful he may be in other respects, people are slow to bring him business, if he cannot make a speech. And yet there is not a more fatal error to young lawyers, than relying too much on speech-making. If any one, upon his rare powers of speaking, shall claim exemption from the drudgery of the law, his case is a failure in advance.

Discourage litigation. Persuade your neighbors to compromise whenever you can. Point out to them how the *nominal* winner is often a *real* loser—in fees, and expenses, and waste of time. As a peace-maker the lawyer has a superior opertunity of being a good man. There will still be business enough.

Never stir up litigation. A worse man can scarcely be found than one who does this. Who can be more nearly a fiend than he who habitually overhauls the Register of deeds in search of defects in titles, whereon to stir up strife, and put money in his pocket? A moral tone ought to be infused into the profession, which should drive such men out of it.

The matter of fees is important far beyond the mere question of bread and butter involved. Properly attended to fuller justice is done to both lawyer and client. An exorbitant fee should never be claimed. As a general rule, never take your whole fee in advance, nor any more than a small retainer. When fully paid before hand, you are more than a common mortal if you can feel the same interest in the case, as if something was still in prospect for you, as well as for your client. And when you lack interest in the case, the job will very likely lack skill and diligence in the performance. Settle the *amount* of fee, and take a note in advance. Then you will feel that you are working for something, and you are sure to do your work faithfully and well. Never sell a fee-note— at least not before the consideration service is performed. It leads to negligence and dishonesty—negligence, by losing interest in the case, and dishonesty in refusing to refund, when you have allowed the consideration to fail.

There is a vague popular belief that lawyers are necessarily dishonest. I say *vague,* because when we consider to what extent *confidence,* and *honors* are reposed in, and conferred upon lawyers by the people, it appears improbable that their *impression* of dishonesty is very distinct and vivid. Yet the impression, is common—almost universal. Let no young man, choosing the law for a calling, for a moment yield to this popular belief. Resolve to be honest at all events; and if, in your own judgment, you can not be an honest lawyer, resolve to be honest without being a lawyer. Choose some other occupation, rather than one in the choosing of which you do, in advance, consent to be a knave.

"THE PRESIDENCY ... IS NO BED OF ROSES"

From a Eulogy of Zachary Taylor, Chicago, Illinois

[JULY 25, 1850]

In 1848, Lincoln abandoned his idol, Henry Clay, to support the Mexican War hero Zachary Taylor for president. Lincoln believed only Taylor could defeat the Democrats, and the general went on to do so. Once elected, however, Taylor disappointed Lincoln by denying him a federal appointment he coveted. Nevertheless, when President Taylor died only sixteen months after taking office, Lincoln delivered this eulogy in Chicago. It included his assertion that political institutions were worthless without popular support. Lincoln ended the eulogy by quoting one of his favorite poems, a verse by William Knox.

The Presidency, even to the most experienced politicians, is no bed of roses; and Gen. Taylor like others, found thorns within it. No human being can fill that station and escape censure. Still I hope and believe when Gen. Taylor's official conduct shall come to be viewed in the calm light of history, he will be found to have *deserved* as little as any who have succeeded him.

Upon the death of Gen. Taylor, as it would in the case of the death of any President, we are naturally led to consider what will be its effect, politically, upon the country. I will not pretend to believe that all the wisdom, or all the patriotism of the country, died with Gen. Taylor. But we know that *wisdom* and *patriotism,* in a public office, under institutions like ours, are wholly inefficient and worthless, unless they are sustained by the confidence and devotion of the people. And I confess my apprehensions, that in the death of the late President, we have lost a degree of that confidence and devotion, which will not soon again pertain to any successor. Between public measures regarded as antagonistic, there is often less real difference in its bearing on the public weal, than there is between the dispute being *kept up,* or being *settled* either way. I fear the one *great* question of the day, is not now so likely to be partially acquiesced in by the different sections of the Union, as it would have been, could Gen. Taylor have been spared to us. Yet, under all circumstances, trusting to our Maker, and through his wisdom and beneficence, to the great body of our people, we will not despair, nor despond.

. . . .

The death of the late President may not be without its use, in reminding us, that *we,* too, must die. Death, abstractly considered, is the same with the high as with the low; but practically, we are not so much aroused to the contemplation of our own mortal natures, by the fall of *many* undistinguished, as that of *one* great, and well known, name. By the latter, we are forced to muse, and ponder, sadly.

"Oh, why should the spirit of mortal be proud"

So the multitude goes, like the flower or the weed,
That withers away to let others succeed;
So the multitude comes, even those we behold,
To repeat every tale that has often been told.

For we are the same, our fathers have been,
We see the same sights our fathers have seen;
We drink the same streams and see the same sun
And run the same course our fathers have run.

They loved; but the story *we* cannot unfold;
They scorned, but the heart of the haughty is cold;
They grieved, but no wail from their slumbers will come,
They joyed, but the tongue of their gladness is dumb.

They died! Aye, they died; we things that are now;
That work on the turf that lies on their brow,
And make in their dwellings a transient abode,
Meet the things that they met on their pilgrimage road.

Yea! hope and despondency, pleasure and pain,
Are mingled together in sun-shine and rain;
And the smile and the tear, and the song and the dirge,
Still follow each other, like surge upon surge.

'Tis the wink of an eye, 'tis the draught of a breath,
From the blossoms of health, to the paleness of death.
From the gilded saloon, to the bier and the shroud.
Oh, why should the spirit of mortal be proud!

"PRINCIPLES HELD DEAR"

Resolutions Supporting Hungarian Freedom,
Springfield, Illinois

[JANUARY 9, 1852]

These resolutions were inspired by Hungarian freedom fighter Lajos Kossuth's visit to America. They were adopted by a Springfield meeting that Lincoln addressed. They not only endorsed Kossuth's efforts but also expressed sympathy with the fights for freedom in Germany, France, and Ireland. The Springfielders met a few weeks later to adopt a new resolution inviting Kossuth to their city, but there is no record that he ever paid such a visit.

Whereas, in the opinion of this meeting, the arrival of Kossuth in our country, in connection with the recent events in Hungary, and with the appeal he is now making in behalf of his country, presents an occasion upon which we, the American people, cannot remain silent, without justifying an inference against our continued devotion to the principles of our free institutions, therefore,

Resolved, 1. That it is the right of any people, sufficiently numerous for national independence, to throw off, to revolutionize, their existing form of government, and to establish such other in its stead as they may choose.

2. That it is the duty of our government to neither foment, nor assist, such revolutions in other governments.

3. That, as we may not legally or warrantably interfere abroad, *to aid,* so no other government may interfere abroad, *to suppress* such revolutions; and that we should at once, announce to the world, our determinations to insist upon this *mutuality* of non-intervention, as a sacred principle of the international law.

4. That the late interference of Russia in the Hungarian struggle was, in our opinion, such illegal and unwarrantable interference.

5. That to have resisted Russia in that case, or to resist any power in a like case, would be no violation of our own cherished principles of

non-intervention, but, on the contrary, would be ever meritorious, in us, or any independent nation.

6. That whether we will, in fact, interfere in such case, is purely a question of policy, to be decided when the exigency arrives.

7. That we recognize in Governor Kossuth of Hungary the most worthy and distinguished representative of the cause of civil and religious liberty on the continent of Europe. A cause for which he and his nation struggled until they were overwhelmed by the armed intervention of a foreign despot, in violation of the more sacred principles of the laws of nature and of nations—principles held dear by the friends of freedom everywhere, and more especially by the people of these United States.

8. That the sympathies of this country, and the benefits of its position, should be exerted in favor of the people of every nation struggling to be free; and whilst we meet to do honor to Kossuth and Hungary, we should not fail to pour out the tribute of our praise and approbation to the patriotic efforts of the Irish, the Germans and the French, who have unsuccessfully fought to establish in their several governments the supremacy of the people.

9. That there is nothing in the past history of the British government, or in its present expressed policy, to encourage the belief that she will aid, in any manner, in the delivery of continental Europe from the yoke of despotism; and that her treatment of Ireland, of [Journalist James or perhaps political insurgent Smith—eds.] O'Brien, [patriot and author John—eds.] Mitchell [sic], and other worthy patriots, forces the conclusion that she will join her efforts to the despots of Europe in suppressing every effort of the people to establish free governments, based upon the principles of true religious and civil liberty.

"A DEEP DEVOTION TO THE CAUSE OF HUMAN LIBERTY"

From a Eulogy of Henry Clay, Springfield, Illinois

[JULY 6, 1852]

In years to come, his arch-rival Stephen A. Douglas enjoyed reminding audiences that Lincoln had deserted Henry Clay in 1848, but Lincoln insisted that the Great Compromiser remained his "beau ideal" of a statesman. As president, he told his hero's son: "I recognize his voice, speaking as it ever spoke, for the Union, the Constitution, and the freedom of mankind." Lincoln delivered his eulogy in the state capitol.

On the fourth day of July, 1776, the people of a few feeble and oppressed colonies of Great Britain, inhabiting a portion of the Atlantic coast of North America, publicly declared their national independence, and made their appeal to the justice of their cause, and to the God of battles, for the maintainance of that declaration. That people were few in numbers, and without resources, save only their own wise heads and stout hearts. Within the first year of that declared independence, and while its maintainance was yet problematical—while the bloody struggle between those resolute rebels, and their haughty would-be-masters, was still waging, of undistinguished parents, and in an obscure district of one of those colonies, Henry Clay was born. The infant nation, and the infant child began the race of life together. For three quarters of a century they have travelled hand in hand. They have been companions ever. The nation has passed its perils, and is free, prosperous, and powerful. The child has reached his manhood, his middle age, his old age, and is dead. In all that has concerned the nation the man ever sympathised; and now the nation mourns for the man.

. . . .

Mr. Clay's predominant sentiment, from first to last, was a deep devotion to the cause of human liberty—a strong sympathy with the oppressed every where, and an ardent wish for their elevation. With him, this was a primary and all controlling passion. Subsidiary to this was the conduct of his whole life. He loved his country partly because it was his own country, but mostly because it was a free country; and he burned with a zeal for its advancement, prosperity and glory, because he saw in such, the advancement, prosperity and glory, of human liberty, human right and human nature. He desired the prosperity of his countrymen partly because they were his countrymen, but chiefly to show to the world that freemen could be prosperous.

· · · · · · · · · ·

Having been led to allude to domestic slavery so frequently already, I am unwilling to close without referring more particularly to Mr. Clay's views and conduct in regard to it. He ever was, on principle and in feeling, opposed to slavery. The very earliest, and one of the latest public efforts of his life, separated by a period of more than fifty years, were both made in favor of gradual emancipation of the slaves in Kentucky. He did not perceive, that on a question of human right, the negroes were to be excepted from the human race. And yet Mr. Clay was the owner of slaves. Cast into life where slavery was already widely spread and deeply seated, he did not perceive, as I think no wise man has perceived, how it could be at *once* eradicated, without producing a greater evil, even to the cause of human liberty itself. His feeling and his judgment, therefore, ever led him to oppose both extremes of opinion on the subject. Those who would shiver into fragments the Union of these States; tear to tatters its now venerated constitution; and even burn the last copy of the Bible, rather than slavery should continue a single hour, together with all their more halting sympathisers, have received, and are receiving their just execration; and the name, and opinions, and influence of Mr. Clay, are fully, and, as I trust, effectually and endearingly, arrayed against them. But I would also, if I could, array his name, opinions, and influence against the opposite extreme— against a few, but an increasing number of men, who, for the sake of perpetuating slavery, are beginning to assail and to ridicule the white-man's charter of freedom—the declaration that "all men are created free and equal."

⫸ II ⫷

"ALL WE HAVE EVER HELD SACRED"

Lincoln and Slavery

1854–1857

Lincoln's "lantern jaws" are particularly pronounced in this rustic pose, a daguerreotype made by Johan Carl Frederic Polycarpus Von Schneidau in Chicago, Illinois, in late October 1854—around the time of his major address on the Kansas-Nebraska Act in Peoria. A journalist who saw him speak sometime later described Lincoln's face as "almost grotesquely square, with high cheekbones" and a complexion that made him look "swarthy as an Indian, with wiry, jet-black hair . . . in an unkempt condition." Lincoln's law partner, William H. Herndon, admitted that his hair floated "where his fingers or the winds left it, piled up at random."

(Photograph: Lloyd Ostendorf, Dayton, Ohio)

Introduction

BY WILLIAM E. GIENAPP

"I have always hated slavery," Abraham Lincoln affirmed on one occasion, "I think as much as any Abolitionist." Be that as it may, slavery was not initially a major concern for him, and while he publicly condemned the institution as early as 1837, he firmly opposed the abolitionist movement and its crusade against slavery. As a member of Congress (1847–1849), he steadfastly supported the Wilmot Proviso, which prohibited slavery from all the territory acquired from Mexico, but he refused to join the Free Soil Party in 1848 and instead backed Zachary Taylor, a slaveholder, for president. As he later recalled, he remained quiet under the comforting assumption that the institution would eventually disappear.

Following his retirement from Congress in 1849, Lincoln turned his attention to his legal profession and became a successful attorney. With his political ambitions blocked by the hopelessness of the Whig cause in Illinois, he seemed to have largely lost interest in politics, when passage of the Kansas-Nebraska Act suddenly gave renewed life to the issue of the expansion of slavery. Passed at the behest of the South, this statute repealed the time-honored Missouri Compromise of 1820, which had barred slavery from the northern part of the Louisiana Purchase, in favor of the principle of popular sovereignty, by which the residents of the territories, at some unspecified time, were to decide whether they wanted slavery or not. A storm of protest swept across the North as Whigs, Democrats, and Free Soilers joined in condemning this reckless destruction of what many considered a sacred sectional compact. Led by Senator Stephen A. Douglas of Illinois, the law's

Northern supporters claimed that under popular sovereignty Kansas and Nebraska would become free states, but critics including Lincoln contended that the real purpose of the Kansas-Nebraska Act was to promote the expansion of slavery, especially into Kansas.

"Thunderstruck and stunned," as he put it, by this unexpected re-opening of the slavery controversy, Lincoln took the stump and campaigned across Illinois in 1854, delivering a series of speeches denouncing the repeal of the Missouri Compromise and opposing the expansion of slavery. His most famous address that year, given in Peoria, skillfully dissected Douglas's arguments in favor of the Kansas-Nebraska Act. Now convinced that, far from being on the verge of dying out, slavery had instead become an aggressive force in the nation, Lincoln, who testified that "the repeal of the Missouri compromise aroused him as he had never been before," evidenced a new depth of passion and sense of urgency in his public remarks. For the first time slavery assumed a central place in his thought, and he quickly became a major leader of the anti-Nebraska movement in the state. The practice of law would never again have the same importance in his life.

The four years between the introduction of the Kansas-Nebraska bill in 1854 and his nomination for senator in 1858 were critical for Lincoln's political career, now revitalized by the renewal of the agitation over slavery. The strength of the anti-Nebraska movement in Illinois whetted Lincoln's ambition, and he made a strong bid in 1855 to be elected to the U.S. Senate (a lifelong dream of his), but in the end was defeated. Still, he was reluctant to abandon his long-standing allegiance to the dying Whig Party. "I think I am a whig," he told his old friend Joshua F. Speed in 1855, "but others say there are no whigs."

Unlike many of his party colleagues, however, Lincoln refused to join the anti-Catholic, anti-immigrant Know Nothing Party, which was for a brief time a political power in the nation. Because of the Know Nothings' strength in Illinois, Lincoln expressed his criticism privately, but he made his views clear in a letter to Speed. "I am not a Know-Nothing. That is certain. How could I be? How can anyone who abhors the oppression of negroes be in favor of degrading classes of white people?" Lamenting the country's retreat from the standard unfurled in 1776, Lincoln observed that "as a nation, we began by declaring that *'all men are created equal.'* We now practically read it 'all men are created equal, *except negroes.'* When the Know-Nothings get control, it will read 'all men are created equal, except negroes, *and foreigners, and catholics.'* " At the same time, he held aloof from the new sectional Republican Party, which opposed the expansion of slavery. His opposition helped block temporarily the party's formation in Illinois.

Buffeted by the swirling winds of change sweeping across the political landscape, Lincoln soon found himself torn loose from his traditional political moorings. Early in 1856, with the Whig Party clearly on its deathbed and the presidential election looming on the horizon, he assumed leadership of the drive to organize the Republican Party in Illinois and came close to winning the Republican vice presidential nomination that summer. Actively campaigning for the party's national ticket in the fall, he proclaimed that "the question is simply this: Shall slavery be spread into the new Territories, or not?"

In the aftermath of the Republicans' defeat in their first national campaign, Lincoln consolidated his position in the state party by forcefully opposing the Dred Scott Decision and the admission of Kansas under the proslavery Lecompton Constitution. By the time the Lecompton Constitution was defeated in Congress in the spring of 1858, Lincoln had emerged as his party's leading choice to oppose Stephen A. Douglas in the upcoming senatorial contest. These years formed the vital background for Lincoln's ultimate emergence as a national Republican leader.

Although he continued to refine and develop his arguments, Lincoln's antislavery principles did not significantly change during these years. His opposition to slavery derived from certain fundamental beliefs rooted in the uniqueness of the American experience: the promise of equality, the nature of opportunity in a free society, the Republic's special destiny, and the importance of the Union. Lincoln was not a political philosopher, and none of these ideas was original with him, but he expressed them with unusual eloquence and power. He consistently argued that slavery was a great moral evil, fundamentally incompatible with democracy.

The starting point for Lincoln's attitudes toward slavery, as for most of his political thought, was not the Constitution but the Declaration of Independence. He was careful to insist that the Constitution had to be obeyed and its provisions concerning slavery respected, but for Lincoln the Declaration, with its assertion of human equality, had established the "central ideas" of the Republic. What distinguished the

American Republic in his eyes was that it was based on an idea. Over and over in his speeches during this period, he insisted that slavery violated the American belief in liberty and equality. Calling on his fellow Americans to uphold the principles of the Declaration, Lincoln insisted that "the spirit of seventy-six and the spirit of Nebraska, are utter antagonisms."

Lincoln's emphasis on equality, however, raised the difficult problem of race. Keenly aware of the strong antiblack sentiment in his state, he hastened to deny that he believed in social or political equality for blacks, but he nevertheless insisted that they were included in the Declaration's promise of equality. He repudiated the idea that it was a document only for whites, or that it had relevance only to the situation in 1776. Individuals were not equal in all respects, he explained, but in natural rights—defined by Thomas Jefferson in the Declaration as life, liberty, and the pursuit of happiness—they were equal. While he recognized that inequality continued to exist in America, he argued that the Declaration of Independence "set up a standard maxim for free society," which "though never perfectly attained" should be "revered by all" and "constantly labored for." Until recently, the nation's progress had been steadily toward greater equality in practice. Now the movement to extend slavery threatened to overthrow this progress, and he urged Americans not to give up their old faith of human equality for the new doctrine of slavery's expansion. "Is there no danger to liberty itself," he pointedly asked, "in discarding the . . . first precept of our ancient faith?"

Like most Republicans, Lincoln insisted that the Founding Fathers hoped that slavery would die out and therefore had opposed its expansion. He traced this policy back to Jefferson and the Northwest Ordinance of 1787, which prohibited slavery from the territory north of the Ohio River (from which the state of Illinois, among others, was eventually created). In advancing this argument, Lincoln exaggerated the antislavery doctrines—and especially actions—of the Founders, whose record on slavery was more mixed than he conceded. This theory, however, served the vital purpose of linking opposition to the expansion of slavery to the principles of the American Revolution, thereby enhancing its legitimacy.

Unlike many Republicans, Lincoln charitably refused to condemn Southerners for the institution of slavery. "I have no prejudice against the Southern people," he asserted, observing that "they are just what we would be in their situation." Still, he fully shared the abolitionists' belief that slavery was a "monstrous injustice." He dismissed the pro-slavery argument that slavery was a positive good with the telling comment that "although volume upon volume is written to prove slavery a very good thing, we never hear of the man who wishes to take the good of it, *by being a slave himself.*" "My ancient faith teaches me that 'all men are created equal,'" he declared on another occasion, "and that there can be no moral right in connection with one man's making a slave of another."

Another major theme in Lincoln's antislavery thought was his belief in opportunity. Having overcome the hardship and limited education of his youth, Lincoln placed great emphasis on the necessity of safeguarding opportunity as part of the American heritage. Everyone, he contended, had a right to "make himself," to move up in life as he had done. Unlike other countries, in the United States "we proposed to give *all* a chance." Slavery denied slaves the basic right of self-improvement by robbing them of the fruits of their own labor. Nor did Lincoln restrict this right to males. "In her natural right to eat the bread she earns with her own hands without asking leave of anyone else," Lincoln affirmed, a black woman "is my equal, and the equal of all others."

Lincoln's vision of the good society was essentially one dominated by independent proprietors—the small farmers and shopkeepers who constituted the backbone of free society. He extolled the social mobility of Northern society, insisting that it contained no class of permanent laborers. "The man who labored for another last year, this year labors for himself, and next year will hire others to labor for him." This social ideal, however, was threatened by the expansion of slavery. Unable to compete with slavery, free labor would inevitably be driven out of any territory where slavery existed. Consequently, the question of the expansion of slavery was of vital concern to the whole nation, not just to the residents of the territory. Speaking of the territories, he said, "We want them for the homes of free white people. This they cannot be, to any considerable extent, if slavery shall be planted within them." The preservation of white opportunity required that slavery be kept out of the western territories.

The third fundamental idea reflected in Lincoln's opposition to slavery was the concept of mission. Since the Revolution, Americans had believed that the United States had a unique responsibility to serve as an example for the rest of the world. By demonstrating that democracy was a workable form of government, America represented the best hope for the future. Lincoln wholeheartedly endorsed this idea of a special national purpose, proclaiming that "we stand at once the wonder and admiration of the whole world." To Lincoln, slavery was inconsistent with the national belief in democracy and thus undermined America's moral leadership. The institution "deprives our republican example of its just influence in the world—enables the enemies of free institutions, with plausibility, to taunt us as hypocrites." America could not fulfill its mission if slavery was a permanent institution.

Lincoln designated the right of self-government "the sheet anchor of American republicanism." He denied that the doctrine of popular sovereignty was based on the principle of democracy, for in practice popular sovereignty would allow the first settlers in a territory to decide the question for all future generations. "The first few may get slavery IN, and the subsequent many cannot easily get it OUT." The territorial period was therefore critical: Let slavery into a territory, Lincoln contended, and it would not be subsequently eliminated. But "keep it out until a vote is taken," he added, "and a vote in favor of it, can not be got in any population of forty thousand, on earth, who have been drawn together by the ordinary motives of emigration and settlement."

Closely related to the idea of mission was Lincoln's reverence for the Union. Lincoln was committed to maintaining the Union, the shield and guardian of American liberty. "Much as I hate slavery," he forthrightly explained, "I would consent to the extension of it rather than see the Union dissolved, just as I would consent to any GREAT evil, to avoid a GREATER one." Yet the real threat to the Union, he continued, stemmed from the attempt to extend slavery into the territories, which inflamed passions and recklessly reopened the sectional controversy. Predicting accurately that violence would quickly break out in Kansas between pro- and antislavery partisans following passage of the Kansas-Nebraska Act, he asked prophetically, "Will not the first drop of blood so shed, be the real knell of the Union?"

In formulating a practical program to deal with slavery, Lincoln, despite his moral hatred of the institution, was careful to demand only that slavery not expand further. Calling for restoration of the Missouri Compromise, he denied that the federal government had any power to interfere with slavery in the states where it already existed. And in contrast to many antislavery people, he did not minimize the problem of getting rid of slavery. "If all earthly power were given me," he confessed, "I should not know what to do, as to the existing institution."

The major shift in Lincoln's thinking during this period concerned the precise nature of the threat slavery posed to the Republic. The Supreme Court's Dred Scott Decision in 1857, which declared that Congress had no power to prohibit slavery from the territories, and the struggle over the admission of Kansas under the proslavery Lecompton Constitution the following year, provided the impetus for this critical change.

For Lincoln, the Dred Scott Decision raised disturbing questions about the future place of slavery in the United States. Far from declining, slavery was getting stronger, and as he pondered the significance of the Court's ruling, he increasingly was convinced that it was part of a movement to make slavery a permanent, national institution. The attempt to admit Kansas as a slave state under the Lecompton Constitution, which represented the desire of a small minority of settlers in the territory, intensified his concern. This effort to impose slavery on Kansas would eventually fail, but at the beginning of the struggle in Congress, before the outcome was clear, Lincoln jotted down his thoughts on the crisis confronting the nation. This fragment, which served as the basis for his famous House Divided speech a few months later, heralded a decisive turn in Lincoln's thought on slavery in the Republic.

Previously Lincoln had emphasized the incompatibility of slavery with the ideals of democracy, and had stressed the danger slavery's expansion posed to free labor in the territories. Now as the struggle over the Lecompton Constitution unfolded, Lincoln glimpsed a more ominous threat, not just to the territories, but to the free states as well. Proclaiming that the nation could not endure permanently half slave and half free, Lincoln predicted that either slavery would eventually be abolished, or it would spread everywhere and convert the United States into a great slaveholding empire. "Welcome, or unwelcome, agreeable or disagreeable, whether this shall be an entire slave nation, *is* the issue before us." With the outcome of this struggle clouded in doubt, Lincoln nonetheless reaffirmed his unwavering belief in democracy: "To give the victory to the right," he argued, "not bloody *bullets,* but *peaceful ballots* only, are necessary." Tragically, the escalating conflict between the sections would ultimately destroy this hope for a peaceful solution to the dilemma of slavery.

→≫ ≪←

"WE PROPOSED TO GIVE *ALL* A CHANCE"

Fragments on Slavery

[JULY I, 1854?]

Passage in 1854 of the Kansas-Nebraska Act gave slavery new life north of the cutoff line established thirty-four years earlier under the Missouri Compromise. It also brought Lincoln back into politics as an outspoken opponent of the extension of slavery. Lincoln's private secretary arbitrarily assigned these fragments the date 1854; others have suggested they were written as many as five years later. The beginning of the piece has never been located.

. . . dent truth. Made so plain by our good Father in Heaven, that all *feel* and *understand* it, even down to brutes and creeping insects. The ant, who has toiled and dragged a crumb to his nest, will furiously defend the fruit of his labor, against whatever robber assails him. So plain, that the most dumb and stupid slave that ever toiled for a master, does constantly *know* that he is wronged. So plain that no one, high or low, ever does mistake it, except in a plainly *selfish* way; for although volume upon volume is written to prove slavery a very good thing, we never hear of the man who wishes to take the good of it, *by being a slave himself.*

Most governments have been based, practically, on the denial of equal rights of men, as I have, in part, stated them; *ours* began, by *affirming* those rights. *They* said, some men are too *ignorant,* and *vicious,* to share in government. Possibly so, said we; and, by your system, you would always keep them ignorant, and vicious. We proposed to give *all* a chance; and we expected the weak to grow stronger, the ignorant, wiser; and all better, and happier together.

We made the experiment; and the fruit is before us. Look at it—think of it. Look at it, in it's aggregate grandeur, of extent of country, and numbers of population—of ship, and steamboat, and rail-

---

If A. can prove, however conclusively, that he may, of right, enslave B.—why may not B. snatch the same argument, and prove equally, that he may enslave A?—

You say A. is white, and B. is black. It is *color,* then; the lighter, having the right to enslave the darker? Take care. By this rule, you are to be slave to the first man you meet, with a fairer skin than your own.

You do not mean *color* exactly?—You mean the whites are *intellectually* the superiors of the blacks, and, therefore have the right to enslave them? Take care again. By this rule, you are to be slave to the first man you meet, with an intellect superior to your own.

But, say you, it is a question of *interest;* and, if you can make it your *interest,* you have the right to enslave another. Very well. And if he can make it his interest, he has the right to enslave you.

" 'To Do for the People What Needs to Be Done' "

Fragments on Government

[JULY 1, 1854?]

These famous expressions of political philosophy demonstrated Lincoln's belief that "joint effort" or "combined action" by government was required to help the weakest members of society. Five years later he would admit that "government is not charged with the duty of redressing or preventing all *the wrongs in the world,"* but he added: *"Government rightfully may, and . . . ought to, redress all wrongs which are wrongs to the nation itself."*

The legitimate object of government, is to do for a community of people, whatever they need to have done, but can not do, *at all,* or can not, *so well do,* for themselves—in their separate, and individual capacities.

In all that the people can individually do as well for themselves, government ought not to interfere.

The desirable things which the individuals of a people can not do, or can not well do, for themselves, fall into two classes: those which have relation to *wrongs,* and those which have not. Each of these branch off into an infinite variety of subdivisions.

The first—that in relation to wrongs—embraces all crimes, misdemeanors, and non-performance of contracts. The other embraces all which, in its nature, and without wrong, requires combined action, as public roads and highways, public schools, charities, pauperism, orphanage, estates of the deceased, and the machinery of government itself.

From this it appears that if all men were just, there still would be *some,* though not so *much,* need of government.

Government is a combination of the people of a country to effect certain objects by joint effort. The best framed and best administered governments are necessarily expensive; while by errors in frame and maladministration most of them are more onerous than they need be, and some of them very oppressive. Why, then, should we have government? Why not each individual take to himself the whole fruit of his labor, without having any of it taxed away, in services, corn, or money? Why not take just so much land as he can cultivate with his own hands, without buying it of any one?

The legitimate object of government is "to do for the people what needs to be done, but which they can not, by individual effort, do at all, or do so well, for themselves." There are many such things—some of them exist independently of the injustice in the world. Making and maintaining roads, bridges, and the like; providing for the helpless young and afflicted; common schools; and disposing of deceased men's property, are instances.

But a far larger class of objects springs from the injustice of men. If one people will make war upon another, it is a necessity with that other to unite and coöperate for defense. Hence the military department. If some men will kill, or beat, or constrain others, or despoil them of property, by force, fraud, or noncompliance with contracts, it is a common object with peaceful and just men to prevent it. Hence the criminal and civil departments.

"OUR REPUBLICAN ROBE IS SOILED"

From a Speech on the Kansas-Nebraska Act, Peoria, Illinois

[OCTOBER 16, 1854]

Four years before the famous Lincoln-Douglas campaign debates, Lincoln and Senator Stephen A. Douglas debated the Kansas-Nebraska Act, although not face-to-face. In Peoria, Douglas offered a three-hour-long defense of the new law from 2 to 5 P.M. Lincoln's equally long response, which is excerpted here, began at 7 P.M. after a two-hour recess. It presented Lincoln's most powerful moral case to date against "one man's making a slave of another." Lincoln continued his anti-Nebraska speechmaking across the state, one newspaper commenting, "his eloquence greatly impressed all his hearers."

. . . I wish to MAKE and to KEEP the distinction between the EXISTING institution [slavery—eds.], and the EXTENSION of it, so broad, and so clear, that no honest man can misunderstand me, and no dishonest one, successfully misrepresent me.

In order to [get] a clear understanding of what the Missouri Compromise is, a short history of the preceding kindred subjects will perhaps be proper. When we established our independence, we did not own, or claim, the country to which this compromise applies. Indeed, strictly speaking, the confederacy then owned no country at all; the States respectively owned the country within their limits; and some of them owned territory beyond their strict State limits. . . . These territories, together with the States themselves, constituted all the country over which the confederacy then claimed any sort of jurisdiction. We were then living under the Articles of Confederation, which were superceded by the Constitution several years afterwards. The question of ceding these territories to the general government was set on foot. Mr. Jefferson, the author of the Declaration of Independence, and otherwise a chief actor in the revolution; then a delegate in Congress; afterwards twice President; who was, is, and perhaps will continue to be, the most distinguished politician of our history; a Virginian by birth and continued residence, and withal, a slave-holder; conceived the idea of taking that occasion, to prevent slavery ever going into the north-western territory. He prevailed on the Virginia Legislature to adopt his views, and to cede the territory, making the prohibition of slavery therein, a condition of the deed [Lincoln erred on this point, and later corrected it—eds.]. Congress accepted the cession, with the condition; and in the first Ordinance (which the acts of Congress were then called) for the government of the territory, provided that slavery should never be permitted therein. This is the famed ordinance of '87 so often spoken of. Thenceforward, for sixty-one years, and until in 1848, the last scrap of this territory came into the Union as the State of Wisconsin, all parties acted in quiet obedience to this ordinance. It is now what Jefferson foresaw and intended—the happy home of teeming millions of free, white, prosperous people, and no slave amongst them.

Thus, with the author of the declaration of Independence, the policy of prohibiting slavery in new territory originated. Thus, away back of the constitution, in the pure fresh, free breath of the revolution, the State of Virginia, and the National congress put that policy in practice. Thus through sixty odd of the best years of the republic did that policy steadily work to its great and beneficent end. And thus, in those five states, and five millions of free, enterprising people, we have before us the rich fruits of this policy. But *now* new light breaks upon us. Now congress declares this ought never to have been; and the like of it, must never be again. The sacred right of self government is grossly violated by it! We even find some men, who drew their first breath, and every other breath of their lives, under this very restriction, now live in dread of absolute suffocation, if they should be restricted in the "sacred right" of taking slaves to Nebraska. That *perfect* liberty they sigh for—the liberty of making slaves of other people—Jefferson never thought of; their own father never thought of; they never thought of themselves, a year ago. How fortunate for them, they did not sooner become sensible of their great misery! Oh, how difficult it is to treat with respect, such assaults upon all we have ever really held sacred.

. . . .

I think, and shall try to show, that it [the repeal of the Missouri Compromise—eds.] is wrong; wrong in its direct effect, letting slavery into Kansas and Nebraska—and wrong in its prospective principle, allowing it to spread to every other part of the wide world, where men can be found inclined to take it.

This *declared* indifference, but as I must think, covert *real* zeal for the spread of slavery, I can not but hate. I hate it because of the monstrous injustice of slavery itself. I hate it because it deprives our republican example of its just influence in the world—enables the enemies of free institutions, with plausibility, to taunt us as hypocrites—causes the real friends of freedom to doubt our sincerity, and especially because it forces so many really good men amongst ourselves into an open war with the very fundamental principles of civil liberty—criticising the Declaration of Independence, and insisting that there is no right principle of action but *self-interest*.

Before proceeding, let me say I think I have no prejudice against the Southern people. They are just what we would be in their situation. If slavery did not now exist amongst them, they would not introduce it. If it did now exist amongst us, we should not instantly give it up. This I believe of the masses north and south. Doubtless there are individuals, on both sides, who would not hold slaves under any circumstances; and others who would gladly introduce slavery anew, if it were out of existence. We know that some southern men do free their slaves, go north, and become tip-top abolitionists; while some northern ones go south, and become most cruel slave-masters.

When southern people tell us they are no more responsible for the origin of slavery, than we; I acknowledge the fact. When it is said that the institution exists, and that it is very difficult to get rid of it, in any satisfactory way, I can understand and appreciate the saying. I surely will not blame them for not doing what I should not know how to do myself. If all earthly power were given me, I should not know what to do, as to the existing institution. My first impulse would be to free all the slaves, and send them to Liberia,—to their own native land. But a moment's reflection would convince me, that whatever of high hope, (as I think there is) there may be in this, in the long run, its sudden execution is impossible. If they were all landed there in a day, they would all perish in the next ten days; and there are not surplus shipping and surplus money enough in the world to carry them there in many times ten days. What then? Free them all, and keep them among us as underlings? Is it quite certain that this betters their condition? I think I would not hold one in slavery, at any rate; yet the point is not clear enough for me to denounce people upon. What next? Free them, and make them politically and socially, our equals? My own feelings will not admit of this; and if mine would, we well know that those of the great mass of white people will not. Whether this feeling accords with justice and sound judgment, is not the sole question, if indeed, it is any part of it. A universal feeling, whether well or ill-founded, can not be safely disregarded. We can not, then, make them equals. It does seem to me that systems of gradual emancipation might be adopted; but for their tardiness in this, I will not undertake to judge our brethren of the south.

When they remind us of their constitutional rights, I acknowledge them, not grudgingly, but fully, and fairly; and I would give them any legislation for the reclaiming of their fugitives, which should not, in its stringency, be more likely to carry a free man into slavery, than our ordinary criminal laws are to hang an innocent one.

But all this, to my judgment, furnishes no more excuse for permitting slavery to go into our own free territory, than it would for reviving the African slave trade by law. The law which forbids the bringing of slaves *from* Africa; and that which has so long forbid the taking them *to* Nebraska, can hardly be distinguished on any moral principle; and the repeal of the former could find quite as plausible excuses as that of the latter.

. . . .

But it is said, there now is *no* law in Nebraska on the subject of slavery; and that, in such case, taking a slave there, operates his freedom. That *is* good book-law; but is not the rule of actual practice. Wherever slavery is, it has been first introducted without law. The oldest laws we find concerning it, are not laws introducing it; but *regulating* it, as an already existing thing. A white man takes his slave to Nebraska now; who will inform the negro that he is free? Who will take him before court to test the question of his freedom? In ignorance of his legal emancipation, he is kept chopping, splitting and plowing. Others are brought, and move on in the same track. At last, if ever the time for voting comes, on the question of slavery, the institution already in fact exists in the country, and cannot well be removed. The facts of its presence, and the difficulty of its removal will carry the vote in its favor. Keep it out until a vote is taken, and a vote in favor of it, can not be got in any population of forty thousand, on earth, who have been drawn together by the ordinary motives of emigration and settlement. To get slaves into the country simultaneously with the whites, in the incipient stages of settlement, is the precise stake played for, and won in this Nebraska measure.

. . . .

Equal justice to the south, it is said, requires us to consent to the extending of slavery to new countries. That is to say, inasmuch as you do not object to my taking my hog to Nebraska, therefore I must not object to you taking your slave. Now, I admit this is perfectly logical, if there is no difference between hogs and negroes. But while you thus require me to deny the humanity of the negro, I wish to ask whether you of the south yourselves, have ever been willing to do as much? It is kindly provided that of all those who come into the world, only a small percentage are natural tyrants. That percentage is no larger in the slave States than in the free. The great majority, south as well as north, have human sympathies, of which they can no more divest themselves than they can of their sensibility to physical pain. These sympathies in the bosoms of the southern people, manifest in many ways, their sense of the wrong of slavery, and their consciousness that, after all, there is humanity in the negro. If they deny this, let me address them a few plain questions. In 1820 you joined the north, almost unanimously, in declaring the African slave trade piracy, and in annexing to it the punishment of death. Why did you do this? If you did not feel that it was wrong, why did you join in providing that men should be hung for it? The practice was no more than bringing wild negroes from Africa, to sell to such as would buy them. But you never thought of hanging men for catching and selling wild horses, wild buffaloes or wild bears. . . .

And yet again; there are in the United State and territories, including the District of Columbia, 433,643 free blacks. At $500 per head they are worth over two hundred millions of dollars. How comes this vast amount of property to be running about without owners? We do not see free horses or free cattle running at large. How is this? All these free blacks are the descendants of slaves, or have been slaves themselves, and they would be slaves now, but for SOMETHING which has operated on their white owners, inducing them, at vast pecuniary sacrifices, to liberate them. What is that SOMETHING? Is there any mistaking it? In all these cases it is your sense of justice, and human sympathy, continually telling you, that the poor negro has some natural right to himself—that those who deny it, and make mere merchandise of him, deserve kickings, contempt and death.

And now, why will you ask us to deny the humanity of the slave? and estimate him only as the equal of the hog? Why ask us to do what you will not do yourselves? Why ask us to do for *nothing,* what two hundred million of dollars could not induce you to do?

But one great argument in the support of the repeal of the Missouri Compromise, is still to come. That argument is "the sacred right of self government." It seems our distinguished Senator [Douglas] has found great difficulty in getting his antagonists, even in the Senate to meet him fairly on this argument. Some poet has said

"Fools rush in where angels fear to tread."

At the hazzard of being thought one of the fools of this quotation, I meet that argument—I rush in, I take that bull by the horns.

I trust I understand, and truly estimate the right of self-government. My faith in the proposition that each man should do precisely as he pleases with all which is exclusively his own, lies at the foundation of the sense of justice there is in me. I extend the principles to communities of men, as well as to individuals. I so extend it, because it is politically wise, as well as naturally just: politically wise, in saving us from broils about matters which do not concern us. Here, or at Washington, I would not trouble myself with the oyster laws of Virginia, or the cranberry laws of Indiana.

The doctrine of self-government is right—absolutely and eternally right—but it has no just application, as here attempted. Or perhaps I should rather say that whether it has such just application depends upon whether a negro is *not* or *is* a man. If he is *not* a man, why in that case, he who *is* a man may, as a matter of self-government, do just as he pleases with him. But if the negro *is* a man, is it not to that extent, a total destruction of self-government, to say that he too shall not govern *himself?* When the white man governs himself that is self-government; but when he governs himself, and also governs *another* man, that is *more* than self-government—that is despotism. If the negro is a *man,* why then my ancient faith teaches me that "all men are created equal;" and that there can be no moral right in connection with one man's making a slave of another.

Judge Douglas frequently, with bitter irony and sarcasm, paraphrases our argument by saying "The white people of Nebraska are good enough to govern themselves, *but they are not good enough to govern a few miserable negroes*!!"

Well I doubt not that the people of Nebraska are, and will continue to be as good as the average of people elsewhere. I do not say the contrary. What I do say is, that no man is good enough to govern another man, *without that other's consent.* I say this is the leading principle—the sheet anchor of American republicanism. Our Declaration of Independence says:

"We hold these truths to be self evident: that all men are created equal; that they are endowed by their Creator with certain inalienable rights; that among these are life, liberty and the pursuit of happiness. That to secure these rights, governments are instituted among men, DERIVING THEIR JUST POWERS FROM THE CONSENT OF THE GOVERNED."

I have quoted so much at this time merely to show that according to our ancient faith, the just powers of governments are derived from the consent of the governed. Now the relation of masters and slaves is, PRO TANTO [to that extent—eds.], a total violation of this principle. The master not only governs the slave without his consent; but he governs him by a set of rules altogether different from those which he prescribes for himself. Allow ALL the governed an equal voice in the government, and that, and that only is self-government.

Let it not be said I am contending for the establishment of political and social equality between the whites and blacks. I have already said the contrary. I am not now combating the argument of NECESSITY, arising from the fact that the blacks are already amongst us; but I am combating what is set up as MORAL argument for allowing them to be taken where they have never yet been—arguing against the EXTENSION of a bad thing, which where it already exists, we must of necessity, manage as we best can.

In support of his application of the doctrine of self-government, Senator Douglas has sought to bring to his aid the opinions and examples of our revolutionary fathers. I am glad he has done this. I love the sentiments of those old-time men; and shall be most happy to abide by their opinions. He shows us that when it was in contemplation for the colonies to break off from Great Britain, and set up a new government for themselves, several of the states instructed their delegates to go for the measure PROVIDED EACH STATE SHOULD BE ALLOWED TO REGULATE ITS DOMESTIC CONCERNS IN ITS OWN WAY. I do not quote; but this in substance. This was right. I see nothing objectionable in it. I also think it probable that it had some reference to the existence of slavery amongst them. I will not deny that it had. But had it, in any reference to the carrying of slavery into NEW COUNTRIES? That is the question; and we will let the fathers themselves answer it.

This same generation of men, and mostly the same individuals of the generation, who declared this principle—who declared independence—who fought the war of the revolution through—who afterwards made the constitution under which we still live—these same men passed the ordinance of '87, declaring that slavery should never go to the northwest territory. I have no doubt Judge Douglas thinks they were very inconsistent in this. It is a question of discrimination between them and him. But there is not an inch of ground left for his claiming that their opinions—their example—their authority—are on his side in this controversy.

Again, is not Nebraska, while a territory, a part of us? Do we not own the country? And if we surrender the control of it, do we not surrender the right of self-government? It is part of ourselves. If you say we shall not control it because it is ONLY part, the same is true of every other part; and when all the parts are gone, what has become of the whole? What is then left of us? What use for the general government, when there is nothing left for it [to] govern?

But you say this question should be left to the people of Nebraska, because they are more particularly interested. If this be the rule, you must leave it to each individual to say for himself whether he will have slaves. What better moral right have thirty-one citizens of Nebraska to say, that the thirty-second shall not hold slaves, than the people of the thirty-one States have to say that slavery shall not go into the thirty-second State at all ? . . .

Another important objection to this application of the right of self-government, is that it enables the first FEW, to deprive the succeeding MANY, of a free exercise of the right of self-government. The first few may get slavery IN, and the subsequent many cannot easily get it OUT. How common is the remark now in the slave States—"If we were only clear of our slaves, how much better it would be for us." They are actually deprived of the privilege of governing themselves as they would, by the action of a very few, in the beginning. The same thing was true of the whole nation at the time our constitution was formed.

Whether slavery shall go into Nebraska, or other new territories, is not a matter of exclusive concern to the people who may go there. The whole nation is interested that the best use shall be made of these territories. We want them for the homes of free white people. This they cannot be, to any considerable extent, if slavery shall be planted within them. Slave States are places for poor white people to remove FROM; not to remove TO. New free States are the places for poor people to go to and better their condition. For this use, the nation needs these territories.

. . . .

Finally, I insist, that if there is ANY THING which it is the duty of the WHOLE PEOPLE to never entrust to any hands but their own, that thing is the preservation and perpetuity, of their own liberties, and institutions. And if they shall think, as I do, that the extension of slavery endangers them, more than any, or all other causes, how recreant to themselves, if they submit the question, and with it, the fate of their country, to a mere hand-full of men, bent only on temporary self-interest. If this question of slavery extension were an insignificant one—one having no power to do harm—it might be shuffled aside in this way. But being, as it is, the great Behemoth of danger, shall the strong gripe of the nation be loosened upon him, to entrust him to the hands of such feeble keepers?

I have done with this mighty argument, of self-government. Go, sacred thing! Go in peace.

But Nebraska is urged as a great Union-saving measure. Well I too, go for saving the Union. Much as I hate slavery, I would consent to the extension of it rather than see the Union dissolved, just as I would consent to any GREAT evil, to avoid a GREATER one. But when I go to Union saving, I must believe, at least, that the means I employ has some adaptation to the end. To my mind, Nebraska has no such adaptation.

"It hath no relish of salvation in it."

[Hamlet on his uncle's misdeeds—eds.]

It is an aggravation, rather, of the only one thing which ever endangers the Union. When it came upon us, all was peace and quiet. The nation was looking to the forming of new bonds of Union; and a long course of peace and prosperity seemed to lie before us. In the whole range of possibility, there scarcely appears to me to have been any thing, out of which the slavery agitation could have been revived, except the very project of repealing the Missouri compromise. Every inch of territory we owned, already had a definite settlement of the slavery question, and by which, all parties were pledged to abide. Indeed, there was no uninhabited country on the continent, which we could acquire; if we except some extreme northern regions, which are wholly out of the question. In this state of case, the genius of Discord himself, could scarcely have invented a way of again getting us by the ears, but by turning back and destroying the peace measures of the past. The councils of that genius seem to have prevailed, the Missouri compromise was repealed; and here we are, in the midst of a new slavery agitation, such, I think, as we have never seen before. Who is responsible for this? Is it those who resist the measure; or those who, causelessly, brought it forward, and pressed it through, having reason to know, and, in fact, knowing it must and would be so resisted? It could not but be expected by its author, that it would be looked upon as a measure for the extension of slavery, aggravated by a gross breach of faith. Argue as you will, and long as you will, this is the naked FRONT and ASPECT, of the measure. And in this aspect, it could not but produce agitation. Slavery is founded in the selfishness of man's nature—opposition to it, is his love of justice. These principles are an eternal antagonism; and when brought into collision so fiercely, as slavery extension brings them, shocks, and throes, and convulsions must ceaselessly follow. Repeal the Missouri compromise—repeal all compromises—repeal the declaration of independence—repeal all past history, you still can not repeal human nature. It still will be the abundance of man's heart, that slavery extension is wrong; and out of the abundance of his heart, his mouth will continue to speak.

The structure, too, of the Nebraska bill is very peculiar. The people are to decide the question of slavery for themselves; but WHEN they are to decide; or HOW they are to decide; or whether, when the question is once decided, it is to remain so, or is it to be subject to an indefinite succession of new trials, the law does not say, Is it to be decided by the first dozen settlers who arrive there? or is it to await the arrival of a hundred? Is it to be decided by a vote of the people? or a vote of the legislature? or, indeed by a vote of any sort? To these questions, the law gives no answer. There is a mystery about this; for when a member proposed to give the legislature express authority to exclude slavery, it was hooted down by the friends of the bill. This fact is worth remembering. Some yankees, in the east, are sending emigrants to Nebraska, to exclude slavery from it; and, so far as I can judge, they expect the question to be decided by voting, in some way or other. But the Missourians are awake too. They are within a stone's throw of the contested ground. They hold meetings, and pass resolutions, in which not the slightest allusion to voting is made. They resolve that slavery already exists in the territory; that more shall go there; that they, remaining in Missouri will protect it; and that abolitionists shall be hung, or driven away. Through all this, bowie-knives and six-shooters are seen plainly enough; but never a glimpse of the ballot-box. And, really, what is to be the result of this? Each party WITHIN, having numerous and determined backers WITHOUT, is it not probable that the contest will come to blows, and bloodshed? Could there be a more apt invention to bring about collision and violence, on the slavery question, than this Nebraska project is? I do not charge, or believe, that such was intended by Congress; but if they had literally formed a ring, and placed champions within it to fight out the controversy, the fight could be no more likely to come off, than it is. And if this fight should begin, is it likely to take a very peaceful, Union-saving turn? Will not the first drop of blood so shed, be the real knell of the Union?

. . . .

I particularly object to the NEW position which the avowed principle of this Nebraska law gives to slavery in the body politic. I object to it because it assumes that there CAN be MORAL RIGHT in the enslaving of one man by another. I object to it as a dangerous dalliance for a few people—a sad evidence that, feeling prosperity we forget right—that liberty, as a principle, we have ceased to revere. I object to it because the fathers of the republic eschewed, and rejected it. The argument of "Necessity" was the only argument they ever admitted in favor of slavery; and so far, and so far only as it carried them, did they ever go. They found the institution existing among us, which they could not help; and they cast blame upon the British King for having permitted its introduction. BEFORE the constitution, they prohibited its introduction into the north-western Territory—the only country we owned, then free from it. AT the framing and adoption of the constitution, they forbore to so much as mention the word "slave" or "slavery" in the whole instrument. In the provision for the recovery of fugitives, the slave is spoken of as a "PERSON HELD TO SERVICE OR LABOR." In that prohibiting the abolition of the African slave trade for twenty years, that trade is spoken of as "The migration or importation of such persons as any of the States NOW EXISTING, shall think proper to admit," &c. These are the only provisions alluding to slavery. Thus, the thing is hid away, in the constitution, just as an afflicted man hides away a wen or a cancer, which he dares not cut out at once, lest he bleed to death; with the promise, nevertheless, that the cutting may begin at the end of a given time. Less than this our fathers COULD not do; and MORE they WOULD not do. Necessity drove them so far, and farther, they would not go. But this is not all. The earliest Congress, under the constitution, took the same view of slavery. They hedged and hemmed it in to the narrowest limits of necessity.

. . . Thus we see, the plain unmistakable spirit of that age, towards slavery, was hostility to the PRINCIPLE, and toleration, ONLY BY NECESSITY.

But NOW it is to be transformed into a "sacred right." Nebraska brings it forth, places it on the high road to extension and perpetuity; and, with a pat on its back, says to it, "Go, and God speed you." Henceforth it is to be the chief jewel of the nation—the very figure-head of the ship of State. Little by little, but steadily as man's march to the grave, we have been giving up the OLD for the NEW faith. Near eighty years ago we began by declaring that all men are created equal; but now from that beginning we have run down to the other declaration, that for SOME men to enslave OTHERS is a "sacred right of self-government." These principles can not stand together. They are as opposite as God and mammon; and whoever holds to the one, must despise the other. When [John] Pettit [Democratic senator from Indiana—eds.], in connection with his support of the Nebraska bill, called the Declaration of Independence "a self-evident lie" he only did what consistency and candor require all other Nebraska men to do. Of the forty odd Nebraska Senators who sat present and heard him, no one rebuked him. Nor am I apprized that any Nebraska newspaper, or any Nebraska orator, in the whole nation, has ever yet rebuked him. If this had been said among [Francis] Marion's [Revolutionary War military hero—eds.] men, Southerners though they were, what would have become of the man who said it? If this had been said to the men who captured [Major John] André [British officer who negotiated treachery with Benedict Arnold—eds.], the man who said it, would probably have been hung sooner than André was. If it had been said in old Independence Hall, seventy-eight years ago, the very door-keeper would have throttled the man, and thrust him into the street.

Let no one be deceived. The spirit of seventy-six and the spirit of Nebraska, are utter antagonisms; and the former is being rapidly displaced by the latter.

Fellow countrymen—Americans south, as well as north, shall we make no effort to arrest this? Already the liberal party throughout the world, express the apprehension "that the one retrograde institution in America, is undermining the principles of progress, and fatally violating the noblest political system the world ever saw." This is not the taunt of enemies, but the warning of friends. Is it quite safe to disregard it—to despise it? Is there no danger to liberty itself, in discarding the earliest practice, and first precept of our ancient faith? In our greedy chase to make profit of the negro, let us beware, lest we "cancel and tear to pieces" even the white man's charter of freedom.

Our republican robe is soiled, and trailed in the dust. Let us repurify it. Let us turn and wash it white, in the spirit, if not the blood, of the Revolution. Let us turn slavery from its claims of "moral right," back upon its existing legal rights, and its arguments of "necessity." Let us return it to the position our fathers gave it; and there let it rest in peace. Let us re-adopt the Declaration of Independence, and with it, the practices, and policy, which harmonize with it. Let north and south— let all Americans—let all lovers of liberty everywhere—join in the great and good work. If we do this, we shall not only have saved the Union; but we shall have so saved it, as to make, and to keep it, forever worthy of the saving. We shall have so saved it, that the succeeding millions of free happy people, the world over, shall rise up, and call us blessed, to the latest generations.

"No Peaceful Extinction of Slavery in Prospect"

Letter to George Robertson

[AUGUST 15, 1855]

In this letter to a Kentucky jurist, Lincoln painted a grim picture of the sectional crisis, asking, "Can we . . . continue together . . . half slave, and half free?" He would eloquently answer the question himself in his House Divided speech three years later. The book to which he referred was a collection of Robertson's speeches on slavery.

Hon: Geo. Robertson   Springfield, Ills.
Lexington, Ky.   Aug. 15. 1855

My dear Sir:

The volume you left for me has been received. I am really grateful for the honor of your kind remembrance, as well as for the book. The partial reading I have already given it, has afforded me much of both pleasure and instruction. It was new to me that the exact question which led to the Missouri compromise, has arisen before it arose in regard to Missouri; and that you had taken so prominent a part in it.

Your short, but able and patriotic speech upon that occasion, has not been improved upon since, by those holding the same views; and, with all the lights you then had, the views you took appear to me as very reasonable.

You are not a friend of slavery in the abstract. In that speech you spoke of *"the peaceful extinction of slavery"* and used other expressions indicating your belief that the thing was, at some time, to have an end. Since then we have had thirty six years of experience; and this experience has demonstrated, I think, that there is no peaceful extinction of slavery in prospect for us. The signal failure of Henry Clay, and other good and great men, in 1849, to effect any thing in favor of gradual emancipation in Kentucky, together with a thousand other signs, extinguishes that hope utterly. On the question of liberty, as a principle, we are not what we have been. When we were the political slaves of King George, and wanted to be free, we called the maxim that "all men are created equal" a self evident truth; but now when we have grown fat, and have lost all dread of being slaves ourselves, we have become so greedy to be *masters* that we call the same maxim "a self evident lie" The fourth of July has not quite dwindled away; it is still a great day—*for burning fire-crackers*!!!

That spirit which desired the peaceful extinction of slavery, has itself become extinct, with the *occasion,* and the *men* of the Revolution. Under the impulse of that occasion, nearly half the states adopted systems of emancipation at once; and it is a significant fact, that not a single state has done the like since. So far as peaceful, voluntary emancipation is concerned, the condition of the negro slave in America, scarcely less terrible to the contemplation of a free mind, is now so fixed, and hopeless of change for the better, as that of the lost souls of the finally impenitent. The Autocrat of all the Russians will resign his crown, and proclaim his subjects free republicans sooner than will our American masters voluntarily give up their slaves.

Our political problem now is "Can we, as a nation, continue together *permanently—forever*—half slave, and half free?" The problem is too mighty for me. May God, in his mercy, superintend the solution. Your much obliged friend, and humble servant

A. LINCOLN—

"I AM NOT A KNOW-NOTHING"

Letter to Joshua F. Speed

[AUGUST 24, 1855]

This deservedly famous defense of Lincoln's antislavery position ends with a ringing denunciation of the growing Know Nothing movement, whose followers favored restricting the political rights of immigrants, especially Roman Catholics. But Lincoln, who did not go out of his way to make his aversion public, soon realized that the new Republican Party would have to absorb the distasteful Know Nothings if it was ever to defeat the Democrats. His assertion that the Kansas-Nebraska Act had been "conceived in violence" calls to mind the mobocratic passions against which he had warned in his Lyceum Address seventeen years earlier. Speed, the man to whom this letter was written, was the only intimate friend Lincoln ever had.

Springfield, Aug: 24, 1855

Dear Speed:

You know what a poor correspondent I am. Ever since I received your very agreeable letter of the 22nd. of May I have been intending to write you in answer to it. You suggest that in political action now, you and I would differ. I suppose we would; not quite as much, however, as you may think. You know I dislike slavery; and you fully admit the abstract wrong of it. So far there is no cause of difference. But you say that sooner than yield your legal right to the slave—especially at the bidding of those who are not themselves interested, you would see the Union dissolved. I am not aware that *any one* is bidding you to yield that right; very certainly *I* am not. I leave that matter entirely to yourself. I also acknowledge *your* rights and *my* obligations, under the constitution, in regard to your slaves. I confess I hate to see the poor creatures hunted down, and caught, and carried back to their stripes, and unrewarded toils; but I bite my lip and keep quiet. In 1841 you and I had together a tedious low-water trip, on a Steam Boat from Louisville to St. Louis. You may remember, as I well do, that from Louisville to the mouth of the Ohio, there were, on board, ten or a dozen slaves, shackled together with irons. That sight was a continual torment to me; and I see something like it every time I touch the Ohio, or any other slave-border. It is hardly fair for you to assume, that I have no interest in a thing which has, and continually exercises, the power of making me miserable. You ought rather to appreciate how much the great body of the Northern people do crucify their feelings, in order to maintain their loyalty to the constitution and the Union.

I do oppose the extension of slavery, because my judgment and feelings so prompt me; and I am under no obligation to the contrary. If for this you and I must differ, differ we must. You say if you were President, you would send an army and hang the leaders of the Missouri outrages upon the Kansas elections; still, if Kansas fairly votes herself a slave state, she must be admitted, or the Union must be dissolved. But how if she votes herself a slave state *unfairly*—that is, by the very means for which you say you would hang men? Must she still be admitted, or the Union be dissolved? That will be the phase of the question when it first becomes a practical one. In your assumption that there may be a *fair* decision of the slavery question in Kansas, I plainly see you and I would differ about the Nebraska-law. I look upon that enactment not as a *law,* but as *violence* from the beginning. It was conceived in violence, passed in violence, is maintained in violence, and is being executed in violence. I say it was *conceived* in violence, because the destruction of the Missouri Compromise, under the circumstances, was nothing less than violence. It was *passed* in violence, because it could not have passed at all but for the votes of many members, in violent disregard of the known will of their constituents. It is *maintained* in violence because the elections since, clearly demand it's repeal, and this demand is openly disregarded. *You* say men ought to be hung for the way they are executing that law; and *I* say the way it is being executed is quite as good as any of its antecedents. It is being executed in the precise way which was intended from the first; else why does no Nebraska man express astonishment or condemnation? Poor [Andrew] Reeder [governor of Kansas Territory—eds.] is the only public man who has been silly enough to believe that any thing like fairness was ever intended; and he has been bravely undeceived.

That Kansas will form a Slave constitution, and, with it, will ask to be admitted into the Union, I take to be an already settled question; and so settled by the very means you so pointedly condemn. By every principle of law, ever held by any court, North or South, every negro taken to Kansas is free; yet in utter disregard of this—in the spirit of violence merely—that beautiful Legislature gravely passes a law to hang men who shall venture to inform a negro of his legal rights. This is the substance, and real object of the law. If, like Haman, they should hang upon the gallows of their own building, I shall not be among the mourners for their fate.

In my humble sphere, I shall advocate the restoration of the Missouri Compromise, so long as Kansas remains a territory; and when, by all these foul means, it seeks to come into the Union as a Slave-state, I shall oppose it. I am very loth, in any case, to withhold my assent to the enjoyment of property *acquired,* or *located,* in good faith; but I do not admit that *good faith,* in taking a negro to Kansas, to be held in slavery, is a *possibility* with any man. Any man who has sense enough to be the controller of his own property, has too much sense to misunderstand the outrageous character of this whole Nebraska business. But I digress. In my opposition to the admission of Kansas I shall have some company; but we may be beaten. If we are, I shall not, on that account, attempt to dissolve the Union. On the contrary, if we succeed, there will be enough of us to take care of the Union. I think it probable, however, we shall be beaten. Standing as a unit among yourselves, you can, directly, and indirectly, bribe enough of our men to carry the day—as you could on an open proposition to establish monarchy. Get hold of some man in the North, whose position and ability is such, that he can make the support of your measure—whatever it may be—a *democratic party necessity,* and the thing is done. *Apropos* of this, let me tell you an anecdote. Douglas introduced the Nebraska bill in January. In February afterwards, there was a call session of the Illinois Legislature. Of the one hundred members composing the two branches of that body, about seventy were democrats. These latter held a caucus, in which the Nebraska bill was talked of, if not formally discussed. It was thereby discovered that just three, and no more, were in favor of the measure. In a day or two Douglas' orders came on to have resolutions passed approving the bill; and they were passed by large majorities!!! The truth of this is vouched for by a bolting democratic member. The masses too, democratic as well as whig, were even, nearer unanamous against it; but as soon as the party necessity of supporting it, became apparent, the way the democracy began to see the *wisdom* and *justice* of it, was perfectly astonishing.

You say if Kansas fairly votes herself a free state, as a christian you will rather rejoice at it. All decent slave-holders *talk* that way; and I do not doubt their candor. But they never *vote* that way. Although in a private letter, or conversation, you will express your preference that Kansas shall be free, you would vote for no man for Congress who would say the same thing publicly. No such man could be elected from any district in any slave-state. You think [Benjamin] Stringfellow & Co [a leader of the proslavery forces in Kansas—eds.] ought to be hung; and yet, at the next presidential election you will vote for the exact type and representative of Stringfellow. The slave-breeders and slave-traders, are a small, odious and detested class, among you; and yet in politics, they dictate the course of all of you, and are as completely your masters, as you are the masters of your own negroes.

You enquire where I now stand. That is a disputed point. I think I am a whig; but others say there are no whigs, and that I am an abolitionist. When I was at Washington I voted for the Wilmot Proviso as good as forty times, and I never heard of any one attempting to unwhig me for that. I now do no more than oppose the *extension* of slavery.

I am not a Know-Nothing. That is certain. How could I be? How can any one who abhors the oppression of negroes, be in favor of degrading classes of white people? Our progress in degeneracy appears to me to be pretty rapid. As a nation, we began by declaring that *"all men are created equal."* We now practically read it "all men are created equal, *except negroes."* When the Know-Nothings get control, it will read "all men are created equal, except negroes, *and foreigners, and catholics."* When it comes to this I should prefer emigrating to some country where they make no pretence of loving liberty—to Russia, for instance, where despotism can be taken pure, and without the base alloy of hypocracy.

Mary [Lincoln] will probably pass a day to two in Louisville in October. My kindest regards to Mrs. Speed. On the leading subject of this letter, I have more of her sympathy than I have of yours.

And yet let [me] say I am   Your friend forever

A. Lincoln—

"THIS GREAT PRINCIPLE OF EQUALITY"

From a Speech at Kalamazoo, Michigan

[AUGUST 27, 1856]

*An audience of some ten thousand listened to this speech at a huge
Republican rally that boasted eight bands and a parade, but an opposition
newspaper reported that Lincoln proved "far too conservative and Union
loving," and at several points was greeted with "emphatic" protests
"against his views." The speech nonetheless featured one of Lincoln's most
clearly stated expressions on the doctrine of opportunity. This excerpt
comes from the text reprinted by the Detroit* **Daily Advertiser,** *with crowd
reaction recorded.*

Fellow countrymen:—Under the Constitution of the U.S. another
Presidential contest approaches us. All over this land—that portion at
least, of which I know much—the people are assembling to consider the
proper course to be adopted by them. One of the first considerations is
to learn what the people differ about. If we ascertain what we differ
about, we shall be better able to decide. The question of slavery, at the
present day, should be not only the greatest question, but very nearly
the sole question. Our opponents, however, prefer that this should not
be the case. To get at this question, I will occupy your attention but a
single moment. The question is simply this:—Shall slavery be spread
into the new Territories, or not? This is the naked question. If we should
support [John C.] Fremont [Republican candidate for president—eds.]
successfully in this, it may be charged that we will not be content with
restricting slavery in the new territories. If we should charge that James
Buchanan, by his platform, is bound to extend slavery into the territories, and that he is in favor of its being thus spread, we should be
puzzled to prove it. We believe it, nevertheless. By taking the issue as
I present it, whether it shall be permitted as an issue, is made up
between the parties. Each takes his own stand. This is the question:
Shall the Government of the United States prohibit slavery in the
United States.

. . . .

Have we no interest in the free Territories of the United States—that they should be kept open for the homes of free white people? As our Northern States are growing more and more in wealth and population, we are continually in want of an outlet, through which it may pass out to enrich our country. In this we have an interest—a deep and abiding interest. There is another thing, and that is the mature knowledge we have—the greatest interest of all. It is the doctrine, that the people are to be driven from the maxims of our free Government, that despises the spirit which for eighty years has celebrated the anniversary of our national independence.

We are a great empire. We are eighty years old. We stand at once the wonder and admiration of the whole world, and we must enquire what it is that has given us so much prosperity, and we shall understand that to give up that one thing, would be to give up all future prosperity. This cause is that every man can make himself. It has been said that such a race of prosperity has been run nowhere else. We find a people on the North-east, who have a different government from ours, being ruled by a Queen. Turning to the South, we see a people who, while they boast of being free, keep their fellow beings in bondage. Compare our Free States with either, shall we say here that we have no interest in keeping that principle alive? Shall we say—"Let it be." No—we have an interest in the maintenance of the principles of the Government, and without this interest, it is worth nothing. I have noticed in Southern newspapers, particularly the Richmond *Enquirer,* the Southern view of the Free States. They insist that slavery has a right to spread. They defend it upon principle. They insist that their slaves are far better off than Northern freemen. What a mistaken view do these men have of Northern laborers! They think that men are always to remain laborers here—but there is no such class. The man who labored for another last year, this year labors for himself, and next year he will hire others to labor for him. These men don't understand when they think in this manner of Northern free labor. When these reasons can be introduced, tell me not that we have no interest in keeping the Territories free for the settlement of free laborers.

I pass, then, from this question. I think we have an ever growing interest in maintaining the free institutions of our country.

. . . .

They tell us that we are in company with men who have long been known as abolitionists. What care we how many may feel disposed to labor for our cause? Why do not you, Buchanan men, come in and use your influence to make our party respectable? [Laughter.] How is the dissolution of the Union to be consummated? They tell us that the Union is in danger. Who will divide it? Is it those who make the charge? Are they themselves the persons who wish to see this result? A majority will never dissolve the Union. Can a minority do it? When this Nebraska bill was first introduced into Congress, the sense of the Democratic party was outraged. That party has ever provided itself, that it was the friend of individual, universal freedom. It was that principle upon which they carried their measures. When the Kansas scheme was conceived, it was natural that this respect and sense should have been outraged. Now I make this appeal to the Democratic citizens here. Don't you find yourself making arguments in support of these measures, which you never would have made before? Did you ever do it before this Nebraska bill compelled you to do it? If you answer this in the affirmative, see how a whole party have been turned away from their love of liberty! And now, my Democratic friends, come forward. Throw off these things, and come to the rescue of this great principle of equality. Don't interfere with anything in the Constitution. That must be maintained, for it is the only safeguard of our liberties. And not to Democrats alone do I make this appeal, but to all who love these great and true principles. Come, and keep coming! Strike, and strike again! So sure as God lives, the victory shall be yours [Great Cheering.]

"FREE SOCIETY IS NOT . . . A FAILURE"

From a Speech at Chicago, Illinois
[DECEMBER 10, 1856]

Lincoln gave this address to three hundred Republicans at a sumptuous political dinner at the Tremont House, replying to this toast amid what

*a friendly newspaper described as "most deafening cheers": "The Union—
the North will maintain it—the South will not depart therefrom." The
month before, ex-president Millard Fillmore, now running as a third-
party, Know Nothing candidate for the White House, had done well
enough to ensure the defeat of the new Republican Party's first presidential
nominee, John C. Frémont, and the election of Democrat James Buchanan.*

Our government rests in public opinion. Whoever can change public
opinion, can change the government, practically just so much. Public
opinion, on any subject, always has a *"central idea,"* from which all its
minor thoughts radiate. That "central idea" in our political public
opinion, at the beginning was, and until recently has continued to be,
"the equality of men." And although it was always submitted patiently
to whatever of inequality there seemed to be as [a] matter of actual
necessity, its constant working has been a steady progress towards the
practical equality of all men. The late Presidential election was a struggle, by one party, to discard that central idea, and to substitute for it
the opposite idea that slavery is right, in the abstract, the workings of
which, as a central idea, may be the perpetuity of human slavery, and
its extension to all countries and colors. Less than a year ago, the
Richmond *Enquirer,* an avowed advocate of slavery, regardless of
color, in order to favor his views, invented the phrase, "State equality,"
and now the President, in his Message, adopts the *Enquirer's* catch-
phrase, telling us the people "have asserted the constitutional equality
of each and all of the States of the Union as States." The President
flatters himself that the new central idea is completely inaugurated; and
so, indeed, it is, so far as the mere fact of a Presidential election can
inaugurate it. To us it is left to know that the majority of the people
have not yet declared for it, and to hope that they never will.

All of us who did not vote for Mr. Buchanan, taken together, are a
majority of four hundred thousand. But, in the late contest we were
divided between Fremont and Fillmore. Can we not come together, for
the future. Let every one who really believes, and is resolved, that free
society is not, *and shall not be,* a failure, and who can conscientiously
declare that in the past contest he has done only what he thought
best—let every such one have charity to believe that every other one

can say as much. Thus let bygones be bygones. Let past differences, as
nothing be; and with steady eye on the real issue, let us reinaugurate
the good old "central ideas" of the Republic. We *can* do it. The human
heart *is* with us—God is with us. We shall again be able not to declare,
that "all States as States, are equal," nor yet that "all citizens as citizens
are equal," but to renew the broader, better declaration, including both
these and much more, that "all *men* are created equal."

"A STANDARD MAXIM
FOR FREE SOCIETY"

*From a Speech on the Dred Scott Decision,
Springfield, Illinois*

[JUNE 26, 1857]

*Another response to a Douglas speech, this was Lincoln's first extensive
attack on the U.S. Supreme Court's Dred Scott Decision, which declared
Negroes ineligible for citizenship. Lincoln repeatedly charged that the
ruling was part of a conspiracy to nationalize slavery. The speech was
delivered, the Chicago* Tribune *reported, with "force and power" but no
"bombast," to a large crowd of Republicans at the state capitol. Copies of
the speech were reprinted and sold by the local pro-Lincoln newspaper. The
New York* Tribune *called it "a masterly effort."*

We believe, as much as Judge Douglas, (perhaps more) in obedience
to, and respect for the judicial department of government. We think its
decisions on Constitutional questions, when fully settled, should control, not only the particular cases decided, but the general policy of the
country, subject to be disturbed only by amendments of the Constitution as provided in that instrument itself. More than this would be
revolution. But we think the Dred Scott decision is erroneous. We know

the court that made it, has often over-ruled its own decisions, and we shall do what we can to have it to over-rule this. We offer no *resistance* to it.

Judicial decisions are of greater or less authority as precedents, according to circumstances. That this should be so, accords both with common sense, and the customary understanding of the legal profession.

If this important decision had been made by the unanimous concurrence of the judges, and without any apparent partisan bias, and in accordance with legal public expectation, and with the steady practice of the departments throughout our history, and had been in no part, based on assumed historical facts which are not really true; or, if wanting in some of these, it had been before the court more than once, and had there been affirmed and re-affirmed through a course of years, it then might be, perhaps would be, factious, nay, even revolutionary, to not acquiesce in it as a precedent.

But when, as it is true we find it wanting in all these claims to the public confidence, it is not resistance, it is not factious, it is not even disrespectful, to treat it as not having yet quite established a settled doctrine for the country. . . .

. . . the Chief Justice does not directly assert, but plainly assumes, as a fact, that the public estimate of the black man is more favorable *now* than it was in the days of Revolution. This assumption is a mistake. In some trifling particulars, the condition of that race has been ameliorated; but, as a whole, in this country, the change between then and now is decidedly the other way; and their ultimate destiny has never appeared so hopeless as in the last three or four years. In two of the five States—New Jersey and North Carolina—that then gave the free negro the right of voting, the right has since been taken away; and in a third—New York—it has been greatly abridged; while it has not been extended, so far as I know, to a single additional State, though the number of the States has more than doubled. In those days, as I understand, masters could, at their own pleasure, emancipate their slaves; but since then, such legal restraints have been made upon emancipation, as to amount almost to prohibition. In those days, Legislatures held the unquestioned power to abolish slavery in their respective States; but now it is becoming quite fashionable for State Constitutions to withhold that power from the Legislatures. In those days, by common consent, the spread of the black man's bondage to new countries was prohibited; but now, Congress decides that it *will* not continue the prohibition, and the Supreme Court decides that it *could* not if it would. In those days, our Declaration of Independence was held sacred by all, and thought to include all; but now, to aid in making the bondage of the negro universal and eternal, it is assailed, and sneered at, and construed, and hawked at, and torn, till, if its framers could rise from their graves, they could not at all recognize it. All the powers of earth seem rapidly combining against him. Mammon is after him; ambition follows, and philosophy follows, and the Theology of the day is fast joining the cry.

. . . .

. . . Now I protest against that counterfeit logic which concludes that, because I do not want a black woman for a *slave* I must necessarily want her for a *wife.* I need not have her for either, I can just leave her alone. In some respects she certainly is not my equal; but in her natural right to eat the bread she earns with her own hands without asking leave of any one else, she is my equal, and the equal of all others.

Chief Justice [Roger B.] Taney, in his opinion in the Dred Scott case, admits that the language of the Declaration is broad enough to include the whole human family, but he and Judge Douglas argue that the authors of that instrument did not intend to include negroes, by the fact that they did not at once, actually place them on an equality with the whites. Now this grave argument comes to just nothing at all, by the other fact, that they did not at once, *or ever afterwards,* actually place all white people on an equality with one or another. And this is the staple argument of both the Chief Justice and the Senator [Douglas— eds.], for doing this obvious violence to the plain, unmistakable language of the Declaration. I think the authors of that notable instrument intended to include *all* men, but they did not intend to declare all men equal *in all respects.* They did not mean to say all were equal in color, size, intellect, moral developments, or social capacity. They defined with tolerable distinctness, in what respects they did consider all men created equal—equal in "certain inalienable rights, among which are life, liberty, and the pursuit of happiness." This they said, and this meant. They did not mean to assert the obvious untruth, that all were then actually enjoying that equality, nor yet, that they were about to confer it immediately upon them. In fact they had no power to confer such a boon. They meant simply to declare the *right,* so that the *enforcement* of it might follow as fast as circumstances should permit. They meant to set up a standard maxim for free society, which should be familiar to all, and revered by all; constantly looked to, constantly labored for, and even though never perfectly attained, constantly approximated, and thereby constantly spreading and deepening its influence, and augmenting the happiness and value of life to all people of all colors everywhere. The assertion that "all men are created equal" was of no practical use in effecting our separation from Great Britain; and it was placed in the Declaration, not for that, but for future use. Its authors meant it to be, thank God, it is now proving itself, a stumbling block to those who in after times might seek to turn a free people back into the hateful paths of despotism. They knew the proneness of prosperity to breed tyrants, and they meant when such should re-appear in this fair land and commence their vocation they should find left for them at least one hard nut to crack.

. . . .

I had thought the Declaration promised something better than the condition of British subjects; but no, it only meant that we should be *equal* to them in their own oppressed and *unequal* condition [Douglas's interpretation—eds.]. According to that, it gave no promise that having kicked off the King and Lords of Great Britain, we should not at once be saddled with a King and Lords of our own.

I had thought the Declaration contemplated the progressive improvement in the condition of all men everywhere; but no, it merely "was adopted for the purpose of justifying the colonists in the eyes of the civilized world in withdrawing their allegiance from the British crown, and dissolving their connection with the mother country" [Lincoln quotes Douglas here—eds.]. Why, that object having been effected some eighty years ago, the Declaration is of no practical use now—mere rubbish—old wadding left to rot on the battle-field after the victory is won.

I understand you are preparing to celebrate the "Fourth," to-morrow week. What for? The doings of that day had no reference to the present; and quite half of you are not even descendants of those who were referred to at that day. But I suppose you will celebrate; and will even go so far as to read the Declaration. Suppose after you read it once in the old fashioned way, you read it once more with Judge Douglas' version. It will then run thus: "We hold these truths to be self-evident that all British subjects who were on this continent eighty-one years ago, were created equal to all British subjects born and *then* residing in Great Britain."

And now I appeal to all—to Democrats as well as others,—are you really willing that the Declaration shall be thus frittered away?—thus left no more at most, than an interesting memorial of the dead past? thus shorn of its vitality, and practical value; and left without the *germ* or even the *suggestion* of the individual rights of man in it?

"NOT *BLOODY BULLETS*, BUT *PEACEFUL BALLOTS*"

From a Draft of a Speech
[DECEMBER 1857?]

The date of this fragment has long been a matter of dispute, with some believing it was prepared for what an eyewitness called Lincoln's "fine Republican speech" in Edwardsville, Illinois, on May 18, 1858, and others arguing it was written as early as December of the previous year. Whenever it was composed, it represented Lincoln's clearest expression yet of the biblical "house divided" warning he would crystallize by the summer of 1858.

Well, I, too, believe in self-government as I understand it; but I do not understand that the privilege one man takes of making a slave of another, or holding him as such, is any part of "self-government." To call it so is, to my mind, simply absurd and ridiculous. I am for the people of the whole nation doing just as they please in all matters which concern the whole nation; for those of each part doing just as they choose in all matters which concern no other part; and for each individual doing just as he chooses in all matters which concern nobody else.

This is the principle. Of course I am content with any exception which the Constitution, or the actually existing state of things, makes a necessity. But neither the principle nor the exception will admit the indefinite spread and perpetuity of human slavery.

. . . .

A house divided against itself cannot stand.

[from the Books of Matthew and Mark—eds.]

I believe the government cannot endure permanently half slave and half free. I expressed this belief a year ago; and subsequent developments have but confirmed me. I do not expect the Union to be dissolved. I do not expect the house to fall; but I do expect it will cease to be divided. It will become all one thing or all the other. Either the opponents of slavery will arrest the further spread of it, and put it in course of ultimate extinction; or its advocates will push it forward so it shall become alike lawful in all the States, old as well as new. Do you doubt it? Study the Dred Scott decision, and then see how little even now remains to be done. That decision may be reduced to three points.

The first is that a negro cannot be citizen. That point is made in order to deprive the negro, in every possible event, of the benefit of that provision of the United States Constitution which declares that "the citizens of each State shall be entitled to all privileges and immunities of citizens in the several States."

The second point is that the United States Constitution protects slavery, as property, in all the United States territories, and that neither Congress, nor the people of the Territories, nor any other power, can prohibit it at any time prior to the formation of State constitutions.

This point is made in order that the Territories may safely be filled up with slaves, before the formation of State constitutions, thereby to embarrass the free-State sentiment, and enhance the chances of slave constitutions being adopted.

The third point decided is that the voluntary bringing of Dred Scott into Illinois by his master, and holding him here a long time as a slave, did not operate his emancipation—did not make him free.

This point is made, not to be pressed immediately; but if acquiesced in for a while, then to sustain the logical conclusion that what Dred Scott's master might lawfully do with Dred in the free State of Illinois, every other master may lawfully do with any other one or one hundred slaves in Illinois, or in any other free State. Auxiliary to all this, and working hand in hand with it, the Nebraska doctrine is to educate and mold public opinion to "not care whether slavery is voted up or voted down." At least Northern public opinion must cease to care anything about it. Southern public opinion may, without offense, continue to care as much as it pleases.

Welcome, or unwelcome, agreeable, or disagreeable, whether this shall be an entire slave nation, *is* the issue before us. Every incident— every little shifting of scenes or of actors—only clears away the intervening trash, compacts and consolidates the opposing hosts, and brings them more and more distinctly face to face. The conflict will be a severe one; and it will be fought through by those who *do* care for the result, and not by those who do not care—by those who are *for,* and those who are against a legalized national slavery. The combined charge of Nebraskaism, and Dred Scottism must be repulsed, and rolled back. The deceitful cloak of "self-government" wherewith "the sum of all villanies" seeks to protect and adorn itself, must be torn from it's hateful carcass. That burlesque upon judicial decisions, and slander and profanation upon the honored names, and sacred history of republican America, must be overruled, and expunged from the books of authority.

To give the victory to the right, not *bloody bullets,* but *peaceful ballots* only, are necessary. Thanks to our good old constitution, and organization under it, these alone are necessary. It only needs that every right thinking man, shall go to the polls, and without fear or prejudice, *vote* as he *thinks.*

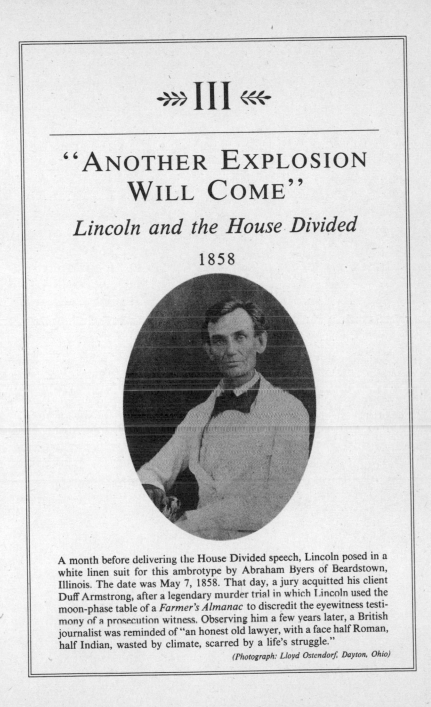

⋙ III ⋘

"ANOTHER EXPLOSION WILL COME"

Lincoln and the House Divided

1858

A month before delivering the House Divided speech, Lincoln posed in a white linen suit for this ambrotype by Abraham Byers of Beardstown, Illinois. The date was May 7, 1858. That day, a jury acquitted his client Duff Armstrong, after a legendary murder trial in which Lincoln used the moon-phase table of a *Farmer's Almanac* to discredit the eyewitness testimony of a prosecution witness. Observing him a few years later, a British journalist was reminded of "an honest old lawyer, with a face half Roman, half Indian, wasted by climate, scarred by a life's struggle."

(Photograph: Lloyd Ostendorf, Dayton, Ohio)

Introduction

BY CHARLES B. STROZIER

The year 1858 was a turning point for Abraham Lincoln. Forced by his own ambition and the approaching senatorial election, Lincoln clarified and focused his developing ideas on democracy. His thinking evolved in the swirl of political debate, especially as a product of his extended dialogue with Stephen A. Douglas.

The year began inauspiciously. Lincoln was busy with his law practice during the winter and spring. As usual he rode the circuit and, with his partner, William Herndon, handled numerous cases. Lincoln was now a leading lawyer, able to command large fees and, through his briefs and arguments, shape law on the frontier. One of his most famous trial cases occurred that spring, when he defended Duff Armstrong in a murder trial. Lincoln interrogated the prime prosecution witness in a particularly clever way. He first had the witness repeat his assertion that he had seen Duff Armstrong commit the murder by the light of the moon. Lincoln then produced an almanac from the period when the murder was supposedly committed, and showed that the moon was barely up in the sky on the night in question. Armstrong was acquitted.

In politics things were going less well. Lincoln was relegated to the role of an observer. He gave no major speeches, and national Republican leaders like William Seward and the influential editor of the New York *Tribune*, Horace Greeley, ignored him. Events seemed to be pushing Lincoln aside. His old colleague and political foe, Illinois senator Stephen A. Douglas, one of the country's leading Democratic politicians, had the limelight.

Douglas was the champion of what he called "popular sovereignty," or the right of local citizens in the territories to decide for themselves on the social and political institutions under which they would live in ways consistent with the Constitution. Douglas had been trying for several years to apply the principle of popular sovereignty to the fierce debate over slavery in the territories as a way of calming tensions—and catapulting himself to the presidency in 1860. His principles—and his ambitions—locked him in mortal combat with the Democratic president, James Buchanan.

The immediate issue was Kansas. There citizens were actually shedding blood over which constitution fairly represented them as they made a bid for statehood. A spurious constitution allowing slavery had been forced through by a handful of unrepresentative electors at Lecompton, the territorial capital. In the fall of 1857, President Buchanan wanted to accept the Lecompton Constitution and move rapidly to make Kansas a state. Free Soilers (those who believed new territories should be secured for free white labor), old Whigs, new Republicans, and a host of others—including Abraham Lincoln—were aghast at what such a development meant, both politically, in terms of shifting power to the South, and symbolically, in giving new life and land for the expansion of the odious institution of slavery.

Douglas opposed Buchanan on the acceptance of the Lecompton Constitution, on the grounds that such a document subverted the principle of popular sovereignty. Douglas made this opposition the heart of a political strategy to redefine the Democratic Party and to gather to himself support from Free Soilers drifting into Republican ranks. Throughout Illinois and the nation, the political debate centered on Douglas and his fierce rivalry with Buchanan. Eastern leaders of the Republican Party came increasingly to feel that Douglas could be a tremendous asset in their campaign to consolidate Northern support for Republicans. They felt it was in their own interest to have Douglas around, keeping the Democratic Party deeply divided. As a result, eastern party leaders did not want Lincoln to oppose Douglas in his upcoming bid for reelection to the United States Senate.

Lincoln opposed this accommodation to Douglas for several reasons. He wanted badly to be a senator in the great tradition of his hero, Henry Clay. From personal experience Lincoln was also aware of the ready opportunism of his old foe, whom he had known since the 1830s. Douglas might well take the prize but once elected do more harm than good for Republican principles. Lincoln knew of the fragility of the Republican Party, which had only taken shape in the mid-1850s. If it waffled on slavery it would lose all sense of its integrity. Lincoln believed strongly that Douglas's doctrine of popular sovereignty was a disastrous and inappropriate policy in dealing with slavery. It contradicted fundamental law as formulated in the Constitution by the founders, as well as our fondest ideals of equality and justice embodied in the Declaration of Independence.

As winter waned, Lincoln determined to oppose Douglas for the Senate race. He began quietly canvassing for support. He examined the 1856 election returns to establish areas of strength and weakness throughout the state and organize an effective campaign. He began noting ideas and speech phrases which he stored on bits of paper stuffed in his stovepipe hat. Perhaps, he speculated, the Lecompton Constitution was only part of a larger conspiracy actually to nationalize slavery. Perhaps even President Buchanan, Douglas, and the Chief Justice of the Supreme Court, Roger B. Taney, were secretly working together to make slavery legal *everywhere.*

By June he was ready. On the sixteenth, in the sultry heat of the legislative chamber in Springfield, Lincoln spoke to the assembled members of the state Republican convention. That afternoon the convention had nominated him as its candidate for the U.S. Senate. Lincoln spoke to accept the nomination and to outline his sense of the future. This extraordinary speech, with its memorable "house divided" phrase and its outline of a dark conspiracy at the highest level to nationalize slavery, immediately shifted the ground of the struggle between himself and Stephen Douglas. Historians have long doubted the existence of an actual plot to nationalize slavery, attributing such an idea largely to Lincoln's heated imagination. But there is no doubt that the speech refocused the debate on slavery as the primary source of crisis in the nation.

Douglas soon took up the challenge of the "house divided" with his own speech in Chicago July 9, which opened his reelection campaign. Before a large and boisterous crowd, Douglas renewed his attack on the Buchanan administration and described himself as a lonely and heroic defender of self-government. He also launched into an extensive refutation of Lincoln's House Divided doctrine, which he described as a radical appeal for sectional war. The founders never intended the country to be all one thing or another, he said, but rather a mixed system with slavery clearly protected constitutionally in the South. Furthermore, Douglas continued, Lincoln favored Negro equality, a view that failed to recognize that this government "was made by the white man, for the benefit of the white man to be administered by the white man."

Lincoln, who had traveled to Chicago to hear the speech, listening to it from the platform at Douglas's invitation, hastily arranged to deliver his own rejoinder the very next day. In that July 10 speech, Lincoln objected strenuously to what he felt were Douglas's misrepresentations of him and of the founding documents. He dwelled at length on the meaning of equality in the Declaration and its simple and clear affirmation of "inalienable" human rights to life, liberty, and the pursuit of happiness. He also took on Douglas's race baiting by agreeing that the government was made for the white man, but he refused to accept that this meant Negroes had no rights at all. In what would become a familiar line, Lincoln noted that just because he would prefer to have a black woman free did not mean that he wanted to marry her. He preferred to grant her more than she currently enjoyed—freedom—while carefully distancing himself from supporting racial equality. Douglas answered Lincoln in speeches in Bloomington on July 16 and Springfield on the following afternoon, while Lincoln in turn responded in a Springfield speech the evening of the seventeenth.

A debate was on. Lincoln's best hope was to engage Douglas relentlessly on the stump. As the underdog, he could only benefit from the exposure of debate with someone as prominent as Douglas. After some discussion with Republican party leaders, Lincoln attempted to formalize his debate with Douglas and challenged him to fifty joint encounters. Douglas accepted the challenge but pared down the number of debates to seven and fixed the format: on an alternating basis, each man spoke for an hour, the other replied for an hour and a half, and the first then had a half-hour rejoinder. The debates began in Ottawa on August 21 and ended in Alton on October 15. They covered the geography of the state, from the Free Soil northern parts, to the proslavery areas of the South (called "Little Egypt"), to the deeply and evenly divided middle sections marked by a band of territory from Charleston to Springfield and extending west to the Mississippi River.

These formal debates—as well as the frequent speechifying in between—have justly entered American folklore as the greatest of their kind. Douglas, although short in stature, was always grand and ostentatious. He rode around the state in special trains draped in banners and arrived in town to the explosion of booming cannons. He sat back in his plush cars, sipping brandy and smoking fine cigars. During the debates themselves, Douglas, who owned slaves in Mississippi, wore what Republican commentators called his "plantation outfit": a wide-brimmed felt hat, a ruffled shirt, and a dark blue coat with shiny buttons, along with light trousers and shined shoes.

Lincoln, for his part, was conspicuously modest and plain in his simple suits and top hats. He often came across as awkward and ungainly. But his relatively high-pitched voice had remarkable carrying power, and his experience as a stump speaker stood him in good stead during the long debates with Douglas. Lincoln also had his own moments of drama: after the Ottawa debate, he was carried off the platform on the shoulders of his supporters; at one point he rode to a debate in a Conestoga wagon drawn by six white horses; he and Douglas were driven to the Galesburg debate on the campus of Knox College in two four-horse carriages driven abreast; and after the Quincy debate there was "a splendid torch-lit procession" in his honor, as reported in the press.

Lincoln had the distinct advantage of the underdog. Just to survive gave him a kind of moral victory, and the publicity of national newspaper coverage was to aid him enormously in the future. He was also a better debater than Douglas. He had a much more subtle grasp of language and could pass easily from humor to eloquence. Douglas had a wooden ear to nuanced phrasing and evocative metaphors, and his comments during the debate were basically variations on the theme of his one set piece. But Douglas was a fierce competitor, alert to Lincoln's own contradictions and confusions, and himself passionately committed to the idea of popular sovereignty. The debates between these two men represented one of the best examples of the workings of our democratic institutions. Seldom has such intelligent political discussion taken place around the truly important issues of the day.

The debates themselves were concerned with one great practical and one great theoretical question. The practical question centered on the constitutional issue of whether federal authority might, indeed should, be used to keep slavery out of the territories. The theoretical question centered on whether slavery was consistent with the institutions of a democratic government. Could free citizens in the territories vote to establish slavery as one of their domestic institutions? Or, are there fundamental rights, as embodied in the founding documents, that precluded the exercise of a doctrine like popular sovereignty in relation to slavery?

For his part Douglas tried to persuade voters that Lincoln's views were those of a dangerous radical who sought to abolish slavery and promote racial equality. There was nothing wrong with slavery, Douglas argued, and no reason why the country could not remain half free and half slave. Surely the founders intended such diversity by building protection of the institution of slavery into the Constitution. Nor were they hypocrites, Douglas maintained. Most important founders themselves owned slaves, and when they talked of realizing human equality in the Declaration, they had in mind only the white man. In Douglas's view, Lincoln wanted "amalgamation" of the races, to make the white man the servant of blacks, which would lead to the dreaded intermarriage. Finally, Douglas argued that Lincoln's absolute political views pushed toward sectional strife and the possibility of war. Douglas cared little whether slavery was voted up or down, as he put it. Let the people decide; that's what democracy is all about.

Lincoln, in turn, sought to move away from everything that linked him to radicalism, especially abolitionist ideas. In several of the debates he reaffirmed his support of the Fugitive Slave Law. He also repeatedly stated his belief that slavery was constitutionally protected in the South, and somewhat mournfully articulated his own sense of *white superiority,* stated most fully in the Charleston debate. But Lincoln also wisely moved beyond defensively warding off Douglas's attacks. To succeed he needed to undermine Douglas's newly won status as a Free Soiler by clarifying how wide a moral and political chasm separated Republicans from Democrats. To accomplish this, Lincoln forced Douglas to repeat his conviction that slavery could be kept out of the territories by a vote of the people (the famous "Freeport doctrine"), a position that infuriated Southern Democrats and was to compromise Douglas's aspirations for the presidency.

Lincoln also moved vigorously to define the moral odiousness of slavery. There could be no compromise on an institution that corrupts all participants in it: "As I would not be a *slave,* so I would not be a *master.* This expresses my idea of democracy. Whatever differs from this, to the extent of the difference is no democracy." Furthermore, free men everywhere must be attuned to the vitality and virulence of slavery and the leaders who sought to promote it into a national institution. As he said in the House Divided speech, and repeated in other ways during the debates: "We shall *lie down* pleasantly dreaming that the *people of Missouri* are on the verge of making their state *free;* and *we shall awake* to the *reality,* instead that the *Supreme Court* has made *Illinois* a *slave* state." Slavery must be contained in the South, where Lincoln believed it would eventually wither away. It should not be allowed into the territories. Popular sovereignty was a valid democratic practice, but not if it contradicted fundamental law. Basic human rights could not be voted up or down by a majority.

Lincoln's most tenuous positions during the debates were those that dealt with equality. Modern readers might well wonder why, if slavery was so evil in Lincoln's mind, blacks should be excluded from full social and political equality with whites. Why was this just and humane man so stunningly explicit about not wanting, even in a theoretical sense, to make blacks his equal? The answer lies in part in the politics of what was possible for Lincoln in 1858. America was a land with legalized slavery, one in which most Southerners *and* Northerners assumed white supremacy and detested blacks. One important source of free-soil sentiment was thus a desire to keep slavery out of the territories so that they would not be overrun by blacks.

Lincoln, it seems, did not share such harsh views, and was himself without malice toward anyone. But as a politician in a land of racial hatred, he necessarily moved toward the passions of the voters. It also seems fair to say that Lincoln harbored distinct ambivalences about full equality between blacks and whites. In 1858, Lincoln stated his beliefs about the inequality of the races repeatedly and with conviction; however regretfully, modern readers should grant that he was not a man to lie. But he never catered to race baiting, and in fact pushed his constituents toward much more humane positions. Slavery as an institution, he said, is morally wrong, a stance that severely challenged the pragmatic Douglas and appealed to the better human instincts of his listeners. Furthermore, in arguing that Negroes should be granted "life, liberty, and the pursuit of happiness," as described in the Declaration, Lincoln was pushing for more than they currently enjoyed in American society—a politically perilous view that risked association with the abolitionists. As the great black intellectual and former slave, Frederick Douglass later put it, Lincoln was always devoted entirely to the welfare of whites. He was willing to postpone, deny, or sacrifice the rights of blacks. He came to the presidency opposed only to the spread of slavery. His patriotic dreams embraced only whites. He supported the Fugitive Slave Law and would have eagerly suppressed any uprising. Whites were his natural children; blacks were his only by adoption. Yet, "measuring him by the sentiment of his country . . . he was swift, zealous, radical, and determined."

Despite all his efforts, Lincoln lost the election. In the popular vote of some 250,000, he polled 4,000 more votes than Douglas. But in those days the state legislatures elected senators (the popular election of senators came only in 1913 with the 17th Amendment). Some seats were held over, there was a suggestion of possible fraud, and a few districts were perhaps gerrymandered, though the real reason for Lincoln's loss seems to have been the difficulty of adequately assuring representation of the popular will through indirect electoral proceedings in such a close contest. So Lincoln, with 50 percent of the vote, received only 47 percent of what might be called the electoral vote. Stephen Douglas retained his position as senator from Illinois.

On the surface, Lincoln's life returned to normal. He resumed his active practice of law, noting, "I have been on expenses so long without earning any thing that I am absolutely without money now for even household purposes." But a deep sadness set in. Lincoln's most positive account of the campaign was itself mournful. "I am glad I made the late race," he wrote an old friend. "It gave me a hearing on the great and durable questions of the age, which I could have had in no other way; and though I now sink out of view, and shall be forgotten, I believe I have made some marks which will tell for the cause of liberty long after I am gone." It was his second major political defeat in four years. He told some visitors: "I feel like the boy who stubbed his toe. I am too big to cry and too badly hurt to laugh."

But neither Lincoln, nor the country, would ever again be quite the same.

→≫ ≪←

"GOVERNMENT CANNOT ENDURE . . . HALF *SLAVE* AND HALF *FREE*"

The House Divided Speech, Springfield, Illinois

[JUNE 16, 1858]

With this speech, Lincoln closed the Republican state convention that had nominated him for the United States Senate, and launched his campaign against incumbent Stephen A. Douglas on both political and moral grounds. The Republican Chicago Tribune lauded the speech as "logical and masterly . . . a powerful summing up of the issues before the people"; Springfield's Democratic paper, on the other hand, criticized one inelegant phrase in the speech, "a living dog is better than a dead lion," sneering: "We have no reason to question Mr. Lincoln's estimation of himself." Some of Lincoln's own supporters thought the new Senate candidate had gone too far with the House Divided speech. It was "imprudent and impolitic," one supporter remembered warning, for Lincoln to assume "such a radical position." But Don E. Fehrenbacher has suggested that Lincoln was intentionally seeking through the speech "to polarize public opinion and to elicit a clear-cut decision" on the slavery issue. He believes Lincoln assumed that the South would come to accept the Republicans' position peaceably once they took power. If such was the case, Lincoln overplayed his hand.

Mr. PRESIDENT and Gentlemen of the Convention.

If we could first know *where* we are, and *whither* we are tending, we could then better judge *what* to do, and *how* to do it.

We are now far into the *fifth* year, since a policy was initiated, with the *avowed* object, and *confident* promise, of putting an end to slavery agitation.

Under the operation of that policy, that agitation has not only, *not ceased,* but has *constantly augmented.*

In *my* opinion, it *will* not cease, until a *crisis* shall have been reached, and passed.

"A house divided against itself cannot stand."

I believe this government cannot endure, permanently half *slave* and half *free*.

I do not expect the Union to be *dissolved*—I do not expect the house to *fall*—but I *do* expect it will cease to be divided.

It will become *all* one thing, or *all* the other.

Either the *opponents* of slavery, will arrest the further spread of it, and place it where the public mind shall rest in the belief that it is in course of ultimate extinction; or its *advocates* will push it forward, till it shall become alike lawful in *all* the States, *old* as well as *new*—*North* as well as *South*.

Have we no *tendency* to the latter condition?

Let anyone who doubts, carefully contemplate that now almost complete legal combination—piece of *machinery* so to speak—compounded of the Nebraska doctrine, and the Dred Scott decision. Let him consider not only *what work* the machinery is adapted to do, and *how well* adapted; but also, let him study the *history* of its construction, and trace, if he can, or rather *fail,* if he can, to trace the evidences of design, and concert of action, among its chief bosses, from the beginning.

The new year of 1854 found slavery excluded from more than half the States by State Constitutions, and from most of the national territory by Congressional prohibition.

Four days later, commenced the struggle, which ended in repealing that Congressional prohibition.

This opened all the national territory to slavery; and was the first point gained.

But, so far, *Congress* only, had acted; and an *indorsement* by the people, *real* or apparent, was indispensable, to *save* the point already gained, and give chance for more.

This necessity had not been overlooked; but had been provided for, as well as might be, in the notable argument of *"squatter sovereignty,"* otherwise called *"sacred right of self government,"* which latter phrase, though expressive of the only rightful basis of any government, was so perverted in this attempted use of it as to amount to just this: That if any *one* man, choose to enslave *another,* no *third* man shall be allowed to object.

That argument was incorporated into the Nebraska bill itself, in the language which follows: *"It being the true intent and meaning of this act not to legislate slavery into any Territory or state, nor to exclude it therefrom; but to leave the people thereof perfectly free to form and regulate their domestic institutions in their own way, subject only to the Constitution of the United States."*

Then opened the roar of loose declamation in favor of "Squatter Sovereignty," and "Sacred right of self government."

"But," said opposition members, "let us be more *specific*—let us *amend* the bill so as to expressly declare that the people of the territory *may* exclude slavery." "Not we," said the friends of the measure; and down they voted the amendment.

While the Nebraska bill was passing through congress, a *law case,* involving the question of a negro's freedom, by reason of his owner having voluntarily taken him first into a free state and then a territory covered by the congressional prohibition, and held him as a slave, for a long time in each, was passing through the U.S. Circuit Court for the District of Missouri; and both Nebraska bill and law suit were brought to a decision in the same month of May, 1854. The negro's name was "Dred Scott," which name now designates the decision finally made in the case.

Before the *then* next Presidential election, the law case came *to,* and was argued *in* the Supreme Court of the United States; but the *decision* of it was deferred until *after* the election. Still, *before* the election, Senator [Lyman] Trumbull [Republican from Illinois—eds.], on the floor of the Senate, requests the leading advocate of the Nebraska bill to state *his opinion* whether the people of a territory can constitutionally exclude slavery from their limits; and the latter answers, "That is a question for the Supreme Court."

The election came. Mr. Buchanan was elected, and the *indorsement,* such as it was, secured. That was the *second* point gained. The indorsement, however, fell short of a clear popular majority by nearly four hundred thousand votes, and so, perhaps, was not overwhelmingly reliable and satisfactory.

The *outgoing* President, in his last annual message, as impressively as possible *echoed back* upon the people the *weight* and *authority* of the indorsement.

The Supreme Court met again; *did not* announce their decision, but ordered a re-argument.

The Presidential inauguration came, and still no decision of the court; but the *incoming* President, in his inaugural address, fervently exhorted the people to abide by the forthcoming decision, *whatever it might be.*

Then, in a few days, came the decision.

The reputed author of the Nebraska bill finds an early occasion to make a speech at this capitol indorsing the Dred Scott Decision, and vehemently denouncing all opposition to it.

The new President, too, seizes the early occasion of the Silliman letter [written by President Buchanan to defend his Kansas policies—eds.] to *indorse* and strongly *construe* that decision, and to express his *astonishment* that any different view had ever been entertained.

At length a squabble springs up between the President and the author of the Nebraska bill, on the *mere* question of *fact,* whether the Lecompton constitution [passed by a proslavery convention in Kansas the year before—eds.] was or was not, in any just sense, made by the people of Kansas; and in that squabble the latter declares that all he wants is a fair vote for the people, and that he *cares* not whether slavery be voted *down* or voted *up.* I do not understand his declaration that he cares not whether slavery be voted down or voted up, to be intended by him other than as an *apt definition* of the *policy* he would impress upon the public mind—the *principle* for which he declares he has suffered much, and is ready to suffer to the end.

And well may he cling to that principle. If he has any parental feeling, well may he cling to it. That principle, is the only *shred* left of his original Nebraska doctrine. Under the Dred Scott decision, "squatter sovereignty" squatted out of existence, tumbled down like temporary scaffolding—like the mould at the foundry served through one blast and fell back into loose sand—helped to carry an election, and then was kicked to the winds. His late *joint* struggle with the Republicans, against the Lecompton Constitution, involves nothing of the original Nebraska doctrine. That struggle was made on a point, the right of a people to make their own constitution, upon which he and the Republicans have never differed.

The several points of the Dred Scott decision, in connection with Senator Douglas' "care not" policy, constitute the piece of machinery, in its *present* state of advancement. This was the third point gained.

The *working* points of that machinery are:

First, that no negro slave, imported as such from Africa, and no descendant of such slave can ever be a *citizen* of any State, in the sense of that term as used in the Constitution of the United States.

This point is made in order to deprive the negro, in every possible event, of the benefit of this provision of the United States Constitution, which declares that—

"The citizens of each State shall be entitled to all privileges and immunities of citizens in the several States."

Secondly, that "subject to the Constitution of the United States," neither *Congress* nor a *Territorial Legislature* can exclude slavery from any United States territory.

This point is made in order that individual men may *fill up* the territories with slaves, without danger of losing them as property, and thus to enhance the chances of *permanency* to the institution through all the future.

Thirdly, that whether the holding a negro in actual slavery in a free State, makes him free, as against the holder, the United States courts will not decide, but will leave to be decided by the courts of any slave State the negro may be forced into by the master.

This point is made, not to be pressed *immediately;* but, if acquiesced in for a while, and apparently *indorsed* by the people at an election, *then* to sustain the logical conclusion that what Dred Scott's master might lawfully do with Dred Scott, in the free State of Illinois, every other master may lawfully do with any other *one* or one *thousand* slaves, in Illinois, or in any other free State.

Auxiliary to all this, and working hand in hand with it, the Nebraska doctrine, or what is left of it, is to *educate* and *mould* public opinion, at least *Northern* public opinion, to not *care* whether slavery is voted *down* or voted *up.*

This shows exactly where we now *are;* and *partially* also, whither we are tending.

It will throw additional light on the latter, to go back, and run the mind over the string of historical facts already stated. Several things will *now* appear less *dark* and *mysterious* than they did *when* they were transpiring. The people were to be left "perfectly free" "subject only to the Constitution." What the *Constitution* had to do with it, outsiders could not *then* see. Plainly enough *now,* it was an exactly fitted *niche* for the Dred Scott decision to afterwards come in, and declare the *perfect freedom* of the people, to be just no freedom at all.

Why was the amendment, expressly declaring the right of the people to exclude slavery, voted down? Plainly enough *now,* the adoption of it, would have spoiled the niche for the Dred Scott decision.

Why was the court decision held up? Why, even a Senator's individual opinion withheld, till *after* the Presidential election? Plainly enough *now,* the speaking out *then* would have damaged the *"perfectly free"* argument upon which the election was to be carried.

Why the *outgoing* President's felicitation on the indorsement? Why the delay of a reargument? Why the incoming President's *advance* exhortation in favor of the decision?

These things *look* like the cautious *patting* and *petting* a spirited horse, preparatory to mounting him, when it is dreaded that he may give the rider a fall.

And why the hasty after indorsements of the decision by the President and others?

We cannot absolutely know that all these exact adaptations are the result of preconcert. But when we see a lot of framed timbers, different portions of which we know have been gotten out at different times and places and by different workmen—Stephen, Franklin, Roger and James [Douglas, Pierce, Taney, and Buchanan—eds.], for instance—and we see these timbers joined together, and see they exactly make the frame of a house or a mill, all the tenons and mortises exactly fitting, and all the lengths and proportions of the different pieces exactly adapted to their respective places, and not a piece too many or too few—not omitting even scaffolding—or, if a single piece be lacking, we can see the place in the frame exactly fitted and prepared to yet bring such piece in—in *such* a case, we find it impossible to not *believe* that Stephen and Franklin and Roger and James all understood one another from the beginning, and all worked upon a common *plan* or *draft* drawn up before the first lick was struck.

It should not be overlooked that, by the Nebraska bill, the people of a *State* as well as *Territory,* were to be left *"perfectly free"* *"subject only to the Constitution."*

Why mention a *State?* They were legislating for *territories,* and not *for* or *about* States. Certainly the people of a State *are* and *ought to be* subject to the Constitution of the United States; but why is mention of this *lugged* into this merely *territorial* law? Why are the people of a *territory* and the people of a *state* therein *lumped* together, and their relation to the Constitution therein treated as being *precisely* the same?

While the opinion of *the Court,* by Chief Justice Taney, in the Dred Scott case, and the separate opinions of all the concurring Judges, expressly declare that the Constitution of the United States neither permits Congress nor a Territorial legislature to exclude slavery from any United States territory, they all *omit* to declare whether or not the same Constitution permits a *state,* or the people of a State, to exclude it.

Possibly, this was a mere *omission;* but who can be *quite* sure, if [Supreme Court Justice John] McLean or [Justice Benjamin R.] Curtis [dissenters in the Dred Scott case—eds.] had sought to get into the opinion a declaration of unlimited power in the people of a *state* to exclude slavery from their limits, just as [Senator Salmon P.] Chase and [Congressman Daniel] Macy sought to get such declaration, in behalf of the people of a territory, into the Nebraska bill—I ask, who can be quite *sure* that it would not have been voted down, in the one case, as it had been in the other.

The nearest approach to the point of declaring the power of a State over slavery, is made by Judge [Samuel] Nelson. He approaches it more than once, using the precise idea, and *almost* the language too, of the Nebraska act. On one occasion his exact language is, "except in cases where the power is restrained by the Constitution of the United States, the law of the State is supreme over the subject of slavery within its jurisdiction."

In what *cases* the power of the *states is* so restrained by the U.S. Constitution, is left an *open* question, precisely as the same question, as to the restraint on the power of the *territories* was left open in the Nebraska act. Put *that* and *that* together, and we have another nice little niche, which we may, ere long, see filled with another Supreme Court decision, declaring that the Constitution of the United States does not permit a *state* to exclude slavery from its limits.

And this may especially be expected if the doctrine of "care not whether slavery be voted *down* or voted *up,*" shall gain upon the public mind sufficiently to give promise that such a decision can be maintained when made.

Such a decision is all that slavery now lacks of being alike lawful in all the States.

Welcome or unwelcome, such decision *is* probably coming, and will soon be upon us, unless the power of the present political dynasty shall be met and overthrown.

We shall *lie down* pleasantly dreaming that the people of *Missouri* are on the verge of making their State *free;* and we shall *awake* to the *reality,* instead, that the *Supreme* Court has made *Illinois* a *slave* State.

To meet and overthrow the power of that dynasty, is the work now before all those who would prevent that consummation.

That is *what* we have to do.

But *how* can we best do it?

There are those who denounce us *openly* to their *own* friends, and yet whisper *us softly,* that *Senator Douglas* is the *aptest* instrument there is, with which to effect that object. *They* do *not* tell us, nor has *he* told us, that he *wishes* any such object to be effected. They wish us to *infer* all, from the facts, that he now has a little quarrel with the present head of the dynasty; and that he has regularly voted with us, on a single point, upon which, he and we, have never differed.

They remind us that *he* is a *very great* man, and that the largest of *us* are very small ones. Let this be granted. But "a *living dog* is better than a *dead lion.*" Judge Douglas, if not a *dead* lion, *for this work,* is at least a *caged* and *toothless* one. How can he oppose the advances of slavery? He don't *care* anything about it. His avowed *mission is impressing* the "public heart" to *care* nothing about it.

A leading Douglas Democratic newspaper thinks Douglas' superior talent will be needed to resist the revival of the African slave trade.

Does Douglas believe an effort to revive that trade is approaching? He has not said so. Does he *really* think so? But if it is, how can he resist it? For years he has labored to prove it a *sacred right* of white men to take negrò slaves into the new territories. Can he possibly show that it is *less* a sacred right to *buy* them where they can be bought cheapest? And, unquestionably they can be bought *cheaper in Africa* than in *Virginia.*

He has done all in his power to reduce the whole question of slavery to one of a mere *right of property;* and as such, how can *he* oppose the foreign slave trade—how can he refuse that trade in that "property" shall be "perfectly free"—unless he does it as a *protection* to the home production? And as the home *producers* will probably not *ask* the protection, he will be wholly without a ground of opposition.

Senator Douglas holds, we know, that a man may rightfully be *wiser to-day* than he was *yesterday*—that he may rightfully *change* when he finds himself wrong.

But, can we for that reason, run ahead, and *infer* that he *will* make any particular change, of which he, himself, has given no intimation? Can we *safely* base *our* action upon any such *vague* inference?

Now, as ever, I wish to not *misrepresent* Judge Douglas' *position,* question his *motives,* or do ought that can be personally offensive to him.

Whenever, *if ever,* he and we can come together on *principle* so that *our great cause* may have assistance from *his great ability,* I hope to have interposed no adventitious obstacle.

But clearly, he is not *now* with us—he does not *pretend* to be—he does not *promise* to *ever* be.

Our cause, then, must be intrusted to, and conducted by its own undoubted friends—those whose hands are free, whose hearts are in the work—who *do care* for the result.

Two years ago the Republicans of the nation mustered over thirteen hundred thousand strong.

We did this under the single impulse of resistance to a common danger, with every external circumstance against us.

Of *strange, discordant,* and even, *hostile* elements, we gathered from the four winds, and *formed* and fought the battle through, under the constant hot fire of a disciplined, proud, and pampered enemy.

Did we brave all *then,* to *falter* now?—*now*—when that same enemy is *wavering,* dissevered and belligerent?

The result is not doubtful. We shall not fail—if we stand firm, we shall not fail.

Wise counsels may *accelerate* or *mistakes delay* it, but sooner or later the victory is *sure* to come.

"THE ELECTRIC CORD IN THAT DECLARATION"

*From a Speech in Reply to
Senator Stephen A. Douglas, Chicago, Illinois*

[JULY 10, 1858]

Douglas opened his reelection campaign with a speech from the balcony of Chicago's Tremont House on July 9, and Lincoln spoke there the next night. The Tribune *described the challenger's audience as only "three-fourths as large as" Douglas's but "four times" as enthusiastic. Lincoln used a humorous touch to deflate Douglas's warnings that Lincoln's policies would result in racial "amalgamation"—the pre–Civil War term for interracial marriage or cohabitation. This concluding excerpt is from the newspaper reprint that Lincoln pasted in his debates scrapbook.*

We were often—more than once at least—in the course of Judge Douglas' speech last night, reminded that this government was made for white men—that he believed it was made for white men. Well, that is putting it into a shape in which no one wants to deny it, but the Judge then goes into his passion for drawing inferences that are not warranted. I protest, now and forever, against that counterfeit logic which presumes that because I do not want a negro woman for a slave, I do necessarily want her for a wife. [Laughter and cheers.] My understanding is that I need not have her for either, but as God made us separate, we can leave one another alone and do one another much good thereby. There are white men enough to marry all the white women, and enough black men to marry all the black women, and in God's name let them be so married. The Judge regales us with the terrible enormities that take place by the mixture of races; that the inferior race bears the superior down. Why, Judge, if we will not let them get together in the Territories, they won't mix there. [Immense applause.]

A voice—"Three cheers for Lincoln." [The cheers were given with a hearty good will.]

Mr. Lincoln—I should say at least that that is a self evident truth.

Now, it happens that we meet together once every year, sometimes about the 4th of July, for some reason or other. These 4th of July gatherings I suppose have their uses. If you will indulge me, I will state what I suppose to be some of them.

We are now a mighty nation, we are thirty—or about thirty millions of people, and we own and inhabit about one-fifteenth part of the dry land of the whole earth. We run our memory back over the pages of history for about eighty-two years and we discover that we were then a very small people in point of numbers, vastly inferior to what we are now, with a vastly less extent of country,—with vastly less of everything we deem desirable among men,—we look upon the change as exceedingly advantageous to us and to our posterity, and we fix upon something that happened away back, as in some way or other being connected with this rise of prosperity. We find a race of men living in that day whom we claim as our fathers and grandfathers; they were iron men; they fought for the principle that they were contending for; and we understood that by what they then did it has followed that the degree of prosperity that we now enjoy has come to us. We hold this annual celebration to remind ourselves of all the good done in this process of time of how it was done and who did it, and how we are historically connected with it; and we go from these meetings in better humor with ourselves—we feel more attached the one to the other, and more firmly bound to the country we inhabit. In every way we are better men in the age, and race, and country in which we live for these celebrations. But after we have done all this we have not yet reached the whole. There is something else connected with it. We have besides these men—descended by blood from our ancestors—among us perhaps half our people who are not descendants at all of these men, they are men who have come from Europe—German, Irish, French and Scandinavian—men that have come from Europe themselves, or whose ancestors have come hither and settled here, finding themselves our equals in all things. If they look back through this history to trace their connection with those days by blood, they find they have none, they cannot carry themselves back into that glorious epoch and make themselves feel that they are part of us, but when they look through that old Declaration of Independence they find that those old men say that "We hold these truths to be self-evident, that all men are created equal," and then they feel that that moral sentiment taught in that day evidences their relation to those men, that it is the father of all moral principle in them, and that they have a right to claim it as though they were blood of the blood, and flesh of the flesh of the men who wrote the Declaration, [loud and long continued applause] and so they are. That is the electric cord in that Declaration that links the hearts of patriotic and liberty-loving men together, that will link those patriotic hearts as long as the love of freedom exists in the minds of men throughout the world. [Applause.]

Now, sirs, for the purpose of squaring things with this idea of "don't care if slavery is voted up or voted down," for sustaining the Dred Scott Decision [A voice—"Hit him again"], for holding that the Declaration of Independence did not mean anything at all, we have Judge Douglas giving his exposition of what the Declaration of Independence means, and we have him saying that the people of America are equal to the people of England. According to his construction, you Germans are not connected with it. Now I ask you in all soberness, if all these things, if indulged in, if ratified, if confirmed and endorsed, if taught to our children, and repeated to them, do not tend to rub out the sentiment of liberty in the country, and to transform this Government into a government of some other form. Those arguments that are made, that the inferior race are to be treated with as much allowance as they are capable of enjoying; that as much is to be done for them as their condition will allow. What are these arguments? They are the arguments that kings have made for enslaving the people in all ages of the world. You will find that all the arguments in favor of king-craft were of this class; they always bestrode the necks of the people, not that they wanted to do it, but because the people were better off for being ridden. That is their argument, and this argument of the Judge is the same old serpent that says you work and I eat, you toil and I will enjoy the fruits of it. Turn in [it—eds.] whatever way you will—whether it come from the mouth of a King, an excuse for enslaving the people of his country, or from the mouth of men of one race as a reason for enslaving the men of another race, it is all the same old serpent, and I hold if that course of argumentation that is made for the purpose of convincing the public mind that we should not care about this, should be granted, it does not stop with the negro. I should like to know if taking this old Declaration of Independence, which declares that all men are equal upon principle and making exceptions to it, where will it stop. If one man says it does not mean a negro, why may not another say it does not mean some other man? If that declaration is not the truth, let us get the Statute book, in which we find it and tear it out! Who is so bold as to do it! [Voices—"me" "no one," &c.] If it is not true let us tear it out! [cries of "no, no,"] let us stick to it then, [cheers]. Let us stand firmly by it then. [Applause]

It may be argued that there are certain conditions that make necessities and impose them upon us, and to the extent that a necessity is imposed upon a man he must submit to it. I think that was the condition in which we found ourselves when we established this government. We had slavery among us, we could not get our constitution unless we permitted them to remain in slavery, we could not secure the good we did secure if we grasped for more, and having by necessity submitted to that much, it does not destroy the principle that is the charter of our liberties. Let that charter stand as our standard.

My friend has said to me that I am a poor hand to quote Scripture. I will try it again, however. It is said in one of the admonitions of the Lord, "As your Father in Heaven is perfect, be ye also perfect." The Savior, I suppose, did not expect that any human creature could be perfect as the Father in Heaven; but He said, "As your Father in Heaven is perfect, be ye also perfect." He set that up as a standard, and he who did most towards reaching that standard, attained the highest degree of moral perfection. So I say in relation to the principle that all men are created equal, let it be as nearly reached as we can. If we cannot give freedom to every creature, let us do nothing that will impose slavery upon any other creature. [Applause.] Let us then turn this government back into the channel in which the framers of the Constitution originally placed it. Let us stand firmly by each other. If we do not do so we are turning in the contrary direction, that our friend Judge Douglas proposes—not intentionally—as working in the traces [that] tend to make this one universal slave nation [A voice—"that is so."]. He is one that runs in that direction, and as such I resist him.

My friends, I have detained you about as long as I desired to do, and I have only to say, let us discard all this quibbling about this man and the other man—this race and that race and the other race being inferior, and therefore they must be placed in an inferior position—discarding our standard that we have left us. Let us discard all these things, and unite as one people throughout this land, until we shall once more stand up declaring that all men are created equal.

My friends, I could not, without launching off upon some new topic, which would detain you too long, continue to-night. [cries of "go on."] I thank you for this most extensive audience that you have furnished me to-night. I leave you, hoping that the lamp of liberty will burn in your bosoms until there shall no longer be a doubt that all men are created free and equal.

[Mr. Lincoln retired amid a perfect torrent of applause and cheers.]

"FIGHT THIS BATTLE UPON PRINCIPLE"

From a Speech in Reply to Douglas, Springfield, Illinois

[JULY 17, 1858]

For a time, Lincoln continued to follow his better-financed Senate oppo-nent around the state, seeking to capitalize on Douglas's press coverage and crowds. On July 16, Lincoln heard Douglas speak in Bloomington. The next morning he was again on hand to hear his foe in a neighboring town, but refused entreaties from the crowd that he respond then and there. That same afternoon Douglas spoke in a Springfield grove: Lincoln finally replied with this speech at the state capitol in the evening. The text of these excerpts follows an 1858 pamphlet reprint, and like the previous speech was pasted by Lincoln into his debates scrapbook. No formal debates had yet been scheduled.

There is still another disadvantage under which we labor, and to which I will ask your attention. It arises out of the relative positions of the two persons who stand before the State as candidates for the Senate. Senator Douglas is of world wide renown. All the anxious politicians of his party, or who have been of his party for years past, have been looking upon him as certainly, at no very distant day, to be the President of the United States. They have seen in his round, jolly, fruitful face, postoffices, landoffices, marshalships, and cabinet appointments, chargeships and foreign missions, bursting and sprouting out in wonderful exuberance ready to be laid hold of by their greedy hands. [Great laughter.] And as they have been gazing upon this attractive picture so long, they cannot, in the little distraction that has taken place in the party, bring themselves to give up the charming hope; but with greedier anxiety they rush about him, sustain him, and give him marches, triumphal entries, and receptions beyond what even in the days of his highest prosperity they could have brought about in his favor. On the contrary nobody has ever expected me to be President. In my poor, lean, lank, face, nobody has ever seen that any cabbages were sprouting out. [Tremendous cheering and laughter.] These are disadvantages all, taken together, that the Republicans labor under. *We* have to fight this battle upon principle, and upon principle alone. I am, in a certain sense, made the standard-bearer in behalf of the Republicans. I was made so merely because there had to be some one so placed—I being in no wise, preferable to any other one of the twenty-five—perhaps a hundred we have in the Republican ranks. Then I say I wish it to be distinctly understood and borne in mind, that we have to fight this battle without many—perhaps without any—of the external aids which are brought to bear against us. So I hope those with whom I am surrounded have principle enough to nerve themselves for the task and leave nothing undone, that can be fairly done to bring about the right result.

. . . .

Last night Judge Douglas tormented himself with horrors about my disposition to make negroes perfectly equal with white men in social and political relations. He did not stop to show that I have said any such thing, or that it legitimately follows from any thing I have said, but he rushes on with his assertions. I adhere to the Declaration of Independence. If Judge Douglas and his friends are not willing to stand by it, let them come up and amend it. Let them make it read that all men are created equal except negroes. Let us have it decided, whether the Declaration of Independence in this blessed year of 1858, shall be thus amended. In his construction of the Declaration last year he said it only meant that Americans in America were equal to Englishmen in England. Then, when I pointed out to him that by that rule he excludes the Germans, the Irish, the Portuguese, and all the other people who have come amongst us since the Revolution, he reconstructs his construction. In his last speech he tells us it meant Europeans.

I press him a little further, and ask if it meant to include the Russians in Asia? or does he mean to exclude that vast population from the principles of our Declaration of Independence? I expect ere long he will introduce another amendment to his definition. He is not at all particular. He is satisfied with any thing which does not endanger the nationalizing of negro slavery. It may draw white men down, but it must not lift negroes up. Who shall say, "I am the superior, and you are the inferior?"

My declarations upon this subject of negro slavery may be misrepresented, but can not be misunderstood. I have said that I do not understand the Declaration to mean that all men were created equal in all respects. They are not our equal in color; but I suppose that it does mean to declare that all men are created equal in some respects; they are equal in their right to "life, liberty, and the pursuit of happiness." Certainly the negro is not our equal in color—perhaps not in many other respects; still, in the right to put into his mouth the bread that his own hands have earned, he is the equal of every other man, white or black. In pointing out that more has been given you, you can not be justified in taking away the little which has been given him. All I ask for the negro is that if you do not like him, let him alone. If God gave him but little, that little let him enjoy.

"THIS EXPRESSES MY IDEA OF DEMOCRACY"

Definition of Democracy

[AUGUST 1, 1858?]

No one knows for certain when this undated fragment was written. Roy P. Basler, editor of Lincoln's Collected Works, *assigned it the date of August 1, 1858, by "pure conjecture," and no one has offered a convincing alternative since. Years later, Mary Lincoln gave the handwritten piece to a woman who had campaigned for the former First Lady's release from an insane asylum.*

As I would not be a *slave*, so I would not be a *master*. This expresses my idea of democracy. Whatever differs from this, to the extent of the difference, is no democracy.

"RETURN TO THE FOUNTAIN"

From a Speech at Lewistown, Illinois

[AUGUST 17, 1858]

Six thousand spectators jammed the Lewistown public square to hear Lincoln "quietly, coolly, but boldly and manfully discharging his arguments" in this speech, reported the Illinois State Journal. *The imperfect text from which this excerpt is taken was transcribed by a newspaper reporter on the scene.*

The Declaration of Independence (said Mr. L.) was formed by the representatives of American liberty from thirteen States of the confederacy—twelve of which were slaveholding communities. We need not discuss the way or the reason of their becoming slaveholding communities. It is sufficient for our purpose that *all of them* greatly deplored the evil and that they placed a provision in the Constitution which they supposed would gradually remove the disease by cutting off its source. This was the abolition of the slave trade. So general was conviction—the public determination—to abolish the African slave trade, that the provision which I have referred to as being placed in the Constitution, declared that it should *not* be abolished prior to the year 1808. A constitutional provision was necessary to prevent the people, through Congress, from putting a stop to the traffic immediately at the close of the war. Now, if slavery had been a good thing, would the Fathers of the Republic have taken a step calculated to diminish its beneficent influences among themselves, and snatch the boon wholly from their posterity? These communities, by their representatives in old Independence Hall, said to the whole world of men: "We hold these truths to be self evident: that all men are created equal; that they are endowed by their Creator with certain unalienable rights; that among these are life, liberty and the pursuit of happiness." This was their majestic interpretation of the economy of the Universe. This was their lofty, and wise, and noble understanding of the justice of the Creator to His creatures. [Applause.] Yes, gentlemen, to *all* His creatures, to the whole great family of man. In their enlightened belief, nothing stamped with the Divine image and likeness was sent into the world to be trodden on, and degraded, and imbruted by its fellows. They grasped not only the whole race of man then living, but they reached forward and seized upon the farthest posterity. They erected a beacon to guide their children and their children's children, and the countless myriads who should inhabit the earth in other ages. Wise statesmen as they were, they knew the tendency of prosperity to breed tyrants, and so they established these great self-evident truths, that when in the distant future some man, some faction, some interest, should set up the doctrine that none but rich men, or none but white men, were entitled to life, liberty and the pursuit of happiness, their posterity might look up again to the Declaration of Independence and take courage to renew the battle which their fathers began—so that truth, and justice, and mercy, and all the humane and Christian virtues might not be extinguished from the land; so that no man would hereafter dare to limit and circumscribe the great principles on which the temple of liberty was being built. [Loud cheers.]

Now, my countrymen (Mr. Lincoln continued with great earnestness,) if you have been taught doctrines conflicting with the great landmarks of the Declaration of Independence; if you have listened to suggestions which would take away from its grandeur, and mutilate the fair symmetry of its proportions; if you have been inclined to believe that all men are *not* created equal in those inalienable rights enumerated by our chart of liberty, let me entreat you to come back. Return to the fountain whose waters spring close by the blood of the Revolution. Think nothing of me—take no thought for the political fate of any man whomsoever—but come back to the truths that are in the Declaration of Independence. You may do anything with me you choose, if you will but heed these sacred principles. You may not only defeat me for the Senate, but you may take me and put me to death. While pretending no indifference to earthly honors, I *do claim* to be actuated in this contest by something higher than an anxiety for office. I charge you to drop every paltry and insignificant thought for any man's success. It is nothing; I am nothing; Judge Douglas is nothing. *But do not destroy that immortal emblem of Humanity the Declaration of American Independence.*

"I CLAIM NO ... EXEMPTION FROM PERSONAL AMBITION"
Fragments for a Speech
[AUGUST 21, 1858?]

Lincoln likely prepared this draft for his first debate with Senator Douglas at Ottawa, Illinois. Only two pages in Lincoln's hand survive.

Allow me now, in my own way, to state with what aims and objects I did enter upon this campaign. I claim no extraordinary exemption from personal ambition. That I like preferment as well as the average of men may be admitted. But I protest I have not entered upon this hard contest solely, or even chiefly, for a mere personal object. I clearly see, as I think, a powerful plot to make slavery universal and perpetual in this nation. The effort to carry that plot through will be persistent and long continued, extending far beyond the senatorial term for which Judge Douglas and I are just now struggling. I enter upon the contest to contribute my humble and temporary mite in opposition to the effort.

. . . .

Judge Douglas is a man of large influence. His bare opinion goes far to fix the opinion of others. Besides this, thousands hang their hopes upon forcing their opinions to agree with his. It is a party necessity with them to *say* they agree with him; and there is danger they will repeat the saying till they really come to believe it. Others dread, and shrink from his denunciations, his sarcasms, and his ingenious misrepresentations. The susceptable young hear lessons from him, such as their fathers never heared [*sic*] when they were young.

If, by all these means, he shall succeed in moulding public sentiment to a perfect accordance with his own—in bringing all men to indorse all court decisions, without caring to know whether they are right or wrong—in bringing all tongues to as perfect a silence as his own, as to there being any wrong in slavery—in bringing all to declare, with him, that they care not whether slavery be voted down or voted up—that if any people want slaves they have a right to have them—that negroes are not men—have no part in the declaration of Independence—that there is no moral question about slavery—that liberty and slavery are perfectly consistent—indeed, necessary accompaniaments—that for a strong man to declare himself the *superior* of a weak one, and thereupon enslave the weak one, is the very *essence* of liberty—the most sacred right of self-government—when, I say, public sentiment shall be brought to all this, in the name of heaven, what barrier will be left against slavery being made lawful every where? Can you find *one* word of his, opposed to it? Can you *not* find many strongly favoring it? If for his life—for his eternal salvation—he was solely striving for that end, could he find any means so well adapted to reach the end?

If our Presidential election, by a mere plurality, and of doubtful significance, brought one Supreme Court decision, that no power can exclude slavery from a Teritory; how much much [*sic*] more shall a public sentiment, in exact accordance with the sentiments of Judge Douglas bring another that no power can exclude it from a State?

And then, the negro bring doomed, and damned, and forgotten, to everlasting bondage, is the white man quite certain that the tyrant demon will not turn upon him too?

"THE MORAL LIGHTS AROUND US"

Extracts from the Lincoln-Douglas Debates: From Lincoln's Reply, First Debate, Ottawa, Illinois

[AUGUST 21, 1858]

On July 24, Lincoln formally asked Douglas "to divide time, and address the same audiences." Though reluctant to share the spotlight, the senator was even more reluctant to duck a direct challenge. Douglas ultimately accepted but named the sites: Ottawa on August 21, Freeport on August 27, Jonesboro on September 15, Charleston on September 18, Galesburg on October 7, Quincy on October 13, and Alton on October 15. Douglas hoped to use the debates to portray Lincoln as a dangerous radical; Lincoln planned to assail the Douglas doctrine of popular sovereignty, which offered citizens of each new territory the right to choose or reject slavery for themselves. Proof of the public interest in the campaign came when ten to twelve thousand people turned out for the first debate at Ottawa, eighty miles southwest of Chicago, a town with only six thousand citizens of its own. Douglas's opening speech called for "confining citizenship to white men," not "inferior races," and charged that Lincoln was an out-and-out abolitionist. Lincoln's reply was rather defensive. Some of his supporters fretted that he had been bested, but after the three-hour session, his backers lifted him to their shoulders and carried him off in triumph. All the extracts from Lincoln's debate remarks have been taken from newspaper reprints he preserved in a scrapbook.

. . . I have no purpose to introduce political and social equality between the white and black races. There is a physical difference between the two, which in my judgment will probably forever forbid their living together upon the footing of perfect equality, and inasmuch as it becomes a necessity that there must be a difference, I, as well as Judge Douglas, am in favor of the race to which I belong, having the superior position. I have never said anything to the contrary, but I hold that notwithstanding all this, there is no reason in the world why the negro is not entitled to all the natural rights enumerated in the Declaration of Independence, the right to life, liberty and the pursuit of happiness. [Loud cheers.] I hold that he is as much entitled to these as the white man. I agree with Judge Douglas he is not my equal in many respects—certainly not in color, perhaps not in moral or intellectual endowment. But in the right to eat the bread, without leave of anybody else, which his own hand earns, *he is my equal, and the equal of Judge Douglas, and the equal of every living man.* [Great applause.]

. . . Henry Clay, my beau ideal of a statesman, the man for whom I fought all my humble life—Henry Clay once said of a class of men who would repress all tendencies to liberty and ultimate emancipation, that they must, if they would do this, go back to the era of our Independence, and muzzle the cannon which thunders its annual joyous return; they must blow out the moral lights around us; they must penetrate the human soul, and eradicate there the love of liberty; and then and not till then, could they perpetuate slavery in this country! [Loud cheers.] To my thinking, Judge Douglas is, by his example and vast influence, doing that very thing in this community, [cheers,] when he says that the negro has nothing in the Declaration of Independence. Henry Clay plainly understood the contrary. Judge Douglas is going back to the era of our Revolution, and to the extent of his ability, muzzling the cannon which thunders its annual joyous return. When he invites any people willing to have slavery, to establish it, he is blowing out the moral lights around us. [Cheers.] When he says he "cares not whether slavery is voted down or voted up,"—that it is a sacred right of self government,—he is in my judgment penetrating the human soul and eradicating the light of reason and the love of liberty in this American people. [Enthusiastic and continued applause.] And now I will only say that when, by all these means and appliances, Judge Douglas shall succeed in bringing public sentiment to an exact accordance with his own views—when these vast assemblages shall echo back all these sentiments—when they shall come to repeat his views and to avow his principles, and to say all that he says on these mighty questions—then it needs only the formality of the second Dred Scott decision, which he endorses in advance, to make slavery alike lawful in all the States—old as well as new, North as well as South.

My friends, that ends the chapter. The Judge can take his half-hour.

"OUR RELIANCE IS IN THE LOVE OF LIBERTY"

From a Speech at Edwardsville, Illinois

[SEPTEMBER 11, 1858]

Between debate appearances, Lincoln continued to deliver campaign speeches on his own. He gave one rousing address on what a reporter called a "quiet autumn day in the quaint old town" of Edwardsville, a few miles east of the Mississippi River. This was his conclusion, as reported five days later in the Alton, Illinois, Weekly Courier.

My friends, I have endeavored to show you the logical consequences of the Dred Scott decision, which holds that the people of a Territory cannot prevent the establishment of Slavery in their midst. I have stated what cannot be gainsayed—that the grounds upon which this decision is made are equally applicable to the Free States as to the Free Territories, and that the peculiar reasons put forth by Judge Douglas for endorsing this decision, commit him in advance to the next decision, and to all other decisions emanating from the same source. Now, when by all these means you have succeeded in dehumanizing the negro; when you have put him down, and made it forever impossible for him to be but as the beasts of the field; when you have extinguished his soul, and placed him where the ray of hope is blown out in darkness like that which broods over the spirits of the damned; are you quite sure the demon which you have roused *will not turn and rend you?* What constitutes the bulwark of our own liberty and independence? It is not our frowning battlements, our bristling sea coasts, the guns of our war steamers, or the strength of our gallant and disciplined army. These are not our reliance against a resumption of tyranny in our fair land. All of them may be turned against our liberties, without making us stronger or weaker for the struggle. Our reliance is in the *love of liberty* which God has planted in our bosoms. Our defense is in the preservation of the spirit which prizes liberty as the heritage of all men, in all lands, every where. Destroy this spirit, and you have planted the seeds of despotism around your own doors. Familiarize yourselves with the chains of bondage, and you are preparing your own limbs to wear them. Accustomed to trample on the rights of those around you, you have lost the genius of your own independence, and become the fit subjects of the first cunning tyrant who rises. And let me tell you, all these things are prepared for you with the logic of history, if elections shall promise that the next Dred Scott decision and all future decisions will be quietly acquiesced in by the people. [Loud applause.]

"NEVER HAVE HAD A BLACK WOMAN FOR EITHER A SLAVE OR A WIFE"

Extracts from the Lincoln-Douglas Debates:
From Lincoln's Speech, Fourth Debate, Charleston, Illinois

[SEPTEMBER 18, 1858]

At Charleston Lincoln responded, before twelve thousand people, to charges made in the Jonesboro debate three days earlier that he favored black-white equality. Judging from the laughter reported when he rejected the idea, many voters did not take the charge seriously. (Lincoln knew his audience: back in 1848, 95 percent of the voters in this heavily Democratic county had voted to bar Negroes from Illinois altogether.) The crowd was so large Lincoln asked for "profound silence" before he spoke, but inevitably these opening remarks were interrupted frequently by cheers and laughter.

While I was at the hotel to-day an elderly gentleman called upon me to know whether I was really in favor of producing a perfect equality between the negroes and white people. [Great laughter.] While I had not proposed to myself on this occasion to say much on that subject, yet as the question was asked me I thought I would occupy perhaps five minutes in saying something in regard to it. I will say then that I am not, nor ever have been in favor of bringing about in any way the social and political equality of the white and black races, [applause]—that I am not nor ever have been in favor of making voters or jurors of negroes, nor of qualifying them to hold office, nor to intermarry with white people; and I will say in addition to this that there is a physical difference between the white and black races which I believe will for ever forbid the two races living together on terms of social and political equality. And inasmuch as they cannot so live, while they do remain together there must be the position of superior and inferior, and I as much as any other man am in favor of having the superior position assigned to the white race. I say upon this occasion I do not perceive that because the white man is to have the superior position the negro should be denied everything. I do not understand that because I do not want a negro woman for a slave I must necessarily want her for a wife. [Cheers and laughter.] My understanding is that I can just let her alone. I am now in my fiftieth year, and I certainly never have had a black woman for either a slave or a wife. So it seems to me quite possible for us to get along without making either slaves or wives of negroes. I will add to this that I have never seen to my knowledge a man, woman or child who was in favor of producing a perfect equality, social and political, between negroes and white men. I recollect of but one distinguished instance that I ever heard of so frequently as to be entirely satisfied of its correctness—and that is the case of Judge Douglas' old friend Col. Richard M. Johnson [former vice president who was believed to have had a black mistress—eds.] [Laughter.] I will also add to the remarks I have made, (for I am not going to enter at large upon this subject,) that I have never had the least apprehension that I or my friends would marry negroes if there was no law to keep them from it, [laughter] but as Judge Douglas and his friends seem to be in great apprehension that they might, if there were no law to keep them from it, [roars of laughter] I give him the most solemn pledge that I will to the very last stand by the law of this State, which forbids the marrying of white people with negroes. [Continued laughter and applause.] I will add one further word, which is this, that I do not understand there is any place where an alteration of the social and political relations of the negro and the white man can be made except in the State Legislature— not in the Congress of the United States—and as I do not really apprehend the approach of any such thing myself, and as Judge Douglas seems to be in constant horror that some such danger is rapidly approaching, I propose as the best means to prevent it that the Judge be kept at home and placed in the State Legislature to fight the measure. [Uproarious laughter and applause.] I do not propose dwelling longer at this time on this subject.

"*GIVE* TO HIM THAT IS NEEDY"

Fragment on Slavery

[OCTOBER 1, 1858?]

The "Rev. Dr. Ross" to whom Lincoln referred here is likely the Alabama minister Frederick A. Ross, author of the 1857 tract **Slavery Ordained by God**.

Suppose it is true, that the negro is inferior to the white, in the gifts of nature; is it not the exact reverse justice that the white should, for that reason, take from the negro, any part of the little which has been given him? *"Give* to him that is needy" is the christian rule of charity; but "Take from him that is needy" is the rule of slavery.

PRO-SLAVERY THEOLOGY

The sum of pro-slavery theology seems to be this: "Slavery is not universally *right,* nor yet universally *wrong;* it is better for *some* people to be slaves; and, in such cases, it is the Will of God that they be such."

Certainly there is no contending against the Will of God; but still there is some difficulty in ascertaining, and applying it, to particular cases. For instance we will suppose the Rev. Dr. Ross has a slave named Sambo, and the question is "Is it the Will of God that Sambo shall remain a slave, or be set free?" The Almighty gives no audable answer to the question, and his revelation—the Bible—gives none—or, at most, none but such as admits of a squabble, as to it's meaning. No one thinks of asking Sambo's opinion on it. So, at last, it comes to this, that *Dr. Ross* is to decide the question. And while he consider[s] it, he sits in the shade, with gloves on his hands, and subsists on the bread that Sambo is earning in the burning sun. If he decides that God Wills Sambo to continue a slave, he thereby retains his own comfortable position; but if he decides that God will's Sambo to be free, he thereby has to walk out of the shade, throw off his gloves, and delve for his own bread. Will Dr. Ross be actuated by that perfect impartiality, which has ever been considered most favorable to correct decisions?

But, slavery is good for some people!!! As a *good* thing, slavery is strikingly perculiar, in this, that it is the only good thing which no man ever seeks the good of, *for himself.*

Nonsense! Wolves devouring lambs, not because it is good for their own greedy maws, but because it [is] good for the lambs!!!

" 'HE TREMBLED FOR HIS COUNTRY' "

Extracts from the Lincoln-Douglas Debates: From Lincoln's Reply, Fifth Debate, Galesburg, Illinois

[OCTOBER 7, 1858]

Some fifteen thousand spectators attended the fifth joint debate at Knox College in Galesburg in west central Illinois, the largest crowd of the Lincoln-Douglas confrontations. Lincoln again took the offensive, arguing the natural right of Negroes to enjoy the blessings of the Declaration of Independence, with Douglas insisting that its authors meant only "white men . . . of European birth, and European descent, when they declared the equality of all men." Lincoln's reply included the following.

The Judge has alluded to the Declaration of Independence, and insisted that negroes are not included in that Declaration; and that it is a slander upon the framers of that instrument, to suppose that negroes were meant therein; and he asks you: Is it possible to believe that Mr. Jefferson, who penned the immortal paper, could have supposed himself applying the language of that instrument to the negro race, and yet held a portion of that race in slavery? Would he not at once have freed them? I only have to remark upon this part of the Judge's speech, (and that, too, very briefly, for I shall not detain myself, or you, upon that point for any great length of time,) that I believe the entire records of the world, from the date of the Declaration of Independence up to within three years ago, may be searched in vain for one single affirmation, from one single man, that the negro was not included in the Declaration of Independence. I think I may defy Judge Douglas to show that he ever said so, that Washington ever said so, that any President ever said so, that any member of Congress ever said so, or that any living man upon the whole earth ever said so, until the necessities of the present policy of the Democratic party, in regard to slavery, had to invent that affirmation. [Tremendous applause.] And I will remind Judge Douglas and this audience, that while Mr. Jefferson was the owner of slaves, as undoubtedly he was, in speaking upon this very subject, he used the strong language that "he trembled for his country when he remembered that God was just;" and I will offer the highest premium in my power to Judge Douglas if he will show that he, in all his life, ever uttered a sentiment at all akin to that of Jefferson. [Great applause and cries of "Hit him again," "good," "good."]

. . . .

Now a few words in regard to these extracts from speeches of mine, which Judge Douglas has read to you, and which he supposes are in very great contrast to each other [the "electric cord" speech in Chicago July 10, and the Charleston debate speech September 18—eds.]. Those speeches have been before the public for a considerable time, and if they have any inconsistency in them, if there is any conflict in them the public have been able to detect it. When the Judge says, in speaking on this subject, that I make speeches of one sort for the people of the Northern end of the State, and of a different sort for the Southern people, he assumes that I do not understand that my speeches will be put in print and read North and South. I knew all the while that the speech that I made at Chicago and the one I made at Jonesboro and the one at Charleston, would all be put in print and all the reading and intelligent men in the community would see them and know all about my opinions. And I have not supposed, and do not now suppose, that there is any conflict whatever between them. ["They are all good speeches!" "Hurrah for Lincoln!"] But the Judge will have it that if we do not confess that there is a sort of inequality between the white and black races, which justifies us in making them slaves, we must, then, insist that there is a degree of equality that requires us to make them our wives. [Loud applause, and cries, "Give it to him;" "Hit him again."] Now, I have all the while taken a broad distinction in regard to that matter; and that is all there is in these different speeches which he arrays here, and the entire reading of either of the speeches will show that that distinction was made. Perhaps by taking two parts of the same speech, he could have got up as much of a conflict as the one he has found. I have all the while maintained, that in so far as it should be insisted that there was an equality between the white and black races that should produce a perfect social and political equality, it was an impossibility. This you have seen in my printed speeches, and with it I have said, that in their right to "life, liberty and the pursuit of happiness," as proclaimed in that old Declaration, the inferior races are our equals. [Long-continued cheering.] And these declarations I have constantly made in reference to the abstract moral question, to contemplate and consider when we are legislating about any new country which is not already cursed with the actual presence of the evil—slavery. I have never manifested any impatience with the necessities that spring from the actual presence of black people amongst us, and the actual existence of slavery amongst us where it does already exist; but I have insisted that, in legislating for new countries, where it does not exist, there is no just rule other than that of moral and abstract right! With reference to those new countries, those maxims as to the right of a people to "life, liberty and the pursuit of happiness," were the just rules to be constantly referred to. There is no misunderstanding this, except by men interested to misunderstand it. [Applause.] I take it that I have to address an intelligent and reading community, who will peruse what I say, weigh it, and then judge whether I advance improper or unsound views, or whether I advance hypocritical, and deceptive, and contrary views in different portions of the country. I believe myself to be guilty of no such thing as the latter, though, of course, I cannot claim that I am entirely free from all error in the opinions I advance.

"THE ETERNAL STRUGGLE"

Extracts from the Lincoln-Douglas Debates: From Lincoln's Reply, Seventh and Final Debate, Alton, Illinois

[OCTOBER 15, 1858]

After a rousing sixth debate in Democratic Quincy, Lincoln and Douglas met for their seventh and final time in front of the city hall in Alton, a river town twenty-five miles north of St. Louis. Only five thousand attended. Lincoln spent the remaining two weeks of the Senate campaign speaking throughout the state. After Lincoln's defeat, the pro-Republican Chicago Tribune *predicted, "his speeches will become landmarks in our political history," adding: "Long live Honest Old Abe!"*

. . . He [Douglas] says that upon the score of equality, slaves should be allowed to go in a new Territory, like other property. This is strictly logical if there is no difference between it and other property. If it and other property are equal, his argument is entirely logical. But if you insist that one is wrong and the other right, there is no use to institute a comparison between right and wrong. You may turn over everything in the Democratic policy from beginning to end, whether in the shape it takes on the statute book, in the shape it takes in the Dred Scott decision, in the shape it takes in conversation or the shape it takes in short maxim-like arguments—it everywhere carefully excludes the idea that there is anything wrong in it.

That is the real issue. That is the issue that will continue in this country when these poor tongues of Judge Douglas and myself shall be silent. It is the eternal struggle between these two principles—right and wrong—throughout the world. They are the two principles that have stood face to face from the beginning of time; and will ever continue to struggle. The one is the common right of humanity and the other the divine right of kings. It is the same principle in whatever shape it develops itself. It is the same spirit that says, "You work and toil and earn bread, and I'll eat it." [Loud applause.] No matter in what shape it comes, whether from the mouth of a king who seeks to bestride the people of his own nation and live by the fruit of their labor, or from one race of men as an apology for enslaving another race, it is the same tyrannical principle. I was glad to express my gratitude at Quincy, and I re-express it here to Judge Douglas—*that he looks to no end of the institution of slavery.* That will help the people to see where the struggle really is. It will hereafter place with us all men who really do wish the wrong may have an end. And whenever we can get rid of the fog which obscures the real question— when we can get Judge Douglas and his friends to avow a policy looking to its perpetuation—we can get out from among them that class of men and bring them to the side of those who treat it as a wrong. Then there will soon be an end of it, and that end will be its "ultimate extinction." Whenever the issue can be distinctly made, and all extraneous matter thrown out so that men can fairly see the real difference between the parties, this controversy will soon be settled, and it will be done peaceably too. There will be no war, no violence. It will be placed again where the wisest and best men of the world, placed it. [Congressman Preston] Brooks of South Carolina once declared that when this Constitution was framed, its framers did not look to the institution existing until this day. When he said this, I think he stated a fact that is fully borne out by the history of the times. But he also said they were better and wiser men than the men of these days; yet the men of these days had experience which they had not, and by the invention of the cotton gin it became a necessity in this country that slavery should be perpetual. I now say that willingly or unwillingly, purposely or without purpose, Judge Douglas has been the most prominent instrument in changing the position of the institution of slavery which the fathers of the government expected to come to an end ere this—*and putting it upon Brooks' cotton gin basis,* [Great applause,]—placing it where he openly confesses he has no desire there shall ever be an end of it. [Renewed applause.]

"THE FIGHT MUST GO ON"

Letter to Henry Asbury

[NOVEMBER 19, 1858]

Lincoln wrote this letter just weeks after his defeat in the 1858 Senate election. Attorney Henry Asbury was a Lincoln supporter from the debate town of Quincy.

Springfield,
Novr. 19, 1858

Henry Asbury, Esq

My dear Sir

Yours of the 13th. was received some days ago. The fight must go on. The cause of civil liberty must not be surrendered at the end of *one,* or even, one *hundred* defeats. Douglas had the ingenuity to be supported in the late contest both as the best means to *break down,* and to *uphold* the Slave interest. No ingenuity can keep those antagonistic elements in harmony long. Another explosion will soon come. Yours truly

A. LINCOLN—

⋙ IV ⋘

"RIGHT MAKES MIGHT"
Lincoln and the Race for President
1859–1860

Only hours before delivering his Cooper Union address in New York City in February 1860, Lincoln posed for this flattering photograph at the Mathew Brady Gallery on Broadway. Seeing him not long thereafter, a London *Times* correspondent was struck by his "ill-fitting, wrinkled suit of black," which he thought resembled "an undertaker's uniform at a funeral." Even Brady could not disguise the fact that his subject's suit badly needed pressing. Nonetheless, this photograph soon inspired countless engraved and lithographed Lincoln campaign portraits, banners, and broadsides. Brady himself insisted it "was the means of his election" as president. All Lincoln would concede—with somewhat forced folksiness—was that Brady "got my shaddow, and can multiply copies indefinitely."

(Photograph: Louis A. Warren Lincoln Library and Museum)

Introduction

BY RICHARD NELSON CURRENT

Lincoln had lost the contest with Douglas, and yet he had won. Though failing to get the senatorship in 1858, he laid the basis for his election to the presidency in 1860. By his eloquent defense of Republican principles, he had gained the recognition of party leaders throughout the North. At the same time, he had weakened the presidential chances of his rival by compelling him to elaborate on his doctrine of popular sovereignty and thereby alienate most of his followers in the South.

While Lincoln's prospects for the Republican nomination were improving, so were the party's prospects for victory in the next election. The party was broadening its base of support. Originally, it had appealed to voters on the single issue of excluding slavery from the territories. As the economic recession following the financial panic of 1857 continued, the Republicans added to their free-soil demand a number of proposals to stimulate prosperity. These included an increase in tariffs to protect American manufacturers from foreign competition, grants of public land to provide both "homesteads" for farmers and endowments for agricultural colleges, and government aid for transportation improvements, especially for the construction of a railroad to the Pacific coast.

The Republicans were gaining on the Democrats in the North. The Democratic Party continued to suffer from the internecine conflict between its two leaders, President Buchanan and Senator Douglas, the one trying to force slavery upon the settlers of Kansas Territory, the other trying to give them a real choice in accordance with the principle of popular sovereignty. Republicans showed their growing strength in the congressional elections of 1858, when (despite Lincoln's loss to Douglas in Illinois) they carried nearly every Northern state. They won a plurality in the new House of Representatives, the first session of which was to meet in December 1859.

In October 1859 occurred an event that greatly alarmed white Southerners and intensified their fear of the rapidly multiplying Republicans. This was John Brown's raid. Brown, after murdering five proslavery settlers in Kansas, moved back east to resume his private war against slavery. With eighteen followers, five of them black, he attacked the federal arsenal at Harpers Ferry, on the northern edge of Virginia, in the hope of obtaining guns. He planned to arm escaping slaves and send them out on forays to liberate additional slaves. But he got nowhere. Ten of his followers, including two of his sons, were killed at the arsenal. He himself and six others were captured and hanged.

Panic swept through the Southern states, and they began to build up their military forces to deal with expected slave insurrections. Southern whites thought that every Republican was a potential John Brown or, at least, that the party's antislavery propaganda had encouraged him and would encourage other such fanatics. Some prominent Northerners praised him. The famous philosopher Ralph Waldo Emerson, for one, said Brown would make the gallows "as glorious as the cross." All this tended to embarrass Republicans, since it made them appear to be dangerous radicals and disturbers of the peace.

When Congress met, just a few days after Brown was hanged, the Southern members were in a bitter mood. Again and again they and the Republicans nearly came to blows. The Republicans kept trying to enact their economic program—their tariff, homestead, Pacific railroad, and college land-grant bills—but were repeatedly frustrated by Southern votes or presidential vetoes. The 1859–1860 session ended with Republicans more determined than ever to get control of both Congress and the presidency in the 1860 election.

Lincoln had been slow to announce himself as a contender for the presidential nomination, though some newspapers in Illinois had come out, soon after his defeat for the Senate, with the headline "Lincoln for President!" When his friend Jesse W. Fell told him he would make a strong candidate, Lincoln replied that there were much better-known men under consideration, and for a while he put off Fell's request for an autobiographical sketch that would serve as the basis for a campaign biography. He may have hesitated because of modesty, yet he was doing what any smart and ambitious man in his place would have done. He would have hurt his chances if he had seemed eager for the office or if he had allowed himself to become conspicuous as a target for rival contenders.

But Lincoln was soon making himself and his Republican doctrines better known through public speeches and public letters. He received many invitations to speak, and he accepted most of them, even though this meant neglecting his law practice—which he had already neglected too long while campaigning for the Senate. During 1859 he traveled four thousand miles and spoke to twenty-three audiences in Illinois, Indiana, Ohio, Iowa, Wisconsin, and Kansas. Early in 1860, he made his longest single speaking tour, going all the way from Illinois to New York and New England.

Some of his speeches were supposedly nonpolitical, but even in them he managed to expound his party's principles. In a lecture on discoveries and inventions, which he gave at Illinois College and elsewhere, he called for emancipation from "slavery of the mind" and for the establishment of "freedom of thought." In an address at the Wisconsin state fair he praised free labor and denied the Southerners' " 'mud-sill' theory" that wage earners were no better off than slaves. Thus he reaffirmed the Republican belief in material progress and personal advancement under a free-labor, capitalist system.

Lincoln reemphasized this theme in a speech at Hartford, Connecticut, where shoemakers were on strike. He said he was "glad to know that there is a system where the laborer can strike if he wants to!" He repeated this statement the next day at New Haven, and went on to declare: "When one starts poor, as most do in the race of life, free society is such that he knows he can better his condition; he knows there is no fixed condition of labor for his whole life." He added: "I want every man to have the chance—and I believe a black man is entitled to it. . . ." He did not need to point out that Southerners had a very different conception of the ideal society.

At times, Lincoln resumed his debate with Douglas, whom he expected to be the Democratic nominee for president. Douglas was going about making speeches in support of popular sovereignty, his proposal for allowing the people of a territory to decide whether or not to permit slavery there. Lincoln said he himself believed in "a genuine popular sovereignty" that would allow "each man" to do as he pleased "with all those things which exclusively concern[ed] him." But slavery, he insisted, was a serious evil that concerned everybody.

While drawing a line between himself and both the Douglas Democrats and the Buchanan Democrats, Lincoln also made clear his difference from the nativists, or so-called Know Nothings. Some Republicans thought their party ought to combine with the nativist party, which remained strong in certain states—especially in Massachusetts, which had restricted the right of immigrants to vote or hold office. In a public letter to a German-American politician in Illinois, Lincoln said he would agree to Republican "fusion" with another party only if it could "be had on republican grounds," and he expressed his opposition to antiforeigner measures of the kind that Massachusetts had recently adopted.

Lincoln was hoping that his party would get many votes from both nativists and the foreign-born, especially the Germans. He also hoped to attract many Democrats. In a widely published letter, he praised their founder, Thomas Jefferson, endorsed Jefferson's principles of free government, and argued that the Republican Party was the real Jeffersonian party.

If the Republicans were to make the broadest possible appeal, they would have to counteract charges of dangerous and divisive radicalism. In particular, they would have to disavow John Brown and his Harpers Ferry raid. Accordingly, Lincoln denounced Brown for his lawlessness and violence, though praising him for his courage. Lincoln pointed out that, anyhow, the raid had posed no real threat to Southerners or their slave system. "It was an attempt by white men to get up a revolt among slaves, in which the slaves refused to participate," he explained at Cooper Union in New York City on February 27, 1860.

At Cooper Union he also argued, on the basis of careful historical research, that the Republicans were taking a perfectly constitutional position in advocating free soil. They were proposing nothing new. They were merely asking to leave slavery where the framers of the Constitution had left it—as an evil to be tolerated but not extended. *"Let us have faith that right makes might,"* Lincoln concluded, to rousing cheers.

While gaining recognition through such public appearances, Lincoln advanced his own and his party's cause in other ways. His Cooper

Union address was printed and widely circulated, as were his 1858 debates with Douglas. He finally provided the autobiography that Fell had requested. He carried on an extensive correspondence with Republican politicians throughout the North, counseling with them about the party's tactics. In his correspondence he intimated that none of the leading contenders (he did not refer to himself) could carry Illinois, whose electoral votes seemed indispensable for a Republican victory in the presidential election.

The preconvention favorite was William H. Seward, U.S. senator from New York and former governor of the state. Seward was the most prominent Republican in the entire country, yet he had a number of handicaps as a possible presidential candidate. The most serious of these was a reputation for radicalism—a reputation he did not really deserve. It was due to incautious remarks he had made. He had said there was a "higher law" than the Constitution—the law of God— which prohibited slavery in the territories. He had also said there was an "irrepressible conflict" between the North and the South, between a civilization based on free labor and one based on slavery.

Lincoln himself had earlier spoken of a "house divided" between freedom and slavery, and had declared that such a house could not stand forever; it must eventually become all free or all slave. But somehow Lincoln appeared to be less radical than Seward, and certainly he had much less of a public record to defend. He had another advantage: As a result of the efforts of his friends, the nominating convention was to be held in Chicago, in his home state, where his supporters could most effectively make their voices heard.

By the time the convention met, in May 1860, he already had the entire Illinois delegation and a number of delegates from other states committed to him. He also had a plan for attracting still other delegates after they had voted once or twice for their respective favorites. "Our policy, then," he explained confidentially, "is to give no offense to others—leave them in a mood to come to us, if they shall be compelled to give up their first love."

Lincoln's managers at the convention, with his old friend David Davis at their head, carried out what was essentially his own strategy. They persuaded as many delegations as possible to adopt him as a second choice. Davis promised some of the contenders high places in the prospective Lincoln administration if they would transfer their followers to Lincoln at the appropriate time. The strategy worked. On the first ballot Seward led but had no majority. On the third ballot Lincoln was nominated. Waiting in Springfield, he received the news by telegraph and then formal notification from a convention committee that called on him.

Lincoln was also given an official copy of the party platform. This stated the Republican position clearly enough on certain issues. It favored a tariff increase, homesteads, and federal funds for a Pacific railroad. It opposed new restrictions on the political rights of immigrants. It declared that neither Congress nor the people of a territory could "give legal existence" to slavery in the territory. Thus it repudiated both the Douglas doctrine of popular sovereignty and the Southern view that slavery could not constitutionally be excluded from the West.

On the question of slavery in the Southern states, however, the platform appeared to be somewhat contradictory. It pledged the party not to interfere with the "domestic institutions" of any state. But it also quoted from the Declaration of Independence to reaffirm the idea that "all men are created equal" and have certain rights, including the right to liberty. This would seem to imply that the continued existence of slavery anywhere in the country was contrary to the principles of the Republican Party.

Lincoln accepted the nomination, endorsed the platform, and prepared for the campaign. But he was not going to make any campaign speeches. It was not yet customary for a presidential candidate to go out stumping in his own behalf. Besides, it would not have been to Lincoln's advantage to do so. He was seeking the votes of various and conflicting groups—former Whigs and former Democrats, nativists and immigrants, protectionists and free traders, abolitionists and free-soilers. An appeal to one group was sure to antagonize another. Lincoln's confidential advice to his fellow politicians was this: We "should look beyond our noses, and at least say *nothing* on points where it is probable we shall disagree."

Running against Lincoln was Douglas, as had been expected, but Douglas was not the only opposing candidate. The Democratic Party had split. Southern delegates at its convention had refused to accept the "Douglas platform," which called for popular sovereignty. They held a separate convention, nominated John C. Breckinridge of Kentucky (the incumbent vice president), and adopted a platform denying the power of Congress or territorial governments to exclude slavery from the territories.

Still a fourth candidate was in the field. Some former Whigs and Know Nothings had formed what they called the Constitutional Union Party. Nominating John Bell of Tennessee, they evaded the slavery issue and simply declared themselves in favor of the Constitution, the Union, and the laws.

None of the parties or candidates advocated disunion, however, and each of them claimed to be taking a perfectly legal and constitutional stand. Disregarding custom and campaigning vigorously for himself, Douglas contended that only *his* election would guarantee the preservation of the Union. Prominent Southern politicians were warning that their states would secede from the Union if Lincoln should be elected (those states would probably have been just as likely to secede had Douglas won).

The prosecessionists repeated the charge that Lincoln and the Republicans were abolitionists at heart and, once in office, would take steps against slavery and would even foment slave insurrections. Southern opponents of secession begged Lincoln to speak out and reassure slaveowners, but he persisted in refusing to make any public statements during the campaign. He thought that there was no real danger of disunion and that, in any case, he had already made his views adequately known through his published speeches and letters.

While Lincoln remained silent, Republicans were busily campaigning for him throughout the North. They stressed different issues in different areas. For example, they promised a high protective tariff in Pennsylvania, where industrialists and their workers considered it essential to their prosperity, but they said little about it in Illinois and other states where it was less popular. The Republican campaigners generally insisted, however, that their party offered no threat to slavery in the South.

On election day nobody voted for Lincoln in the South, where his name did not even appear on the ballot; and only a few voted for him in the border slave states. However, he received pluralities in California and Oregon, and a clear majority cast their ballots for him in every other free state except New Jersey. In the country as a whole, he received just under 40 percent of the popular vote. Still, he got a majority of the electoral vote, and so he won the election. But his party failed to win a majority of the seats in either house of Congress.

Thus the Republicans could expect to control only one of the three branches of the federal government—the executive, but not the legislative or the judicial branch. They would not yet be in a position to carry out any part of their program. Nevertheless, the Southern secessionists determined to make good their recent threats of disunion. South Carolina led off by promptly scheduling a popular convention to arrange for the secession of that state.

No sooner was Lincoln elected than he had to face the worrisome prospect of presiding over a country in the throes of dissolution.

→>> <<←

"SOLE HOPE OF THE *FUTURE*"

*From a Lecture on Discoveries and Inventions,
Jacksonville, Decatur, and Springfield*

[FEBRUARY 11, 1859]

"I am not a professional lecturer," Lincoln maintained after delivering this talk. He thought it "a rather poor one," though it brought forth "hearty bursts of applause," according to a newspaper report. Cleverly politicizing his topic, Lincoln began the lecture by pretending to praise "Young America." This was a slogan of Stephen A. Douglas and other jingoistic Democrats who advocated territorial expansion for the United States and the overthrow of monarchy in Europe. They contended that anyone opposing them must be an "Old Fogy" who objected to all progress. Lincoln was actually making sly fun of some of the "Young America" notions. He proceeded to argue that real progress depended on "useful discoveries and inventions."

We have all heard of Young America. He is the most *current* youth of the age. Some think him conceited, and arrogrant; but has he not reason to entertain a rather extensive opinion of himself? Is he not the inventor and owner of the *present,* and sole hope of the *future?* Men, and things, everywhere, are ministering unto him. Look at his apparel, and you shall see cotten fabrics from Manchester and Lowell; flax-linen from Ireland; wood-cloth from [Spain;] silk from France; furs from the Arctic regions, with a buffalo-robe from the Rocky Mountains, as a general out-sider. At his table, besides plain bread and meat made at home, are sugar from Louisiana; coffee and fruits from the tropics; salt from Turk's Island; fish from New-foundland; tea from China, and spices from the Indies. The whale of the Pacific furnishes his candle-light; he has a diamond-ring from Brazil; a gold-watch from California, and a spanish cigar from Havanna. He not only has a present supply of all these, and much more; but thousands of hands are engaged in producing fresh supplies, and other thousands, in bringing them to him. The iron horse is panting, and impatient, to carry him everywhere, in no time; and the lightening stands ready harnessed to take and bring his tidings in a trifle less than no time. He owns a large part of the world, by right of possessing it; and all the rest by right of *wanting* it, and *intending* to have it. As Plato had for the immortality of the soul, so Young America has "a pleasing hope—a fond desire—a longing after" teritory. He has a great passion—a perfect rage—for the *"new";* particularly new men for office, and the new earth mentioned in the revelations, in which, being no more sea, there must be about three times as much land as in the present. He is a great friend of humanity; and his desire for land is not selfish, but merely an impulse to extend the area of freedom. He is very anxious to fight for the liberation of enslaved nations and colonies, provided, always, they *have* land, and have *not* any liking for his interference. As to those who have no land, and would be glad of help from any quarter, he considers, *they* can afford to wait a few hundred years longer. In knowledge he is particularly rich. He knows all that can possibly be known; inclines to believe in spiritual rappings, and is the unquestioned inventor of *"Manifest Destiny."* His horror is for all that is old, particularly "Old Fogy"; and if there be any thing old which he can endure, it is only old whiskey and old tobacco.

If the said Young America really is, as he claims to be, the owner of all present, it must be admitted that he has considerable advantage of Old Fogy. Take, for instance, the first of all fogies, father Adam. There he stood, a very perfect physical man, as poets and painters inform us; but he must have been very ignorant, and simple in his habits. He had had no sufficient time to learn much by observation; and he had no near neighbors to teach him anything. No part of his breakfast had been brought from the other side of the world; and it is quite probable, he had no conception of the world having any other side. In all of these things, it is very plain, he was no equal of Young America; the most that can be said is, that *according to his chance* he may have quite as much of a man as his very self-complaisant descendant. Little as was what he knew, let the Youngster discard all he had learned from others, and then show, if he can, any advantage on his side. In the way of *land,* and *live stock,* Adam was quite in the ascendant. He had dominion over all the earth, and all the living things upon, and round about it. The land has been sadly divided out since; but never fret, young America will *re-annex* it.

The great difference between Young America and Old Fogy, is the result of *Discoveries, Inventions,* and *Improvements.* These, in turn, are the result of *observation, reflection* and *experiment.* For instance, it is quite certain that ever since water has been boiled in covered vessels, men have seen the lids of the vessels rise and fall a little, with a sort of fluttering motion, by force of the steam; but so long as this was not specially observed, and reflected and experimented upon, it came to nothing. At length however, after many thousand years, some man observes this long-known effect of hot water lifting a pot-lid, and begins a train of reflection upon it. He says "Why, to be sure, the force that lifts the pot-lid, will lift any thing else, which is no heavier than the pot-lid." "And, as man has much hard lifting to do, can not this hot-water power be made to help him?" He has become a little excited on the subject, and he fancies he hears a voice answering "Try me[.]" He does try it; and the *observation, reflection,* and *trial* gives to the world the control of that tremendous, and now well known agent, called steam-power. This is not the actual history in detail, but the general principle.

But was this first inventor of the application of steam, wiser or more ingenious than those who had gone before him? Not at all. Had he not learned much of them, he never would have succeeded—probably, never would have thought of making the attempt. To be fruitful in invention, it is indispensable to have a *habit* of observation and reflection; and this *habit*, our steam friend acquired, no doubt, from those who, to him, were old fogies. But for the difference in *habit* of observation, why did yankees, almost instantly, discover gold in California, which had been trodden upon, and over-looked by indians and Mexican greasers, for centuries? Gold-mines are not the only mines overlooked in the same way. There are more mines above the Earth's surface than below it. All nature—the whole world, material, moral, and intellectual,—is a mine; and, in Adam's day, it was a wholly unexplored mine. Now, it was the destined work of Adam's race to develope, by discoveries, inventions, and improvements, the hidden treasures of this mine. But Adam had nothing to turn his attention to the work. If he should do anything in the way of invention, he had first to invent the art of invention—the *instance* at least, if not the *habit* of observation and reflection. As might be expected he seems not to have been a very observing man at first; for it appears he went about naked a considerable length of time, before he even noticed that obvious fact. But when he did observe it, the observation was not lost upon him; for it immediately led to the first of all inventions, of which we have any direct account—the *fig-leaf apron.*

The inclination to exchange thoughts with one another is probably an original impulse of our nature. If I be in pain I wish to let you know it, and to ask your sympathy and assistance; and my pleasurable emotions also, I wish to communicate to, and share with you. But to carry on such communication, some *instrumentality* is indispensable. Accordingly speech—articulate sounds rattled off from the tongue—was used by our first parents, and even by Adam, before the creation of Eve. He gave names to the animals while she was still a bone in his side; and he broke out quite volubly when she first stood before him, the best present of his maker. From this it would appear that speech was not an invention of man, but rather the direct gift of his Creator. But whether Divine gift, or invention, it is still plain that if a mode of communication had been left to invention, *speech* must have been the first, from the superior adaptation to the end, of the organs of speech, over every other means within the whole range of nature. Of the organs of speech the tongue is the principal; and if we shall test it, we shall find the capacities of the tongue, in the utterance of articulate sounds, absolutely wonderful. You can count from one to one hundred, quite distinctly in about forty seconds. In doing this two hundred and eighty three distinct sounds or syllables are uttered, being seven to each second; and yet there shall be enough difference between every two, to be easily recognized by the ear of the hearer. What other *signs* to represent *things* could possibly be produced so rapidly? or, even, if ready made, could be *arranged* so rapidly to express the sense? *Motions* with the hands, are no adequate substitute. *Marks* for the recognition of the eye—*writing*—although a wonderful auxiliary for speech, is no worthy substitute for it. In addition to the more slow and laborious process of getting up a communication in writing, the materials—pen, ink, and paper—are not always at hand. But one always has his tongue with him, and the breath of his life is the ever-ready material with which it works. Speech, then, by enabling different individuals to interchange thoughts, and thereby to combine their powers of observation and reflection, greatly facilitates useful discoveries and inventions. What one observes, and would himself infer nothing from, he tells to another, and that other at once sees a valuable hint in it. A result is thus reached which neither *alone* would have arrived at.

And this reminds me of what I passed unnoticed before, that the very first invention was a joint operation, Eve having shared with Adam in the getting up of the apron. And, indeed, judging from the fact that sewing has come down to our times as "woman's work" it is very probable she took the leading part; he, perhaps, doing no more than to stand by and thread the needle. That proceeding may be reckoned as the mother of all "Sewing societies"; and the first and most perfect "world's fair" all inventions and all inventors then in the world, being on the spot.

But speech alone, valuable as it ever has been, and is, has not advanced the condition of the world much. This is abundantly evident when we look at the degraded condition of all those tribes of human creatures who have no considerable additional means of communicating thoughts. *Writing*—the art of communicating thoughts to the mind, through the eye—is the great invention of the world. Great in the astonishing range of analysis and combination which necessarily underlies the most crude and general conception of it—great, very great in enabling us to converse with the dead, the absent, and the unborn, at all distances of time and of space; and great, not only in its direct benefits, but greatest help, to all other inventions. Suppose the art, with all conception of it, were this day lost to the world, how long, think you, would it be, before even Young America could get up the letter A. with any adequate notion of using it to advantage? The precise period at which writing was invented, is not known; but it certainly was as early as the time of Moses; from which we may safely infer that it's inventors were very old fogies.

. . . .

. . . It is difficult for us, *now* and *here,* to conceive how strong this slavery of the mind was; and how long it did, of necessity, take, to break it's shackles, and to get a habit of freedom of thought, established. It is, in this connection, a curious fact that a new country is most favorable—almost necessary—to the immancipation of thought, and the consequent advancement of civilization and the arts. The human family originated as is thought, somewhere in Asia, and have worked their way princip[al]ly Westward. Just now, in civilization, and the arts, the people of Asia are entirely behind those of Europe; those of the East of Europe behind those of the West of it; while we, here in America, *think* we discover, and invent, and improve, faster than any of them. *They* may think this is arrogance; but they can not deny that Russia has called on us to show her how to build steam-boats and railroads—while in the older parts of Asia, they scarcely know that such things as S.Bs & RR.s. exist. In anciently inhabited countries, the dust of ages—a real downright old-fogyism—seems to settle upon, and smother the intellects and energies of man. It is in this view that I have mentioned the discovery of America as an event greatly favoring and facilitating useful discoveries and inventions.

"HE WHO WOULD *BE* NO SLAVE, MUST CONSENT TO *HAVE* NO SLAVE"

Letter to Boston Republicans

[APRIL 6, 1859]

Lincoln wrote this letter to a group of Bostonians who, like many of his party, were now clamoring to invite him to address them—his defeat by Douglas notwithstanding. So impressed were the Bostonians by this reply that they had it reprinted in Republican newspapers.

Springfield, Ills.
April 6. 1859

Messrs. Henry L. Pierce, & others.

Gentlemen

Your kind note inviting me to attend a Festival in Boston, on the 13th. Inst. in honor of the birth-day of Thomas Jefferson, was duly received. My engagements are such that I can not attend.

Bearing in mind that about seventy years ago, two great political parties were first formed in this country, that Thomas Jefferson was the head of one of them, and Boston the head-quarters of the other, it is both curious and interesting that those supposed to descend politically from the party opposed to Jefferson, should now be celebrating his birth-day in their own original seat of empire, while those claiming political descent from him have nearly ceased to breathe his name everywhere.

Remembering too, that the Jefferson party were formed upon their supposed superior devotion to the *personal* rights of men, holding the rights of *property* to be secondary only, and greatly inferior, and then assuming that the so-called democracy of to-day, are the Jefferson, and their opponents, the anti-Jefferson parties, it will be equally interesting to note how completely the two have changed hands as to the principle upon which they were originally supposed to be divided.

The democracy of to-day hold the *liberty* of one man to be absolutely nothing, when in conflict with another man's right of *property*. Republicans, on the contrary, are for both the *man* and the *dollar;* but in cases of conflict, the man *before* the dollar.

I remember once being much amused at seeing two partially intoxicated men engage in a fight with their great-coats on, which fight, after a long, and rather harmless contest, ended in each having fought himself *out* of his own coat, and *into* that of the other. If the two leading parties of this day are really identical with the two in the days of Jefferson and Adams, they have performed the same feat as the two drunken men.

But soberly, it is now no child's play to save the principles of Jefferson from total overthrow in this nation.

One would start with great confidence that he could convince any sane child that the simpler propositions of Euclid are true; but, nevertheless, he would fail, utterly, with one who should deny the definitions and axioms. The principles of Jefferson are the definitions and axioms of free society. And yet they are denied, and evaded, with no small show of success. One dashingly calls them "glittering generalities"; another bluntly calls them "self evident lies"; and still others insidiously argue that they apply only to "superior races."

These expressions, differing in form, are identical in object and effect—the supplanting the principles of free government, and restoring those of classification, caste, and legitimacy. They would delight a convocation of crowned heads, plotting against the people. They are the van-guard—the miners, and sappers—of returning despotism. We must repulse them, or they will subjugate us.

This is a world of compensations; and he who would *be* no slave, must consent to *have* no slave. Those who deny freedom to others, deserve it not for themselves; and, under a just God, can not long retain it.

All honor to Jefferson—to the man who, in the concrete pressure of a struggle for national independence by a single people, had the coolness, forecast, and capacity to introduce into a merely revolutionary document, an abstract truth, applicable to all men and all times, and so to embalm it there, that to-day, and in all coming days, it shall be a rebuke and a stumbling-block to the very harbingers of re-appearing tyranny and oppression. Your obedient Servant

A. LINCOLN—

"AIM AT THE *ELEVATION* OF MEN"

Letter to Theodore Canisius

[MAY 17, 1859]

Here Lincoln told a German-American publisher that he opposed restrictions on the right to vote. Lincoln was a financial backer of Canisius's paper, the Illinois Staats-Anzeiger, *which published the letter.*

Dr. Theodore Canisius   Springfield, May 17, 1859

Dear Sir:

Your note asking, in behalf of yourself and other german citizens, whether I am for or against the constitutional provision in regard to naturalized citizens, lately adopted by Massachusetts; and whether I am for or against a fusion of the republicans, and other opposition elements, for the canvas of 1860, is received.

Massachusetts is a sovereign and independent state; and it is no privilege of mine to scold her for what she does. Still, if from what she *has done,* an inference is sought to be drawn as to what I *would do,* I may, without impropriety, speak out. I say then, that, as I understand the Massachusetts provision, I am against it's adoption in Illinois, or in any other place, where I have a right to oppose it. Understanding the spirit of our institutions to aim at the *elevation* of men, I am opposed to whatever tends to *degrade* them. I have some little notoriety for commiserating the oppressed condition of the negro; and I should be strangely inconsistent if I could favor any project for curtailing the existing rights of *white men,* even though born in different lands, and speaking different languages from myself.

As to the matter of fusion, I am for it, if it can be had on republican grounds; and I am not for it on any other terms. A fusion on any other terms, would be as foolish as unprincipled. It would lose the whole North, while the common enemy would still carry the whole South. The question of *men* is a different one. There are good patriotic men, and able statesmen, in the South whom I would cheerfully support, if they would now place themselves on republican ground. But I am against letting down the republican standard a hair's breadth.

I have written this hastily, but I believe it answers your questions substantially. Yours truly

A. LINCOLN

"THE MORAL LIGHTS AROUND US"
From a Speech at Columbus, Ohio
[SEPTEMBER 16, 1859]

The opening address in a six-state speaking tour, this speech, delivered from the terrace of the Ohio statehouse, was used by Lincoln to renew his attack on Stephen A. Douglas—"without gloves," according to the influential Washington newspaper, the National Intelligencer. *Although a pro-Douglas Cincinnati paper reported that Lincoln "disappointed his friends" by proving not to be "a very pleasing speaker," others credited his campaigning for bringing about the Republican Party's success in the state's fall elections. He returned home, an Illinois journalist reported, "after electrifying Ohio."*

I believe there is a genuine popular sovereignty. I think a definition of genuine popular sovereignty, in the abstract, would be about this: That each man shall do precisely as he pleases with himself, and with all those things which exclusively concern him. Applied to government, this principle would be, that a general government shall do all those things which pertain to it, and all the local governments shall do precisely as they please in respect to those matters which exclusively concern them. I understand that this government of the United States, under which we live, is based upon this principle; and I am misunderstood if it is supposed that I have any war to make upon that principle.

. . . .

. . . After Judge Douglas has established this proposition [the right of states to run their own affairs—eds.], which nobody disputes or ever has disputed, he proceeds to assume, without proving it, that slavery is one of those little, unimportant, trivial matters which are of just about as much consequence as the question would be to me, whether my neighbor should raise horned cattle or plant tobacco [laughter]; that there is no moral question about it, but that it is altogether a matter of dollars and cents; that when a new territory is opened for settlement, the first man who goes into it may plant there a thing which, like the Canada thistle, or some other of those pests of the soil, cannot be dug out by the millions of men who will come thereafter; that it is one of those little things that is so trivial in its nature that it has no effect upon anybody save the few men who first plant upon the soil; that it is not a thing which in any way affects the family of communities composing these States, nor any way endangers the general government. Judge Douglas ignores altogether the very well known fact, that we have never had a serious menace to our political existence, except it sprang from this thing which he chooses to regard as only upon a par with onions and potatoes. [Laughter.]

. . . .

Now, if you are opposed to slavery honestly, as much as anybody I ask you to note that fact, and the like of which is to follow, to be plastered on, layer after layer, until very soon you are prepared to deal with the negro everywhere as with the brute. If public sentiment has not been debauched already to this point, a new turn of the screw in that direction is all that is wanting; and this is constantly being done by the teachers of this insidious popular sovereignty. You need but one or two turns further until your minds, now ripening under these teachings will be ready for all these things, and you will receive and support, or submit to, the slave trade; revived with all its horrors; a slave code enforced in our territories, and a new Dred Scott decision to bring slavery up into the very heart of the free North. This, I must say, is but carrying out those words prophetically spoken by Mr. Clay, many, many years ago. I believe more than thirty years when he told an audience that if they would repress all tendencies to liberty and ultimate emancipation, they must go back to the era of our independence and muzzle the cannon which thundered its annual joyous return on the Fourth of July; they must blow out the moral lights around us; they must penetrate the human soul and eradicate the love of liberty; but until they did these things, and others eloquently enumerated by him, they could not repress all tendencies to ultimate emancipation.

I ask attention to the fact that in a pre-eminent degree these popular sovereigns are at this work; blowing out the moral lights around us; teaching that the negro is no longer a man but a brute; that the Declaration has nothing to do with him; that he ranks with the crocodile and the reptile; that man, with body and soul, is a matter of dollars and cents. I suggest to this portion of the Ohio Republicans, or Democrats if there be any present, the serious consideration of this fact, that there is now going on among you a steady process of debauching public opinion on this subject. With this my friends, I bid you adieu.

"EQUALITY . . . BEATS INEQUALITY"

Fragment on Free Labor

[SEPTEMBER 17, 1859?]

This fragment may have been prepared for a speech scheduled for Cincinnati, another stop on Lincoln's Ohio speaking tour.

. . . *Equality,* in society, alike beats *inequality,* whether the lat[t]er be of the British aristocratic sort, or of the domestic slavery sort.

We know, Southern men declare that their slaves are better off than hired laborers amongst us. How little they *know,* whereof they *speak!* There is no permanent class of hired laborers amongst us. Twentyfive years ago, I was a hired laborer. The hired laborer of yesterday, labors on his own account to-day; and will hire others to labor for him to-morrow. Advancement—improvement in condition—is the order of things in a society of equals. As Labor is the common *burthen* of our race, so the effect of *some* to shift their share of the burthen on to the shoulders of *others,* is the great, durable, curse of the race. Originally a curse for transgression upon the whole race, when, as by slavery, it is concentrated on a part only, it becomes the double-refined curse of God upon his creatures.

Free labor has the inspiration of hope; pure slavery has no hope. The power of hope upon human exertion, and happiness, is wonderful. The slave-master himself has a conception of it; and hence the system of *tasks* among slaves. The slave whom you can not drive with the lash to break seventy-five pounds of hemp in a day, if you will task him to break a hundred, and promise him pay for all he does over, he will break you a hundred and fifty. You have substituted *hope,* for the *rod.* And yet perhaps it does not occur to you, that to the extent of your gain in the case, you have given up the slave system, and adopted the free system of labor.

"*FREE* LABOR . . . GIVES HOPE TO ALL"

From an Address Before the Wisconsin State Agricultural Society, Milwaukee, Wisconsin

[SEPTEMBER 30, 1859]

This was Lincoln's most comprehensive discussion of labor and capital, and his sharpest criticism of the so-called "mudsill" theory, which held that labor was fixed in its subordinate position for life. Lincoln also took pains to appeal to his audience by extolling the virtues of farming, for which, in reality, he had a disdain bordering on repugnance.

The world is agreed that *labor* is the source from which human wants are mainly supplied. There is no dispute upon this point. From this point, however, men immediately diverge. Much disputation is maintained as to the best way of applying and controlling the labor element. By some it is assumed that labor is available only in connection with capital—that nobody labors, unless somebody else, owning capital, somehow, by the use of that capital, induces him to do it. Having assumed this, they proceed to consider whether it is best that capital shall *hire* laborers, and thus induce them to work by their own consent; or *buy* them, and drive them to it without their consent. Having proceeded so far they naturally conclude that all laborers are necessarily cither *hired* laborers, or *slaves.* They further assume that whoever is once a *hired* laborer, is fatally fixed in that condition for life; and thence again that his condition is as bad as, or worse than that of a slave. This is the *"mud-sill"* theory.

But another class of reasoners hold the opinion that there is no *such* relation between capital and labor, as assumed; and that there is no such thing as a freeman being fatally fixed for life, in the condition of a hired laborer, that both these assumptions are false, and all inferences from them groundless. They hold that labor is prior to, and independent of, capital; that, in fact, capital is the fruit of labor, and could never have existed if labor had not *first* existed—that labor can exist without capital, but capital could never have existed without labor. Hence they hold that labor is the superior—greatly the superior—of capital.

They do not deny that there is, and probably always will be, *a* relation between labor and capital. The error, as they hold, is in assuming that the *whole* labor of the world exists within that relation. A few men own capital; and that few avoid labor themselves, and with their capital, hire, or buy, another few to labor for them. A large majority belong to neither class—neither work for others, nor have others working for them. Even in all our slave States, except South Carolina, a majority of the whole people of all colors, are neither slaves nor masters. In these Free States, a large majority are neither *hirers* nor *hired.* Men, with their families—wives, sons and daughters—work for themselves, on their farms, in their houses and in their shops, taking the whole product to themselves, and asking no favors of capital on the one hand, nor of hirelings or slaves on the other.

. . . The prudent, penniless beginner in the world, labors for wages awhile, saves a surplus with which to buy tools or land, for himself; then labors on his own account another while, and at length hires another new beginner to help him. This, say its advocates, is *free* labor—the just and generous, and prosperous system, which opens the way for all— gives hope to all, and energy, and progress, and improvement of condition to all. If any continue through life in the condition of the hired laborer, it is not the fault of the system, but because of either a dependent nature which prefers it, or improvidence, folly, or singular misfortune. I have said this much about the elements of labor generally, as introductory to the consideration of a new phase which that element is in process of assuming. The old general rule was that *educated* people did not perform manual labor. They managed to eat their bread, leaving the toil of producing it to the uneducated. This was not an insupportable evil to the working bees, so long as the class of drones remained very small. But *now,* especially in these free States, nearly all are educated—quite too nearly all, to leave the labor of the uneducated, in any wise adequate to the support of the whole. It follows from this that henceforth educated people must labor. Otherwise, education itself would become a positive and intolerable evil. No country can sustain, in idleness, more than a small per centage of its numbers. The great majority must labor at something productive. From these premises the problem springs, "How can *labor* and *education* be the most satisfactorily combined?"

By the *"mud-sill"* theory it is assumed that labor and education are incompatible; and any practical combination of them impossible. According to that theory, a blind horse upon a tread-mill, is a perfect illustration of what a laborer should be—all the better for being blind, that he could not tread out of place, or kick understandingly. According to that theory, the education of laborers, is not only useless, but pernicious, and dangerous. In fact, it is, in some sort, deemed a misfortune that laborers should have heads at all. Those same heads are regarded as explosive materials, only to be safely kept in damp places, as far as possible from that peculiar sort of fire which ignites them. A Yankee who could invent a strong *handed* man without a head would receive the everlasting gratitude of the "mud-sill" advocates.

But Free Labor says "no!" Free Labor argues that, as the Author of man makes every individual with one head and one pair of hands, it was probably intended that heads and hands should cooperate as friends; and that that particular head, should direct and control that particular pair of hands. As each man has one mouth to be fed, and one pair of hands to furnish food, it was probably intended that that particular pair of hands should feed that particular mouth—that each head is the natural guardian, director, and protector of the hands and mouth inseparably connected with it; and that being so, every head should be cultivated, and improved, by whatever will add to its capacity for performing its charge. In one word Free Labor insists on universal education. . . .

This leads to the further reflection, that no other human occupation opens so wide a field for the profitable and agreeable combination of labor with cultivated thought, as agriculture. I know of nothing so pleasant to the mind, as the discovery of anything which is at once *new* and *valuable*—nothing which so lightens and sweetens toil, as the hopeful pursuit of such discovery. And how vast, and how varied a field is agriculture, for such discovery. The mind, already trained to thought, in the country school, or higher school, cannot fail to find there an exhaustless source of profitable enjoyment. Every blade of grass is a study; and to produce two, where there was but one, is both a profit and a pleasure. And not grass alone; but soils, seeds, and seasons—hedges, ditches, and fences, draining, droughts, and irrigation—plowing, hoeing, and harrowing—reaping, mowing, and threshing—saving crops, pests of crops, diseases of crops, and what will prevent or cure them—implements, utensils, and machines, their relative merits, and [how] to improve them—hogs, horses, and cattle—sheep, goats, and poultry—trees, shrubs, fruits, plants, and flowers—the thousand things of which these are specimens—each a world of study within itself.

. . . .

It is said an Eastern monarch once charged his wise men to invent him a sentence, to be ever in view, and which should be true and appropriate in all times and situations. They presented him the words: *"And this, too, shall pass away."* How much it expresses! How chastening in the hour of pride!—how consoling in the depths of affliction! "And this, too, shall pass away." And yet let us hope it is not *quite* true. Let us hope, rather, that by the best cultivation of the physical world, beneath and around us; and the intellectual and moral world within us, we shall secure an individual, social, and political prosperity and happiness, whose course shall be onward and upward, and which, while the earth endures, shall not pass away.

"LET US STAND BY OUR DUTY"

From an Address at Cooper Union, New York City

[FEBRUARY 27, 1860]

Probably the most important speech of his career to date, the Cooper Union address triumphantly introduced Lincoln to the eastern Republican establishment, and invigorated his chances for the presidency. "No man ever before made such an impression on his first appeal to a New York audience," the New York Tribune *reported. A preface to the speech, published in September 1860, called it "an historical work—brief, complete, profound, impartial, truthful—which will survive the time and the occasion that called it forth." But in a letter to his wife, Lincoln conceded only that the appearance "went off passably well." The first section of the address was devoted to proving that the nation's founders anticipated the eventual extinction of slavery; these are the words that followed.*

If any man at this day sincerely believes that a proper division of local from federal authority, or any part of the Constitution, forbids the Federal Government to control as to slavery in the federal territories, he is right to say so, and to enforce his position by all truthful evidence and fair argument which he can. But he has no right to mislead others, who have less access to history, and less leisure to study it, into the false belief that "our fathers, who framed the Government under which we live," were of the same opinion—thus substituting falsehood and deception for truthful evidence and fair argument. If any man at this day sincerely believes "our fathers who framed the Government under which we live," used and applied principles, in other cases, which ought to have led them to understand that a proper division of local from federal authority or some part of the Constitution, forbids the Federal Government to control as to slavery in the federal territories, he is right to say so. But he should, at the same time, brave the responsibility of declaring that, in his opinion, he understands their principles better than they did themselves; and especially should he not shirk that responsibility by asserting that they "understood the question just as well, and even better, than we do now."

But enough! *Let all who believe that "our fathers, who framed the Government under which we live, understood this question just as well, and even better, than we do now," speak as they spoke, and act as they acted upon it. This is all Republicans ask—all Republicans desire—in relation to slavery. As those fathers marked it, so let it be again marked, as an evil not to be extended, but to be tolerated and protected only because of and so far as its actual presence among us makes that toleration and protection a necessity. Let all the guaranties those fathers gave it, be, not grudgingly, but fully and fairly maintained.* For this Republicans contend, and with this, so far as I know or believe, they will be content.

And now, if they would listen—as I suppose they will not—I would address a few words to the Southern people.

I would say to them:—You consider yourselves a reasonable and a just people; and I consider that in the general qualities of reason and justice you are not inferior to any other people. Still, when you speak of us Republicans, you do so only to denounce us as reptiles, or, at the best, as no better than outlaws. You will grant a hearing to pirates or murderers, but nothing like it to "Black Republicans." In all your contentions with one another, each of you deems an unconditional condemnation of "Black Republicanism" as the first thing to be attended to. Indeed, such condemnation of us seems to be an indispensable prerequisite—license, so to speak—among you to be admitted or permitted to speak at all. Now, can you, or not, be prevailed upon to pause and to consider whether this is quite just to us, or even to yourselves? Bring forward your charges and specifications, and then be patient long enough to hear us deny or justify.

You say we are sectional. We deny it. That makes an issue; and the burden of proof is upon you. You produce your proof; and what is it? Why, that our party has no existence in your section—gets no votes in your section. The fact is substantially true; but does it prove the issue? If it does, then in case we should, without change of principle, begin to get votes in your section, we should thereby cease to be sectional. You cannot escape this conclusion; and yet, are you willing to abide by it? If you are, you will probably soon find that we have ceased to be sectional, for we shall get votes in your section this very year. You will then begin to discover, as the truth plainly is, that your proof does not touch the issue. The fact that we get no votes in your section, is a fact of your making, and not of ours. And if there be fault in that fact, that fault is primarily yours, and remains so until you show that we repel you by some wrong principle or practice. If we do repel you by any wrong principle or practice, the fault is ours; but this brings you to where you ought to have started—to a discussion of the right or wrong of our principle. If our principle, put in practice, would wrong your section for the benefit of ours, or for any other object, then our principle, and we with it, are sectional, and are justly opposed and denounced as such. Meet us, then, on the question of whether our principle, put in practice, would wrong your section; and so meet us as if it were possible that something may be said on our side. Do you accept the challenge? No! Then you really believe that the principle which "our fathers who framed the Government under which we live" thought so clearly right as to adopt it, and indorse it again and again, upon their official oaths, is in fact so clearly wrong as to demand your condemnation without a moment's consideration.

Some of you delight to flaunt in our faces the warning against sectional parties given by Washington in his Farewell Address. Less than eight years before Washington gave that warning, he had, as President of the United States, approved and signed an act of Congress, enforcing the prohibition of slavery in the Northwestern Territory, which act embodied the policy of the Government upon that subject up to and at the very moment he penned that warning; and about one year after he penned it, he wrote La Fayette that he considered that prohibition a wise measure, expressing in the same connection his hope that we should at some time have a confederacy of free States.

Bearing this in mind, and seeing that sectionalism has since arisen upon this same subject, is that warning a weapon in your hands against us, or in our hands against you? Could Washington himself speak, would he cast the blame of that sectionalism upon us, who sustain his policy, or upon you who repudiate it? We respect that warning of Washington, and we commend it to you, together with his example pointing to the right application of it.

But you say you are conservative—eminently conservative—while we are revolutionary, destructive, or something of the sort. What is conservatism? Is it not adherence to the old and tried, against the new and untried? We stick to, contend for, the identical old policy on the point in controversy which was adopted by "our fathers who framed the Government under which we live;" while you with one accord

reject, and scout, and spit upon that old policy, and insist upon substituting something new. True, you disagree among yourselves as to
what that substitute shall be. You are divided on new propositions and
plans, but you are unanimous in rejecting and denouncing the old
policy of the fathers. Some of you are for reviving the foreign slave
trade; some for a Congressional Slave-Code for the Territories; some for
Congress forbidding the Territories to prohibit Slavery within their
limits; some for maintaining Slavery in the Territories through the
judiciary; some for the "gur-reat pur-rinciple" that "if one man would
enslave another, no third man should object," fantastically called "Popular Sovereignty;" but never a man among you in favor of federal
prohibition of slavery in federal territories, according to the practice of
"our fathers who framed the Government under which we live." Not
one of all your various plans can show a precedent or an advocate in
the century within which our Government originated. Consider, then,
whether your claim of conservatism for yourselves, and your charge of
destructiveness against us, are based on the most clear and stable foundations.

Again, you say we have made the slavery question more prominent
than it formerly was. We deny it. We admit that it is more prominent,
but we deny that we made it so. It was not we, but you, who discarded
the old policy of the fathers. We resisted, and still resist, your innovation; and thence comes the greater prominence of the question. Would
you have that question reduced to its former proportions? Go back to
that old policy. What has been will be again, under the same conditions.
If you would have the peace of the old times, readopt the precepts and
policy of the old times.

You charge that we stir up insurrections among your slaves. We deny
it; and what is your proof? Harper's Ferry! John Brown!! John Brown
was no Republican; and you have failed to implicate a single Republican in his Harper's Ferry enterprise. If any member of our party is
guilty in that matter, you know it or you do not know it. If you do know
it, you are inexcusable for not designating the man and proving the fact.
If you do not know it, you are inexcusable for asserting it, and especially
for persisting in the assertion after you have tried and failed to make
the proof. You need not be told that persisting in a charge which one
does not know to be true, is simply malicious slander.

Some of you admit that no Republican designedly aided or encouraged the Harper's Ferry affair; but still insist that our doctrines and declarations necessarily lead to such results. We do not believe it. We know we hold to no doctrine, and make no declaration, which were not held to and made by "our fathers who framed the Government under which we live." You never dealt fairly by us in relation to this affair. When it occurred, some important State elections were near at hand, and you were in evident glee with the belief that, by charging the blame upon us, you could get an advantage of us in those elections. The elections came, and your expectations were not quite fulfilled. Every Republican man knew that, as to himself at least, your charge was a slander, and he was not much inclined by it to cast his vote in your favor. Republican doctrines and declarations are accompanied with a continual protest against any interference whatever with your slaves, or with you about your slaves. Surely, this does not encourage them to revolt. True, we do, in common with "our fathers, who framed the Government under which we live," declare our belief that slavery is wrong; but the slaves do not hear us declare even this. For anything we say or do, the slaves would scarcely know there is a Republican party. I believe they would not, in fact, generally know it but for your misrepresentations of us, in their hearing. In your political contests among yourselves, each faction charges the other with sympathy with Black Republicanism; and then, to give point to the charge, defines Black Republicanism to simply be insurrection, blood and thunder among the slaves.

Slave insurrections are no more common now than they were before the Republican party was organized. What induced the Southampton insurrection [Nat Turner's 1831 slave revolt—eds.], twenty-eight years ago, in which, at least, three times as many lives were lost as at Harper's Ferry? You can scarcely stretch your very elastic fancy to the conclusion that Southampton was "got up by Black Republicanism." In the present state of things in the United States, I do not think a general, or even a very extensive slave insurrection, is possible. The indispensable concert of action cannot be attained. The slaves have no means of rapid communication; nor can incendiary freemen, black or white, supply it. The explosive materials are everywhere in parcels; but there neither are, nor can be supplied, the indispensable connecting trains.

Much is said by Southern people about the affection of slaves for their masters and mistresses; and a part of it, at least, is true. A plot for an

uprising could scarcely be devised and communicated to twenty individuals before some one of them, to save the life of a favorite master
or mistress, would divulge it. This is the rule; and the slave revolution
in Hayti [a bloody 1791 uprising—eds.] was not an exception to it, but
a case occurring under peculiar circumstances. The gunpowder plot of
British history, though not connected with slaves, was more in point.
In that case, only about twenty were admitted to the secret; and yet one
of them, in his anxiety to save a friend, betrayed the plot to that friend,
and, by consequence, averted the calamity. Occasional poisonings from
the kitchen, and open or stealthy assassinations in the field, and local
revolts extending to a score or so, will continue to occur as the natural
results of slavery; but no general insurrection of slaves, as I think, can
happen in this country for a long time. Whoever much fears, or much
hopes for such an event, will be alike disappointed.

In the language of Mr. Jefferson, uttered many years ago, "It is still
in our power to direct the process of emancipation, and deportation,
peaceably, and in such slow degrees, as that the evil will wear off
insensibly; and their places be, *pari passu* [at an equal pace—eds.], filled
up by free white laborers. If, on the contrary, it is left to force itself on,
human nature must shudder at the prospect held up."

Mr. Jefferson did not mean to say, nor do I, that the power of
emancipation is in the Federal Government. He spoke of Virginia; and,
as to the power of emancipation, I speak of the slaveholding States only.
The Federal Government, however, as we insist, has the power of
restraining the extension of the institution—the power to insure that a
slave insurrection shall never occur on any American soil which is now
free from slavery.

John Brown's effort was peculiar. It was not a slave insurrection. It
was an attempt by white men to get up a revolt among slaves, in which
the slaves refused to participate. In fact, it was so absurd that the slaves,
with all their ignorance, saw plainly enough it could not succeed. That
affair, in its philosophy, corresponds with the many attempts, related
in history, at the assassination of kings and emperors. An enthusiast
broods over the oppression of a people till he fancies himself commis-
sioned by Heaven to liberate them. He ventures the attempt, which ends
in little else than his own execution. Orsini's attempt on Louis Napoleon, and John Brown's attempt at Harper's Ferry were, in their philosophy, precisely the same. The eagerness to cast blame on old England

in the one case, and on New England in the other, does not disprove the sameness of the two things.

And how much would it avail you, if you could, by the use of John Brown, [Hinton Rowan] Helper's Book [*The Impending Crisis of the South, and How to Meet It,* an 1857 antislavery tract—eds.], and the like, break up the Republican organization? Human action can be modified to some extent, but human nature cannot be changed. There is a judgment and a feeling against slavery in this nation, which cast at least a million and a half of votes. You cannot destroy that judgment and feeling—that sentiment—by breaking up the political organization which rallies around it. You can scarcely scatter and disperse an army which has been formed into order in the face of your heaviest fire; but if you could, how much would you gain by forcing the sentiment which created it out of the peaceful channel of the ballot-box, into some other channel? What would that other channel probably be? Would the number of John Browns be lessened or enlarged by the operation?

But you will break up the Union rather than submit to a denial of your Constitutional rights.

That has a somewhat reckless sound; but it would be palliated, if not fully justified, were we proposing, by the mere force of numbers, to deprive you of some right, plainly written down in the Constitution. But we are proposing no such thing.

When you make these declarations, you have a specific and well-understood allusion to an assumed Constitutional right of yours, to take slaves into the federal territories, and to hold them there as property. But no such right is specially written in the Constitution. That instrument is literally silent about any such right. We, on the contrary, deny that such a right has any existence in the Constitution, even by implication.

Your purpose, then, plainly stated, is that you will destroy the Government, unless you be allowed to construe and enforce the Constitution as you please, on all points in dispute between you and us. You will rule or ruin in all events.

This, plainly stated, is your language. Perhaps you will say the Supreme Court has decided the disputed Constitutional question in your favor. Not quite so. But waiving the lawyer's distinction between dictum and decision, the Court have decided the question for you in a sort of way. The Court have substantially said, it is your Constitutional right to take slaves into the federal territories, and to hold them there as property. When I say the decision was made in a sort of way, I mean it was made in a divided Court, by a bare majority of the Judges, and they not quite agreeing with one another in the reasons for making it; that it is so made as that its avowed supporters disagree with one another about its meaning, and that it was mainly based upon a mistaken statement of fact—the statement in the opinion that "the right of property in a slave is distinctly and expressly affirmed in the Constitution."

An inspection of the Constitution will show that the right of property in a slave is not "*distinctly* and *expressly* affirmed" in it. Bear in mind, the Judges do not pledge their judicial opinion that such right is *impliedly* affirmed in the Constitution; but they pledge their veracity that it is "*distinctly* and *expressly*" affirmed there—"distinctly," that is, not mingled with anything else—"expressly," that is, in words meaning just that, without the aid of any inference, and susceptible of no other meaning.

If they had only pledged their judicial opinion that such right is affirmed in the instrument by implication, it would be open to others to show that neither the word "slave" nor "slavery" is to be found in the Constitution, nor the word "property" even, in any connection with language alluding to the things slave, or slavery, and that wherever in that instrument the slave is alluded to, he is called a "person;"—and wherever his master's legal right in relation to him is alluded to, it is spoken of as "service or labor which may be due,"—as a debt payable in service or labor. Also, it would be open to show, by contemporaneous history, that this mode of alluding to slaves and slavery, instead of speaking of them, was employed on purpose to exclude from the Constitution the idea that there could be property in man.

To show all this, is easy and certain.

When this obvious mistake of the Judges shall be brought to their notice, is it not reasonable to expect that they will withdraw the mistaken statement, and reconsider the conclusion based upon it?

And then it is to be remembered that "our fathers, who framed the Government under which we live"—the men who made the Constitution—decided this same Constitutional question in our favor, long ago—decided it without division among themselves, when making the decision; without division among themselves about the meaning of it after it was made, and, so far as any evidence is left, without basing it upon any mistaken statement of facts.

Under all these circumstances, do you really feel yourselves justified to break up this Government, unless such a court decision as yours is, shall be at once submitted to as a conclusive and final rule of political action? But you will not abide the election of a Republican President! In that supposed event, you say, you will destroy the Union; and then, you say, the great crime of having destroyed it will be upon us! That is cool. A highwayman holds a pistol to my ear, and mutters through his teeth, "Stand and deliver, or I shall kill you, and then you will be a murderer!"

To be sure, what the robber demanded of me—my money—was my own; and I had a clear right to keep it; but it was no more my own than my vote is my own; and the threat of death to me, to extort my money, and the threat of destruction to the Union, to extort my vote, can scarcely be distinguished in principle.

A few words now to Republicans. *It is exceedingly desirable that all parts of this great Confederacy shall be at peace, and in harmony, one with another. Let us Republicans do our part to have it so. Even though much provoked, let us do nothing through passion and ill temper. Even though the southern people will not so much as listen to us, let us calmly consider their demands, and yield to them if, in our deliberate view of our duty, we possibly can.* Judging by all they say and do, and by the subject and nature of their controversy with us, let us determine, if we can, what will satisfy them.

Will they be satisfied if the Territories be unconditionally surrendered to them? We know they will not. In all their present complaints against us, the Territories are scarcely mentioned. Invasions and insurrections are the rage now. Will it satisfy them, if, in the future, we have nothing to do with invasions and insurrections? We know it will not. We so know, because we know we never had anything to do with invasions and insurrections; and yet this total abstaining does not exempt us from the charge and the denunciation.

The question recurs, what will satisfy them? Simply this: We must not only let them alone, but we must, somehow, convince them that we do let them alone. This, we know by experience, is no easy task. We have been so trying to convince them from the very beginning of our organization, but with no success. In all our platforms and speeches we have constantly protested our purpose to let them alone; but this has had no tendency to convince them. Alike unavailing to convince them, is the fact that they have never detected a man of us in any attempt to disturb them.

These natural, and apparently adequate means all failing, what will convince them? This, and this only: cease to call slavery *wrong,* and join them in calling it *right.* And this must be done thoroughly—done in *acts* as well as in *words.* Silence will not be tolerated—we must place ourselves avowedly with them. Senator Douglas's new sedition law must be enacted and enforced, suppressing all declarations that slavery is wrong, whether made in politics, in presses, in pulpits, or in private. We must arrest and return their fugitive slaves with greedy pleasure. We must pull down our Free State constitutions. The whole atmosphere must be disinfected from all taint of opposition to slavery, before they will cease to believe that all their troubles proceed from us.

I am quite aware they do not state their case precisely in this way. Most of them would probably say to us, "Let us alone, *do* nothing to us, and *say* what you please about slavery." But we do let them alone—have never disturbed them—so that, after all, it is what we say, which dissatisfies them. They will continue to accuse us of doing, until we cease saying.

I am also aware they have not, as yet, in terms, demanded the overthrow of our Free-State Constitutions. Yet those Constitutions declare the wrong of slavery, with more solemn emphasis, than do all other sayings against it; and when all these other sayings shall have been silenced, the overthrow of these Constitutions will be demanded, and nothing be left to resist the demand. It is nothing to the contrary, that they do not demand the whole of this just now. Demanding what they do, and for the reason they do, they can voluntarily stop nowhere short of this consummation. Holding, as they do, that slavery is morally right, and socially elevating, they cannot cease to demand a full national recognition of it, as a legal right, and a social blessing.

Nor can we justifiably withhold this, on any ground save our conviction that slavery is wrong. If slavery is right, all words, acts, laws, and constitutions against it, are themselves wrong, and should be silenced, and swept away. If it is right, we cannot justly object to its nationality—its universality; if it is wrong, they cannot justly insist upon its extension—its enlargement. All they ask, we could readily grant, if we thought slavery right; all we ask, they could as readily grant, if they thought it wrong. Their thinking it right, and our thinking it wrong, is the precise fact upon which depends the whole controversy. Thinking it right, as they do, they are not to blame for desiring its full recognition, as being right; but, thinking it wrong, as we do, can we yield to them? Can we cast our votes with their view, and against our own? In view of our moral, social, and political responsibilities, can we do this?

Wrong as we think slavery is, we can yet afford to let it alone where it is, because that much is due to the necessity arising from its actual presence in the nation; but can we, while our votes will prevent it, allow it to spread into the National Territories, and to overrun us here in these Free States? If our sense of duty forbids this, then let us stand by our duty, fearlessly and effectively. Let us be diverted by none of those sophistical contrivances wherewith we are so industriously plied and belabored—contrivances such as groping for some middle ground between the right and the wrong, vain as the search for a man who should be neither a living man nor a dead man—such as a policy of "don't care" on a question about which all true men do care—such as Union appeals beseeching true Union men to yield to Disunionists, reversing the divine rule, and calling, not the sinners, but the righteous to repentance—such as invocations to Washington, imploring men to unsay what Washington said, and undo what Washington did.

Neither let us be slandered from our duty by false accusations against us, nor frightened from it by menaces of destruction to the Government nor of dungeons to ourselves. LET US HAVE FAITH THAT RIGHT MAKES MIGHT, AND IN THAT FAITH, LET US, TO THE END, DARE TO DO OUR DUTY AS WE UNDERSTAND IT.

"THE LABORER CAN STRIKE
IF HE WANTS TO"

From a Speech at Hartford, Connecticut

[MARCH 5, 1860]

Following the Cooper Union address, Lincoln headed into New England, ostensibly to visit his son at boarding school, but also to deliver a series of political speeches in Rhode Island, Connecticut, and New Hampshire— most of them distillations of his New York talk. Commenting on the local shoe workers' strike, Lincoln offered his support "in a humorous and philosophical manner," according to the Hartford Press, *at one point affecting a hilarious regional accent. But the strain on the undeclared presidential aspirant was beginning to show. A Hartford paper noted disdainfully that he arrived in town wearing a "dirty shirt." "I have been unable to escape this toil," Lincoln wrote to his wife. "If I had foreseen it, I think I would not have come east at all."*

The proposition that there is a struggle between the white man and the negro contains a falsehood. There is *no* struggle between them. It assumes that unless the white man enslaves the negro, the negro will enslave the white man. In that case, I think I would go for enslaving the black man, in preference to being enslaved myself. As the learned Judge of a certain Court is said to have decided—"When a ship is wrecked at sea, and two men seize upon one plank which is capable of sustaining but one of them, either of them can rightfully push the other off!" There is, however, no such controversy here.

. . . .

Now they [the Democrats—eds.] are going to work at [attacking— eds.] the shoe strike. I don't know that it comes into Connecticut. It goes into New Hampshire. A Democratic Senator gets up in the Senate Chamber and pompously announces that "I cannot dawt thot this strike is *the* thresult of the onforchunit wahfar brought aboat boy this sucktional contrvussy!" Now whether this is so or not, I know one thing—*there is a strike!* And I am glad to know that there is a system of labor where the laborer can strike if he wants to! I would to God that such a system prevailed all over the world.

"ALLOW THE HUMBLEST MAN AN EQUAL CHANCE"

From a Speech at New Haven, Connecticut

[MARCH 6, 1860]

In New Haven, Lincoln continued to speak out in sympathy with striking shoe workers. Lincoln's son Robert believed his father's New England speeches "the most important in his political career."

. . . *I am glad to see that a system of labor prevails in New England under which laborers* CAN *strike* when they want to [Cheers,] where they are not obliged to work under all circumstances, and are not tied down and obliged to labor whether you pay them or not! [Cheers.] I *like* the system which lets a man quit when he wants to, and wish it might prevail everywhere. [Tremendous applause.] One of the reasons why I am opposed to Slavery is just here. What is the true condition of the laborer? I take it that it is best for all to leave each man free to acquire property as fast as he can. Some will get wealthy. I don't believe in a law to prevent a man from getting rich; it would do more harm than good. So while we do not propose any war upon capital, we do wish to allow the humblest man an equal chance to get rich with everybody else. [Applause.] When one starts poor, as most do in the race of life, free society is such that he knows he can better his condition; he knows that there is no fixed condition of labor, for his whole life. I am not ashamed to confess that twenty five years ago I was a hired laborer, mauling rails, at work on a flat-boat—just what might happen to any poor man's son! [Applause.] I want every man to have the chance—and I believe a black man is entitled to it—in which he *can* better his condition—when he may look forward and hope to be a hired laborer this year and the next, work for himself afterward, and finally to hire men to work for him! That is the true system.

"I ACCEPT THE NOMINATION"

Letter to George Ashmun

[MAY 23, 1860]

Lincoln's formal acceptance of the Republican nomination for president signaled an end to his active campaigning and oratory on national issues for a full ten months. "It would be improper for me to write, or say anything to, or for the public," he confided—embracing the traditional invisible role of mid-nineteenth-century presidential candidates.

Hon: George Ashmun: Springfield, Ills. May 23. 1860
President of the Republican National Convention.

Sir: I accept the nomination tendered me by the Convention over which you presided, and of which I am formally apprized in the letter of yourself and others, acting as a committee of the convention, for that purpose.

The declaration of principles and sentiments, which accompanies your letter, meets my approval; and it shall be my care not to violate, or disregard it, in any part.

Imploring the assistance of Divine Providence, and with due regard to the views and feelings of all who were represented in the convention; to the rights of all the states, and territories, and people of the nation; to the inviolability of the constitution, and the perpetual union, harmony, and prosperity of all, I am most happy to co-operate for the practical success of the principles declared by the convention. Your obliged friend, and fellow citizen

A. LINCOLN

"WORK, WORK, WORK, IS THE MAIN THING"
Letter to John M. Brockman
[SEPTEMBER 25, 1860]

Even as a candidate for the White House, Lincoln continued to earn his living as an attorney. Here he advised a young Illinois teacher with dreams of entering the law. The young man did not become a lawyer, but he did become a politician.

J. M. Brockman, Esq   Springfield, Ills. Sep. 25. 1860

Dear Sir: Yours of the 24th. asking "the best mode of obtaining a thorough knowledge of the law" is received. The mode is very simple, though laborious, and tedious. It is only to get the books, and read, and study them carefully. Begin with Blackstone's Commentaries, and after reading it carefully through, say twice, take up Chitty's Pleading, Greenleaf's Evidence, & Story's Equity &c. in succession. Work, work, work, is the main thing. Yours very truly

A. LINCOLN

"I REJOICE WITH YOU IN THE SUCCESS"
Remarks at Springfield, Illinois
[NOVEMBER 20, 1860]

Not only did presidential candidates in Lincoln's day remain silent during campaigns; winners did not declare victory and losers did not concede defeat, as they do with such great pomp today. Lincoln issued no known statement the night of his election, November 6, only these brief acknowledgments to a rally of Republican supporters two weeks later.

FRIENDS AND FELLOW CITIZENS:—Please excuse me, on this occasion, from making a speech. I thank you for the kindness and compliment of this call. I thank you, in common with all others, who have thought fit, by their votes, to indorse the Republican cause. I rejoice with you in the success which has, so far, attended that cause. Yet in all our rejoicing let us neither express, nor cherish, any harsh feeling towards any citizen who, by his vote, has differed with us. Let us at all times remember that all American citizens are brothers of a common country, and should dwell together in the bonds of fraternal feeling.

Let me again beg you to accept my thanks, and to excuse me from further speaking at this time.

"THE TUG HAS TO COME"

Letter to Senator Lyman Trumbull

[DECEMBER 10, 1860]

South Carolina would secede from the Union on December 20, barely a month after Lincoln's election to the presidency. In this letter to one of his closest political associates ten days earlier, Lincoln made clear he would not yield on the slavery issue, no matter what the consequences.

Private, & confidential

Springfield, Ills. Dec. 10. 1860

Hon. L. Trumbull.

My dear Sir:

Let there be no compromise on the question of *extending* slavery. If there be, all our labor is lost, and, ere long, must be done again. The dangerous ground—that into which some of our friends have a hankering to run—is Pop[ular]. Sov[ereignty]. Have none of it. Stand firm. The tug has to come, & better now, than any time hereafter. Yours as ever

A. LINCOLN.

⋙ V ⋘

"HOUR OF TRIAL"

Lincoln and Union

1861

President-elect Abraham Lincoln sat for this Alexander Gardner photograph soon after arriving in Washington, D.C., in late February 1861. Within a week he would deliver his first inaugural address and assume the presidency. At the gallery, as Gardner fussed over his camera equipment, Lincoln became "wholly absorbed in deep thought . . . oblivious to his surroundings," according to an eyewitness. By the time Gardner was ready to make his picture, Lincoln's expression had frozen into the mask his private secretary, John G. Nicolay, described as "that serious, faraway look that with prophetic intuitions beheld the awful panorama of war, and heard the cry of oppression and suffering."

(Photograph: Library of Congress)

Introduction

BY JAMES M. McPHERSON

At its core, the American Civil War was a struggle over the meaning of liberty and democracy. Both sides professed to be fighting for the heritage of freedom and self-government bequeathed to them by their forefathers in the Revolution of 1776.

When the "Black Republican" Abraham Lincoln won the presidential election in 1860 on a platform of excluding slavery from the territories, he received not a single electoral vote from any of the fifteen slave states and no popular votes from ten of them. Southern secessionists thereupon branded Lincoln "King Abraham I," compared him with George III, and took their states out of the Union in the name of independence from a tyrannical government that no longer represented their interests or respected their rights. Southerners were a "liberty loving people," declared an Alabama secessionist; therefore "the same spirit of freedom and independence that impelled our Fathers to the separation from the British Government, will induce the liberty loving people of the Southern States to a separation" from the oppressive United States government. From "the high and solemn motive of defending and protecting the rights . . . which our fathers bequeathed to us," said President Jefferson Davis of the Confederate States of America, after his government had precipitated war by ordering its army to fire on American troops at Fort Sumter, let us "renew such sacrifices as our fathers made to the holy cause of constitutional liberty."

Confederates fighting for their independence not only wrapped themselves in the mantle of 1776; in a bid for the sympathy of European liberals, they also compared themselves to nationality groups on the continent that had struggled heroically for self-determination: the Netherlands against Spain in the seventeenth century; Greece against Turkey in the 1820s; Hungary against the Hapsburg empire in 1848; Poland against rule by Russia, Prussia, and Austria through most of its recent history. So long as the South could divert attention from its own enslavement of four million black people, the Confederacy won some support to this view of itself as a small country fighting for independence from an alien government ruled by Abraham Lincoln. Even as late as 1989, a prominent editor of a well-known American publishing house, when approached about this book on Lincoln and democracy, confessed himself "puzzled" by such a project. "Lincoln is not, after all," he said, "best remembered for his efforts on behalf of self-determination: just the opposite I would have thought."

The editor had conveniently forgotten about slavery, just as Confederate propagandists in Europe conveniently ignored it. But Lincoln and his fellow Republicans who led a struggle to preserve the Union in the name of freedom did not ignore it. Slavery was a "monstrous injustice," said Lincoln many times. It "deprives our republican example of its just influence in the world—enables the enemies of free institutions, with plausibility, to taunt us as hypocrites." For Confederates to invoke liberty and self-determination to identify themselves with the Revolutionary fathers of 1776, wrote the pro-Lincoln editor and poet William Cullen Bryant, "is a libel upon the whole character and conduct of the men of '76." They fought "to establish the rights of man . . . and principles of universal liberty." The Confederacy declared its independence "not in the interest of a general humanity, but of a domestic despotism. . . . Their motto is not liberty, but slavery." If Lincoln is "best remembered" for any one thing, it is for striking the shackles from four million slaves and ending the "monstrous injustice" of slavery.

But in 1861, Union war aims did not yet include the abolition of slavery; those aims were simply to suppress the insurrection of eleven Confederate states and thereby preserve the integrity of the United States. For Lincoln, even apart from the question of slavery, this made the cause of Union the cause of liberty and democracy. In Lincoln's eyes, the *Union,* not the Confederacy, embodied the ideals of 1776. The republic established by the Founding Fathers as a bulwark of liberty was a fragile experiment in a world bestrode by kings, emperors, tsars, dictators, and theories of aristocracy. Americans were painfully aware that most republics through history had eventually collapsed or been overthrown. Americans alive in 1861 had seen two French republics rise and fall, several nationalist republics spring up in 1848 and succumb to counterrevolution, and republics in Latin America come and go with bewildering rapidity. In this atmosphere of counterrevolution and reaction, Lincoln would say, in late 1862, that the United States represented the "last best, hope" for the survival of republican liberty. But the success of secession—the cleaving of the United States in two—would destroy that hope. It would set a fatal precedent by which the minority could secede from the Union whenever it did not like what the majority stood for, until the United States fragmented into a multitude of petty, squabbling autocracies. Thus "our example for more than eighty years," said Lincoln's predecessor James Buchanan in his last message to Congress, on December 3, 1860, "would not only be lost, but it would be quoted as conclusive proof that man is unfit for self-government."

Lincoln agreed. "The central idea pervading this struggle," he said in 1861, "is the necessity that is upon us of proving that popular government is not an absurdity." European conservatives and monarchists regularly predicted the demise of this upstart democracy in North America. They were rubbing their hands with glee at the apparent fulfillment of their prediction by secession of the Confederate states. "We must settle this question now, whether in a free government the minority have the right to break up the government whenever they choose," said Lincoln. "If we fail it will go far to prove the incapability of the people to govern themselves." The contest, he said on another occasion in 1861, was "not altogether for today—it is for a vast future also." It "embraces more than the fate of these United States. It presents to the whole family of man, the question whether a constitutional republic, or a democracy," a nation "conceived in Liberty, and dedicated to the proposition that all men are created equal"—as Lincoln would express it two years later at Gettysburg—"can long endure."

Lincoln's inaugural address as president on March 4, 1861, was the most important such statement in American history. It had one theme and two variations. The theme was Lincoln's determination to preserve an undivided American nation. The variations offered both a sword and an olive branch. The sword was the president's pledge to "hold, occupy and possess" the national property in Confederate states that still remained under the control of the federal government—principally Fort Sumter in Charleston harbor. Lincoln also expressed an intention to "take care, as the Constitution itself expressly enjoins upon me, that the laws of the Union be faithfully executed in all the States." Nevertheless, as a gesture of conciliation, the President said that whenever "in any interior locality" the hostility to the United States government was "so great and so universal, as to prevent competent resident citizens from holding the Federal offices," he would suspend government activities "for the time." And he promised not to use force against the Southern people except in self-defense: "The government will not assail *you*. You can have no conflict, without being yourselves the aggressors." Nevertheless, Lincoln stood firm on the inviolability of the Union. "*You* have no oath registered in Heaven to destroy the government, while *I* shall have the most solemn one to 'preserve, protect and defend' it."

Above all, Lincoln appealed to the South's shared memories of the struggle for independence and nationhood. Do not destroy this great experiment in democratic self-government, he urged. "We are not enemies, but friends," he told the Southern people, whom he still considered part of the American people. "We must not be enemies. Though passion may have strained, it must not break our bonds of affection. The mystic chords of memory, stretching from every battle-field, and patriot grave, to every living heart and hearthstone, all over this broad land, will yet swell the chorus of the Union, when again touched, as surely they will be, by the better angels of our nature."

Lincoln's eloquence went for naught on this occasion. Confederates considered his determination to hold Fort Sumter a provocation for war. On April 12, they opened fire on the fort, compelling its surrender after a bombardment of two days. This caused the Lincoln administration to call out the militia to suppress the "insurrection," which in turn drove four more states into asserting their rights of secession and revolution to go out of the Union. The stage was set for the most destructive war in the Western world between the end of the Napoleonic Wars in 1815 and the onset of World War I a century later. It was a war that did preserve the American nation, but at a cost of at least 620,000 lives. Without paying that cost, however, the United States might well have ceased to exist—might have been destroyed by a revolution that would have established a precedent for future secessions which would have fragmented the country into several pieces.

Lincoln did not deny to the South or to any other part of the American polity the right of revolution for just cause. The United States had been founded on that right. But that phrase, "for just cause," was crucial. As Lincoln expressed it in the summer of 1861, "the right of revolution, is never a legal right . . . At most, it is but a moral right, when exercised for a morally justifiable cause. When exercised without such a cause revolution is no right, but simply a wicked exercise of physical power." In Lincoln's view, secession was just such a wicked exercise. The South had no justifiable cause. Indeed, the reason Southern states seceded was to escape the threat to the future of slavery that they feared Lincoln's election portended. It was "strange," said Lincoln of secessionists, "that any men should dare to ask a just God's assistance in wringing their bread from the sweat of other men's faces." Secession was a counterrevolution by slaveholders against the ideology of freedom, the dignity of labor, and the chance for upward mobility for workingmen represented by Lincoln's Republican Party. "This is essentially a People's contest," said Lincoln of the Union cause on July 4, 1861, the eighty-fifth anniversary of American independence. "It is a struggle for maintaining in the world, that form, and substance of government, whose leading object is, to elevate the condition of men— to lift artificial weights from all shoulders—to clear the paths of laudable pursuit for all—to afford all, an unfettered start, and a fair chance, in the race of life."

Under Lincoln's leadership, the Union would triumph in the Civil War over the slaveholding Confederacy, which represented the opposite philosophy. This triumph ensured the survival of the United States as a beacon light to all peoples struggling for democracy and self-determination.

→>> <<←

"THE PRINCIPLE THAT CLEARS THE *PATH* FOR ALL"

Fragment on the Constitution and the Union

[JANUARY 1861?]

Lincoln may have been moved to record these thoughts after corresponding with Alexander H. Stephens of Georgia, a onetime congressional colleague of Lincoln's, soon to become vice president of the Confederacy.

All this is not the result of accident. It has a philosophical cause. Without the *Constitution* and the *Union,* we could not have attained the result; but even these, are not the primary cause of our great prosperity. There is something back of these, entwining itself more closely about the human heart. That something, is the principle of "Liberty to all"—the principle that clears the *path* for all—gives *hope* to all—and, by consequence, *enterprize,* and *industry* to all.

The *expression* of that principle, in our Declaration of Independence, was most happy, and fortunate. *Without* this, as well as *with* it, we could have declared our independence of Great Britain; but *without* it, we could not, I think, have secured our free government, and consequent prosperity. No oppressed, people will *fight,* and *endure,* as our fathers did, without the promise of something better, than a mere change of masters.

The assertion of that *principle,* at *that time,* was *the* word, *"fitly spoken"* which has proved an "apple of gold" to us. The *Union,* and the *Constitution,* are the *picture of silver,* subsequently framed around it. The picture was made, not to *conceal,* or *destroy* the apple; but to *adorn,* and *preserve* it. The *picture* was made *for* the apple—*not* the apple for the picture.

So let us act, that neither *picture,* or *apple* shall ever be blurred, or bruised or broken.

That we may so act, we must study, and understand the points of danger.

"IF WE SURRENDER, IT IS THE END OF US"

Letter to James T. Hale

[JANUARY 11, 1861]

Pennsylvania congressman Hale, a fellow Republican, had proposed a constitutional amendment barring Congress from abolishing slavery in territories south of latitude 36°31'. He thought it would placate the South and save the Union. Lincoln rejected the idea.

Confidential.

Hon. J. T. Hale   Springfield, Ill.   Jan'y. 11th 1861.

My dear Sir—

Yours of the 6th is received. I answer it only because I fear you would misconstrue my silence. What is our present condition? We have just carried an election on principles fairly stated to the people. Now we are told in advance, the government shall be broken up, unless we surrender to those we have beaten, before we take the offices. In this they are either attempting to play upon us, or they are in dead earnest. Either way, if we surrender, it is the end of us, and of the government. They will repeat the experiment upon us *ad libitum* [in accordance with desire—eds.]. A year will not pass, till we shall have to take Cuba as a condition upon which they will stay in the Union. They now have the Constitution, under which we have lived over seventy years, and acts of Congress of their own framing, with no prospect of their being changed; and they can never have a more shallow pretext for breaking up the government, or extorting a compromise, than now. There is, in my judgment, but one compromise which would really settle the slavery question, and that would be a prohibition against acquiring any more territory. Yours very truly,

A. LINCOLN.

"WITH A TASK BEFORE ME"

Farewell Address at Springfield, Illinois

[FEBRUARY 11, 1861]

Lincoln bade farewell to his Springfield neighbors with an emotional address delivered from the back of the train that was to take him on the first leg of his long journey to Washington. Asked to write out the apparently impromptu remarks after his departure, he greatly improved the version recorded by newspaper stenographers at the depot. This is the version he composed aboard the train. Although most historians cite this text today, the first version was quoted in most nineteenth-century biographies. In the words of a local newspaper, Lincoln had never spoken with more "simple touching eloquence," although another journalist insisted Lincoln could not be heard above "the incorrigible hissing of the locomotive." Though not strictly a statement on democracy, the address reflected Lincoln's grave view of the burdens he would soon undertake to preserve democracy.

My friends—No one, not in my situation, can appreciate my feeling of sadness at this parting. To this place, and the kindness of these people, I owe every thing. Here I have lived a quarter of a century, and have passed from a young to an old man. Here my children have been born, and one is buried. I now leave, not knowing when, or whether ever, I may return, with a task before me greater than that which rested upon Washington. Without the assistance of that Divine Being, who ever attended him, I cannot succeed. With that assistance I cannot fail. Trusting in Him, who can go with me, and remain with you and be every where for good, let us confidently hope that all will yet be well. To His care commending you, as I hope in your prayers you will commend me, I bid you an affectionate farewell[.]

"Liberty, for Yourselves, and Not for Me"

Reply to Governor Oliver P. Morton, Indianapolis, Indiana

[FEBRUARY 11, 1861]

En route to Washington, Lincoln was called on to speak from trains, train platforms, hotels, and government buildings. But even as he was breaking his long public silence, he was still reluctant to say anything new or provocative. These remarks, delivered from the rear platform of his train, gave him the opportunity both to reassure the South that he was no threat and to underscore his belief in the sanctity of the Union.

Gov. Morton and Fellow Citizens of the State of Indiana:

Most heartily do I thank you for this magnificent reception, and while I cannot take to myself any share of the compliment thus paid, more than that which pertains to a mere instrument, an accidental instrument, perhaps I should say, of a great cause, I yet must look upon it as a most magnificent reception, and as such, most heartily do I thank you for it.

You have been pleased to address yourselves to me chiefly in behalf of this glorious Union in which we live, in all of which you have my hearty sympathy, and, as far as may be within my power, will have, one and inseparably, my hearty consideration. While I do not expect, upon this occasion, or on any occasion, till after I get to Washington, to attempt any lengthy speech, I will only say that to the salvation of this Union there needs but one single thing—the hearts of a people like yours. [Applause.] When the people rise in masses in behalf of the Union and the liberties of their country, truly may it be said, "The gates of hell shall not prevail against them." [Renewed applause.]

In all the trying positions in which I shall be placed, and doubtless I shall be placed in many trying ones, my reliance will be placed upon you and the people of the United States—and I wish you to remember now and forever, that it is your business, and not mine; that if the union of these States, and the liberties of this people, shall be lost, it is but little to any one man of fifty-two years of age, but a great deal to the thirty millions of people who inhabit these United States, and to their posterity in all coming time. It is your business to rise up and preserve the Union and liberty, for yourselves, and not for me. I desire they shall be constitutionally preserved.

I, as already intimated, am but an accidental instrument, temporary, and to serve but for a limited time, but I appeal to you again to constantly bear in mind that with you, and not with politicians, not with Presidents, not with office-seekers, but with you, is the question, "Shall the Union and shall the liberties of this country be preserved to the latest generation?" [Loud and prolonged applause.]

"THERE IS BUT LITTLE HARM I CAN DO"

From a Speech at Lawrenceburg, Indiana

[FEBRUARY 12, 1861]

Protesting, "I have no speech to give you," Lincoln nonetheless offered Lawrenceburg, on his fifty-second birthday, an eloquent little greeting from the rear platform of his train. This was his conclusion, as recorded by an Ohio newspaper.

If the politicians and leaders of parties were as true as the PEOPLE, there would be little fear that the peace of the country would be disturbed. I have been selected to fill an important office for a brief period, and am now, in your eyes, invested with an influence which will soon pass away; but should my administration prove to be a very wicked one, or what is more probable, a very foolish one, if you, the PEOPLE, are but true to yourselves and to the Constitution, there is but little harm I can do, *thank God!*

"GIVE THE GREATEST GOOD
TO THE GREATEST NUMBER"

From a Speech to Germans at Cincinnati, Ohio

[FEBRUARY 12, 1861]

German-Americans had been ardent Lincoln supporters in the 1860 cam-
paign; from the balcony of his hotel in Cincinnati Lincoln gave this
address to two thousand members of the German Industrial Association.
A Columbus newspaper teased that "Abe . . . don't make as many jokes
as he did. He fears that he will get things mixed up. . . ."

I agree with you, Mr. Chairman, that the working men are the basis of all governments, for the plain reason that they are the most numerous, and as you added that those were the sentiments of the gentlemen present, representing not only the working class, but citizens of other callings than those of the mechanic, I am happy to concur with you in these sentiments, not only of the native born citizens, but also of the Germans and foreigners from other countries.

Mr. Chairman, I hold that while man exists, it is his duty to improve not only his own condition, but to assist in ameliorating mankind; and therefore, without entering upon the details of the question, I will simply say, that I am for those means which will give the greatest good to the greatest number.

In regard to the Homestead Law, I have to say that in so far as the Government lands can be disposed of, I am in favor of cutting up the wild lands into parcels, so that every poor man may have a home.

In regard to the Germans and foreigners, I esteem them no better than other people, nor any worse. [Cries of good.] It is not my nature, when I see a people borne down by the weight of their shackles—the oppression of tyranny—to make their life more bitter by heaping upon them greater burdens; but rather would I do all in my power to raise the yoke, than to add anything that would tend to crush them.

Inasmuch as our country is extensive and new, and the countries of

Europe are densely populated, if there are any abroad who desire to make this the land of their adoption, it is not in my heart to throw aught in their way, to prevent them from coming to the United States.

"THE MAJORITY SHALL RULE"

From a Speech at Steubenville, Ohio

[FEBRUARY 14, 1861]

A recurring theme of Lincoln's early inaugural journey speeches was his own unimportance: it was the Constitution and the Union that mattered, not the new president. Here he responded to an address of welcome, one of seven talks he made that day.

... Though the people have made me by electing me, the instrument to carry out the wishes expressed in the address, I greatly fear that I shall not be the repository of the ability to do so. Indeed I know I shall not, more than in purpose, unless sustained by the great body of the people, and by the Divine Power, without whose aid we can do nothing. We everywhere express devotion to the Constitution. I believe there is no difference in this respect, whether on this or on the other side of this majestic stream [the Ohio River, which separated Ohio from what was then Virginia—eds.]. I understand that on the other side, among our dissatisfied brethren, they are satisfied with the Constitution of the United States, if they can have their rights under the Constitution. The question is, as to what the Constitution means—"What are their rights under the Constitution?" That is all. To decide that, who shall be the judge? Can you think of any other, than the voice of the people? If the majority does not control, the minority must—would that be right? Would that be just or generous? Assuredly not! Though the majority may be wrong, and I will not undertake to say that they were not wrong in electing me, yet we must adhere to the principle that the majority shall rule. By your Constitution you have another chance in four years. No great harm can be done by us in that time—in that time there can be nobody hurt. If anything goes wrong, however, and you find you have made a mistake, elect a better man next time. There are plenty of them.

"THE SHIP CAN BE SAVED, WITH THE CARGO"

Reply to Mayor Fernando Wood, City Hall, New York

[FEBRUARY 20, 1861]

President-elect Lincoln received a rousing reception in New York City, even though its mayor had earlier proposed seceding from the Union and setting up a free city. This was Lincoln's subtle response, couched in the metaphor of the ship of state. Mayor Fernando Wood later supported the war effort—for a time, anyway.

MR. MAYOR—It is with feelings of deep gratitude that I make my acknowledgment for this reception which has been given me in the great commercial city of New York. I cannot but remember that this is done by a people who do not by a majority agree with me in political sentiments. It is the more grateful because in this reception I see that, in regard to the great principles of our government, the people are very nearly or quite unanimous.

In reference to the difficulties that confront us at this time, and of which your Honor thought fit to speak so becomingly, and so justly as I suppose, I can only say that I fully concur in the sentiments expressed by the Mayor. In my devotion to the Union I hope I am behind no man in the Union; but as to the wisdom with which to conduct affairs tending to the preservation of the Union, I fear that even too great confidence may have been reposed in me. I am sure I bring a heart devoted to the work.

There is nothing that can ever bring me willingly to consent to the destruction of this Union, under which not only the commercial city of New York, but the whole country has acquired its greatness, unless it were to be that thing for which the Union itself was made. I understand a ship to be made for the carrying and preservation of the cargo, and so long as the ship can be saved, with the cargo, it should never be abandoned. This Union should likewise never be abandoned unless it fails and the probability of its preservation shall cease to exist without throwing the passengers and cargo overboard. So long, then, as it is possible that the prosperity and the liberties of the people can be preserved in the Union, it shall be my purpose at all times to preserve it. Thanking you for the reception given me, allow me to come to a close.

"In Accordance with the Original Idea"

Address to the State Senate, Trenton, New Jersey
[FEBRUARY 21, 1861]

Greeted in New Jersey's state capital with a thirty-four-gun salute—one for each state—Lincoln gave several speeches in the city where George Washington had defeated the Hessians in 1776, resolving to preserve the fruits of Washington's victory.

MR. PRESIDENT AND GENTLEMEN OF THE SENATE OF THE STATE OF NEW-JERSEY: I am very grateful to you for the honorable reception of which I have been the object. I cannot but remember the place that New-Jersey holds in our early history. In the early Revolutionary struggle, few of the States among the old Thirteen had more of the battle-fields of the country within their limits than old New-Jersey. May I be pardoned if, upon this occasion, I mention that away back in my childhood, the earliest days of my being able to read, I got hold of a small book, such a one as few of the younger members have ever seen, "Weem's Life of Washington." I remember all the accounts there given of the battle fields and struggles for the liberties of the country, and none fixed themselves upon my imagination so deeply as the struggle here at Trenton, New-Jersey. The crossing of the river; the contest with the Hessians; the great hardships endured at that time, all fixed themselves on my memory more than any single revolutionary event; and you all know, for you have all been boys, how these early impressions last longer than any others. I recollect thinking then, boy even though I was, that there must have been something more than common that those men struggled for. I am exceedingly anxious that that thing which they struggled for; that something even more than National Independence; that something that held out a great promise to all the people of the world to all time to come; I am exceedingly anxious that this Union, the Constitution, and the liberties of the people shall be perpetuated in accordance with the original idea for which that struggle was made, and I shall be most happy indeed if I shall be an humble instrument in the hands of the Almighty, and of this, his almost chosen people, for perpetuating the object of that great struggle. You give me this reception, as I understand, without distinction of party. I learn that this body is composed of a majority of gentlemen who, in the exercise of their best judgment in the choice of a Chief Magistrate, did not think I was the man. I understand, nevertheless, that they came forward here to greet me as the constitutional President of the United States—as citizens of the United States, to meet the man who, for the time being, is the representative man of the nation, united by a purpose to perpetuate the Union and liberties of the people. As such, I accept this reception more gratefully than I could do did I believe it was tendered to me as an individual.

"I WOULD RATHER BE ASSASSINATED"

Speech in Independence Hall, Philadelphia, Pennsylvania

[FEBRUARY 22, 1861]

A visit to Independence Hall, the cradle of American democracy, inspired the most memorable speech of Lincoln's inaugural journey, a moving tribute to the founders and the "hope" they gave "to the world." The speech was reprinted the next day in the Philadelphia Inquirer. *Two years later, when an artist proposed painting a portrait of Lincoln to hang in the building, the usually modest president understandably accepted. But the result was never displayed there.*

I am filled with deep emotion at finding myself standing here in the place where were collected together the wisdom, the patriotism, the devotion to principle, from which sprang the institutions under which we live. You have kindly suggested to me that in my hands is the task of restoring peace to our distracted country. I can say in return, sir, that all the political sentiments I entertain have been drawn, so far as I have been able to draw them, from the sentiments which originated, and were given to the world from this hall in which we stand. I have never had a feeling politically that did not spring from the sentiments embodied in the Declaration of Independence. (Great cheering.) I have often pondered over the dangers which were incurred by the men who assembled here and adopted that Declaration of Independence—I have pondered over the toils that were endured by the officers and soldiers of the army, who achieved that Independence. (Applause.) I have often inquired of myself, what great principle or idea it was that kept this Confederacy so long together. It was not the mere matter of the separation of the colonies from the mother land; but something in that Declaration giving liberty, not alone to the people of this country, but hope to the world for all future time. (Great applause.) It was that which gave promise that in due time the weights should be lifted from the shoulders of all men, and that *all* should have an equal chance. (Cheers.) This is the sentiment embodied in that Declaration of Independence.

Now, my friends, can this country be saved upon that basis? If it can, I will consider myself one of the happiest men in the world if I can help to save it. If it can't be saved upon that principle, it will be truly awful. But, if this country cannot be saved without giving up that principle—I was about to say I would rather be assassinated on this spot than to surrender it. (Applause.)

Now, in my view of the present aspect of affairs, there is no need of bloodshed and war. There is no necessity for it. I am not in favor of such a course, and I may say in advance, there will be no blood shed unless it be forced upon the Government. The Government will not use force unless force is used against it. (Prolonged applause and cries of "That's the proper sentiment.")

My friends, this is a wholly unprepared speech. I did not expect to be called upon to say a word when I came here—I supposed I was merely to do something towards raising a flag. I may, therefore, have said something indiscreet, (cries of "no, no"), but I have said nothing but what I am willing to live by, and, in the pleasure of Almighty God, die by.

"Plain As a Turnpike Road"

*Informal Remarks to Delegates to the Peace Conference,
Willard's Hotel, Washington*

[FEBRUARY 23, 1861]

> *On his first night in Washington, the President-elect received delegates from a conference organized "to bring back the cotton states that had already begun seceding." Years later, Lucius Crittenden, a delegate from Vermont, recalled the statements Lincoln made to a disgruntled Virginian.*

My course is as plain as a turnpike road. It is marked out by the Constitution. I am in no doubt which way to go. Suppose now we all stop discussing and try the experiment of obedience to the Constitution and the laws. Don't you think it would work?

. . . .

Your slaves have been returned, yes, from the shadow of Faneuil Hall in the heart of Boston. Our people do not like the work, I know. They will do what the law commands, but they will not volunteer to act as tip-staves or bum-bailiffs [contemptuous slang for constables and deputies—eds.]. The instinct is natural to the race. Is it not true of the South? Would you join in the pursuit of a fugitive slave if you could avoid it? Is such the work of gentlemen?

. . . .

We do maintain the freedom of the press—we deem it necessary to a free government. Are we peculiar in that respect? Is not the same doctrine held in the South?

. . . .

If I shall ever come to the great office of President of the United States, I shall take an oath. I shall swear that I will faithfully execute the office of President of the United States, of all the United States, and that I will, to the best of my ability, preserve, protect, and defend the Constitution of the United States. This is a great and solemn duty. With the support of the people and the assistance of the Almighty I shall undertake to perform it. I have full faith that I shall perform it. It is not the Constitution as I would like to have it, but as it *is,* that is to be defended. The Constitution will not be preserved and defended until it is enforced and obeyed in every part of every one of the United States. It must be so respected, obeyed, enforced, and defended, let the grass grow where it may.

. . . .

In a choice of evils, war may not always be the worst. Still I would do all in my power to avert it, except to neglect a Constitutional duty. As to slavery, it must be content with what it has. The voice of the civilized world is against it; it is opposed to its growth or extension. Freedom is the natural condition of the human race, in which the Almighty intended men to live. Those who fight the purposes of the Almighty will not succeed. They always have been, they always will be, beaten.

"THE MOMENTOUS ISSUE OF CIVIL WAR"

First Inaugural Address, Washington

[MARCH 4, 1861]

Lincoln hoped his conciliatory inaugural address, delivered before some thirty thousand listeners, would stem the tide of secession. But one hostile newspaper, focusing instead on Lincoln's pledge to hold government-owned Southern property, declared the speech "coercive," and predicted that "civil war will be inaugurated forthwith." Lincoln's voice "rang out, clear and resonant, above the vast throngs," his secretary remembered. Another eyewitness recalled its being received in "profound silence." The magnificent peroration was proposed by incoming secretary of state William H. Seward, but brilliantly rewritten by Lincoln. The speech was composed long before the invention of copying machines, even carbon paper, so when Lincoln's son temporarily misplaced the manuscript during the inaugural journey he received a public scolding from his father.

Fellow citizens of the United States:

In compliance with a custom as old as the government itself, I appear before you to address you briefly, and to take, in your presence, the oath prescribed by the Constitution of the United States, to be taken by the President "before he enters on the execution of his office."

I do not consider it necessary, at present, for me to discuss those matters of administration about which there is no special anxiety, or excitement.

Apprehension seems to exist among the people of the Southern States, that by the accession of a Republican Administration, their property, and their peace, and personal security, are to be endangered. There has never been any reasonable cause for such apprehension. Indeed, the most ample evidence to the contrary has all the while existed, and been open to their inspection. It is found in nearly all the published speeches of him who now addresses you. I do but quote from one of those speeches when I declare that "I have no purpose, directly or indirectly, to interfere with the institution of slavery in the States where it exists. I believe I have no lawful right to do so, and I have no inclination to do so." Those who nominated and elected me did so with full knowledge that I had made this, and many similar declarations, and had never recanted them. And more than this, they placed in the platform, for my acceptance, and as a law to themselves, and to me, the clear and emphatic resolution which I now read:

"*Resolved,* That the maintenance inviolate of the rights of the States, and especially the right of each State to order and control its own domestic institutions according to its own judgment exclusively, is essential to that balance of power on which the perfection and endurance of our political fabric depend; and we denounce the lawless invasion by armed force of the soil of any State or Territory, no matter under what pretext, as among the gravest of crimes."

I now reiterate these sentiments: and in doing so, I only press upon the public attention the most conclusive evidence of which the case is susceptible, that the property, peace and security of no section are to be in anywise endangered by the now incoming Administration. I add too, that all the protection which, consistently with the Constitution and the laws, can be given, will be cheerfully given to all the States when lawfully demanded, for whatever cause—as cheerfully to one section, as to another.

There is much controversy about the delivering up of fugitives from service or labor. The clause I now read is as plainly written in the Constitution as any other of its provisions:

"No person held to service or labor in one State, under the laws thereof, escaping into another, shall, in consequence of any law or regulation therein, be discharged from such service or labor, but shall be delivered up on claim of the party to whom such service or labor may be due."

It is scarcely questioned that this provision was intended by those who made it, for the reclaiming of what we call fugitive slaves; and the intention of the law-giver is the law. All members of Congress swear their support to the whole Constitution—to this provision as much as to any other. To the proposition, then, that slaves whose cases come within the terms of this clause, "shall be delivered up," their oaths are unanimous. Now, if they would make the effort in good temper, could they not, with nearly equal unanimity, frame and pass a law, by means of which to keep good that unanimous oath?

There is some difference of opinion whether this clause should be enforced by national or by state authority; but surely that difference is not a very material one. If the slave is to be surrendered, it can be of but little consequence to him, or to others, by which authority it is done. And should any one, in any case, be content that his oath shall go unkept, on a merely unsubstantial controversy as to *how* it shall be kept?

Again, in any law upon this subject, ought not all the safeguards of liberty known in civilized and humane jurisprudence to be introduced, so that a free man be not, in any case, surrendered as a slave? And might it not be well, at the same time, to provide by law for the enforcement of that clause in the Constitution which guaranties that "The citizens of each State shall be entitled to all previleges and immunities of citizens in the several States?"

I take the official oath to-day, with no mental reservations, and with no purpose to construe the Constitution or laws, by any hypercritical rules. And while I do not choose now to specify particular acts of Congress as proper to be enforced, I do suggest, that it will be much safer for all, both in official and private stations, to conform to, and abide by, all those acts which stand unrepealed, than to violate any of them, trusting to find impunity in having them held to be unconstitutional.

It is seventy-two years since the first inauguration of a President under our national Constitution. During that period fifteen different and greatly distinguished citizens, have, in succession, administered the executive branch of the government. They have conducted it through many perils; and, generally, with great success. Yet, with all this scope for precedent, I now enter upon the same task for the brief constitutional term of four years, under great and peculiar difficulty. A disruption of the Federal Union heretofore only menaced, is now formidably attempted.

I hold, that in contemplation of universal law, and of the Constitution, the Union of these States is perpetual. Perpetuity is implied, if not expressed, in the fundamental law of all national governments. It is safe to assert that no government proper, ever had a provision in its organic law for its own termination. Continue to execute all the express provisions of our national Constitution, and the Union will endure forever—it being impossible to destroy it, except by some action not provided for in the instrument itself.

Again, if the United States be not a government proper, but an association of States in the nature of contract merely, can it, as a contract, be peaceably unmade, by less than all the parties who made it? One party to a contract may violate it—break it, so to speak; but does it not require all to lawfully rescind it?

Descending from these general principles, we find the proposition that, in legal contemplation, the Union is perpetual, confirmed by the history of the Union itself. The Union is much older than the Constitution. It was formed in fact, by the Articles of Association in 1774. It was matured and continued by the Declaration of Independence in 1776. It was further matured and the faith of all the then thirteen States expressly plighted and engaged that it should be perpetual, by the Articles of Confederation in 1778. And finally, in 1787, one of the declared objects for ordaining and establishing the Constitution, was *"to form a more perfect union."*

But if destruction of the Union, by one, or by a part only, of the States, be lawfully possible, the Union is *less* perfect than before the Constitution, having lost the vital element of perpetuity.

It follows from these views that no State, upon its own mere motion, can lawfully get out of the Union,—that *resolves* and *ordinances* to that effect are legally void; and that acts of violence, within any State or States, against the authority of the United States, are insurrectionary or revolutionary, according to circumstances.

I therefore consider that, in view of the Constitution and the laws, the Union is unbroken; and, to the extent of my ability, I shall take care, as the Constitution itself expressly enjoins upon me, that the laws of the Union be faithfully executed in all the States. Doing this I deem to be only a simple duty on my part; and I shall perform it, so far as practicable, unless my rightful masters, the American people, shall withhold the requisite means, or in some authoritative manner, direct the contrary. I trust this will not be regarded as a menace, but only as the declared purpose of the Union that it *will* constitutionally defend, and maintain itself.

In doing this there needs to be no bloodshed or violence; and there shall be none, unless it be forced upon the national authority. The power confided to me, will be used to hold, occupy, and possess the property, and places belonging to the government, and to collect the duties and imposts; but beyond what may be necessary for these objects, there will be no invasion—no using of force against, or among the people anywhere. Where hostility to the United States, in any interior locality, shall be so great and so universal, as to prevent competent resident citizens from holding the Federal offices, there will be no attempt to force obnoxious strangers among the people for that object. While the strict legal right may exist in the government to enforce the exercise of these offices, the attempt to do so would be so irritating, and so nearly impracticable with all, that I deem it better to forego, for the time, the uses of such offices.

The mails, unless repelled, will continue to be furnished in all parts of the Union. So far as possible, the people everywhere shall have that sense of perfect security which is most favorable to calm thought and reflection. The course here indicated will be followed, unless current events, and experience, shall show a modification, or change, to be proper; and in every case and exigency, my best discretion will be exercised, according to circumstances actually existing, and with a view and a hope of a peaceful solution of the national troubles, and the restoration of fraternal sympathies and affections.

That there are persons in one section, or another who seek to destroy the Union at all events, and are glad of any pretext to do it, I will neither affirm or deny; but if there be such, I need address no word to them. To those, however, who really love the Union, may I not speak?

Before entering upon so grave a matter as the destruction of our national fabric, with all its benefits, its memories, and its hopes, would it not be wise to ascertain precisely why we do it? Will you hazard so desperate a step, while there is any possibility that any portion of the ills you fly from, have no real existence? Will you, while the certain ills you fly to, are greater than all the real ones you fly from? Will you risk the commission of so fearful a mistake?

All profess to be content in the Union, if all constitutional rights can be maintained. Is it true, then, that any right, plainly written in the Constitution, has been denied? I think not. Happily the human mind is so constituted, that no party can reach to the audacity of doing this. Think, if you can, of a single instance in which a plainly written provision of the Constitution has ever been denied. If, by the mere force of numbers, a majority should deprive a minority of any clearly written constitutional right, it might, in a moral point of view, justify revolution—certainly would, if such right were a vital one. But such is not our case. All the vital rights of minorities, and of individuals, are so plainly assured to them, by affirmations and negations, guarranties and prohibitions, in the Constitution, that controversies never arise concerning them. But no organic law can ever be framed with a provision specifically applicable to every question which may occur in practical administration. No foresight can anticipate, nor any document of reasonable length contain express provisions for all possible questions. Shall fugitives from labor be surrendered by national or by State authority? The Constitution does not expressly say. *May* Congress prohibit slavery in the territories? The Constitution does not expressly say. *Must* Congress protect slavery in the territories? The Constitution does not expressly say.

From questions of this class spring all our constitutional controversies, and we divide upon them into majorities and minorities. If the minority will not acquiesce, the majority must, or the government must cease. There is no other alternative; for continuing the government, is acquiescence on one side or the other. If a minority, in such case, will secede rather than acquiesce, they make precedent which, in turn, will divide and ruin them; for a minority of their own will secede from them, whenever a majority refuses to be controlled by such minority. For instance, why may not any portion of a new confederacy, a year or two hence, arbitrarily secede again, precisely as portions of the present Union now claim to secede from it. All who cherish disunion sentiments, are now being educated to the exact temper of doing this. Is there such perfect identity of interests among the States to compose a new Union, as to produce harmony only, and prevent renewed secession?

Plainly, the central idea of secession, is the essence of anarchy. A majority, held in restraint by constitutional checks, and limitations, and always changing easily, with deliberate changes of popular opinions and sentiments, is the only true sovereign of a free people. Whoever rejects it, does, of necessity, fly to anarchy or to despotism. Unanimity is impossible; the rule of a minority, as a permanent arrangement, is wholly inadmissable; so that, rejecting the majority principle, anarchy, or despotism in some form, is all that is left.

I do not forget the position assumed by some, that constitutional questions are to be decided by the Supreme Court; nor do I deny that such decisions must be binding in any case, upon the parties to a suit, as to the object of that suit, while they are also entitled to very high respect and consideration, in all paralel cases, by all other departments of the government. And while it is obviously possible that such decision may be erroneous in any given case, still the evil effect following it, being limited to that particular case, with the chance that it may be over-ruled, and never become a precedent for other cases, can better be borne than could the evils of a different practice. At the same time the candid citizen must confess that if the policy of the government, upon vital questions, affecting the whole people, is to be irrevocably fixed by decisions of the Supreme Court, the instant they are made, in ordinary litigation between parties, in personal actions, the people will have ceased, to be their own rulers, having, to that extent, practically resigned their government, into the hands of that eminent tribunal. Nor is there, in this view, any assault upon the court, or the judges. It is a duty, from which they may not shrink, to decide cases properly brought before them; and it is no fault of theirs, if others seek to turn their decisions to political purposes.

One section of our country believes slavery is *right*, and ought to be extended, while the other believes it is *wrong*, and ought not to be extended. This is the only substantial dispute. The fugitive slave clause of the Constitution, and the law for the suppression of the foreign slave trade, are each as well enforced, perhaps, as any law can ever be in a community where the moral sense of the people imperfectly supports the law itself. The great body of the people abide by the dry legal obligation in both cases, and a few break over in each. This, I think, cannot be perfectly cured; and it would be worse in both cases *after* the separation of the sections, than before. The foreign slave trade, now imperfectly suppressed, would be ultimately revived without restriction, in one section; while fugitive slaves, now only partially surrendered, would not be surrendered at all, by the other.

Physically speaking, we cannot separate. We cannot remove our respective sections from each other, nor build an impassable wall between them. A husband and wife may be divorced, and go out of the presence, and beyond the reach of each other; but the different parts of our country cannot do this. They cannot but remain face to face; and intercourse, either amicable or hostile, must continue between them. Is it possible then to make that intercourse more advantageous, or more satisfactory, *after* separation than *before?* Can aliens make treaties easier than friends can make laws? Can treaties be more faithfully enforced between aliens, than laws can among friends? Suppose you go to war, you cannot fight always; and when, after much loss on both sides, and no gain on either, you cease fighting, the identical old questions, as to terms of intercourse, are again upon you.

This country, with its institutions, belongs to the people who inhabit it. Whenever they shall grow weary of the existing government, they can exercise their *constitutional* right of amending it, or their *revolutionary* right to dismember, or overthrow it. I can not be ignorant of the fact that many worthy, and patriotic citizens are desirous of having the national constitution amended. While I make no recommendation of amendments, I fully recognize the rightful authority of the people over the whole subject, to be exercised in either of the modes prescribed in the instrument itself; and I should, under existing circumstances, favor, rather than oppose, a fair opportunity being afforded the people to act upon it.

I will venture to add that, to me, the convention mode seems preferable, in that it allows amendments to originate with the people themselves, instead of only permitting them to take, or reject, propositions, originated by others, not especially chosen for the purpose, and which might not be precisely such, as they would wish to either accept or refuse. I understand a proposed amendment to the Constitution—which amendment, however, I have not seen, has passed Congress, to the effect that the federal government, shall never interfere with the domestic institutions of the States, including that of persons held to service. To avoid misconstruction of what I have said, I depart from my purpose not to speak of particular amendments, so far as to say that, holding such a provision to now be implied constitutional law, I have no objection to its being made express, and irrevocable.

The Chief Magistrate derives all his authority from the people, and they have conferred none upon him to fix terms for the separation of the States. The people themselves can do this also if they choose; but the executive, as such, has nothing to do with it. His duty is to administer the present government, as it came to his hands, and to transmit it, unimpaired by him, to his successor.

Why should there not be a patient confidence in the ultimate justice of the people? Is there any better, or equal hope, in the world? In our present differences, is either party without faith of being in the right? If the Almighty Ruler of nations, with his eternal truth and justice, be on your side of the North, or on yours of the South, that truth, and that justice, will surely prevail, by the judgment of this great tribunal, the American people.

By the frame of the government under which we live, this same people have wisely given their public servants but little power for mischief; and have, with equal wisdom, provided for the return of that little to their own hands at very short intervals.

While the people retain their virtue, and vigilence, no administration, by any extreme of wickedness or folly, can very seriously injure the government, in the short space of four years.

My countrymen, one and all, think calmly and *well,* upon this whole subject. Nothing valuable can be lost by taking time. If there be an object to *hurry* any of you, in hot haste, to a step which you would never take *deliberately,* that object will be frustrated by taking time; but no good object can be frustrated by it. Such of you as are now dissatisfied, still have the old Constitution unimpaired, and, on the sensitive point, the laws of your own framing under it; while the new administration will have no immediate power, if it would, to change either. If it were admitted that you who are dissatisfied, hold the right side in the dispute, there still is no single good reason for precipitate action. Intelligence, patriotism, Christianity, and a firm reliance on Him, who has never yet forsaken this favored land, are still competent to adjust, in the best way, all our present difficulty.

In *your* hands, my dissatisfied fellow countrymen, and not in *mine,* is the momentous issue of civil war. The government will not assail *you.* You can have no conflict, without being yourselves the aggressors. *You* have no oath registered in Heaven to destroy the government, while *I* shall have the most solemn one to "preserve, protect and defend" it.

I am loth to close. We are not enemies, but friends. We must not be enemies. Though passion may have strained, it must not break our bonds of affection. The mystic chords of memory, stretching from every battle-field, and patriot grave, to every living heart and hearthstone, all over this broad land, will yet swell the chorus of the Union, when again touched, as surely they will be, by the better angels of our nature.

"I HOPE WE HAVE A GOVERNMENT AND A PRESIDENT"

Reply to a Pennsylvania Delegation, the White House

[MARCH 5, 1861]

Lincoln received delegates from several states at the White House on his first full day as president. He welcomed a group of Pennsylvanians with this reaffirmation of the right of dissent.

Mr. Chairman and Gentlemen of the Pennsylvania Delegation:—As I have so frequently said heretofore, when I have had occasion to address the people of the Keystone, in my visits to that State, I can now but repeat the assurance of my gratification at the support you gave me at the late election, and at the promise of a continuation of that support which is now tendered to me.

Allusion has been made to the hope that you entertain that you have a President and a Government. In respect to that I wish to say to you, that in the position I have assumed I wish to do no more than I have ever given reason to believe I would do. I do not wish you to believe that I assume to be any better than others who have gone before me. I prefer rather to have it understood that if we ever have a Government on the principles we prefer, we should remember while we exercise our opinion, that others have also rights to the exercise of their opinions, and we should endeavor to allow these rights, and act in such a manner as to create no bad feeling. I hope we have a Government and a President. I hope and wish it to be understood that there may be allusion to no unpleasant differences.

We must remember that the people of all the States are entitled to all the privileges and immunities of the citizens of the several States. We should bear this in mind, and act in such a way as to say nothing insulting or irritating. I would inculcate this idea, so that we may not, like Pharisees, set ourselves up to be better than other people.

Now my friends, my public duties are pressing today, and will prevent my giving more time to you. Indeed, I should not have left them now, but I could not well deny myself to so large and respectable a body.

"THE PERPETUITY OF POPULAR GOVERNMENT"

Proclamation Calling Out the Militia, and Convening a Special Session of Congress

[APRIL 15, 1861]

After thirty-four hours of rebel bombardment, Fort Sumter in Charleston, South Carolina, was evacuated by Union forces on April 14, igniting the Civil War. Lincoln summoned his cabinet for a late-night session, and the following morning issued this call for troops, couching it in terms of preserving democracy. While the North generally applauded the proclamation, a New Orleans newspaper called it the "insolent" response of a "Military Dictator."

April 15, 1861

By the President of the United States

A Proclamation.

Whereas the laws of the United States have been for some time past, and now are opposed, and the execution thereof obstructed, in the States of South Carolina, Georgia, Alabama, Florida, Mississippi, Louisiana and Texas, by combinations too powerful to be suppressed by the ordinary course of judicial proceedings, or by the powers vested in the Marshals by law,

Now therefore, I, Abraham Lincoln, President of the United States, in virtue of the power in me vested by the Constitution, and the laws, have thought fit to call forth, and hereby do call forth, the militia of the several States of the Union, to the aggregate number of seventy-five thousand, in order to suppress said combinations, and to cause the laws to be duly executed. The details, for this object, will be immediately communicated to the State authorities through the War Department.

I appeal to all loyal citizens to favor, facilitate and aid this effort to maintain the honor, the integrity, and the existence of our National Union, and the perpetuity of popular government; and to redress wrongs already long enough endured.

I deem it proper to say that the first service assigned to the forces hereby called forth will probably be to re-possess the forts, places, and property which have been seized from the Union; and in every event, the utmost care will be observed, consistently with the objects aforesaid, to avoid any devastation, any destruction of, or interference with, property, or any disturbance of peaceful citizens in any part of the country.

And I hereby command the persons composing the combinations aforesaid to disperse, and retire peaceably to their respective abodes within twenty days from this date.

Deeming that the present condition of public affairs presents an extraordinary occasion, I do hereby, in virtue of the power in me vested by the Constitution, convene both Houses of Congress. Senators and Representatives are therefore summoned to assemble at their respective chambers, at 12 o'clock, noon, on Thursday, the fourth day of July, next, then and there to consider and determine, such measures, as, in their wisdom, the public safety, and interest may seem to demand.

In Witness Whereof I have hereunto set my hand, and caused the Seal of the United States to be affixed.

> Done at the city of Washington this fifteenth day of April in the year of our Lord One thousand, Eight hundred and Sixty-one, and of the Independence of the United States the Eighty-fifth.

ABRAHAM LINCOLN

By the President
WILLIAM H. SEWARD, Secretary of State.

"WE *CAN* NOT PERMANENTLY PREVENT THEIR ACTION"

Letter to General Winfield Scott

[APRIL 25, 1861]

Eleven days after the outbreak of war, federal troops had still not arrived to protect Washington, prompting an anguished Lincoln to exclaim, "I begin to believe there is no North." To make matters worse, Maryland seemed poised to follow other Southern states out of the Union, a decision that would have completely isolated the capital. Despite the crisis, Lincoln was still expressing reluctance, as of April 25, to block Maryland's likely secession.

Lieutenant General Scott   Washington, April 25- 1861.

My dear Sir:

The Maryland Legislature assembles to-morrow at Anapolis; and, not improbably, will take action to arm the people of that State against the United States. The question has been submitted to, and considered by me, whether it would not be justifiable, upon the ground of necessary defence, for you, as commander in Chief of the United States Army, to arrest, or disperse the members of that body. I think it would *not* be justifiable; nor, efficient for the desired object.

First, they have a clearly legal right to assemble; and, we can not know in advance, that their action will not be lawful, and peaceful. And if we wait until they shall *have* acted, their arrest, or dispersion, will not lessen the effect of their action.

Secondly, we *can* not permanently prevent their action. If we arrest them, we can not long hold them as prisoners; and when liberated, they will immediately re-assemble, and take their action. And, precisely the same if we simply disperse them. They will immediately re-assemble in some other place.

I therefore conclude that it is only left to the commanding General to watch, and await their action, which, if it shall be to arm their people against the United States, he is to adopt the most prompt, and efficient means to counteract, even, if necessary, to the bombardment of their cities—and in the extremist necessity, the suspension of the writ of habeas corpus. Your Obedient Servant

ABRAHAM LINCOLN.

"SUSPEND THE WRIT OF HABEAS CORPUS"
Letter to General Winfield Scott
[APRIL 27, 1861]

Two days after instructing General Winfield Scott to do no more than watch and wait in Maryland, Lincoln suspended the privilege of the writ of habeas corpus there. The army proceeded to arrest prosecession Marylanders, including legislators suspected of willingness to vote the state out of the Union. Maryland did not secede.

April 27, 1861

To the Commanding General of the Army of the United States:

You are engaged in repressing an insurrection against the laws of the United States. If at any point on or in the vicinity of the military line, which is now used between the City of Philadelphia and the City of Washington, via Perryville, Annapolis City, and Annapolis Junction, you find resistance which renders it necessary to suspend the writ of Habeas Corpus for the public safety, you, personally or through the officer in command at the point where the resistance occurs, are authorized to suspend that writ.

ABRAHAM LINCOLN

"THE CENTRAL IDEA PERVADING THIS STRUGGLE"

Informal Comments on Popular Government, the White House

[MAY 7, 1861]

Lincoln made these remarks to his junior White House secretary, John M. Hay—later a U.S. secretary of state. Hay recorded them in his diary.

For my part, I consider the central idea pervading this struggle is the necessity that is upon us, of proving that popular government is not an absurdity. We must settle this question now, whether in a free government the minority have the right to break up the government whenever they choose. If we fail it will go far to prove the incapability of the people to govern themselves. There may be one consideration used in stay of such final judgment, but that is not for us to use in advance.

That is, that there exists in our case, an instance of so vast and farreaching a disturbing element, which the history of no other free nation will probably ever present. That, however, is not for us to say at present. Taking the government as we found it we will see if the majority can preserve it.

"A POLISH GENTLEMAN ... HIGHLY RECOMMENDED"

Letter to Secretary of War Simon Cameron

[MAY 20, 1861]

Once the war began, Lincoln was ready and willing to accept military help from nationalized Americans. Allen, a Polish-American New York merchant, received approval in July to raise an infantry regiment.

Executive Mansion
May 20, 1861

Hon. Sec. of War:

My dear Sir:

Col. Julian Allen, a Polish gentleman, naturalized, proposes raising a Regiment of our citizens of his nationality, to serve in our Army. He proposes getting them from the different States, without particular order, as can be most conveniently done, and organizing them here, so that they, as a Regiment, will hail from no particular State. Mr. Allen is highly recommended, as you will see by his testimonials. If he so raises and tenders a Regiment, I am in favor of accepting it, unless there be some objection which does not occur to me. Yours truly,

A. LINCOLN.

"THIS IS ... A PEOPLE'S CONTEST"

From a Message to Congress in Special Session

[JULY 4, 1861]

With the attack on Fort Sumter, Lincoln believed "the last ray of hope for preserving the Union peaceably expired." His extraordinary war message to Congress was, in historian Don E. Fehrenbacher's words, an effort at "mobilizing the national will" to put down the rebellion. Lincoln forcefully defined the war to come as a struggle to save democracy itself and its promise of a "fair chance in the race of life" for every American. When it was delivered, however, one Baltimore newspaper, The South, *thought it proved that Lincoln was either "a disgusting fool" or "the equal, in despotic wickedness, of Nero or any of the other tyrants who have polluted this earth."*

. . . this issue embraces more than the fate of these United States. It presents to the whole family of man, the question, whether a constitutional republic, or a democracy—a government of the people, by the same people—can, or cannot, maintain its territorial integrity, against its own domestic foes. It presents the question, whether discontented individuals, too few in numbers to control administration, according to organic law, in any case, can always, upon the pretences made in this case, or on any other pretences, or arbitrarily, without any pretence, break up their Government, and thus practically put an end to free government upon the earth. It forces us to ask: "Is there, in all republics, this inherent, and fatal weakness?" "Must a government, of necessity, be too *strong* for the liberties of its own people, or too *weak* to maintain its own existence?"

So viewing the issue, no choice was left but to call out the war power of the Government; and so to resist force, employed for its destruction, by force, for its preservation.

. . . .

Soon after the first call for militia, it was considered a duty to authorize the Commanding General, in proper cases, according to his discretion, to suspend the privilege of the writ of habeas corpus; or, in other words, to arrest, and detain, without resort to the ordinary processes and forms of law, such individuals as he might deem dangerous to the public safety. This authority has purposely been exercised but very sparingly. Nevertheless, the legality and propriety of what has been done under it, are questioned; and the attention of the country has been called to the proposition that one who is sworn to "take care that the laws be faithfully executed," should not himself violate them. Of course some consideration was given to the questions of power, and propriety, before this matter was acted upon. The whole of the laws which were required to be faithfully executed, were being resisted, and failing of execution, in nearly one-third of the States. Must they be allowed to finally fail of execution, even had it been perfectly clear, that by the use of the means necessary to their execution, some single law, made in such extreme tenderness of the citizen's liberty, that practically, it relieves more of the guilty, than of the innocent, should, to a very limited extent, be violated? To state the question more directly, are all the laws, *but one,* to go unexecuted, and the government itself go to pieces, lest that one be violated? Even in such a case, would not the official oath be broken, if the government should be overthrown, when it was believed that disregarding the single law, would tend to preserve it? But it was not believed that this question was presented. It was not believed that any law was violated. The provision of the Constitution that "The privilege of the writ of habeas corpus, shall not be suspended unless when, in cases of rebellion or invasion, the public safety may require it," is equivalent to a provision—is a provision—that such privilege may be suspended when, in cases of rebellion, or invasion, the public safety *does* require it. It was decided that we have a case of rebellion, and that the public safety does require the qualified suspension of the privilege of the writ which was authorized to be made.

. . . .

It is now recommended that you give the legal means for making this contest a short, and a decisive one; that you place at the control of the government, for the work, at least four hundred thousand men, and four hundred millions of dollars. That number of men is about one tenth of those of proper ages within the regions where, apparently, *all* are willing to engage; and the sum is less than a twentythird part of the money value owned by the men who seem ready to devote the whole.

A debt of six hundred millions of dollars *now,* is a less sum per head, than was the debt of our revolution, when we came out of that struggle; and the money value in the country now, bears even a greater proportion to what it was *then,* than does the population. Surely each man has as strong a motive *now,* to *preserve* our liberties, as each had *then,* to *establish* them.

A right result, at this time, will be worth more to the world, than ten times the men, and ten times the money. The evidence reaching us from the country, leaves no doubt, that the material for the work is abundant; and that it needs only the hand of legislation to give it legal sanction, and the hand of the Executive to give it practical shape and efficiency. One of the greatest perplexities of the government, is to avoid receiving troops faster than it can provide for them. In a word, the people will save their government, if the government itself, will do its part, only indifferently well.

It might seem, at first thought, to be of little difference whether the present movement at the South be called "secession" or "rebellion." The movers, however, well understand the difference. At the beginning, they knew they could never raise their treason to any respectable magnitude, by any name which implies *violation* of law. They knew their people possessed as much of moral sense, as much of devotion to law and order, and as much pride in, and reverence for, the history, and government, of their common country, as any other civilized, and patriotic people. They knew they could make no advancement directly in the teeth of these strong and noble sentiments. Accordingly they commenced by an insidious debauching of the public mind. They invented an ingenious sophism, which, if conceded, was followed by perfectly logical steps, through all the incidents, to the complete destruction of the Union. The sophism itself is, that any state of the Union may, *consistently* with the national Constitution, and therefore *lawfully,* and *peacefully,* withdraw from the Union, without the consent of the Union, or of any other state. The little disguise that the supposed right is to be exercised only for just cause, themselves to be the sole judge of its justice, is too thin to merit any notice.

With rebellion thus sugar-coated, they have been drugging the public mind of their section for more than thirty years; and, until at length, they have brought many good men to a willingness to take up arms against the government the day *after* some assemblage of men have enacted the farcical pretence of taking their State out of the Union, who could have been brought to no such thing the day *before*.

This sophism derives much—perhaps the whole—of its currency, from the assumption, that there is some omnipotent, and sacred supremacy, pertaining to a *State*—to each State of our Federal Union. Our States have neither more, nor less power, than that reserved to them, in the Union, by the Constitution—no one of them ever having been a State *out* of the Union. The original ones passed into the Union even *before* they cast off their British colonial dependence; and the new ones each came into the Union directly from a condition of dependence, excepting Texas. And even Texas, in its temporary independence, was never designated a State. The new ones only took the designation of States, on coming into the Union, while that name was first adopted for the old ones, in, and by, the Declaration of Independence. Therein the "United Colonies" were declared to be "Free and Independent States"; but, even then, the object plainly was not to declare their independence of *one another*, or of the *Union;* but directly the contrary, as their mutual pledge, and their mutual action, before, at the time, and afterwards, abundantly show. The express plighting of faith, by each and all of the original thirteen, in the Articles of Confederation, two years later, that the Union shall be perpetual, is most conclusive. Having never been States, either in substance, or in name, *outside* of the Union, whence this magical omnipotence of "State rights," asserting a claim of power to lawfully destroy the Union itself? Much is said about the "sovereignty" of the States; but the word, even, is not in the national Constitution; nor, as is believed, in any of the State constitutions. What is a "sovereignty," in the political sense of the term? Would it be far wrong to define it "A political community, without a political superior?" Tested by this, no one of our States, except Texas, ever was a sovereignty. And even Texas gave up the character on coming into the Union; by which act, she acknowledged the Constitution of the United States, and the laws and treaties of the United States made in pursuance of the Constitution, to be, for her, the supreme law of the land. The States have their *status* IN the Union, and they have no other *legal status.* If they break from this, they can only do so against law, and by revolution. The Union, and not themselves separately, procured their independence, and their liberty. By conquest, or purchase, the Union gave each of them, whatever of independence, and liberty, it has. The

Union is older than any of the States; and, in fact, it created them as States. Originally, some dependent colonies made the Union; and, in turn, the Union threw off their old dependence, for them, and made them States, such as they are. Not one of them ever had a State constitution, independent of the Union. Of course, it is not forgotten that all the new States framed their constitutions, before they entered the Union; nevertheless, dependent upon, and preparatory to, coming into the Union.

Unquestionably the States have the powers, and rights, reserved to them in, and by the National Constitution; but among these, surely, are not included all conceivable powers, however mischievous, or destructive; but, at most, such only, as were known in the world, at the time, as governmental powers; and certainly, a power to destroy the government itself, had never been known as a governmental—as a merely administrative power. This relative matter of National power, and State rights, as a principle, is no other than the principle of *generality,* and *locality.* Whatever concerns the whole, should be confided to the whole—to the general government; while, whatever concerns *only* the State, should be left exclusively, to the State. This is all there is of original principle about it. Whether the National Constitution, in defining boundaries between the two, has applied the principle with exact accuracy, is not to be questioned. We are all bound by that defining, without question.

What is now combatted, is the position that secession is *consistent* with the Constitution—is *lawful,* and *peaceful.* It is not contended that there is any express law for it; and nothing should ever be implied as law, which leads to unjust, or absurd consequences. The nation purchased, with money, the countries out of which several of these States were formed. Is it just that they shall go off without leave, and without refunding? The nation paid very large sums, (in the aggregate, I believe, nearly a hundred millions) to relieve Florida of the aboriginal tribes. Is it just that she shall now be off without consent, or without making any return? The nation is now in debt for money applied to the benefit of these so-called seceding States, in common with the rest. Is it just, either that creditors shall go unpaid, or the remaining States pay the whole? A part of the present national debt was contracted to pay the old debts of Texas. Is it just that she shall leave, and pay no part of this herself?

Again, if one State may secede, so may another; and when all shall have seceded, none is left to pay the debts. Is this quite just to creditors? Did we notify them of this sage view of ours, when we borrowed their money? If we now recognize this doctrine, by allowing the seceders to go in peace, it is difficult to see what we can do, if others choose to go, or to extort terms upon which they will promise to remain.

The seceders insist that our Constitution admits of secession. They have assumed to make a National Constitution of their own, in which, of necessity, they have either *discarded,* or *retained,* the right of secession, as they insist, it exists in ours. If they have discarded it, they thereby admit that, on principle, it ought not to be in ours. If they have retained it, by their own construction of ours they show that to be consistent they must secede from one another, whenever they shall find it the easiest way of settling their debts, or effecting any other selfish, or unjust object. The principle itself is one of disintegration, and upon which no government can possibly endure.

If all the States, save one, should assert the power to *drive* that one out of the Union, it is presumed the whole class of seceder politicians would at once deny the power, and denounce the act as the greatest outrage upon State rights. But suppose that precisely the same act, instead of being called "driving the one out," should be called "the seceding of the others from that one," it would be exactly what the seceders claim to do; unless, indeed, they make the point, that the one, because it is a minority, may rightfully do, what the others, because they are a majority, may not rightfully do. These politicians are subtle, and profound, on the rights of minorities. They are not partial to that power which made the Constitution, and speaks from the preamble, calling itself "We, the People."

.   .   .   .

It may be affirmed, without extravagance, that the free institutions we enjoy, have developed the powers, and improved the condition, of our whole people, beyond any example in the world. Of this we now have a striking, and an impressive illustration. So large an army as the government has now on foot, was never before known, without a soldier in it, but who had taken his place there, of his own free choice. But more than this: there are many single Regiments whose members, one and another, possess full practical knowledge of all the arts, sciences, professions, and whatever else, whether useful or elegant, is known in the world; and there is scarcely one, from which there could not be selected, a President, a Cabinet, a Congress, and perhaps a Court, abundantly competent to administer the government itself. Nor do I say this is not true, also, in the army of our late friends, now adversaries, in this contest; but if it is, so much better the reason why the government, which has conferred such benefits on both them and us, should not be broken up. Whoever, in any section, proposes to abandon such a government, would do well to consider, in deference to what principle it is, that he does it—what better he is likely to get in its stead—whether the substitute will give, or be intended to give, so much of good to the people. There are some foreshadowings on this subject. Our adversaries have adopted some Declarations of Independence; in which, unlike the good old one, penned by Jefferson, they omit the words "all men are created equal." Why? They have adopted a temporary national constitution, in the preamble of which, unlike our good old one, signed by Washington, they omit "We, the People," and substitute "We, the deputies of the sovereign and independent States." Why? Why this deliberate pressing out of view, the rights of men, and the authority of the people?

This is essentially a People's contest. On the side of the Union, it is a struggle for maintaining in the world, that form, and substance of government, whose leading object is, to elevate the condition of men— to lift artificial weights from all shoulders—to clear the paths of laudable pursuit for all—to afford all, an unfettered start, and a fair chance, in the race of life. Yielding to partial, and temporary departures, from necessity, this is the leading object of the government for whose existence we contend.

I am most happy to believe that the plain people understand, and appreciate this. It is worthy of note, that while in this, the government's hour of trial, large numbers of those in the Army and Navy, who have been favored with the offices, have resigned, and proved false to the hand which had pampered them, not one common soldier, or common sailor is known to have deserted his flag.

Great honor is due to those officers who remain true, despite the example of their treacherous associates; but the greatest honor, and most important fact of all, is the unanimous firmness of the common soldiers, and common sailors. To the last man, so far as known, they have successfully resisted the traitorous efforts of those, whose commands, but an hour before, they obeyed as absolute law. This is the patriotic instinct of the plain people. They understand, without an argument, that destroying the government, which was made by Washington, means no good to them.

Our popular government has often been called an experiment. Two points in it, our people have already settled—the successful *establishing,* and the successful *administering* of it. One still remains—its successful *maintenance* against a formidable internal attempt to overthrow it. It is now for them to demonstrate to the world, that those who can fairly carry an election, can also suppress a rebellion—that ballots are the rightful, and peaceful, successors of bullets; and that when ballots have fairly, and constitutionally, decided, there can be no successful appeal, back to bullets; that there can be no successful appeal, except to ballots themselves, at succeeding elections. Such will be a great lesson of peace; teaching men that what they cannot take by an election, neither can they take it by a war—teaching all, the folly of being the beginners of a war.

Lest there be some uneasiness in the minds of candid men, as to what is to be the course of the government, towards the Southern States, *after* the rebellion shall have been suppressed, the Executive deems it proper to say, it will be his purpose then, as ever, to be guided by the Constitution, and the laws; and that he probably will have no different understanding of the powers, and duties of the Federal government, relatively to the rights of the States, and the people, under the Constitution, than that expressed in the inaugural address.

He desires to preserve the government, that it may be administered for all, as it was administered by the men who made it. Loyal citizens everywhere, have the right to claim this of their government; and the government has no right to withhold, or neglect it. It is not perceived that, in giving it, there is any coercion, any conquest, or any subjugation, in any just sense of those terms.

The Constitution provides, and all the States have accepted the provision, that "The United States shall guarantee to every State in this Union a republican form of government." But, if a State may lawfully go out of the Union, having done so, it may also discard the republican form of government; so that to prevent its going out, is an indispensable *means,* to the *end,* of maintaining the guaranty mentioned; and when an end is lawful and obligatory, the indispensable means to it, are also lawful, and obligatory.

It was with the deepest regret that the Executive found the duty of employing the war-power, in defence of the government, forced upon him. He could but perform this duty, or surrender the existence of the government. No compromise, by public servants, could, in this case, be a cure; not that compromises are not often proper, but that no popular government can long survive a marked precedent, that those who carry an election, can only save the government from immediate destruction, by giving up the main point, upon which the people gave the election. The people themselves, and not their servants, can safely reverse their own deliberate decisions. As a private citizen, the Executive could not have consented that these institutions shall perish; much less could he, in betrayal of so vast, and so sacred a trust, as these free people had confided to him. He felt that he had no moral right to shrink; nor even to count the chances of his own life, in what might follow. In full view of his great responsibility, he has, so far, done what he had deemed his duty. You will now, according to your own judgment, perform yours. He sincerely hopes that your views, and your action, may so accord with his, as to assure all faithful citizens, who have been disturbed in their rights, of a certain, and speedy restoration to them, under the Constitution, and the laws.

And having thus chosen our course, without guile, and with pure purpose, let us renew our trust in God, and go forward without fear, and with manly hearts.

ABRAHAM LINCOLN

"ALLOW NO MAN TO BE SHOT"

Letter to General John C. Frémont

[SEPTEMBER 2, 1861]

The 1856 Republican presidential candidate, John C. Frémont, was now a Union general. He overstepped his authority by proclaiming the confiscation of the property of Confederate sympathizers in Missouri, including property in slaves. His emancipation edict was designed to curtail guerrilla warfare in the West, but also to curry favor with Republican abolitionists. Still worried about holding the border states in the Union, Lincoln was not ready for such a move, especially if it was, in his word, "political." He gently rebuked "the Pathfinder of the West" with this letter, which reflected Lincoln's determination that the civilian authority, and not the military, make policy. But Frémont refused to heed the request, and a few days later Lincoln sent a more direct order.

Private and confidential.

Major General Fremont: Washington D.C. Sept. 2, 1861.

My dear Sir:

Two points in your proclamation of August 30th give me some anxiety. First, should you shoot a man, according to the proclamation, the Confederates would very certainly shoot our best man in their hands in retaliation; and so, man for man, indefinitely. It is therefore my order that you allow no man to be shot, under the proclamation, without first having my approbation or consent.

Secondly, I think there is great danger that the closing paragraph, in relation to the confiscation of property, and the liberating slaves of traiterous owners, will alarm our Southern Union friends, and turn them against us—perhaps ruin our rather fair prospect for Kentucky. Allow me therefore to ask, that you will as of your own motion, modify that paragraph so as to conform to the *first* and *fourth* sections of the act of Congress, entitled, "An act to confiscate property used for insurrectionary purposes," approved August, 6th, 1861, and a copy of which act I herewith send you. This letter is written in a spirit of caution and not of censure.

I send it by a special messenger, in order that it may certainly and speedily reach you. Yours very truly

A. LINCOLN

"I CANNOT ASSUME THIS RECKLESS POSITION"

Letter to Orville H. Browning

[SEPTEMBER 22, 1861]

A longtime ally of Lincoln in Illinois politics, Browning was named to fill Stephen A. Douglas's Senate seat after Douglas's sudden death in 1861. He then disappointed Lincoln by siding with Frémont's Missouri initiatives. Lincoln's response focused not only on "principle" but on his fear that border slave states like Kentucky and Maryland might yet follow the Southern states out of the Union if provoked. A month after writing this letter, Lincoln relieved Frémont of command in the West. The "Hurlbut" mentioned in the last paragraph was widely rumored a drunkard; but he did not offer to resign for more than two years.

Private & confidential.

Executive Mansion
Washington Sept. 22d 1861.

Hon. O. H. Browning

My dear Sir

Yours of the 17th is just received; and coming from you, I confess it astonishes me. That you should object to my adhering to a law, which you had assisted in making, and presenting to me, less than a month before, is odd enough. But this is a very small part. Genl. Fremont's proclamation, as to confiscation of property, and the liberation of slaves, is *purely political,* and not within the range of *military* law, or necessity. If a commanding General finds a necessity to seize the farm of a private owner, for a pasture, an encampment, or a fortification, he has the right to do so, and to so hold it, as long as the necessity lasts; and this is within military law, because within military necessity. But to say the farm shall no longer belong to the owner, or his heirs forever; and this as well when the farm is not needed for military purposes as when it is, is purely political, without the savor of military law about it. And the same is true of slaves. If the General needs them, he can seize them, and use them; but when the need is past, it is not for him to fix their permanent future condition. That must be settled according to laws made by law-makers, and not by military proclamations. The proclamation in the point in question, is simply "dictatorship." It assumes that the general may do *anything* he pleases—confiscate the lands and free the slaves of *loyal* people, as well as of disloyal ones. And going the whole figure I have no doubt would be more popular with some thoughtless people, than that which has been done! But I cannot assume this reckless position; nor allow others to assume it on my responsibility. You speak of it as being the only means of *saving* the government. On the contrary it is itself the surrender of the government. Can it be pretended that it is any longer the government of the U.S.—any government of Constitution and laws,—wherein a General, or a President, may make permanent rules of property by proclamation?

I do not say Congress might not with propriety pass a law, on the point, just such as General Fremont proclaimed. I do not say I might not, as a member of Congress, vote for it. What I object to, is, that I as President, shall expressly or impliedly seize and exercise the permanent legislative functions of the government.

So much as to principle. Now as to policy. No doubt the thing was popular in some quarters, and would have been more so if it had been a general declaration of emancipation. The Kentucky Legislature would not budge till that proclamation was modified; and Gen. [Robert] Anderson [commander of Union forces in Kentucky—eds.] telegraphed me that on the news of Gen. Fremont having actually issued deeds of manumission, a whole company of our Volunteers threw down their arms and disbanded. I was so assured, as to think it probable, that the very arms we had furnished Kentucky would be turned against us. I think to lose Kentucky is nearly the same as to lose the whole game. Kentucky gone, we can not hold Missouri, nor, as I think, Maryland.

These all against us, and the job on our hands is too large for us. We would as well consent to separation at once, including the surrender of this capitol. On the contrary, if you will give up your restlessness for new positions, and back me manfully on the grounds upon which you and other kind friends gave me the election, and have approved in my public documents, we shall go through triumphantly.

You must not understand I took my course on the proclamation *because* of Kentucky. I took the same ground in a private letter to General Fremont before I heard from Kentucky.

You think I am inconsistent because I did not also forbid Gen. Fremont to shoot men under the proclamation. I understand that part to be within military law; but I also think, and so privately wrote Gen. Fremont, that it is impolitic in this, that our adversaries have the power, and will certainly exercise it, to shoot as many of our men as we shoot of theirs. I did not say this in the public letter, because it is a subject I prefer not to discuss in the hearing of our enemies.

There has been no thought of removing Gen. Fremont on any ground connected with his proclamation; and if there has been any wish for his removal on any ground, our mutual friend Sam. Glover can probably tell you what it was. I hope no real necessity for it exists on any ground.

Suppose you write to [General Stephen] Hurlbut and get him to resign. Your friend as ever

A. LINCOLN

"WANTING TO WORK IS SO RARE"

Letter to George D. Ramsay

[OCTOBER 17, 1861]

Lincoln's undying belief in the work ethic was reflected in this job reference directed to the commander of the Washington arsenal, where war had made jobs plentiful.

Majr. Ramsay

Executive Mansion
October 17, 1861

My dear Sir

The lady—bearer of this—says she has two sons who want to work. Set them at it, if possible. Wanting to work is so rare a merit, that it should be encouraged. Yours truly

A. LINCOLN

"THE CAPACITY OF MAN FOR SELF-GOVERNMENT"

Reply to Edward Count Piper, the White House

[NOVEMBER 8, 1861]

During the early months of his presidency, Lincoln was required to exchange formal greetings with an endless procession of diplomats. These are his remarks to the minister resident from Sweden and Norway.

November 8, 1861.

Sir:

I receive with great pleasure a Minister from Sweden. That pleasure was enhanced by the information which preceded your arrival here, that his Majesty, your sovereign, had selected you to fill the mission upon the grounds of your derivation from an ancestral stock, identified with the most glorious era in your country's noble history, and your own eminent social and political standing in Sweden.

This country, Sir, maintains, and means to maintain, the rights of human nature and the capacity of man for self-government. The history of Sweden proves that this is the faith of the people of Sweden, as we know that it is the faith and practice of their respected Sovereign. Rest assured, therefore, that we shall be found always just and fraternal in our transactions with your Government, and that nothing will be omitted on my part to make your residence in this capital agreeable to yourself and satisfactory to your Government.

"THE STRUGGLE OF TODAY . . . FOR A VAST FUTURE ALSO"

From the Annual Message to Congress

[DECEMBER 3, 1861]

Personally delivered State of the Union messages were not yet part of American government tradition during Lincoln's time. Annual messages from the president, as they were then called, were merely transmitted to Capitol Hill and read by a clerk. One can only imagine how Lincoln's highly personal style suffered in the delivery. This, his first annual message, focused on the threat of foreign intervention; boasted of a $2.257 million budget surplus; and, in the extract presented here, turned to a favorite Lincoln theme: the relationship between labor and capital. The New York **Tribune** *commended the President for recognizing that the rebellion constituted "a war upon the . . . political franchises of the poor."*

It continues to develop that the insurrection is largely, if not exclusively, a war upon the first principle of popular government—the rights of the people. Conclusive evidence of this is found in the most grave and maturely considered public documents, as well as in the general tone of the insurgents. In those documents we find the abridgment of the existing right of suffrage and the denial to the people of all right to participate in the selection of public officers, except the legislative[,] boldly advocated, with labored arguments to prove that large control of the people in government, is the source of all political evil. Monarchy itself is sometimes hinted at as a possible refuge from the power of the people.

In my present position, I could scarcely be justified were I to omit raising a warning voice against this approach of returning despotism.

It is not needed, nor fitting here, that a general argument should be made in favor of popular institutions; but there is one point, with its connexions, not so hackneyed as most others, to which I ask a brief attention. It is the effort to place *capital* on an equal footing with, if not above *labor,* in the structure of government. It is assumed that labor is available only in connexion with capital; that nobody labors unless somebody else, owning capital, somehow by the use of it, induces him to labor. This assumed, it is next considered whether it is best that capital shall *hire* laborers, and thus induce them to work by their own consent, or *buy* them, and drive them to it without their consent. Having proceeded so far, it is naturally concluded that all laborers are either *hired* laborers, or what we call slaves. And further it is assumed that whoever is once a hired laborer, is fixed in that condition for life.

Now, there is no such relation between capital and labor as assumed; nor is there any such thing as a free man being fixed for life in the condition of a hired laborer. Both these assumptions are false, and all inferences from them are groundless.

Labor is prior to, and independent of, capital. Capital is only the fruit of labor, and could never have existed if labor had not first existed. Labor is the superior of capital, and deserves much the higher consideration. Capital has its rights, which are as worthy of protection as any other rights. Nor is it denied that there is, and probably always will be, a relation between labor and capital, producing mutual benefits. The error is in assuming that the whole labor of community exists within that relation. A few men own capital, and that few avoid labor themselves, and, with their capital, hire or buy another few to labor for them. A large majority belong to neither class—neither work for others, nor have others working for them. In most of the southern States, a majority of the whole people of all colors are neither slaves nor masters; while in the northern a large majority are neither hirers nor hired. Men with their families—wives, sons, and daughters—work for themselves, on their farms, in their houses, and in their shops, taking the whole product to themselves, and asking no favors of capital on the one hand, nor of hired laborers or slaves on the other. It is not forgotten that a considerable number of persons mingle their own labor with capital— that is, they labor with their own hands, and also buy or hire others to labor for them; but this is only a mixed, and not a distinct class. No principle stated is disturbed by the existence of this mixed class.

Again: as has already been said, there is not, of necessity, any such thing as the free hired laborer being fixed to that condition for life. Many independent men everywhere in these States, a few years back in their lives, were hired laborers. The prudent, penniless beginner in the world, labors for wages awhile, saves a surplus with which to buy tools or land for himself; then labors on his own account another while, and at length hires another new beginner to help him. This is the just, and generous, and prosperous system, which opens the way to all—gives hope to all, and consequent energy, and progress, and improvement of condition to all. No men living are more worthy to be trusted than those who toil up from poverty—none less inclined to take, or touch, aught which they have not honestly earned. Let them beware of surrendering a political power which they already possess, and which, if surrendered, will surely be used to close the door of advancement against such as they, and to fix new disabilities and burdens upon them, till all of liberty shall be lost.

From the first taking of our national census to the last are seventy years; and we find our population at the end of the period eight times as great as it was at the beginning. The increase of those other things which men deem desirable has been even greater. We thus have at one view, what the popular principle applied to government, through the machinery of the States and the Union, has produced in a given time; and also what, if firmly maintained, it promises for the future. There are already among us those, who, if the Union be preserved, will live to see it contain two hundred and fifty millions. The struggle of today, is not altogether for today—it is for a vast future also. With a reliance on Providence, all the more firm and earnest, let us proceed in the great task which events have devolved upon us.

ABRAHAM LINCOLN

⇛ VI ⇚

"FOREVER FREE"
Lincoln and Liberty
1862–1863

The author of the Emancipation Proclamation eyed the camera with an expression combining both belligerence and cunning for this photograph by Lewis E. Walker of Washington, taken sometime in 1863. Observing him for the first time not long before, writer Nathaniel Hawthorne saw in his "sallow, queer" countenance an unmistakable "expression of homely sagacity, that seems weighted with the rich results of village experience." Lincoln's face, he thought—as this picture testifies—reflected a "tact and wisdom that are akin to craft."

(Photograph: Lloyd Ostendorf, Dayton, Ohio)

Introduction

BY MARK E. NEELY, JR.

Had Abraham Lincoln died at the end of 1861, historians would remember his brief presidential term as a dismal failure. He adhered stubbornly to his political party's platform until the nation was on the brink of civil war, and proved frighteningly willing to risk war in the Fort Sumter crisis despite his country's notorious military unpreparedness. Unable to find a competent military commander once war began, he therefore failed to lead his government to significant military victories. He even declared a laughably ineffectual naval blockade regarded as of questionable legality by his own secretary of the navy. Historians would point to Lincoln's year as commander in chief as proof that a civilian, inexperienced in military affairs, was bound to fail miserably in this, the greatest role given a president by the U.S. Constitution.

To incompetence historians would add the charge of failure of moral leadership. Despite some high-sounding phrases spoken as a Republican candidate in years past, President Lincoln in fact disallowed practical measures taken by General John C. Frémont to undermine slavery in the United States. Before 1862, Abraham Lincoln seemed an unprincipled political weakling, well-meaning perhaps but administratively unprepared. He appeared to be as unready to master the sectional crisis as his disastrous presidential predecessors, the Democrats Franklin Pierce and James Buchanan.

Historians might find in Lincoln as he appeared in 1861 not only the floundering successor of Pierce and Buchanan but also the arch-bourgeois forerunner of a long line of Republican presidents. Later in the nineteenth century they would so encourage industrial capitalism that critics would call the whole era "the Great Barbecue." Lincoln did little directly to implement his capitalistic vision in 1861, but he did not really have to in order to get his way. Like-minded Republicans, thoroughly convinced that a capitalistic free-labor system was superior to the traditional slave-labor system of their adversaries in the war, went promptly to work to put their economic system in place. Republicans had raised the tariff in the special session of Congress called by Lincoln in July 1861 (with most of the free-trading Southerners gone), and a Pacific Rail Road Bill, drawn to the specifications of corporate interests, was in the works.

Hints of financial corruption accompanied the frenzied Republican attempts to develop the economy and mobilize Northern industrial production for war. Lincoln may have run for office as "Honest Abe," but his secretary of war, Simon Cameron, would leave office in February 1862 under a cloud of suspicion of financial malfeasance and with a well-merited reputation for administrative incompetence. The President even had to get the Republican-dominated Congress to cover up his own wife's cost overruns—some $20,000 at a time when soldiers needed blankets—in redecorating the executive mansion in luxurious style. Lincoln had used his cronies, relatives, and influential private persons rather than government officials to discharge many government functions, including handling government money. He maintained that he did so because the government departments early in the war were still staffed with potentially disloyal Southerners, but he admitted that many of his actions were "without any authority of law."

From the beginning, Lincoln had interpreted the Constitution and laws in a way that increased presidential power. Despite a record of moderation on constitutional matters before the war, he had suspended the privilege of the writ of habeas corpus in certain areas less than two weeks after Fort Sumter fell. Then he turned over the program of military arrests of civilians made possible by this controversial policy to a man who quickly gained a reputation as an unfeelingly ruthless tyrant, Secretary of State William H. Seward. By contrast with Lincoln's seeming weakness, however, Seward certainly looked like the strong man of the administration in its first year, as many observers had expected him to be all along. He gained credit for the administration's only triumph, if it may be called that: keeping Great Britain from intervening on the side of the Confederacy after the crisis over the steamer *Trent* in November and December 1861.

But Abraham Lincoln did not die in 1861, and he is generally remembered as the greatest American president rather than one of the worst. Many of the reasons for that more favorable appraisal can be found in the events of 1862 and 1863. In those years, he laid solid claim to world reputation as a statesman and moral leader. His armies began to win battles. And he gained a more assured voice. By the time Lincoln climbed onto the steam train to ride to Gettysburg, Pennsylvania, to deliver what would become the most famous speech in all American history—perhaps in all modern history—some shrewd observers knew that this man was marked for success, even world renown.

Nevertheless, success had been slow coming, and 1862 did not begin much better than 1861. Foremost in President Lincoln's thoughts, always, was the war. Nearly every policy, nearly every administrative action, nearly every change of personnel, nearly every word expressed, was shaped by the necessity of winning the war in order to have anything of value left at the end of his administration—a country, democracy, liberty.

When Lincoln first began to move toward ending slavery, he did so more from despair than from hope: he did it because the war continued to go badly. When he recommended that the border states adopt gradual emancipation, he depicted this policy as "one of the most efficient means of self-preservation" for "the federal government." Apparently, Lincoln believed this sincerely. And if that part of his argument for compensated emancipation was sincere, so too may have been his early support of colonization, expressed to a delegation of reluctant border state politicians, on July 12, 1862. He told those defenders of slave interests, skeptical that freed black people would ever leave this country for another, that once "numbers shall be large enough to be company and encouragement for one another, the freed people will not be so reluctant to go." When a group of black leaders came to see him the following August, the President spoke to them in brutally frank terms and—somewhat as he spoke to Indian delegations—in extremely simple language, telling them that the war showed "our white men cutting one another's throats." "It is better for us both," he told them in chilling terms, "to be separated."

All the while, Lincoln had sitting in his desk his draft of a proclamation that would have thrilled the black leaders had he shown it to them, a document meant to free most of the slaves on the North American continent. This document, too, had been written less from optimism than from pessimism. Discouraged when the border state representatives in Congress spurned his proposals for compensated emancipation and disturbed by the continuing lack of success by Union military forces operating in Virginia, Lincoln "felt that we had reached the end of our rope on the plan of operations we had been pursuing." The President decided that military necessity demanded that he lay a "strong hand on the colored element" in order to weaken the stubbornly powerful Confederacy by threatening to free its black labor force. Although practical military considerations seemed paramount with Lincoln, other factors helped shape the famous proclamation, most notably the Constitution of the United States.

Unlike many politicians of his contentious generation, Lincoln rarely reached first for a copy of the Constitution when a political problem arose. He sought practical solutions first, but it did matter to him that these solutions square with the fundamental law of the land. Though in 1861 he thought the Constitution left no room for any presidential proclamation abolishing slave property (any such measure would be "dictatorship," he said), Lincoln came around to the view that it was possible for the commander in chief to issue a legal proclamation of emancipation as a military necessity. People who read closely his public letter of August 22, 1862, might have noticed, despite its generally discouraging tone in regard to the abolition of slavery, that Lincoln revealed for the first time a newfound belief that the Constitution would permit abolition as a means of saving the Union from destruction in war. The resulting proclamation, written, as Karl Marx noted, in the uninspiring language of a pettifogging lawyer, exempted areas of the Confederacy already under Union control: in Lincoln's view these did not require emancipation to bring about military victory. The President felt he had "no constitutional or legal justification" other than military necessity. To include areas under the proclamation where such a justification did not apply would put him "in the boundless field of absolutism."

The preliminary Emancipation Proclamation, issued September 22, 1862, threatened only to free slaves in those Southern states that persisted in rebellion against the national government one hundred days later, on January 1, 1863. Before that ominous deadline, Lincoln seems to have worried about precisely what the "will of God" pointed to as the outcome of this bloody human contest. Since youth Lincoln had been a philosophical fatalist, in the commonsense meaning of the term, and he now emphasized as much as ever his own impotence in the sweep of history. He nevertheless initiated what seemed like one last attempt to stave off what very few white persons, North or South, had desired in 1861: the immediate abolition of slavery in most of the United States. The President proposed to Congress on December 1, 1862, a constitutional amendment offering compensation to the masters of slaves in any state that adopted a program of emancipation to take effect by 1900, thirty-eight years in the future. No one took advantage of the offer.

However hesitant the steps taken toward it, the Emancipation Proclamation, once issued, gave Abraham Lincoln a solid claim on a worldwide reputation for statesmanship. The many limitations and fine points in the proclamation provided fuel for Lincoln's critics during the war and right into the present day, but while he lived, those critics were mostly conservatives who were not going to admire *any* policy that led to freeing black people. Likewise, in Lincoln's own day most political liberals—and, perhaps more important, most black people themselves—praised the proclamation. They noticed, as Marx did, that despite the dreary, legalistic language, the document carried genuinely "historic content." And the proclamation was nothing if not politically courageous. In a confidential letter of rather dispirited tone, Lincoln told his vice president, Hannibal Hamlin, who had written to congratulate him on the proclamation, that after almost a week's trial the only effects had been to depress the stock market and cause volunteering for service in the armies to diminish. "The North responds to the proclamation sufficiently in breath," Lincoln complained with a rare touch of bitterness, "but breath alone kills no rebels."

If the President appeared to lack confidence in his proclamation at first, he gained it steadily thereafter. And this was but part of a general growth in assurance as Lincoln handled the difficult tasks of office in 1862 and 1863. Readers will detect this confidence in his surer voice in the selections that follow, as historians find it in his deft handling of political problems in this period. When, for example, Lincoln felt compelled to remind a general (Joseph Hooker) that he knew of his mutterings of the country's need for a dictator, he wrote a letter so adroitly phrased that the red-faced and blustering soldier's gentle reaction was to characterize the reprimand as "just such a letter as a 'father might write to his son.' "

Lincoln could be tough, too. Two days after he issued the preliminary Emancipation Proclamation, the President also suspended the writ of habeas corpus across the whole United States and stipulated that civilians could be tried by military courts. Emancipation proved so startling to the American public that this sweeping restriction of civil liberties went virtually unnoticed at first. But the arrest of a prominent leader of the Democratic opposition, Clement Vallandigham of Ohio, in May 1863, brought extensive public protests. Lincoln defended his policy in a public letter of June 12, 1863. The effect of this defense of the administration's unpopular and potentially embarrassing willingness to allow the military to arrest thousands of civilians without charge was evidently potent. The letter probably convinced none of the opposition party, of course, but it reassured doubters in Lincoln's own party and it further embellished the President's increasingly forceful image. Unlike his first defense of the policy, made back on July 4, 1861, this one had the common touch, and the phrase about the simpleminded soldier boy and the wily agitator has often been quoted. Close readers of the President's statements would have seen in his June 29, 1863, defense of the same policy not only a forceful personality but a statesman with quite expansive views of executive power in wartime: Lincoln still thought the president was "the man who holds the power," though a friendly Congress, dominated by Republicans since secession, had passed a bill the previous spring purportedly legalizing the very power Lincoln now claimed to have held all along.

One thing still eluded Lincoln's grasp: decisive military victory in the Civil War. Even by the late autumn of 1863, his armies in the East—the ones most watched by Lincoln and by world opinion—had merely halted their string of losses to Confederate armies of inferior size. At most, Union armies in the East could claim only to have repelled invasions of the North by the South on two occasions. The first of these successes, the bloody Battle of Antietam of September 17, 1862, cost more American lives than any other single day in the war but turned back General Robert E. Lee's invasion of Maryland. The second, the Battle of Gettysburg of July 1–3, 1863, inflicting terrible casualties on Lee's army, turned back an invasion of Pennsylvania. In the western theater, Union armies were more successful, driving deep into Confederate territory and cutting off all of the Confederacy west of the Mississippi River by gaining military control of the river with the fall of Vicksburg on July 4, 1863.

Lincoln could not yet foresee victory. Military force had not been able to deny the Confederacy's claim to nationhood, though its borders were shrinking. Until that question was settled, Lincoln's mission remained incomplete. But despite his seeming uncertainty about God's will, Lincoln occasionally spoke in 1862 and 1863 as though he had a clear sense of that mission: "In *giving* freedom to the *slave,* we *assure* freedom to the *free*—honorable alike in what we give, and what we preserve. We shall nobly save, or meanly lose, the last best, hope of earth."

→>> <<←

"THE PRINCIPLE OF THE EQUAL RIGHTS OF MEN"

Greetings to the Minister from Peru, the White House

[MARCH 4, 1862]

Like most of Lincoln's remarks and replies to visiting diplomats, these greetings may have been drafted by Secretary of State Seward. But it was Lincoln who personally delivered them when Federico Barreda arrived at the White House—on the day of Lincoln's first anniversary as president—to present his credentials as the new minister to the United States from Peru.

The United States have no enmities, animosities, or rivalries, and no interests which conflict with the welfare, safety and rights or interests of any other nation. Their own prosperity, happiness and aggrandizement are sought most safely and advantageously through the preservation, not only of peace on their own part, but peace among all other nations. But while the United States are thus a friend to all other nations, they do not seek to conceal the fact that they cherish especial sentiments of friendship for, and sympathies with, those who, like themselves, have founded their institutions on the principle of the equal rights of men; and such nations, being more prominently neighbors of the United States, the latter are co-operating with them in establishing civilization and culture on the American continent. Such being the general principles which govern the United States in their foreign relations, you may be assured, sir, that in all things this government will deal justly, frankly, and, if it be possible, even liberally, with Peru, whose liberal sentiments towards us you have so kindly expressed.

"GRADUAL ... EMANCIPATION, IS BETTER FOR ALL"

Message to Congress

[MARCH 6, 1862]

Lincoln hoped the loyal slave states could be encouraged to launch a program of voluntary, compensated emancipation. This message to Congress on the subject also contained a thinly veiled warning of what might yet be imposed on the disloyal states—involuntarily—if the war went on.

Fellow-citizens of the Senate, and House of Representatives,

I recommend the adoption of a Joint Resolution by your honorable bodies which shall be substantially as follows:

"Resolved that the United States ought to co-operate with any state which may adopt gradual abolishment of slavery, giving to such state pecuniary aid, to be used by such state in it's discretion, to compensate for the inconveniences public and private, produced by such change of system."

If the proposition contained in the resolution does not meet the approval of Congress and the country, there is the end; but if it does command such approval, I deem it of importance that the states and people immediately interested, should be at once distinctly notified of the fact, so that they may begin to consider whether to accept or reject it. The federal government would find it's highest interest in such a measure, as one of the most efficient means of self-preservation. The leaders of the existing insurrection entertain the hope that this government will ultimately be forced to acknowledge the independence of some part of the disaffected region, and that all the slave states North of such part will then say "the Union, for which we have struggled, being already gone, we now choose to go with the Southern section." To deprive them of this hope, substantially ends the rebellion; and the initiation of emancipation completely deprives them of it, as to all the states initiating it. The point is not that *all* the states tolerating slavery would very soon, if at all, initiate emancipation; but that, while the offer is equally made to all, the more Northern shall, by such initiation, make it certain to the more Southern, that in no event, will the former ever join the latter, in their proposed confederacy. I say "initiation" because, in my judgment, gradual, and not sudden emancipation, is better for all. In the mere financial, or pecuniary view, any member of Congress, with the census-tables and Treasury-reports before him, can readily see for himself how very soon the current expenditures of this war would purchase, at fair valuation, all the slaves in any named State. Such a proposition, on the part of the general government, sets up no claim of a right, by federal authority, to interfere with slavery within state limits, referring, as it does, the absolute control of the subject, in each case, to the state and it's people, immediately interested. It is proposed as a matter of perfectly free choice with them.

In the annual message last December, I thought fit to say "The Union must be preserved; and hence all indispensable means must be employed." I said this, not hastily, but deliberately. War has been made, and continues to be, an indispensable means to this end. A practical re-acknowledgement of the national authority would render the war unnecessary, and it would at once cease. If, however, resistance continues, the war must also continue; and it is impossible to foresee all the incidents, which may attend and all the ruin which may follow it. Such as may seem indispensable, or may obviously promise great efficiency towards ending the struggle, must and will come.

The proposition now made, though an offer only, I hope it may be esteemed no offence to ask whether the pecuniary consideration tendered would not be of more value to the States and private persons concerned, than are the institution, and property in it, in the present aspect of affairs.

While it is true that the adoption of the proposed resolution would be merely initiatory, and not within itself a practical measure, it is recommended in the hope that it would soon lead to important practical results. In full view of my great responsibility to my God, and to my country, I earnestly beg the attention of Congress and the people to the subject.

ABRAHAM LINCOLN

"GOVERNMENT WAS SAVED
FROM OVERTHROW"

From a Message to the Senate and House of Representatives

[MAY 26, 1862]

On April 30, the House passed a resolution censuring outgoing secretary of war Simon Cameron for having given New Yorker Alexander Cummings unrestricted authority to use public money to buy emergency military supplies in the early days of the Rebellion. Refusing to allow Cameron to take the blame for a decision for which he felt "equally responsible," Lincoln sent a message to Congress recounting those days of crisis, when he had to choose between letting "the government fall at once into ruin" or "availing myself of the broader powers conferred by the Constitution in cases of insurrection. . . ." In this extract from the message, he defends some of his actions.

The several departments of the government at that time contained so large a number of disloyal persons that it would have been impossible to provide safely, through official agents only, for the performance of the duties thus confided to citizens favorably known for their ability, loyalty, and patriotism.

The several orders issued upon these occurrences were transmitted by private messengers, who pursued a circuitous way to the seaboard cities, inland, across the States of Pennsylvania and Ohio and the northern lakes. I believe that by these and other similar measures taken in that crisis, some of which were without any authority of law, the government was saved from overthrow. I am not aware that a dollar of the public funds thus confided without authority of law to unofficial persons was either lost or wasted, although apprehensions of such misdirection occurred to me as objections to those extraordinary proceedings, and were necessarily overruled.

"OUR COMMON COUNTRY IS IN GREAT PERIL"

From an Appeal to Border State Representatives on Compensated Emancipation, the White House

[JULY 12, 1862]

Eager to promote his plan for voluntary emancipation, Lincoln summoned to the White House a delegation of border state congressmen and senators, and read this formal appeal to them. (As early as 1861 he had personally drafted a bill for compensated emancipation in the border state of Delaware, although its state legislature never considered it.) Two days after this appeal, a majority voted to reject Lincoln's proposal. In ten days, Lincoln would reveal to his cabinet his Emancipation Proclamation.

Gentlemen. After the adjournment of Congress, now very near, I shall have no opportunity of seeing you for several months. Believing that you of the border-states hold more power for good than any other equal numbers of members, I feel it a duty which I can not justifiably waive, to make this appeal to you. I intend no reproach or complaint when I assure you that in my opinion, if you all had voted for the resolution in the gradual emancipation message of last March, the war would now be substantially ended. And the plan therein proposed is yet one of the most potent, and swift means of ending it. Let the states which are in rebellion see, definitely and certainly, that, in no event, will the states you represent ever join their proposed Confederacy, and they can not, much longer maintain the contest. But you can not divest them of their hope to ultimately have you with them so long as you show a determination to perpetuate the institution within your own states. Beat them at elections, as you have overwhelmingly done, and, nothing daunted, they still claim you as their own. You and I know what the lever of their power is. Break that lever before their faces, and they can shake you no more forever.

Most of you have treated me with kindness and consideration; and I trust you will not now think I improperly touch what is exclusively your own, when, for the sake of the whole country I ask "Can you, for your states, do better than to take the course I urge?["] Discarding *punctillio,* and maxims adapted to more manageable times, and looking only to the unprecedentedly stern facts of our case, can you do better in any possible event? You prefer that the constitutional relation of the states to the nation shall be practically restored, without disturbance of the institution; and if this were done, my whole duty, in this respect, under the constitution, and my oath of office, would be performed. But it is not done, and we are trying to accomplish it by war. The incidents of the war can not be avoided. If the war continue long, as it must, if the object be not sooner attained, the institution in your states will be extinguished by mere friction and abrasion—by the mere incidents of the war. It will be gone, and you will have nothing valuable in lieu of it. Much of it's value is gone already. How much better for you, and for your people, to take the step which, at once, shortens the war, and secures substantial compensation for that which is sure to be wholly lost in any other event. How much better to thus save the money which else we sink forever in the war. How much better to do it while we can, lest the war ere long render us pecuniarily unable to do it. How much better for you, as seller, and the nation as buyer, to sell out, and buy out, that without which the war could never have been, than to sink both the thing to be sold, and the price of it, in cutting one another's throats.

I do not speak of emancipation *at once,* but of a *decision* at once to emancipate *gradually.* Room in South America for colonization, can be obtained cheaply, and in abundance; and when numbers shall be large enough to be company and encouragement for one another, the freed people will not be so reluctant to go. . . .

. . . You are patriots and statesmen; and, as such, I pray you, consider this proposition; and, at the least, commend it to the consideration of your states and people. As you would perpetuate popular government for the best people in the world, I beseech you that you do in no wise omit this. Our common country is in great peril, demanding the loftiest views, and boldest action to bring it speedy relief. Once relieved, it's form of government is saved to the world; it's beloved history, and cherished memories, are vindicated; and it's happy future fully assured, and rendered inconceivably grand. To you, more than to any others, the privilege is given, to assure that happiness, and swell that grandeur, and to link your own names therewith forever.

"A FIT AND NECESSARY MILITARY MEASURE"

First Draft of the Emancipation Proclamation

[JULY 22, 1862]

President Lincoln first read this initial draft of his Emancipation Proclamation at a momentous cabinet meeting which artist Francis B. Carpenter later apotheosized as "a scene second only in historical importance and interest to that of the Declaration of Independence." Even so, the meeting failed to produce a publicly announced proclamation, because Lincoln's ministers convinced him there to defer it. Postmaster General Blair, for one, argued that it would jeopardize pro-Lincoln candidates in upcoming elections. And Secretary of State Seward warned that the proclamation would be viewed as the government's "last shriek, on the retreat" if it was announced without a Union battlefield victory to back it up. "I do not want to issue a document that the whole world . . . must necessarily see as inoperative, like the Pope's bull against the comet," Lincoln conceded. He tabled the document, labeling this draft "Emancipation Proclamation as first sketched and shown to the Cabinet in July 1862." Three days later he did issue the first paragraph only as a proclamation to suppress insurrection. The Emancipation Proclamation would not be reconsidered for nearly two months.

In pursuance of the sixth section of the act of congress entitled "An act to suppress insurrection and to punish treason and rebellion, to seize and confiscate property of rebels, and for other purposes" Approved July 17. 1862, and which act, and the Joint Resolution explanatory thereof, are herewith published, I, Abraham Lincoln, President of the United States, do hereby proclaim to, and warn all persons within the contemplation of said sixth section to cease participating in, aiding, countenancing, or abetting the existing rebellion, or any rebellion against the government of the United States, and to return to their proper allegiance to the United States, on pain of the forfeitures and seizures, as within and by said sixth section provided.

And I hereby make known that it is my purpose, upon the next meeting of congress, to again recommend the adoption of a practical measure for tendering pecuniary aid to the free choice or rejection, of any and all States which may then be recognizing and practically sustaining the authority of the United States, and which may then have voluntarily adopted, or thereafter may voluntarily adopt, gradual abolishment of slavery within such State or States—that the object is to practically restore, thenceforward to be maintain[ed], the constitutional relation between the general government, and each, and all the states, wherein that relation is now suspended, or disturbed; and that, for this object, the war, as it has been, will be, prossecuted. And, as a fit and necessary military measure for effecting this object, I, as Commander-in-Chief of the Army and Navy of the United States, do order and declare that on the first day of January in the year of Our Lord one thousand, eight hundred and sixtythree, all persons held as slaves within any state or states, wherein the constitutional authority of the

United States shall not then be practically recognized, submitted to, and maintained, shall then, thenceforward, and forever, be free.

"YOUR RACE ARE SUFFERING"

From an Address on Colonization to a Committee of Black Leaders, the White House

[AUGUST 14, 1862]

In the precise language of the lawyer and the vague tone of a master politician, Lincoln here urged a delegation of black leaders to take advantage of $600,000 in congressional appropriations to fund colonization in Africa and the Caribbean. Lincoln did not fully abandon his interest in emigration of freed slaves until 1863 or 1864, even though he spent only $38,000 of the available money. Although historians have long debated the President's personal inclinations on the issue, some suggesting that he saw colonization as a necessary postscript to emancipation, his parsimony may suggest he never fully embraced the racist colonization scheme, but merely used it to calm white fears of postwar "amalgamation"—the antebellum term for interracial marriage. Besides, unknown to the White House visitors to whom he read this message, Lincoln had already drafted an Emancipation Proclamation.

Perhaps you have long been free, or all your lives. Your race are suffering, in my judgment, the greatest wrong inflicted on any people. But even when you cease to be slaves, you are yet far removed from being placed on an equality with the white race. You are cut off from many of the advantages which the other race enjoy. The aspiration of men is to enjoy equality with the best when free, but on this broad continent, not a single man of your race is made the equal of a single man of ours. Go where you are treated the best, and the ban is still upon you.

I do not propose to discuss this, but to present it as a fact with which we have to deal. I cannot alter it if I would. It is a fact, about which we all think and feel alike, I and you. We look to our condition, owing to the existence of the two races on this continent. I need not recount to you the effects upon white men, growing out of the institution of Slavery. I believe in its general evil effects on the white race. See our present condition—the country engaged in war!—our white men cutting one another's throats, none knowing how far it will extend; and then consider what we know to be the truth. But for your race among us there could not be war, although many men engaged on either side do not care for you one way or the other. Nevertheless, I repeat, without the institution of Slavery and the colored race as a basis, the war could not have an existence.

It is better for us both, therefore, to be separated. I know that there are free men among you, who even if they could better their condition are not as much inclined to go out of the country as those, who being slaves could obtain their freedom on this condition. I suppose one of the principal difficulties in the way of colonization is that the free colored man cannot see that his comfort would be advanced by it. You may believe you can live in Washington or elsewhere in the United States the remainder of your life [as easily], perhaps more so than you can in any foreign country, and hence you may come to the conclusion that you have nothing to do with the idea of going to a foreign country. This is (I speak in no unkind sense) an extremely selfish view of the case.

. . . There is much to encourage you. For the sake of your race you should sacrifice something of your present comfort for the purpose of being as grand in that respect as the white people. It is a cheering thought throughout life that something can be done to ameliorate the condition of those who have been subject to the hard usage of the world. It is difficult to make a man miserable while he feels he is worthy of himself, and claims kindred to the great God who made him . . .

"My Paramount Object in This Struggle"

Reply to Horace Greeley's "Prayer of Twenty Millions"

[AUGUST 22, 1862]

A New York Tribune *editorial by its editor, Horace Greeley, had charged Lincoln with being "strangely and disastrously remiss" in not more aggressively pursuing emancipation. Although he had already determined to issue an Emancipation Proclamation—waiting only for the right moment to make it public—Lincoln evidently saw in a response to the editorial a useful opportunity to nurture support for his forthcoming edict in terms of saving the Union, rather than of compassion.*

Executive Mansion,
Washington, August 22, 1862.

Hon. Horace Greely:

Dear Sir

I have just read yours of the 19th. addressed to myself through the New-York Tribune. If there be in it any statements, or assumptions of fact, which I may know to be erroneous, I do not, now and here, controvert them. If there be in it any inferences which I may believe to be falsely drawn, I do not, now and here, argue against them. If there be perceptable in it an impatient and dictatorial tone, I waive it in deference to an old friend, whose heart I have always supposed to be right.

As to the policy I "seem to be pursuing" as you say, I have not meant to leave any one in doubt.

I would save the Union. I would save it the shortest way under the Constitution. The sooner the national authority can be restored; the nearer the Union will be "the Union as it was." If there be those who would not save the Union, unless they could at the same time *save* slavery, I do not agree with them. If there be those who would not save the Union unless they could at the same time *destroy* slavery, I do not agree with them. My paramount object in this struggle *is* to save the

Union, and is *not* either to save or to destroy slavery. If I could save the Union without freeing *any* slave I would do it, and if I could save it by freeing *all* the slaves I would do it; and if I could save it by freeing some and leaving others alone I would also do that. What I do about slavery, and the colored race, I do because I believe it helps to save the Union; and what I forbear, I forbear because I do *not* believe it would help to save the Union. I shall do *less* whenever I shall believe what I am doing hurts the cause, and I shall do *more* whenever I shall believe doing more will help the cause. I shall try to correct errors when shown to be errors; and I shall adopt new views so fast as they shall appear to be true views.

I have here stated my purpose according to my view of *official* duty; and I intend no modification of my oft-expressed *personal* wish that all men every where could be free. Yours,

A. LINCOLN

"GOD WILLS THIS CONTEST"

Meditation on the Divine Will

[SEPTEMBER 2, 1862?]

Lincoln never joined a church, but his son Willie's tragic death in February 1862 propelled him toward deeper thought about divine providence. He was careful not to claim that God favored the Union, as this fragment shows. Besides, he wrote it soon after the Second Battle of Bull Run, a major Union defeat.

The will of God prevails. In great contests each party claims to act in accordance with the will of God. Both *may* be, and one *must* be wrong. God can not be *for,* and *against* the same thing at the same time. In the present civil war it is quite possible that God's purpose is something different from the purpose of either party—and yet human instrumentalities, working just as they do, are of the best adaptation to effect His purpose. I am almost ready to say this is probably true—that God wills this contest, and wills that it shall not end yet. By this mere quiet power, on the minds of the now contestants, He could have either *saved* or *destroyed* the Union without a human contest. Yet the contest began. And having begun He could give the final victory to either side any day. Yet the contest proceeds.

"THE TIME HAS COME NOW"

Remarks at Cabinet Meeting, the White House

[SEPTEMBER 22, 1862]

On September 17, Union forces turned back the Confederate army at Antietam. At a cabinet meeting five days later, after reading aloud a chapter from a humorous book, Lincoln told his ministers he intended to issue an Emancipation Proclamation forthwith. The remarks of the President that follow were recorded by Secretary of the Treasury Salmon P. Chase. Another cabinet diarist, Navy Secretary Gideon Welles, remembered Lincoln saying he "made a vow, a covenant, that if God gave us victory in the approaching battle, he would consider it an indicator of God's will," adding: "God decided the question in favor of the slaves."

Gentlemen: I have, as you are aware, thought a great deal about the relation of this war to Slavery; and you all remember that, several weeks ago, I read to you an Order I had prepared on this subject, which, on account of objections made by some of you, was not issued. Ever since then, my mind has been much occupied with this subject, and I have thought all along that the time for acting on it might very probably come. I think the time has come now. I wish it were a better time. I wish that we were in a better condition. The action of the army against the rebels has not been quite what I should have best liked. But they have been driven out of Maryland, and Pennsylvania is no longer in danger of invasion. When the rebel army was at Frederick, I determined, as soon as it should be driven out of Maryland, to issue a Proclamation of Emancipation such as I thought most likely to be useful. I said nothing to any one; but I made the promise to myself, and (hesitating a little)—to my Maker. The rebel army is now driven out, and I am going to fulfill that promise. I have got you together to hear what I have written down. I do not wish your advice about the main matter—for that I have determined for myself. This I say without intending any thing but respect for any one of you. But I already know the views of each on this question. They have been heretofore expressed, and I have considered them as thoroughly and carefully as I can. What I have written is that which my reflections have determined me to say. If there is anything in the expressions I use, or in any other minor matter, which anyone of you thinks had best be changed, I shall be glad to receive the suggestions. One other observation I will make. I know very well that many others might, in this matter, as in others, do better than I can; and if I were satisfied that the public confidence was more fully possessed by any one of them than by me, and knew of any Constitutional way in which he could be put in my place, he should have it. I would gladly yield it to him. But though I believe that I have not so much of the confidence of the people as I had some time since, I do not know that, all things considered, any other person has more; and, however this may be, there is no way in which I can have any other man put where I am. I am here. I must do the best I can, and bear the responsibility of taking the course which I feel I ought to take.

"THENCEFORWARD, AND FOREVER FREE"

Preliminary Emancipation Proclamation

[SEPTEMBER 22, 1862]

The proclamation was in the form of a warning to Southerners to end the rebellion by "a hundred days fair notice," as Lincoln later put it, or face the confiscation of their slave property "forever." Americans today tend to take the proclamation for granted, focusing on the fact that it addressed slavery only where Lincoln had no enforceable authority. But Lincoln limited its scope to areas still in rebellion, because he justified the measure as an exercise of his war power. Contemporaries viewed it as genuinely revolutionary, as press coverage makes clear. "No event in the history of this country since the Declaration of Independence itself," one newspaper said, "has exacted so profound attention." Critics, meanwhile, expressed "alarm and dismay," with a Richmond paper branding the President "Coward, assassin, savage. . . ."

By the President of the United States of America

A Proclamation.

I, Abraham Lincoln, President of the United States of America, and Commander-in-chief of the Army and Navy thereof, do hereby proclaim and declare that hereafter, as heretofore, the war will be prosecuted for the object of practically restoring the constitutional relation between the United States, and each of the states, and the people thereof, in which states that relation is, or may be suspended, or disturbed.

That it is my purpose, upon the next meeting of Congress to again recommend the adoption of a practical measure tendering pecuniary aid to the free acceptance or rejection of all slave-states, so called, the people whereof may not then be in rebellion against the United States, and which states, may then have voluntarily adopted, or thereafter may voluntarily adopt, immediate, or gradual abolishment of slavery within their respective limits; and that the effort to colonize persons of African descent, with their consent, upon this continent, or elsewhere, with the previously obtained consent of the Governments existing there, will be continued.

That on the first day of January in the year of our Lord, one thousand eight hundred and sixty-three, all persons held as slaves within any state, or designated part of a state, the people whereof shall then be in rebellion against the United States shall be then, thenceforward, and forever free; and the executive government of the United States, including the military and naval authority thereof, will recognize and maintain the freedom of such persons, and will do no act or acts to repress such persons, or any of them, in any efforts they may make for their actual freedom.

That the executive will, on the first day of January aforesaid, by proclamation, designate the States, and parts of states, if any, in which the people thereof respectively, shall then be in rebellion against the United States; and the fact that any state, or the people thereof shall, on that day be, in good faith represented in the Congress of the United States, by members chosen thereto, at elections wherein a majority of the qualified voters of such state shall have participated, shall, in the absence of strong countervailing testimony, be deemed conclusive evidence that such state and the people thereof, are not then in rebellion against the United States.

That attention is hereby called to an act of Congress entitled "An act to make an additional Article of War" approved March 13, 1862, and which act is in the words and figure following:

Be it enacted by the Senate and House of Representatives of the United States of America in Congress assembled, That hereafter the following shall be promulgated as an additional article of war for the government of the army of the United States, and shall be obeyed and observed as such:

Article—. All officers or persons in the military or naval service of the United States are prohibited from employing any of the forces under their respective commands for the purpose of returning fugitives from service or labor, who may have escaped from any persons to whom such service or labor is claimed to be due, and any officer who shall be found guilty by a court-martial of violating this article shall be dismissed from the service.

Sec. 2. *And be it further enacted,* That this act shall take effect from and after its passage.

Also to the ninth and tenth sections of an act entitled "An Act to suppress Insurrection, to punish Treason and Rebellion, to seize and confiscate property of rebels, and for other purposes," approved July 17, 1862, and which sections are in the words and figures following:

Sec. 9. *And be it further enacted,* That all slaves of persons who shall hereafter be engaged in rebellion against the government of the United States, or who shall in any way give aid or comfort thereto, escaping from such persons and taking refuge within the lines of the army; and all slaves captured from such persons or deserted by them and coming under the control of the government of the United States; and all slaves of such persons found *on* (or) being within any place occupied by rebel forces and afterwards occupied by the forces of the United States, shall be deemed captives of war, and shall be forever free of their servitude and not again held as slaves.

Sec. 10. *And be it further enacted,* That no slave escaping into any State, Territory, or the District of Columbia, from any other State, shall be delivered up, or in any way impeded or hindered of his liberty, except for crime, or some offence against the laws, unless the person claiming said fugitive shall first make oath that the person to whom the labor or service of such fugitive is alleged to be due is his lawful owner, and has not borne arms against the United States in the present rebellion, nor in any way given aid and comfort thereto; and no person engaged in the military or naval service of the United States shall, under any pretence whatever, assume to decide on the validity of the claim of any person to the service or labor of any other person, or surrender up any such person to the claimant, on pain of being dismissed from the service.

And I do hereby enjoin upon and order all persons engaged in the military and naval service of the United States to observe, obey, and enforce, within their respective spheres of service, the act, and sections above recited.

And the executive will in due time recommend that all citizens of the United States who shall have remained loyal thereto throughout the

rebellion, shall (upon the restoration of the constitutional relation between the United States, and their respective states, and people, if that
relation shall have been suspended or disturbed) be compensated for all
losses by acts of the United States, including the loss of slaves.

    In witness whereof, I have hereunto set my hand, and caused
the seal of the United States to be affixed.

    Done at the City of Washington, this twenty second day of
September, in the year of our Lord, one thousand eight hundred
and sixty two, and of the Independence of the United States, the
eighty seventh.

By the President: ABRAHAM LINCOLN
    WILLIAM H. SEWARD, Secretary of State.

"TO SUPPRESS THE INSURRECTION"

Proclamation Suspending the Writ of Habeas Corpus

[SEPTEMBER 24, 1862]

*Only two days after issuing one proclamation promising a new freedom,
Lincoln issued another suppressing an old one—suspending the privilege
of the writ of habeas corpus nationwide. Among the "arbitrary arrests"
it triggered were those of spies and traitors, but also political foes. Lincoln's suspension of the writ was his most controversial decision—it
earned him from some the label of tyrant—but he insisted that without
the suspension, habeas corpus would have been saved but the country
would have been destroyed. Congress validated the suspension in March
1863 and Lincoln issued yet another, broader presidential suspension that
September.*

By the President of the United States of America:

A Proclamation.

Whereas, it has become necessary to call into service not only volunteers but also portions of the militia of the States by draft in order to suppress the insurrection existing in the United States, and disloyal persons are not adequately restrained by the ordinary processes of law from hindering this measure and from giving aid and comfort in various ways to the insurrection;

Now, therefore, be it ordered, first, that during the existing insurrection and as a necessary measure for suppressing the same, all Rebels and Insurgents, their aiders and abettors within the United States, and all persons discouraging volunteer enlistments, resisting militia drafts, or guilty of any disloyal practice, affording aid and comfort to Rebels against the authority of the United States, shall be subject to martial law and liable to trial and punishment by Courts Martial or Military Commission:

Second. That the Writ of Habeas Corpus is suspended in respect to all persons arrested, or who are now, or hereafter during the rebellion shall be, imprisoned in any fort, camp, arsenal, military prison, or other place of confinement by any military authority or by the sentence of any Court Martial or Military Commission.

In witness whereof, I have hereunto set my hand, and caused the seal of the United States to be affixed.

Done at the City of Washington this twenty fourth day of September, in the year of our Lord one thousand eight hundred and sixty-two, and of the Independence of the United States the 87th.

By the President: ABRAHAM LINCOLN.

WILLIAM H. SEWARD, Secretary of State.

"BREATH ALONE KILLS NO REBELS"

Letter to Vice President Hannibal Hamlin

[SEPTEMBER 28, 1862]

On September 25 the vice president sent Lincoln his "sincere thanks for your Emancipation Proclamation," adding: "It will stand as the great act of the age. It will prove to be wise in statesmanship as it is patriotic. It will be enthusiastically approved and sustained, and future generations will, as I do, say God bless you for this great and noble act." But his confidential reply revealed a Lincoln far from certain about the enthusiastic approval of his countrymen. Six days after the proclamation was issued, Lincoln was clearly worried about his action—revealing both uncertainty and surprising vulnerability in this frank letter.

(*Strictly private.*)

Executive Mansion,
Washington, September 28, 1862.

My Dear Sir:

Your kind letter of the 25th is just received. It is known to some that while I hope something from the proclamation, my expectations are not as sanguine as are those of some friends. The time for its effect southward has not come; but northward the effect should be instantaneous.

It is six days old, and while commendation in newspapers and by distinguished individuals is all that a vain man could wish, the stocks have declined, and troops come forward more slowly than ever. This, looked soberly in the face, is not very satisfactory. We have fewer troops in the field at the end of six days than we had at the beginning—the attrition among the old outnumbering the addition by the new. The North responds to the proclamation sufficiently in breath; but breath alone kills no rebels.

I wish I could write more cheerfully; nor do I thank you the less for the kindness of your letter. Yours very truly,

A. LINCOLN.

"A FIERY TRIAL"

Reply to a Quaker Prayer
[OCTOBER 26, 1862]

Eliza P. Gurney, wife of an English Quaker leader, visited the White House to pray for wisdom "from on high" for the President. Lincoln responded with this declaration of faith, which was transcribed by an eyewitness.

I am glad of this interview, and glad to know that I have your sympathy and prayers. We are indeed going through a great trial—a fiery trial. In the very responsible position in which I happen to be placed, being a humble instrument in the hands of our Heavenly Father, as I am, and as we all are, to work out his great purposes, I have desired that all my works and acts may be according to his will, and that it might be so, I have sought his aid—but if after endeavoring to do my best in the light which he affords me, I find my efforts fail, I must believe that for some purpose unknown to me, He wills it otherwise. If I had had my way, this war would never have been commenced; If I had been allowed my way this war would have been ended before this, but we find it still continues; and we must believe that He permits it for some wise purpose of his own, mysterious and unknown to us; and though with our limited understandings we may not be able to comprehend it, yet we cannot but believe, that he who made the world still governs it.

"WE CANNOT ESCAPE HISTORY"

From the Annual Message to Congress

[DECEMBER 1, 1862]

With the Emancipation Proclamation due to take effect in rebellious states in a month, Lincoln devoted much of his second annual message to the issue of slavery in loyal states: a plan for compensated, gradual emancipation, and colonization of freedmen "with their own consent." The message ended with one of the most eloquent passages Lincoln ever composed.

Our national strife springs not from our permanent part; not from the land we inhabit; not from our national homestead. There is no possible severing of this, but would multiply, and not mitigate, evils among us. In all its adaptations and aptitudes, it demands union, and abhors separation. In fact, it would, ere long, force reunion, however much of blood and treasure the separation might have cost.

Our strife pertains to ourselves—to the passing generations of men; and it can, without convulsion, be hushed forever with the passing of one generation.

In this view, I recommend the adoption of the following resolution and articles amendatory to the Constitution of the United States.

"Resolved by the Senate and House of Representatives of the United States of America in Congress assembled, (two thirds of both houses concurring,) That the following articles be proposed to the legislatures (or conventions) of the several States as amendments to the Constitution of the United States, all or any of which articles when ratified by three-fourths of the said legislatures (or conventions) to be valid as part or parts of the said Constitution, viz:

"Article_____.

"Every State, wherein slavery now exists, which shall abolish the same therein, at any time, or times, before the first day of January, in the year of our Lord one thousand and nine hundred, shall receive compensation from the United States as follows, to wit:

"The President of the United States shall deliver to every such State, bonds of the United States, bearing interest at the rate of _____ per cent, per annum, to an amount equal to the aggregate sum of _____ for each slave shown to have been therein, by the eig[h]th census of the United States, said bonds to be delivered to such State by instalments, or in one parcel, at the completion of the abolishment, accordingly as the same shall have been gradual, or at one time, within such State; and interest shall begin to run upon any such bond, only from the proper time of its delivery as aforesaid. Any State having received bonds as aforesaid, and afterwards reintroducing or tolerating slavery therein, shall refund to the United States the bonds so received, or the value thereof, and all interest paid thereon.

"Article_____.

"All slaves who shall have enjoyed actual freedom by the chances of the war, at any time before the end of the rebellion, shall be forever free; but all owners of such, who shall not have been disloyal, shall be compensated for them, at the same rates as is provided for States adopting abolishment of slavery, but in such way, that no slave shall be twice accounted for.

"Article_____.

"Congress may appropriate money, and otherwise provide, for colonizing free colored persons, with their own consent, at any place or places without the United States."

I beg indulgence to discuss these proposed articles at some length. Without slavery the rebellion could never have existed; without slavery it could not continue.

Among the friends of the Union there is great diversity, of sentiment, and of policy, in regard to slavery, and the African race amongst us. Some would perpetuate slavery; some would abolish it suddenly, and without compensation; some would abolish it gradually, and with compensation; some would remove the freed people from us, and some would retain them with us; and there are yet other minor diversities. Because of these diversities, we waste much strength in struggles among ourselves. By mutual concession we should harmonize, and act together. This would be compromise; but it would be compromise among the friends, and not with the enemies of the Union. These articles are intended to embody a plan of such mutual concessions. If the plan shall be adopted, it is assumed that emancipation will follow, at least, in several of the States.

As to the first article, the main points are: first, the emancipation; secondly, the length of time for consummating it—thirty-seven years; and thirdly, the compensation.

The emancipation will be unsatisfactory to the advocates of perpetual slavery; but the length of time should greatly mitigate their dissatisfaction. The time spares both races from the evils of sudden derangement—in fact, from the necessity of any derangement—while most of those whose habitual course of thought will be disturbed by the measure will have passed away before its consummation. They will never see it. Another class will hail the prospect of emancipation, but will deprecate the length of time. They will feel that it gives too little to the now living slaves. But it really gives them much. It saves them from the vagrant destitution which must largely attend immediate emancipation in localities where their numbers are very great; and it gives the inspiring assurance that their posterity shall be free forever. The plan leaves to each State, choosing to act under it, to abolish slavery now, or at the end of the century, or at any intermediate time, or by degrees, extending over the whole or any part of the period; and it obliges no two states to proceed alike. It also provides for compensation, and generally the mode of making it. This, it would seem, must further mitigate the dissatisfaction of those who favor perpetual slavery, and especially of those who are to receive the compensation. Doubtless some of those who are to pay, and not to receive will object. Yet the measure is both just and economical. In a certain sense the liberation of slaves is the destruction of property—property acquired by descent, or by purchase, the same as any other property. It is no less true for having been often said, that the people of the south are not more responsible for the original introduction of this property, than are the people of the north; and when it is remembered how unhesitatingly we all use cotton and sugar, and share the profits of dealing in them, it may not be quite safe to say, that the south has been more responsible than the north for its continuance. If then, for a common object, this property is to be sacrificed is it not just that it be done at a common charge?

And if, with less money, or money more easily paid, we can preserve the benefits of the Union by this means, than we can by the war alone, is it not also economical to do it? Let us consider it then.

. . . .

As to the second article, I think it would be impracticable to return to bondage the class of persons therein contemplated. Some of them, doubtless, in the property sense, belong to loyal owners; and hence, provision is made in this article for compensating such.

The third article relates to the future of the freed people. It does not oblige, but merely authorizes, Congress to aid in colonizing such as may consent. This ought not to be regarded as objectionable, on the one hand, or on the other, in so much as it comes to nothing, unless by the mutual consent of the people to be deported, and the American voters, through their representatives in Congress.

I cannot make it better known than it already is, that I strongly favor colonization. And yet I wish to say there is an objection urged against free colored persons remaining in the country, which is largely imaginary, if not sometimes malicious.

It is insisted that their presence would injure, and displace white labor and white laborers. If there ever could be a proper time for mere catch arguments, that time surely is not now. In times like the present, men should utter nothing for which they would not willingly be responsible through time and in eternity. Is it true, then, that colored people can displace any more white labor, by being free, than by remaining slaves? If they stay in their old places, they jostle no white laborers; if they leave their old places, they leave them open to white laborers. Logically, there is neither more nor less of it. Emancipation, even without deportation, would probably enhance the wages of white labor, and, very surely, would not reduce them. Thus, the customary amount of labor would still have to be performed; the freed people would surely not do more than their old proportion of it, and very probably, for a time, would do less, leaving an increased part to white laborers, bringing their labor into greater demand, and, consequently, enhancing the wages of it. With deportation, even to a limited extent, enhanced wages to white labor is mathematically certain. Labor is like any other commodity in the market—increase the demand for it, and you increase the price of it. Reduce the supply of black labor, by colonizing the black laborer out of the country, and, by precisely so much, you increase the demand for, and wages of, white labor.

But it is dreaded that the freed people will swarm forth, and cover the whole land? Are they not already in the land? Will liberation make them any more numerous? Equally distributed among the whites of the whole country, and there would be but one colored to seven whites. Could the one, in any way, greatly disturb the seven? There are many communities now, having more than one free colored person, to seven whites; and this, without any apparent consciousness of evil from it. The District of Columbia, and the States of Maryland and Delaware, are all in this condition. The District has more than one free colored to six whites; and yet, in its frequent petitions to Congress, I believe it has never presented the presence of free colored persons as one of its grievances. But why should emancipation south, send the free people north? People, of any color, seldom run, unless there be something to run from. *Heretofore* colored people, to some extent, have fled north from bondage; and *now,* perhaps, from both bondage and destitution. But if gradual emancipation and deportation be adopted, they will have neither to flee from. Their old masters will give them wages at least until new laborers can be procured; and the freed men, in turn, will gladly give their labor for the wages, till new homes can be found for them, in congenial climes, and with people of their own blood and race.

. . . .

Is it doubted, then, that the plan I propose, if adopted, would shorten the war, and thus lessen its expenditure of money and of blood? Is it doubted that it would restore the national authority and national prosperity, and perpetuate both indefinitely? Is it doubted that we here— Congress and Executive—can secure its adoption? Will not the good people respond to a united, and earnest appeal from us? Can we, can they, by any other means, so certainly, or so speedily, assure these vital objects? We can succeed only by concert. It is not "can *any* of us *imagine* better?" but "can we *all* do better?" Object whatsoever is possible, still the question recurs "can we do better?" The dogmas of the quiet past, are inadequate to the stormy present. The occasion is piled high with difficulty, and we must rise with the occasion. As our case is new, so we must think anew, and act anew. We must disenthrall ourselves, and then we shall save our country.

Fellow-citizens, *we* cannot escape history. We of this Congress and this administration, will be remembered in spite of ourselves. No personal significance, or insignificance, can spare one or another of us. The fiery trial through which we pass, will light us down, in honor or dishonor, to the latest generation. We *say* we are for the Union. The world will not forget that we say this. We know how to save the Union. The world knows we do know how to save it. We—even *we here*—hold the power, and bear the responsibility. In *giving* freedom to the *slave,* we *assure* freedom to the *free*—honorable alike in what we give, and what we preserve. We shall nobly save, or meanly lose, the last best, hope of earth. Other means may succeed; this could not fail. The way is plain, peaceful, generous, just—a way which, if followed, the world will forever applaud, and God must forever bless.

ABRAHAM LINCOLN

"THE PROMISE MUST NOW BE KEPT"

*Informal Remarks to Witnesses at the Signing
of the Final Emancipation Proclamation, the White House*

[JANUARY 1, 1863]

Lincoln's remarks at the signing of the Emancipation Proclamation were reported by artist Francis B. Carpenter, who interviewed eyewitnesses when he worked in the White House for six months in 1864 to create a painting of Lincoln's first reading of the proclamation to his cabinet.

[The final Proclamation was signed on New Year's Day, 1863. The President remarked . . . the same evening, that the signature appeared somewhat tremulous and uneven.] "Not," said he, "because of any uncertainty or hesitation on my part; but it was just after the public reception, and three hours' hand-shaking is not calculated to improve a man's chirography." Then changing his tone, he added: "The South had fair warning, that if they did not return to their duty, I should strike at this pillar of their strength. The promise must now be kept, and I shall never recall one word. . . .

.   .   .   .

". . . I have been shaking hands since nine o'clock this morning, and my right arm is almost paralyzed. If my name ever goes into history it will be for this act, and my whole soul is in it. If my hand trembles when I sign the Proclamation, all who examine the document hereafter will say, 'He hesitated.' "

[He then turned to the table, took up the pen again, and slowly, firmly wrote that "Abraham Lincoln" with which the whole world is now familiar. He looked up, smiled, and said: "That will do."]

"SINCERELY BELIEVED TO BE . . . AN ACT OF JUSTICE"

Final Emancipation Proclamation

[JANUARY 1, 1863]

The final proclamation has been criticized for its legalistic prose. Historian Richard Hofstadter went so far as to complain that it had "all the moral grandeur of a bill of lading." But as historian LaWanda Cox has pointed out, Lincoln wanted to make sure blacks would be able to rely on a legally sound proclamation if their freedom was challenged later in the courts. As the New York Times *reported on New Year's Eve, the President felt blacks could best preserve their new liberty with "a proclamation proceeding as a war measure from the Commander-in-Chief of the Army . . . not one issuing from the bosom of philanthropy." Its legal language notwithstanding, the text of the proclamation was reproduced by several engravers and lithographers, and the results published as parlor decorations for the American home.*

By the President of the United States of America:

A Proclamation.

Whereas, on the twentysecond day of September, in the year of our Lord one thousand eight hundred and sixty two, a proclamation was issued by the President of the United States, containing, among other things, the following, towit:

"That on the first day of January, in the year of our Lord one thousand eight hundred and sixty-three, all persons held as slaves within any state or designated part of a State, the people whereof shall then be in rebellion against the United States, shall be then, thenceforward, and forever free; and the Executive Government of the United States, including the military and naval authority thereof, will recognize and maintain the freedom of such persons, and will do no act or acts to repress such persons, or any of them, in any efforts they may make for their actual freedom.

"That the Executive will, on the first day of January aforesaid, by proclamation, designate the States and parts of States, if any, in which the people thereof, respectively, shall then be in rebellion against the United States; and the fact that any State, or the people thereof, shall on that day be, in good faith, represented in the Congress of the United States by members chosen thereto at elections wherein a majority of the qualified voters of such State shall have participated, shall, in the absence of strong countervailing testimony, be deemed conclusive evidence that such State, and the people thereof, are not then in rebellion against the United States."

Now, therefore I, Abraham Lincoln, President of the United States, by virtue of the power in me vested as Commander-in-Chief of the Army and Navy of the United States in time of actual armed rebellion against authority and government of the United States, and as a fit and necessary war measure for suppressing said rebellion, do, on this first day of January, in the year of our Lord one thousand eight hundred and sixty three, and in accordance with my purpose so to do publicly proclaimed for the full period of one hundred days, from the day first above mentioned, order and designate as the States and parts of States wherein the people thereof respectively, are this day in rebellion against the United States, the following, towit:

Arkansas, Texas, Louisiana, (except the Parishes of St. Bernard, Plaquemines, Jefferson, St. Johns, St. Charles, St. James[,] Ascension, Assumption, Terrebonne, Lafourche, St. Mary, St. Martin, and Orleans, including the City of New-Orleans) Mississippi, Alabama, Florida, Georgia, South-Carolina, North-Carolina, and Virginia, (except the fortyeight counties designated as West Virginia, and also the counties of Berkley, Accomac, Northampton, Elizabeth-City, York, Princess Ann, and Norfolk, including the cities of Norfolk & Portsmouth[)]; and which excepted parts are, for the present, left precisely as if this proclamation were not issued.

And by virtue of the power, and for the purpose aforesaid, I do order and declare that all persons held as slaves within said designated States, and parts of States, are, and henceforward shall be free; and that the Executive government of the United States, including the military and naval authorities thereof, will recognize and maintain the freedom of said persons.

And I hereby enjoin upon the people so declared to be free to abstain from all violence, unless in necessary self-defence; and I recommend to them that, in all cases when allowed, they labor faithfully for reasonable wages.

And I further declare and make known, that such persons of suitable condition, will be received into the armed service of the United States to garrison forts, positions, stations, and other places, and to man vessels of all sorts in said service.

And upon this act, sincerely believed to be an act of justice, warranted by the Constitution, upon military necessity, I invoke the considerate judgment of mankind, and the gracious favor of Almighty God.

In witness whereof, I have hereunto set my hand and caused the seal of the United States to be affixed.

Done at the City of Washington, this first day of January, in the year of our Lord one thousand eight hundred and sixty three, and of the Independence of the United States of America the eighty-seventh.

By the President: ABRAHAM LINCOLN
WILLIAM H. SEWARD, Secretary of State.

"AN INSTANCE OF SUBLIME CHRISTIAN HEROISM"

Reply to the Workingmen of Manchester, England

[JANUARY 19, 1863]

England maintained a tenuous neutrality throughout the Civil War, even though disruption of its cotton imports shut down mills and forced people out of work. On New Year's Eve, a group of workingmen from Manchester, one affected city, agreed at a public meeting to "joyfully honor" Lincoln "for the many decisive steps towards practically exemplifying your belief in the words of your great founders, 'All men are created free and equal . . .'" This is Lincoln's grateful reply, forwarded to the American ambassador to the Court of St. James's.

Executive Mansion, Washington,
January 19, 1863.

To the workingmen of Manchester:

I have the honor to acknowledge the receipt of the address and resolutions which you sent to me on the eve of the new year.

When I came, on the fourth day of March, 1861, through a free and constitutional election, to preside in the government of the United States, the country was found at the verge of civil war. Whatever might have been the cause, or who[se]soever the fault, one duty paramount to all others was before me, namely, to maintain and preserve at once the Constitution and the integrity of the federal republic. A conscientious purpose to perform this duty is a key to all the measures of administration which have been, and to all which will hereafter be pursued. Under our form of government, and my official oath, I could not depart from this purpose if I would. It is not always in the power of governments to enlarge or restrict the scope of moral results which follow the policies that they may deem it necessary for the public safety, from time to time, to adopt.

I have understood well that the duty of self-preservation rests solely with the American people. But I have at the same time been aware that favor or disfavor of foreign nations might have a material influence in enlarging and prolonging the struggle with disloyal men in which the country is engaged. A fair examination of history has seemed to authorize a belief that the past action and influences of the United States were generally regarded as having been beneficent towards mankind. I have therefore reckoned upon the forbearance of nations. Circumstances, to some of which you kindly allude, induced me especially to expect that if justice and good faith should be practiced by the United States, they would encounter no hostile influence on the part of Great Britain. It is now a pleasant duty to acknowledge the demonstration you have given of your desire that a spirit of peace and amity towards this country may prevail in the councils of your Queen, who is respected and esteemed in your own country only more than she is by the kindred nation which has its home on this side of the Atlantic.

I know and deeply deplore the sufferings which the workingmen at Manchester and in all Europe are called to endure in this crisis. It has been often and studiously represented that the attempt to overthrow this government, which was built upon the foundation of human rights, and to substitute for it one which should rest exclusively on the basis of human slavery, was likely to obtain the favor of Europe. Through the actions of our disloyal citizens the workingmen of Europe have been subjected to a severe trial, for the purpose of forcing their sanction to that attempt. Under these circumstances, I cannot but regard your decisive utterance upon the question as an instance of sublime Christian heroism which has not been surpassed in any age or in any country. It is, indeed, an energetic and reinspiring assurance of the inherent power of truth and of the ultimate and universal triumph of justice, humanity, and freedom. I do not doubt that the sentiments you have expressed will be sustained by your great nation, and, on the other hand, I have no hesitation in assuring you that they will excite admiration, esteem, and the most reciprocal feelings of friendship among the American people. I hail this interchange of sentiment, therefore, as an augury that, whatever else may happen, whatever misfortune may befall your country or my own, the peace and friendship which now exist between the two nations will be, as it shall be my desire to make them, perpetual.

Abraham Lincoln.

"I WILL RISK THE DICTATORSHIP"

Letter to General Joseph Hooker

[JANUARY 26, 1863]

After a series of battlefield defeats, Lincoln named "Fighting Joe" Hooker to command the Union army in early 1863. Lincoln then heard that the general entertained Napoleonic ambitions. With this letter, he adroitly affirmed the civilian authority, making light of Hooker's alleged lust for dictatorship.

Executive Mansion,
Major General Hooker: Washington, January 26, 1863.

General.

I have placed you at the head of the Army of the Potomac. Of course I have done this upon what appear to me to be sufficient reasons. And yet I think it best for you to know that there are some things in regard to which, I am not quite satisfied with you. I believe you to be a brave and a skilful soldier, which, of course, I like. I also believe you do not mix politics with your profession, in which you are right. You have confidence in yourself, which is a valuable, if not an indispensable quality. You are ambitious, which, within reasonable bounds, does good rather than harm. But I think that during Gen. [Ambrose] Burnside's command of the Army, you have taken counsel of your ambition, and thwarted him as much as you could, in which you did a great wrong to the country, and to a most meritorious and honorable brother officer. I have heard, in such way as to believe it, of your recently saying that both the Army and the Government needed a Dictator. Of course it was not *for* this, but in spite of it, that I have given you the command. Only those generals who gain successes, can set up dictators. What I now ask of you is military success, and I will risk the dictatorship. The government will support you to the utmost of it's ability, which is neither more nor less than it has done and will do for all commanders. I much fear that the spirit which you have aided to infuse into the Army, of criticising their Commander, and withholding confidence from him, will now turn upon you. I shall assist you as far as I can, to put it down. Neither you, nor Napoleon, if he were alive again, could get any good out of an army, while such a spirit prevails in it.

And now, beware of rashness. Beware of rashness, but with energy, and sleepless vigilance, go forward, and give us victories. Yours very truly

A. LINCOLN

"RESIST . . . SUCH RECOGNITION"

Resolution Condemning Pro-Slavery Nations

[APRIL 15, 1863]

For much of his presidency, Lincoln worried that European nations would intervene in America's Civil War—on the side of the Confederacy. He drafted this resolution in the hope that it would be adopted at pro-Union meetings in England, and at the least influence the British government to remain neutral. Senator Charles Sumner, who was summoned to the White House to receive the resolution, forwarded it to John Bright, a pro-Lincoln member of British Parliament.

Whereas, while *heretofore,* States, and Nations, have tolerated slavery, *recently,* for the first [time] in the world, an attempt has been made to construct a new Nation, upon the basis of, and with the primary, and fundamental object to maintain, enlarge, and perpetuate human slavery, therefore,

Resolved, That no such embryo State should ever be recognized by, or admitted into, the family of christian and civilized nations; and that all ch[r]istian and civilized men everywhere should, by all lawful means, resist to the utmost, such recognition or admission.

"PUBLIC SAFETY DOES REQUIRE THE SUSPENSION"

From a Letter to Albany, New York, Democrats

[JUNE 12, 1863]

*In May, the army arrested former Ohio congressman Clement L. Valland-
igham, a leader of the so-called Copperheads—northern Democrats who
opposed the war and sympathized with the South. His seizure unleashed
angry protests from fellow Democrats throughout the country, including
one group from New York's capital city, Albany. Lincoln's detailed reply
suggested that without his tough action against Copperheads, the rebellion
might succeed. Historian James G. Randall called this "one of those
dignified, carefully worded statements addressed to a person or occasion,
but intended as a kind of state paper." Indeed, it was quickly published
in the press. Lincoln also read it to his cabinet, with Gideon Welles
responding that it had "vigor and ability." But Erastus Corning, to whom
it was addressed, found it "misty and clouded," a "monstrous heresy," and
"a plea for absolute power." The following excerpts are from Lincoln's
handwritten draft.*

Executive Mansion

Hon. Erastus Corning & others   Washington [June 12] 1863.

Gentlemen Your letter of May 19th. inclosing the resolutions of a
public meeting held at Albany, N.Y. on the 16th. of the same month,
was received several days ago.

. . . Prior to my instalation here it had been inculcated that any State
had a lawful right to secede from the national Union; and that it would
be expedient to exercise the right, whenever the devotees of the doctrine
should fail to elect a President to their own liking. I was elected contrary to their liking; and accordingly, so far as it was legally possible,
they had taken seven states out of the Union, had seized many of the
United States Forts, and had fired upon the United States' Flag, all
before I was inaugurated; and, of course, before I had done any official
act whatever. The rebellion, thus began soon ran into the present civil

war; and, in certain respects, it began on very unequal terms between the parties. The insurgents had been preparing for it more than thirty years, while the government had taken no steps to resist them. The former had carefully considered all the means which could be turned to their account. It undoubtedly was a well pondered reliance with them that in their own unrestricted effort to destroy Union, constitution, and law, all together, the government would, in great degree, be restrained by the same constitution and law, from arresting their progress. Their sympathizers pervaded all departments of the government, and nearly all communities of the people. From this material, under cover of "Liberty of speech" "Liberty of the press" and *"Habeas corpus"* they hoped to keep on foot amongst us a most efficient corps of spies, informers, supplyers, and aiders and abettors of their cause in a thousand ways. They knew that in times such as they were inaugerating, by the constitution itself, the "Habeas corpus" might be suspended; but they also knew they had friends who would make a question as to *who* was to suspend it; meanwhile their spies and others might remain at large to help on their cause. Or if, as has happened, the executive should suspend the writ, without ruinous waste of time, instances of arresting innocent persons might occur, as are always likely to occur in such cases; and then a clamor could be raised in regard to this, which might be, at least, of some service to the insurgent cause. It needed no very keen perception to discover this part of the enemies' programme, so soon as by open hostilities their machinery was fairly put in motion. Yet, thoroughly imbued with a reverence for the guaranteed rights of individuals, I was slow to adopt the strong measures, which by degrees I have been forced to regard as being within the exceptions of the constitution, and as indispensable to the public Safety. Nothing is better known to history than that courts of justice are utterly incompetent to such cases. Civil courts are organized chiefly for trials of individuals, or, at most, a few individuals acting in concert; and this in quiet times, and on charges of crimes well defined in the law. Even in times of peace, bands of horse-thieves and robbers frequently grow too numerous and powerful for the ordinary courts of justice. But what comparison, in numbers, have such bands ever borne to the insurgent sympathizers even in many of the loyal states? Again, a jury too frequently have at least one member, more ready to hang the panel than to hang the traitor. And yet again, he who dissuades one man from volunteering, or induces one soldier to desert, weakens the Union cause as much as he who kills a union soldier in battle. Yet this dissuasion, or inducement, may be so conducted as to be no defined crime of which any civil court would take cognizance.

Ours is a case of Rebellion—so called by the resolutions before me—in fact, a clear, flagrant, and gigantic case of Rebellion; and the provision of the constitution that "The previlege of the writ of Habeas Corpus shall not be suspended, unless when in cases of Rebellion or Invasion, the public Safety may require it" is *the* provision which specially applies to our present case. This provision plainly attests the understanding of those who made the constitution that ordinary courts of justice are inadequate to "cases of Rebellion"—attests their purpose that in such cases, men may be held in custody whom the courts acting on ordinary rules, would discharge. Habeas Corpus, does not discharge men who are proved to be guilty of defined crime; and its suspension is allowed by the constitution on purpose that, men may be arrested and held, who can not be proved to be guilty of defined crime, "when, in cases of Rebellion or Invasion the public Safety may require it." This is precisely our present case—a case of Rebellion, wherein the public Safety does require the suspension. Indeed, arrests by process of courts, and arrests in cases of rebellion, do not proceed altogether upon the same basis. The former is directed at the small per centage of ordinary and continuous perpetration of crime; while the latter is directed at sudden and extensive uprisings against the government, which, at most, will succeed or fail, in no great length of time. In the latter case, arrests are made, not so much for what has been done, as for what probably would be done. The latter is more for the preventive, and less for the vindictive, than the former. In such cases the purposes of men are much more easily understood, than in cases of ordinary crime. The man who stands by and says nothing, when the peril of his government is discussed, can not be misunderstood. If not hindered, he is sure to help the enemy. Much more, if he talks ambiguously—talks for his country with "buts" and "ifs" and "ands." Of how little value the constitutional provision I have quoted will be rendered, if arrests shall never be made until defined crimes shall have been committed, may be illustrated by a few notable examples. Gen. John C. Breckienridge, Gen. Robert E. Lee, Gen. Joseph E. Johnston, Gen. John B. Magruder, Gen. William B. Preston, Gen. Simon B. Buckner, and Comodore [Franklin] Buchanan, now occupying the very highest places in the rebel war service, were all within the power of the government since the rebellion began, and were nearly as well known to be traitors then as now. Unquestionably if we had seized and held them, the insurgent cause would be much weaker. But no one of them had then committed any crime defined in the law. Every one of them if arrested would have been discharged on Habeas Corpus, were the writ allowed to operate. In view of these and similar cases, I think the time not unlikely to come when I shall be blamed for having made too few arrests rather than too many.

By the third resolution the meeting indicate their opinion that military arrests may be constitutional in localities where rebellion actually exists; but that such arrests are unconstitutional in localities where rebellion, or insurrection, does not actually exist. They insist that such arrests shall not be made "outside of the lines of necessary military occupation, and the scenes of insurrection[.]" In asmuch, however, as the constitution itself makes no such distinction, I am unable to believe that there is any such constitutional distinction. I concede that the class of arrests complained of, can be constitutional only when, in cases of Rebellion or Invasion, the public Safety may require them; and I insist that in such cases, they are constitutional *wherever* the public safety does require them—as well in places to which they may prevent the rebellion extending, as in those where it may be already prevailing—as well where they may restrain mischievous interference with the raising and supplying of armies, to suppress the rebellion, as where the rebellion may actually be—as well where they may restrain the enticing men out of the army, as where they would prevent mutiny in the army— equally constitutional at all places where they will conduce to the public Safety, as against the dangers of Rebellion or Invasion.

. . . .

I understand the meeting whose resolutions I am considering to be in favor of suppressing the rebellion by military force—by armies. Long experience has shown that armies cannot be maintained unless desertion shall be punished by the severe penalty of death. The case requires, and the law and the constitution sanction, this punishment. Must I shoot a simple-minded soldier boy who deserts, while I must not touch a hair of a wiley agitator who induces him to desert? This is none the less injurious when effected by getting a father, or brother, or friend into a public meeting, and there working upon his feelings till he is persuaded to write the soldier boy, that he is fighting in a bad cause, for a wicked administration of a contemptable government, too weak to arrest and punish him if he shall desert. I think that, in such a case, to silence the agitator, and save the boy is not only constitutional, but, withal a great mercy.

If I be wrong on this question of constitutional power, my error lies in believing that certain proceedings are constitutional when, in cases of rebellion or Invasion, the public Safety requires them, which would not be constitutional when, in absence of rebellion or invasion, the public Safety does not require them—in other words, that the constitution is not in it's application in all respects the same, in cases of Rebellion or invasion, involving the public Safety, as it is in times of profound peace and public security. The constitution itself makes the distinction; and I can no more be persuaded that the government can constitutionally take no strong measure in time of rebellion, because it can be shown that the same could not be lawfully taken in time of peace, than I can be persuaded that a particular drug is not good medicine for a sick man, because it can be shown to not be good food for a well one. Nor am I able to appreciate the danger, apprehended by the meeting, that the American people will, by means of military arrests during the rebellion, lose the right of public discussion, the liberty of speech and the press, the law of evidence, trial by jury, and Habeas corpus, throughout the indefinite peaceful future which I trust lies before them, any more than I am able to believe that a man could contract so strong an appetite for emetics during temporary illness, as to persist in feeding upon them through the remainder of his healthful life.

"THE DECISION IS TO BE MADE"

From a Response to Resolutions from Ohio Democrats

[JUNE 29, 1863]

This is part of Lincoln's reply to an Ohio delegation which arrived in Washington to lodge yet another protest against the Vallandigham arrest.

You ask, in substance, whether I really claim that I may override all the guarrantied rights of individuals, on the plea of conserving the public safety—when I may choose to say the public safety requires it. This question, divested of the phraseology calculated to represent me as struggling for an arbitrary personal prerogative, is either simply a question *who* shall decide, or an affirmation that *nobody* shall decide, what the public safety does require, in cases of Rebellion or invasion. The constitution contemplates the question as likely to occur for decision, but it does not expressly declare who is to decide it. By necessary implication, when Rebellion or Invasion comes, the decision is to be made, from time to time; and I think the man whom, for the time, the people have, under the constitution, made the commander-in-chief, of their Army and Navy, is the man who holds the power, and bears the responsibility of making it. If he uses the power justly, the same people will probably justify him; if he abuses it, he is in their hands, to be dealt with by all the modes they have reserved to themselves in the constitution.

"How Long Ago Is It?— Eighty Odd Years"

Response to a Victory Serenade, the White House

[JULY 7, 1863]

Lincoln was a reluctant and at times a clumsy extemporaneous speaker. Not surprisingly, he failed to rise to the occasion when a crowd of serenaders celebrating the recent Union triumphs at Gettysburg and Vicksburg called for a speech and got the following. But Lincoln did express the basic ideas he would refine into a virtual hymn for his address on the Gettysburg battlefield the following November. This is the New York Times *transcript.*

Fellow-citizens: I am very glad indeed to see you to-night, and yet I will not say I thank you for this call, but I do most sincerely thank Almighty God for the occasion on which you have called. [Cheers.] How long ago is it?—eighty odd years—since on the Fourth of July for the first time in the history of the world a nation by its representatives, assembled and declared as a self-evident truth that "all men are created equal." [Cheers.] That was the birthday of the United States of America. Since then the Fourth of July has had several peculiar recognitions. The two most distinguished men in the framing and support of the Declaration were Thomas Jefferson and John Adams—the one having penned it and the other sustained it the most forcibly in debate—the only two of the fifty-five who sustained it being elected President of the United States. Precisely fifty years after they put their hands to the paper it pleased Almighty God to take both from the stage of action. This was indeed an extraordinary and remarkable event in our history. Another President, five years after, was called from this stage of existence on the same day and month of the year [James Monroe died July 4, 1831—eds.]; and now, on this last Fourth of July just passed, when we have a gigantic Rebellion, at the bottom of which is an effort to overthrow the principle that all men were created equal, we have the surrender of a most powerful position and army on that very day, [cheers] and not only so, but in a succession of battles in Pennsylvania, near to us, through three days, so rapidly fought that they might be called one great battle on the 1st, 2d, and 3d of the month of July; and on the 4th the cohorts of those who opposed the declaration that all men are created equal, "turned tail" and run. [Long and continued cheers.] Gentlemen, this is a glorious theme, and the occasion for a speech, but I am not prepared to make one worthy of the occasion. I would like to speak in terms of praise due to the many brave officers and soldiers who have fought in the cause of the Union and liberties of the country from the beginning of the war. These are trying occasions, not only in success, but for the want of success. I dislike to mention the name of one single officer lest I might do wrong to those I might forget. Recent events bring up glorious names, and particularly prominent ones, but these I will not mention. Having said this much, I will now take the music.

"MY 'PUBLIC-OPINION BATHS' "

Remarks to a Visiting Journalist, the White House

[JULY 25, 1863]

When New York journalist Major Charles G. Halpine visited the White House, he was astounded to find a "crowd of men and women, representing all ranks and classes, who were gathered in the large waiting-room" to see the President. Halpine, who had gained fame as humorist "Miles O'Reilly," suggested that Lincoln ease this burden by routinely screening visitors in advance, the way busy generals in the field did. In this frank and revealing response—"made with half-shut eyes, as if in soliloquy," remembered Halpine—Lincoln explained why he cherished the ritual of his "public days." To Halpine the response revealed "the essentially representative character of his mind and of his administration."

. . . I feel—though the tax on my time is heavy—that no hours of my day are better employed than those which thus bring me again within the direct contact and atmosphere of the average of our whole people. Men moving only in an official circle are apt to become merely official—not to say arbitrary—in their ideas, and are apter and apter, with each passing day, to forget that they only hold power in a representative capacity. Now this is all wrong. I go into these promiscuous receptions of all who claim to have business with me twice each week, and every applicant for audience has to take his turn, as if waiting to be shaved in a barber's shop. Many of the matters brought to my notice are utterly frivolous, but others are of more or less importance, and all serve to renew in me a clearer and more vivid image of that great popular assemblage out of which I sprung, and to which at the end of two years I must return. I tell you . . . that I call these receptions my *"public-opinion baths;"* for I have but little time to read the papers and gather public opinion that way; and though they may not be pleasant in all their particulars, the effect, as a whole, is renovating and invigorating to my perceptions of responsibility and duty."

"THOSE WHO SHALL HAVE TASTED ACTUAL FREEDOM . . . CAN NEVER BE SLAVES"

From a Letter to Stephen A. Hurlbut

[JULY 31, 1863]

The Emancipation Proclamation drew much criticism, North as well as South, not to mention challenges to its legality. In this letter to a general who expressed a wish to resign, Lincoln reaffirmed the inviolability of the proclamation, and his belief that it was lawful. Although Lincoln had wanted General Hurlbut's resignation in 1861, he did not accept it now.

My dear General Hurlbut:

. . . The emancipation proclamation applies to Arkansas. I think it is valid in law, and will be so held by the courts. I think I shall not retract or repudiate it. Those who shall have tasted actual freedom I believe can never be slaves, or quasi slaves again. For the rest, I believe some plan, substantially being gradual emancipation, would be better for both white and black. The Missouri plan, recently adopted, I do not object to on account of the time for *ending* the institution; but I am sorry the *beginning* should have been postponed for seven years, leaving all that time to agitate for the repeal of the whole thing. It should begin at once, giving at least the new-born, a vested interest in freedom, which could not be taken away. If Senator[-elect Silliam K.] Sebastian could come with something of this sort from Arkansas, I at least should take great interest in his case; and I believe a single individual will have scarcely done the world so great a service. See him, if you can, and read this to him; but charge him not to make it public for the present. Write me again. Yours very truly.

A. LINCOLN

"BETTER PREPARED FOR THE NEW"
From a Letter to General Nathaniel P. Banks
[AUGUST 5, 1863]

General Banks had played a major role in Grant's campaign to open the Mississippi River for the Union. In this letter, Lincoln offered both belated thanks and the hope that whites and blacks in conquered Louisiana could somehow begin moving toward a new relationship. It was a major change for Lincoln, who years earlier had admitted in a speech he could foresee no way the races could ever live together "on terms of social and political equality."

Executive Mansion, Washington,
August 5, 1863.

My dear General Banks

Being a poor correspondent is the only apology I offer for not having sooner tendered my thanks for your very successful, and very valuable military operations this year. The final stroke in opening the Mississippi never should, and I think never will, be forgotten.

Recent events in Mexico, I think, render early action in Texas more important than ever. I expect, however, the General-in-Chief, will address you more fully upon this subject.

Governor Boutwell read me to-day that part of your letter to him, which relates to Louisiana affairs. While I very well know what I would be glad for Louisiana to do, it is quite a different thing for me to assume direction of the matter. I would be glad for her to make a new Constitution recognizing the emancipation proclamation, and adopting emancipation in those parts of the state to which the proclamation does not apply. And while she is at it, I think it would not be objectionable for her to adopt some practical system by which the two races could gradually live themselves out of their old relation to each other, and both come out better prepared for the new. Education for young blacks should be included in the plan. After all, the power, or element, of "contract" may be sufficient for this probationary period; and, by it's simplicity, and flexibility, may be the better.

As an anti-slavery man I have a motive to desire emancipation, which pro-slavery men do not have; but even they have strong enough reason to thus place themselves again under the shield of the Union; and to thus perpetually hedge against the recurrence of the scenes through which we are now passing.

Gov. Shepley has informed me that Mr. Durant is now taking a registry, with a view to the election of a Constitutional convention in Louisiana. This, to me, appears proper. If such convention were to ask my views, I could present little else than what I now say to you. I think the thing should be pushed forward, so that if possible, it's mature work may reach here by the meeting of Congress.

For my own part I think I shall not, in any event, retract the emancipation proclamation; nor, as executive, ever return to slavery any person who is free by the terms of that proclamation, or by any of the acts of Congress. . . . Yours very truly

A. LINCOLN

"YOU SAY YOU WILL NOT FIGHT TO FREE NEGROES"

Letter to James C. Conkling

[AUGUST 26, 1863]

Beginning in January, blacks were welcomed into the Union armed forces, and their valor later inspired Lincoln to explore the possibility of giving them the right to vote. But the prospect of fighting to emancipate blacks, much less fighting alongside them, appalled many Northerners who had been perfectly happy fighting only for the idea of preserving the Union. When Conkling, an old Springfield friend, notified Lincoln of a Union rally in his hometown, the President seized the opportunity to provide this spirited defense of his policy on black enlistments. Lincoln crafted the letter to be read aloud at the Springfield meeting, and asked Conkling, whom he considered an able public reader, to do so "very slowly." Novelist Harriet Beecher Stowe, who thought Lincoln's writing generally imbued "with a power of insight and expression," considered this letter a "masterly" product of "a mind both strong and generous."

Executive Mansion,
Washington, August 26, 1863.

Hon. James C. Conkling

My Dear Sir.

Your letter inviting me to attend a mass-meeting of unconditional Union-men, to be held at the Capital of Illinois, on the 3d day of September, has been received.

It would be very agreeable to me, to thus meet my old friends, at my own home; but I can not, just now, be absent from here, so long as a visit there, would require.

The meeting is to be of all those who maintain unconditional devotion to the Union; and I am sure my old political friends will thank me for tendering, as I do, the nation's gratitude to those other noble men, whom no partizan malice, or partizan hope, can make false to the nation's life.

There are those who are dissatisfied with me. To such I would say: You desire peace; and you blame me that we do not have it. But how can we attain it? There are but three conceivable ways. First, to suppress the rebellion by force of arms. This, I am trying to do. Are you for it? If you are, so far we are agreed. If you are not for it, a second way is, to give up the Union. I am against this. Are you for it? If you are, you should say so plainly. If you are not for *force,* nor yet for *dissolution,* there only remains some imaginable *compromise.* I do not believe any compromise, embracing the maintenance of the Union, is now possible. All I learn, leads to a directly opposite belief. The strength of the rebellion, is its military—its army. That army dominates all the country, and all the people, within its range. Any offer of terms made by any man or men within that range, in opposition to that army, is simply nothing for the present; because such man or men, have no power whatever to enforce their side of a compromise, if one were made with them. To illustrate—Suppose refugees from the South, and peace men of the North, get together in convention, and frame and proclaim a compromise embracing a restoration of the Union; in what way can that compromise be used to keep Lee's army out of Pennsylvania? [General George] Meade's army can keep Lee's army out of Pennsylvania; and, I think, can ultimately drive it out of existence. But no paper compromise, to which the controllers of Lee's army are not agreed, can, at all, affect that army. In an effort at such compromise we should waste time, which the enemy would improve to our disadvantage; and that would be all. A compromise, to be effective, must be made either with those who control the rebel army, or with the people first liberated from the domination of that army, by the success of our own army. Now allow me to assure you, that no word or intimation, from that rebel army, or from any of the men controlling it, in relation to any peace compromise, has ever come to my knowledge or belief. All charges and insinuations to the contrary, are deceptive and groundless. And I promise you, that if any such proposition shall hereafter come, it shall not be rejected, and kept a secret from you. I freely acknowledge myself the servant of the people, according to the bond of service—the United States constitution; and that, as such, I am responsible to them.

But, to be plain, you are dissatisfied with me about the negro. Quite likely there is a difference of opinion between you and myself upon that subject. I certainly wish that all men could be free, while I suppose you do not. Yet I have neither adopted, nor proposed any measure, which is not consistent with even your view, provided you are for the Union. I suggested compensated emancipation; to which you replied you wished not to be taxed to buy negroes. But I had not asked you to be taxed to buy negroes, except in such way, as to save you from greater taxation to save the Union exclusively by other means.

You dislike the emancipation proclamation; and, perhaps, would have it retracted. You say it is unconstitutional—I think differently. I think the constitution invests its commander-in-chief, with the law of war, in time of war. The most that can be said, if so much, is, that slaves are property. Is there—has there ever been—any question that by the law of war, property, both of enemies and friends, may be taken when needed? And is it not needed whenever taking it, helps us, or hurts the enemy? Armies, the world over, destroy enemies' property when they can not use it; and even destroy their own to keep it from the enemy. Civilized belligerents do all in their power to help themselves, or hurt the enemy, except a few things regarded as barbarous or cruel. Among the exceptions are the massacre of vanquished foes, and non-combatants, male and female.

But the proclamation, as law, either is valid, or is not valid. If it is not valid, it needs no retraction. If it is valid, it can not be retracted, any more than the dead can be brought to life. Some of you profess to think its retraction would operate favorably for the Union. Why better *after* the retraction, than *before* the issue? There was more than a year and a half of trial to suppress the rebellion before the proclamation issued, the last one hundred days of which passed under an explicit notice that it was coming, unless averted by those in revolt, returning to their allegiance. The war has certainly progressed as favorably for us, since the issue of the proclamation as before. I know as fully as one can know the opinions of others, that some of the commanders of our armies in the field who have given us our most important successes,

believe the emancipation policy, and the use of colored troops, constitute the heaviest blow yet dealt to the rebellion; and that, at least one
of those important successes, could not have been achieved when it was,
but for the aid of black soldiers. Among the commanders holding these
views are some who have never had any affinity with what is called
abolitionism, or with republican party politics; but who hold them
purely as military opinions. I submit these opinions as being entitled to
some weight against the objections, often urged, that emancipation, and
arming the blacks, are unwise as military measures, and were not
adopted, as such, in good faith.

You say you will not fight to free negroes. Some of them seem willing
to fight for you; but, no matter. Fight you, then, exclusively to save the
Union. I issued the proclamation on purpose to aid you in saving the
Union. Whenever you shall have conquered all resistance to the Union,
if I shall urge you to continue fighting, it will be an apt time, then, for
you to declare you will not fight to free negroes.

I thought that in your struggle for the Union, to whatever extent the
negroes should cease helping the enemy, to that extent it weakened the
enemy in his resistance to you. Do you think differently? I thought that
whatever negroes can be got to do as soldiers, leaves just so much less
for white soldiers to do, in saving the Union. Does it appear otherwise
to you? But negroes, like other people, act upon motives. Why should
they do any thing for us, if we will do nothing for them? If they stake
their lives for us, they must be prompted by the strongest motive—even
the promise of freedom. And the promise being made, must be kept.

The signs look better. The Father of Waters again goes unvexed to
the sea. Thanks to the great North-West for it. Nor yet wholly to them.
Three hundred miles up, they met New-England, Empire, Key-Stone,
and Jersey, hewing their way right and left. The Sunny South too, in
more colors than one, also lent a hand. On the spot, their part of the
history was jotted down in black and white. The job was a great national
one; and let none be banned who bore an honorable part in it. And while
those who have cleared the great river may well be proud, even that is
not all. It is hard to say that anything has been more bravely, and well
done, than at Antietam, Murfreesboro, Gettysburg, and on many fields
of lesser note. Nor must Uncle Sam's Web-feet be forgotten. At all the
watery margins they have been present. Not only on the deep sea, the
broad bay, and the rapid river, but also up the narrow muddy bayou,

and wherever the ground was a little damp, they have been, and made their tracks. Thanks to all. For the great republic—for the principle it lives by, and keeps alive—for man's vast future,—thanks to all.

Peace does not appear so distant as it did. I hope it will come soon, and come to stay; and so come as to be worth the keeping in all future time. It will then have been proved that, among free men, there can be no successful appeal from the ballot to the bullet; and that they who take such appeal are sure to lose their case, and pay the cost. And then, there will be some black men who can remember that, with silent tongue, and clenched teeth, and steady eye, and well-poised bayonet, they have helped mankind on to this great consummation; while, I fear, there will be some white ones, unable to forget that, with malignant heart, and deceitful speech, they have strove to hinder it.

Still let us not be over-sanguine of a speedy final triumph. Let us be quite sober. Let us diligently apply the means, never doubting that a just God, in his own good time, will give us the rightful result. Yours very truly

A. LINCOLN.

"THE BOUNDLESS FIELD
OF ABSOLUTISM?"

Draft Letter to Secretary of the Treasury Salmon P. Chase

[SEPTEMBER 2, 1863]

The eight-month-old Emancipation Proclamation applied only to states in rebellion, exempting border slave states and even areas of the Confederacy returned to Union control by January 1, 1863. In this letter, Lincoln defends these restrictions, arguing that to have gone further would have clearly exceeded his constitutional authority. Not until the following summer was Lincoln prepared publicly to support a constitutional amendment abolishing slavery everywhere.

Executive Mansion,

Hon. S. P. Chase.   Washington, September 2. 1863.

My dear Sir:

Knowing your great anxiety that the emancipation proclamation shall now be applied to certain parts of Virginia and Louisiana which were exempted from it last January, I state briefly what appear to me to be difficulties in the way of such a step. The original proclamation has no constitutional or legal justification, except as a military measure. The exemptions were made because the military necessity did not apply to the exempted localities. Nor does that necessity apply to them now any more than it did then. If I take the step must I not do so, without the argument of military necessity, and so, without any argument, except the one that I think the measure politically expedient, and morally right? Would I not thus give up all footing upon constitution or law? Would I not thus be in the boundless field of absolutism? Could this pass unnoticed, or unresisted? Could it fail to be perceived that without any further stretch, I might do the same in Delaware, Maryland, Kentucky, Tennessee, and Missouri; and even change any law in any state? Would not many of our own friends shrink away appalled? Would it not lose us the elections, and with them, the very cause we seek to advance?

"HAS THE MANHOOD OF OUR RACE RUN OUT?"

From an Opinion on the Draft

[SEPTEMBER 14, 1863?]

Mobs in New York City greeted the beginning of conscription by rampaging through the streets, setting fire to a Negro orphanage, and stoning the Tribune. Then some state and federal courts began acting to interfere with the draft on legal grounds. Lincoln prepared this response to the crisis, possibly for a speech he never gave. He did read it to his cabinet on September 15.

It is at all times proper that misunderstanding between the public and the public servant should be avoided; and this is far more important now, than in times of peace and tranquility. I therefore address you without searching for a precedent upon which to do so. Some of you are sincerely devoted to the republican institutions, and territorial integrity of our country, and yet are opposed to what is called the draft, or conscription.

. . . .

. . . The republican institutions, and territorial integrity of our country can not be maintained without the further raising and supporting of armies. There can be no army without men. Men can be had only voluntarily, or involuntarily. We have ceased to obtain them voluntarily; and to obtain them involuntarily, is the draft—the conscription. If you dispute the fact, and declare that men can still be had voluntarily in sufficient numbers prove the assertion by yourselves volunteering in such numbers, and I shall gladly give up the draft. Or if not a sufficient number, but any one of you will volunteer, he for his single self, will escape all the horrors of the draft; and will thereby do only what each one of at least a million of his manly brethren have already done. Their toil and blood have been given as much for you as for themselves. Shall it all be lost rather than you too, will bear your part?

I do not say that all who would avoid serving in the war, are unpatriotic; but I do think every patriot should willingly take his chance under a law made with great care in order to secure entire fairness. This law was considered, discussed, modified, and amended, by congress, at great length, and with much labor; and was finally passed, by both branches, with a near approach to unanimity. At last, it may not be exactly such as any one man out of congress, or even in congress, would have made it. It has been said, and I believe truly, that the constitution itself is not altogether such as any one of it's framers would have preferred. It was the joint work of all; and certainly the better that it was so.

. . . .

The principle of the draft, which simply is involuntary, or enforced service, is not new. It has been practiced in all ages of the world. It was well known to the framers of our constitution as one of the modes of raising armies, at the time they placed in that instrument the provision that "the congress shall have power to raise and support armies." It has been used, just before, in establishing our independence; and it was also used under the constitution in 1812. Wherein is the peculiar hardship now? Shall we shrink from the necessary means to maintain our free government, which our grand-fathers employed to establish it, and our own fathers have already employed once to maintain it? Are we degenerate? Has the manhood of our race run out?

Again, a law may be both constitutional and expedient, and yet may be administered in an unjust and unfair way. This law belongs to a class, which class is composed of those laws whose object is to distribute burthens or benefits on the principle of equality. No one of these laws can ever be practically administered with that exactness which can be conceived of in the mind. A tax law, the principle of which is that each owner shall pay in proproportion [*sic*] to the value of his property, will be a dead letter, if no one can be compelled to pay until it can be shown that every other one will pay in precisely the same proportion according to value; nay even, it will be a dead letter, if no one can be compelled to pay until it is certain that every other one will pay at all—even in unequal proportion. Again the United States House of representatives is constituted on the principle that each member is sent by the same number of people that each other one is sent by; and yet in practice no two of the whole number, much less the whole number, are ever sent by precisely the same number of constituents. The Districts can not be made precisely equal in population at first, and if they could, they would become unequal in a single day, and much more so in the ten years, which the Districts, once made, are to continue. They can not be re-modelled every day; nor, without too much expence and labor, even every year.

This sort of difficulty applies in full force, to the practical administration of the draft law. In fact the difficulty is greater in the case of the draft law. First, it starts with all the inequality of the congressional Districts; but these are based on entire population, while the draft is based upon those only who are fit for soldiers, and such may not bear the same proportion to the whole in one District, that they do in another. Again, the facts must be ascertained, and credit given, for the unequal numbers of soldiers which have already gone from the several Districts. In all these points errors will occur in spite of the utmost fidelity. The government is bound to administer the law with such an approach to exactness as is usual in analagous cases, and as entire good faith and fidelity will reach. If so great departures as to be inconsistent with such good faith and fidelity, or great departures occurring in any way, be pointed out, they shall be corrected; and any agent shown to have caused such departures intentionally, shall be dismissed.

With these views, and on these principles, I feel bound to tell you it is my purpose to see the draft law faithfully executed.

"I DO NOT INTEND TO BE A TYRANT"

Informal Comments to and About Radical Republicans

[SEPTEMBER 30 AND OCTOBER 28, 1863]

The so-called radicals—Republicans with the most liberal attitude toward race—hounded Lincoln on such issues as emancipation, military strategy, and reunification, which most of them insisted be based on strict loyalty tests. For generations, historians have speculated about how Lincoln might have handled this wing of his party had he lived. In the first extract here, Lincoln commented on efforts by radicals from Kansas and Missouri to secure a change in military command. In the second, he hinted that their hostility toward him notwithstanding, he felt their viewpoint was understandable. Both conversations were recorded by Lincoln's private secretary.

My Radical friends will . . . see that I understand and appreciate their position. Still you appear to come before me as my friends, if I agree with you, and not otherwise. I do not here speak of mere personal friendship. When I speak of my friends I mean those who are friendly to my measures, to the policy of the Government. I am well aware that by many, by some even among this delegation—I shall not name them—I have been in public speeches and in printed documents charged with "tyranny and willfulness," with a disposition to make my own personal will supreme. I do not intend to be a tyrant. At all events I shall take care that in my own eyes I do not become one. I have no right to act the tyrant to mere political opponents. If a man votes for supplies of men and money, encourages enlistments, discourages desertions, does all in his power to carry the war on to a successful issue, I have no right to question him for his abstract political opinions. I must make a dividing line somewhere between those who are the opponents of the Government, and those who only approve peculiar features of my Administration while they sustain the Government.

. . . .

They [the radicals] are nearer to me than the other side, in thought and sentiment, though bitterly hostile personally. They are utterly lawless—the unhandiest devils in the world to deal with—but after all their faces are set Zionwards.

⋙ VII ⋘

"FOR US THE LIVING"
Lincoln and Democracy
1863–1865

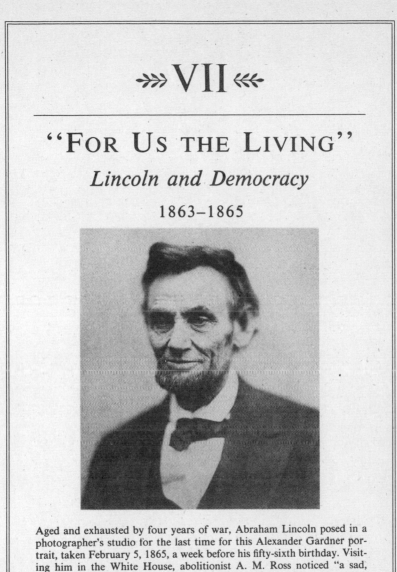

Aged and exhausted by four years of war, Abraham Lincoln posed in a photographer's studio for the last time for this Alexander Gardner portrait, taken February 5, 1865, a week before his fifty-sixth birthday. Visiting him in the White House, abolitionist A. M. Ross noticed "a sad, serious look in his eyes that spoke louder than words of the disappointments, trials, and discouragements he had encountered since the war began. The wrinkles about the eyes and forehead were deeper; the lips were firmer, but indicative of kindness and forbearance. The great struggle," he concluded, "had brought out the hidden riches of his noble nature."

(Photograph: National Portrait Gallery)

Introduction

BY HANS L. TREFOUSSE

By the fall of 1863, Lincoln had arrived at a point in his career that permitted him to develop to the fullest his skills and ideals. Always committed to the democratic process, he now gave his most memorable expression to this faith in the Gettysburg Address; always opposed to slavery, he was now able to carry this opposition to its logical conclusion with the 13th Amendment to the Constitution; always sympathetic to the downtrodden, he could now openly voice his concern for black rights. And while he always had a sound understanding of the necessities of warfare, he could now benefit from his previous experiences and, together with General Ulysses S. Grant, lead the nation to victory.

His long devotion to democracy received its finest expression in the Gettysburg Address. Asked to say a few words on November 19, 1863, on the occasion of the dedication of a national cemetery at the site of the gigantic battle fought there only a few months before, he had given much thought to the preparation of his remarks. But, worried about the illness of his youngest son, Tad, and preoccupied with affairs of state, he had only been able to complete it in the house of his Gettysburg host, the local attorney David Wills, on the night before the ceremony. Wishing to say something that could not be construed as a mere fishing for votes—the affair was much too solemn for that—Lincoln determined to make a firm statement about the purpose of the war.

The result was one of the greatest speeches ever made in the English language. After the main speaker of the day—Edward Everett, the famous orator, former Harvard professor and statesman—had held forth for two hours, the tall, lanky president, dressed in black, mounted the rostrum in the cemetery in the small Pennsylvania town. As members of the cabinet, state, local, and foreign dignitaries looked on, he addressed an audience of fifteen thousand. "Four score and seven years ago," he began in a clear allusion to the Declaration of Independence, "our fathers brought forth on this continent, a new nation, conceived in Liberty, and dedicated to the proposition that all men are created equal." The President's masterful rhetoric cut through all arguments about the nature of the Civil War, a contest to determine whether any nation dedicated to the concepts of freedom and equality could long endure. The war was a struggle for democracy, for if a popular decision by ballots could be challenged by bullets, democratic government was at an end.

The speech of a few paragraphs has rightly remained a classic. Lincoln never failed to remind his correspondents of its implications. Thus he expressed the opinion that the Lord must have loved the common people because he made so many of them, called on laboring folk to support the war effort, and emphasized his belief in the democratic process by running for a second term in the midst of war. To suspend the elections would never have occurred to him; they were mandated by the Constitution and embodied an essential part of the democratic government Lincoln was fighting to preserve. And unlike other wartime leaders, he had no thought of using his military prerogatives to perpetuate himself in power. On the contrary, as he expressed it so well, should he suffer defeat, as seemed likely, he would make every effort to cooperate with his successor to bring the war to a successful conclusion.

His own renomination was attended by difficulty. Salmon P. Chase, his secretary of the treasury, was an open aspirant for the higher office. Various others were also mentioned, and in February 1864, the Pomeroy Circular, a letter to various Republican politicians signed by Senator Samuel Pomeroy of Kansas, urged the nomination of Chase rather than that of the President. Because of the impropriety of a cabinet member conspiring against his chief, the effect of the circular was the opposite of that intended. The Republicans in Ohio, Chase's home state, endorsed Lincoln, and the secretary withdrew, so that the President was renominated in June.

Nevertheless, many radical Republicans, the most advanced wing of the party, some of whom had already put into the field a separate ticket headed by General John C. Frémont, remained dissatisfied. When in

July Lincoln pocket-vetoed the Wade-Davis Bill, a Reconstruction measure more stringent than his own, Senator Benjamin F. Wade of Ohio and Representative Henry Winter Davis of Maryland published the Wade-Davis Manifesto, attacking the President and charging him with improper motives for his failure to sign the bill. At the same time, plans were afoot to substitute another person to head the ticket. However, when the Democrats nominated former Union army commander George B. McClellan on a peace platform, the radicals reconsidered. Lincoln dropped the conservative Montgomery Blair from the cabinet; Frémont withdrew, and the party rallied behind its chief. After a series of federal victories enabled Lincoln to win in November, he could take justifiable pride in the fact that elections had been held in the midst of war.

It was also during this period that the President was finally able to bring to a conclusion his long struggle against slavery. If his constitutional scruples and his sense of timing had prevented him from fulfilling his dream in the early years of the war, in 1864 and 1865 he was no longer constrained by these factors. True, the Emancipation Proclamation had merely been a partial solution; now he was ready to put teeth into it. Making its acceptance one of the conditions of his plan of Reconstruction, he reinforced and reiterated his commitment to it. As he made clear in his famous letter to the Kentucky newspaperman Albert G. Hodges, he had always hated slavery. It was in this spirit that he expressed his approval of the plank in his party's 1864 platform calling for a constitutional amendment to bring about full emancipation and later used all the powers of his office to make possible its passage in the House of Representatives in January 1865. His immortal words in acknowledgment of divine justice in his second inaugural are further proof of his devotion to the cause.

His speech on that occasion ranks with the Gettysburg Address as one of the masterpieces of American oratory. March 4, 1865, the date of the inauguration, was a cold, drizzly day. But shortly after noon, as the President stepped up to the platform erected at the east front of the Capitol, the sun briefly broke through the clouds. "On the occasion corresponding to this four years ago," he recalled, "all thoughts were anxiously directed to an impending civil-war. . . . Both parties deprecated war; but one of them would *make* war rather than let the nation survive, and the other would *accept* war rather than let it perish. And the war came." Then he turned to the cause of the conflict. When Lincoln said, "If we shall suppose that American Slavery is one of those offences which, in the providence of God, must needs come, but which . . . He now wills to remove, and that He gives to both North and South, this terrible war, as the woe due to those by whom the offence came," he left no doubt in the minds of the audience about his utter detestation of human bondage.

But the emancipation of the slaves was no longer enough. What was to become of the blacks once they were free? For a long time, Lincoln had urged that they be colonized abroad. It soon became evident, however, that this was not practical, and although he continued to pay lip service to the idea, probably to assuage conservative critics, he now turned his attention to ways of improving their lot at home. In this spirit, early in 1864, he wrote to Governor Michael Hahn of Louisiana suggesting the extension of the suffrage at least to the "intelligent" and to those who had served as soldiers. He reiterated the same idea to James S. Wadsworth, to whom he stated, "I cannot see, if universal amnesty is granted, how, under the circumstances, I can avoid exacting in return universal suffrage, or, least, suffrage on the basis of intelligence and military service. . . ." And in his last public address, he repeated his admonition in public. "I would myself prefer," he said, speaking to a large crowd from a White House window and recurring to the problem of suffrage for blacks in Louisiana, "that it were now conferred upon the very intelligent, and on those who serve our cause as soldiers." By that time, he had already signed the Freedmen's Bureau Bill setting up an agency designed to ease the blacks' transition from slavery. Lincoln was rapidly moving toward a belief in equal rights, and had he lived, the history of American race relations might well have been different.

Finally, it was during these years that Lincoln displayed his full mastery of his position as commander in chief as well as of the art of politics. He had appointed Ulysses S. Grant commander of the western armies in September 1863. When in the following year Congress conferred on Grant the rank of lieutenant general, Lincoln promoted him to the position of commander of all the armies of the United States. And in this post, the President gave the general his complete support. He sustained him when, in the campaign against Richmond, casualties mounted; despite serious doubts he did not interfere with William T.

Sherman's daring march from Atlanta to the sea; and he was able to witness the triumph of Grant's strategy at Appomattox. It was a record of which he could be proud.

Lincoln also developed fully as a statesman. He evidenced his magnificent sense of timing in the letter to Hodges as well as on April 7, 1864, in his informal remarks to the British abolitionist George Thompson, to whose address to Congress he had listened the day before. Dropping all other business and admitting him immediately to the White House, the President told him, among other things, "that, had the [emancipation] proclamation been issued even six months earlier than it was, public sentiment would not have sustained it." Lincoln's remarks were a model of persuasion and help explain his gradualism in approaching black freedom. Moreover, his astute handling of the Reconstruction problem contributed to the success of the Union's arms. On December 8, 1863, he published his famous 10 percent plan, offering amnesty to all but the leading insurgents, and providing that whenever 10 percent of the voters of 1861 had taken the oath of amnesty, they were entitled to form a new government. The ease with which Southerners could thus come back into the Union has often been contrasted with the more severe terms offered by Congress in later years, but it must be remembered that Lincoln acted in time of war, when it was important to win over as many war-weary insurgents as possible, and not when the country was at peace. He succeeded in establishing loyal governments in Louisiana and Arkansas in 1864, with Tennessee following suit in 1865.

That his policies would have changed with the coming of peace he showed after the fall of Richmond. Visiting the captured city, he was approached by Confederates asking that he permit the reconvening of the state legislature for the purpose of taking Virginia out of the Confederacy. He agreed; but as soon as Confederate general Robert E. Lee surrendered to Grant, the President, mindful of the radicals' objections and no longer constrained by military considerations, withdrew his consent. And if in 1863 his plan did not include black suffrage, by 1865 he urged this innovation upon the reconstructed states.

In the same way that he succeeded in establishing a Reconstruction policy designed to shorten the war, Lincoln also managed to disarm advocates of a compromise peace. Fully aware that the South would never give up its claim to independence, he permitted Francis P. Blair, his conservative adviser, to travel to Richmond to see whether he could obtain peace. The Confederates' intransigence demonstrated the folly of the advocates of a negotiated end to the war, and no harm was done. And the President himself met with Alexander H. Stephens, the vice president of the Confederacy, and two other Southern commissioners in February 1865 on board the *River Queen* at Hampton Roads. The Confederates had instructions to seek peace for "the two countries"; Lincoln, however, insisted on securing an end to the war for "the people of our one common country." The South would not surrender its dream of separate nationhood, just as he would not abandon his vision of perpetual union. Only he knew how to realize it.

What Lincoln would have done with the problem of Reconstruction had he lived will never be known. To be sure, the man who preached "malice toward none" and "charity for all" did not advocate a harsh peace. He wanted the Confederate president to escape "unbeknownst" to him and on April 10, 1865, asked the band playing patriotic tunes in celebration of the victory at Appomattox to play the Southern hymn, "Dixie," as well. But his sense of justice to the blacks, to say nothing of his understanding of national and party needs, would probably have kept him from committing his successor's errors. In fact, it was the President's call for black suffrage in Louisiana in his last speech that led the pro-Confederate actor John Wilkes Booth to decide to carry out his plot to kill him. Lincoln fell victim to Booth's bullet at Ford's Theater on April 14. He died the next day.

His death stunned the nation. The great, good president dead! And murdered on Good Friday! After lying in state in the White House and the rotunda of the Capitol, his remains were carried by funeral train to Springfield for burial. In an unprecedented outpouring of grief, thousands mourned everywhere along the route. He was almost immediately raised to martyrdom and has ever since occupied a position next to Washington in the national pantheon of heroes.

His legacy, however, lived on. Democratic government—"government of the people, by the people, for the people"—not only did not perish from the earth but spread to a large part of the world. Its continued vitality is a tribute to the unique genius who led the United States during the Civil War.

→>> <<←

"NEW BIRTH OF FREEDOM"

The Gettysburg Address

[NOVEMBER 19, 1863]

Four months after the Union repulsed the Confederacy at the decisive Battle of Gettysburg, thousands flocked to the once-unknown Pennsylvania village, which was still littered with stacked coffins and spent shells, to pay tribute to those who had died there. Lincoln was not the principal speaker at the dedication of the soldiers' cemetery that day. Renowned classical orator Edward Everett won that honor; Lincoln was invited to deliver only "a few appropriate remarks." Legend notwithstanding, he did not take the occasion lightly, and he certainly did not compose his address on the bumpy train ride to Pennsylvania the day before the ceremony. Other stubborn myths attending Lincoln's greatest speech suggest it was poorly received by the restless audience and dismissed by all the newspapers of the day—yet one eyewitness heard the talk greeted by "a hurricane of applause," and another by "sobs of smothered emotion." Press reaction divided strictly along party lines. Republican papers praised the address ("a perfect gem"), while Democratic sheets ridiculed it ("silly flat and dishwatery"). Lincoln himself surely realized he had made a success when principal orator Everett wrote him soon afterward: "I should be glad, if I could flatter myself that I came as near to the central idea of the occasion, in two hours, as you did in two minutes." Three times over the next few months Lincoln would be asked to recopy the speech so it could be sold to raise funds for war charities. This is his final copy, slightly altered from the spoken version. It is the only copy to which Lincoln gave a title, and the only one he signed. It was written around March 1864.

Address delivered at the dedication of the Cemetery at Gettysburg.

Four score and seven years ago our fathers brought forth on this continent, a new nation, conceived in Liberty, and dedicated to the proposition that all men are created equal.

Now we are engaged in a great civil war, testing whether that nation, or any nation so conceived and so dedicated, can long endure. We are met on a great battle-field of that war. We have come to dedicate a portion of that field, as a final resting place for those who here gave their lives that that nation might live. It is altogether fitting and proper that we should do this.

But, in a larger sense, we can not dedicate—we can not consecrate—we can not hallow—this ground. The brave men, living and dead, who struggled here have consecrated it, far above our poor power to add or detract. The world will little note, nor long remember what we say here, but it can never forget what they did here. It is for us the living, rather, to be dedicated here to the unfinished work which they who fought here have thus far so nobly advanced. It is rather for us to be here dedicated to the great task remaining before us—that from these honored dead we take increased devotion to that cause for which they gave the last full measure of devotion—that we here highly resolve that these dead shall not have died in vain—that this nation, under God, shall have a new birth of freedom—and that government of the people, by the people, for the people, shall not perish from the earth.

November 19. 1863.

ABRAHAM LINCOLN.

"YOU WILL NOT FIND THAT TO BE AN OBSTACLE"

Informal Remarks to a Lieutenant, the White House

[1863?]

*This story appeared in an 1866 volume by Frank Moore, **Anecdotes, Poetry, and Incidents of the War.** Years earlier, and in a far less jocular mood, Lincoln had placed old Senate rival Stephen A. Douglas on the side of "the divine right of kings," declaring himself, on the other hand, aligned with "the common right of humanity." On another occasion, he equated slavery with a tolerance for royal despotism. "It is the same spirit," he put it, even when it comes "from the mouth of a king who seeks to bestride the people of his nation and live by the fruits of their labor."*

[A lieutenant, whom debts compelled to leave his fatherland and service, succeeded in being admitted to the late President Lincoln, and, by reason of his commendable and winning deportment and intelligent appearance, was promised a lieutenant's commission in a cavalry regiment. He was so enraptured with his success, that he deemed it a duty to inform the President that he belonged to one of the oldest noble houses in Germany.] "O, never mind that," said Mr. Lincoln; "you will not find that to be an obstacle to your advancement."

"THE NEW RECKONING"

From the Annual Message to Congress

[DECEMBER 8, 1863]

Lincoln devoted part of his third annual message to Congress to detailing the progress his administration had made toward ending slavery. He seemed particularly proud that even among border states like Maryland, hitherto rigidly opposed even to restraining "the extension of slavery," the only dispute now centered on "the best mode of removing" slavery altogether. In the sections that follow, Lincoln reiterated that he would never renege on the Emancipation Proclamation; proposed that an oath to obey the proclamation be included in any plan to re-admit rebel states into the Union; defended the use of freed blacks in the Union armed forces; and argued that military force was still needed to restore democracy. One Southern newspaper reacted by branding Lincoln a "Yankee monster of inhumanity and falsehood," but the President's private secretary reported that the message was ecstatically received in Congress, where "men acted as if the millennium had come."

Of those who were slaves at the beginning of the rebellion, full one hundred thousand are now in the United States military service, about one-half of which number actually bear arms in the ranks; thus giving the double advantage of taking so much labor from the insurgent cause, and supplying the places which otherwise must be filled with so many white men. So far as tested, it is difficult to say they are not as good soldiers as any. No servile insurrection, or tendency to violence or cruelty, has marked the measures of emancipation and arming the blacks. These measures have been much discussed in foreign countries, and contemporary with such discussion the tone of public sentiment there is much improved. At home the same measures have been fully discussed, supported, criticised, and denounced, and the annual elections following are highly encouraging to those whose official duty it is to bear the country through this great trial. Thus we have the new reckoning. The crisis which threatened to divide the friends of the Union is past.

. . . .

An attempt to guaranty and protect a revived State government, constructed in whole, or in preponderating part, from the very element against whose hostility and violence it is to be protected, is simply absurd. There must be a test by which to separate the opposing elements, so as to build only from the sound; and that test is a sufficiently liberal one, which accepts as sound whoever will make a sworn recantation of his former unsoundness.

But if it be proper to require, as a test of admission to the political body, an oath of allegiance to the Constitution of the United States, and to the Union under it, why also to the laws and proclamations in regard to slavery? Those laws and proclamations were enacted and put forth for the purpose of aiding in the suppression of the rebellion. To give them their fullest effect, there had to be a pledge for their maintenance. In my judgment they have aided, and will further aid, the cause for which they were intended. To now abandon them would be not only to relinquish a lever of power, but would also be a cruel and an astounding breach of faith. I may add at this point, that while I remain in my present position I shall not attempt to retract or modify the emancipation proclamation; nor shall I return to slavery any person who is free by the terms of that proclamation, or by any of the acts of Congress. For these and other reasons it is thought best that support of these measures shall be included in the oath; and it is believed the Executive may lawfully claim it in return for pardon and restoration of forfeited rights, which he has clear constitutional power to withhold altogether, or grant upon the terms which he shall deem wisest for the public interest.

.   .   .   .

The movements, by State action, for emancipation in several of the States, not included in the emancipation proclamation, are matters of profound gratulation. And while I do not repeat in detail what I have heretofore so earnestly urged upon this subject, my general views and feelings remain unchanged; and I trust that Congress will omit no fair opportunity of aiding these important steps to a great consummation.

In the midst of other cares, however important, we must not lose sight of the fact that the war power is still our main reliance. To that power alone can we look, yet for a time, to give confidence to the people in the contested regions, that the insurgent power will not again overrun them. Until that confidence shall be established, little can be done anywhere for what is called reconstruction. Hence our chiefest care must still be directed to the army and navy, who have thus far borne their harder part so nobly and well. And it may be esteemed fortunate that in giving the greatest efficiency to these indispensable arms, we do also honorably recognize the gallant men, from commander to sentinel, who compose them, and to whom, more than to others, the world must stand indebted for the home of freedom disenthralled, regenerated, enlarged, and perpetuated.

ABRAHAM LINCOLN

"I HAVE NEVER INTERFERED . . . IN ANY CHURCH"

From a Letter to Oliver D. Filley

[DECEMBER 22, 1863]

Filley, a member of the Union Safety Committee of St. Louis, had petitioned Lincoln to restore Rev. Samuel McPheeters as pastor of the city's

Pine Street Church. The minister had been charged by the Union Army
with "sympathy with the rebellion" and expelled by his congregation.
"The assumption that I am keeping Dr. M. from preaching in his church
is monstrous," Lincoln said. In his reply to Filley, Lincoln condemned all
government involvement in church affairs—including any action to re-
store the ousted McPheeters. "You can conceive of my embarrassment,"
Lincoln told his secretary of war when he learned that, contrary to the
sentiments expressed in this letter, Union military forces were seizing other
churches and ousting pastors judged to be disloyal. "The U.S. Government
must not . . . undertake to run the churches," Lincoln had insisted earlier
in the year. This is the final portion of his letter to Filley.

I have never interfered, nor thought of interfering as to who shall or
shall not preach in any church; nor have I knowingly, or believingly,
tolerated any one else to so interfere by my authority. If any one is so
interfering, by color of my authority, I would like to have it specifically
made known to me.

If, after all, what is now sought, is to have me put Dr. M. back over
the heads of a majority of his own congregation, that too, will be
declined. I will not have control of any church on any side. Yours
Respectfully

A. LINCOLN

"COMMON LOOKING PEOPLE ARE THE BEST IN THE WORLD"

Informal Comments to His Secretary, the White House

[DECEMBER 23, 1863]

Frequently quoted, and just as often misquoted, this famous story was first
recorded in the following entry from the diary of White House assistant
secretary John Hay.

The President last night had a dream.

He was in a party of plain people and as it became known who he was they began to comment on his appearance. One of them said, "He is a very common looking man." The President replied, "Common looking people are the best in the world: that is the reason the Lord makes so many of them."

Waking, he remembered it, and told it as rather a neat thing.

"UNIVERSAL AMNESTY . . . WITH UNIVERSAL SUFFRAGE"

From a Letter to General James S. Wadsworth

[JANUARY 1864?]

The original of this letter has never been located. It was published in the New York Tribune *five months after Lincoln's death, along with a questionable concluding paragraph most likely not from Lincoln's pen—and not included here. To the* Southern Advocate, *commenting in September 1865, the letter showed that Lincoln "desired the bestowal of the elective franchise upon the blacks. . . ."*

You desire to know, in the event of our complete success in the field, the same being followed by a loyal and cheerful submission on the part of the South, if universal amnesty should not be accompanied with universal suffrage.

Now, since you know my private inclinations as to what terms should be granted to the South in the contingency mentioned, I will here add, that if our success should thus be realized, followed by such desired results, I cannot see, if universal amnesty is granted, how, under the circumstances, I can avoid exacting in return universal suffrage, or, at least, suffrage on the basis of intelligence and military service. . . .

"KEEP THE JEWEL OF LIBERTY"
Letter to Michael Hahn
[MARCH 13, 1864]

Lincoln's most clear-cut endorsement of enfranchising blacks came in this letter to the newly elected governor of occupied Louisiana, who thought it "mild and graceful." However, despite Lincoln's urgings, when the state adopted its new constitution, it did not provide for the vote for blacks, although it did empower the legislature to grant it to them.

Executive Mansion,
Washington,
March 13, 1864.

Private
Hon. Michael Hahn

My dear Sir:

I congratulate you on having fixed your name in history as the first-free-state Governor of Louisiana. Now you are about to have a Convention which, among other things, will probably define the elective franchise. I barely suggest for your private consideration, whether some of the colored people may not be let in—as, for instance, the very intelligent, and especially those who have fought gallantly in our ranks. They would probably help, in some trying time to come, to keep the jewel of liberty within the family of freedom. But this is only a suggestion, not to the public, but to you alone. Yours truly

A. LINCOLN

"LET NOT HIM WHO IS HOUSELESS PULL DOWN THE HOUSE OF ANOTHER"

*From a Reply to the New York Workingmen's
Democratic Republican Association, the White House*

[MARCH 21, 1864]

According to the New York **Tribune,** *the goal of the group to whom these
remarks were directed was to advance the "morals, position, and loyalty"
of American working people. A delegation visited the White House to
present Lincoln with an honorary membership. This was his reply: an
appeal for unity among all working people.*

Gentlemen of the Committee.

The honorary membership in your Association, as generously tendered, is gratefully accepted.

You comprehend, as your address shows, that the existing rebellion,
means more, and tends to more, than the perpetuation of African
Slavery—that it is, in fact, a war upon the rights of all working people.
. . . None are so deeply interested to resist the present rebellion as
the working people. Let them beware of prejudice, working division and
hostility among themselves. The most notable feature of a disturbance
in your city last summer [the New York City draft riots—eds.], was the
hanging of some working people by other working people. It should
never be so. The strongest bond of human sympathy, outside of the
family relation, should be one uniting all working people, of all nations,
and tongues, and kindreds. Nor should this lead to a war upon property, or the owners of property. Property is the fruit of labor—property
is desirable— —is a positive good in the world. That some should be
rich, shows that others may become rich, and hence is just encouragement to industry and enterprize. Let not him who is houseless pull
down the house of another; but let him labor diligently and build one
for himself, thus by example assuring that his own shall be safe from
violence when built.

"NEVER KNEW A MAN WHO WISHED TO BE . . . A SLAVE"

Fragment on Slavery

[MARCH 22, 1864]

Lincoln probably wrote this fragment as an extended autograph for an album scheduled to be sold for war charity.

I never knew a man who wished to be himself a slave. Consider if you know any *good* thing, that no man desires for himself.
March 22, 1864

A. LINCOLN

"IF SLAVERY IS NOT WRONG, NOTHING IS WRONG"

Letter to Albert G. Hodges

[APRIL 4, 1864]

Hodges, editor of a Frankfort, Kentucky, newspaper, visited the White House to warn that there was "much dissatisfaction" in the state over "the enlistment of slaves as soldiers." Evidently Lincoln's reply pleased Hodges, because he later asked the President to write out a copy of what he had said. Hodges showed the letter to "prominent men" back home, and told Lincoln, "I have met but one as yet who dissents from your reasoning. . . ."

A.G. Hodges, Esq   Executive Mansion,
Frankfort, Ky.   Washington, April 4, 1864.

My dear Sir:

You ask me to put in writing the substance of what I verbally said the other day, in your presence, to Governor [Thomas E.] Bramlette and Senator [Archibald] Dixon. It was about as follows:

"I am naturally anti-slavery. If slavery is not wrong, nothing is wrong. I can not remember when I did not so think, and feel. And yet I have never understood that the Presidency conferred upon me an unrestricted right to act officially upon this judgment and feeling. It was in the oath I took that I would, to the best of my ability, preserve, protect, and defend the Constitution of the United States. I could not take the office without taking the oath. Nor was it my view that I might take an oath to get power, and break the oath in using the power. I understood, too, that in ordinary civil administration this oath even forbade me to practically indulge my primary abstract judgment on the moral question of slavery. I had publicly declared this many times, and in many ways. And I aver that, to this day, I have done no official act in mere deference to my abstract judgment and feeling on slavery. I did understand however, that my oath to preserve the constitution to the best of my ability, imposed upon me the duty of preserving, by every indispensable means, that government—that nation—of which that constitution was the organic law. Was it possible to lose the nation, and yet preserve the constitution? By general law life *and* limb must be protected; yet often a limb must be amputated to save a life; but a life is never wisely given to save a limb. I felt that measures, otherwise unconstitutional, might become lawful, by becoming indispensable to the preservation of the constitution, through the preservation of the nation. Right or wrong, I assumed this ground, and now avow it. I could not feel that, to the best of my ability, I had even tried to preserve the constitution, if, to save slavery, or any minor matter, I should permit the wreck of government, country and Constitution all together. When, early in the war, Gen. Fremont attempted military emancipation, I forbade it, because I did not then think it an indispensable necessity. When a little later, Gen. [Simon] Cameron, then Secretary of War, suggested the arming of the blacks, I objected, because I did not yet think it an indispensable necessity. When, still later, Gen. [David] Hunter attempted military emancipation, I again forbade it, because I did not yet think the indispensable necessity had come. When, in March, and May, and July 1862 I made earnest, and successive appeals to the border states to favor compensated emancipation, I believed the indispensable necessity for military emancipation, and arming the blacks would come, unless averted by that measure. They declined the proposition; and I was, in my best judgment, driven to the alternative of either surrendering the Union, and with it, the Constitution, or of laying strong hand upon the colored element. I chose the latter. In choosing it, I hoped for greater gain than loss; but of this, I was not entirely confident. More than a year of trial now shows no loss by it in our foreign relations, none in our home popular sentiment, none in our white military force,—no loss by it any how or any where. On the contrary, it shows a gain of quite a hundred and thirty thousand soldiers, seamen, and laborers. These are palpable facts, about which, as facts, there can be no cavilling. We have the men; and we could not have had them without the measure.

["]And now let any Union man who complains of the measure, test himself by writing down in one line that he is for subduing the rebellion by force of arms; and in the next, that he is for taking these hundred and thirty thousand men from the Union side, and placing them where they would be but for the measure he condemns. If he can not face his case so stated, it is only because he can not face the truth.["]

I add a word which was not in the verbal conversation. In telling this tale I attempt no compliment to my own sagacity. I claim not to have controlled events, but confess plainly that events have controlled me. Now, at the end of three years struggle the nation's condition is not what either party, or any man devised, or expected. God alone can claim it. Whither it is tending seems plain. If God now wills the removal of a great wrong, and wills also that we of the North as well as you of the South, shall pay fairly for our complicity in that wrong, impartial history will find therein new cause to attest and revere the justice and goodness of God. Yours truly

A. LINCOLN

"THE LIMB MUST BE SACRIFICED"

Informal Remarks on U.S.-British Relations to George Thompson and Others, the White House

[APRIL 7, 1864]

Lincoln was in the audience when English antislavery spokesman George Thompson spoke in the Capitol on April 6. The following day, Thompson visited the White House to assure the President that in his country "the great heart of the masses beat in sympathy with the North." This is Lincoln's reply, as recalled by artist Francis B. Carpenter.

Mr. Thompson the people of Great Britain, and of other foreign governments, were in one great error in reference to this conflict. They seemed to think that, the moment I was President, I had the power to abolish slavery, forgetting that, before I could have any power whatever, I had to take the oath to support the Constitution of the United States, and execute the laws as I found them. When the Rebellion broke out, my duty did not admit of a question. That was, first, by all strictly lawful means to endeavor to maintain the integrity of the government. I did not consider that I had a *right* to touch the "State" institution of "Slavery" until all other measures for restoring the Union had failed. The paramount idea of the constitution is the preservation of the Union. It may not be specified in so many words, but that this was the idea of its founders is evident; for, without the Union, the constitution would be worthless. It seems clear, then, that in the last extremity, if any local institution threatened the existence of the Union, the Executive could not hesitate as to his duty. In our case, the moment came when I felt that slavery must die that the nation might live! I have sometimes used the illustration in this connection of a man with a diseased limb, and his surgeon. So long as there is a chance of the patient's restoration, the surgeon is solemnly bound to try to save both life *and* limb; but when the crisis comes, and the limb must be sacrificed as the only chance of saving the life, no honest man will hesitate.

Many of my strongest supporters urged *Emancipation* before I thought it indispensable, and, I may say, before I thought the country ready for it. It is my conviction that, had the proclamation been issued even six months earlier than it was, public sentiment would not have sustained it. Just so, as to the subsequent action in reference to enlisting blacks in the Border States. The step, taken sooner, could not, in my judgment, have been carried out. A man watches his pear-tree day after day, impatient for the ripening of the fruit. Let him attempt to *force* the process, and he may spoil both fruit and tree. But let him patiently *wait,* and the ripe pear at length falls into his lap! We have seen this great revolution in public sentiment slowly but *surely* progressing, so that, when final action came, the opposition was not strong enough to defeat the purpose. I can now solemnly assert that I have a clear conscience in regard to my action on this momentous question. I have done what no man could have helped doing, standing in my place.

"A GOOD DEFINITION OF THE WORD LIBERTY"

From an Address at "Sanitary Fair," Baltimore, Maryland

[APRIL 18, 1864]

Lincoln made this little speech during one of his rare presidential trips, to Baltimore, for a war charity fair that raised $40,000. Only three years earlier, anti-Union sentiment in Baltimore was running so high that Massachusetts troops on their way to the defense of Washington had been attacked on the streets. When the President-elect himself passed through Baltimore en route to his inauguration, "not one voice broke the stillness to cheer me," Lincoln wrote in a section of this speech he decided to delete. Actually, he had slipped through the city in secret that night because of assassination threats.

. . . The world has never had a good definition of the word liberty, and the American people, just now, are much in want of one. We all declare for liberty; but in using the same *word* we do not all mean the same *thing*. With some the word liberty may mean for each man to do as he pleases with himself, and the product of his labor; while with others the same word may mean for some men to do as they please with other men, and the product of other men's labor. Here are two, not only different, but incompatable things, called by the same name—liberty. And it follows that each of the things is, by the respective parties, called by two different and incompatable names—liberty and tyranny.

The shepherd drives the wolf from the sheep's throat, for which the sheep thanks the shepherd as a *liberator,* while the wolf denounces him for the same act as the destroyer of liberty, especially as the sheep was a black one. Plainly the sheep and the wolf are not agreed upon a definition of the word liberty; and precisely the same difference prevails to-day among us human creatures, even in the North, and all professing to love liberty. Hence we behold the processes by which thousands are daily passing from under the yoke of bondage, hailed by some as the advance of liberty, and bewailed by others as the destruction of all liberty. Recently, as it seems, the people of Maryland have been doing something to define liberty; and thanks to them that, in what they have done, the wolf's dictionary, has been repudiated.

"SO THAT THEY CAN HAVE THE BENEFIT"

Letter to Senator Charles Sumner

[MAY 19, 1864]

In April 1864, Confederate general Nathan Bedford Forrest captured Fort Pillow in Tennessee, inflicting heavy losses on both black and white defenders. Rumors quickly spread that the Union troops had surrendered, only to be killed. Forrest, who denied the stories, did boast that the carnage proved "Negro soldiers cannot cope with Southerners," adding: "The river was dyed with the blood of the slaughter for 200 yards." The Fort Pillow Massacre, as it came to be called, enraged Northerners. Lincoln eventually promised that if the stories were proven, "retribution shall . . . surely come." Here he endorsed the idea of providing pensions to the black victims' widows, even though they had not been married in conventional ceremonies, as the pension law required.

Executive Mansion,
Hon. Charles Sumner,   Washington, May 19, 1864.

My dear Sir:

The bearer of this is the widow of Major [Lionel] Booth, who fell at Fort-Pillow. She makes a point, which I think very worthy of consideration which is, widows and children *in fact,* of colored soldiers who fall in our service, be placed in law, the same as if their marriages were legal, so that they can have the benefit of the provisions made the widows & orphans of white soldiers. Please see & hear Mrs. Booth. Yours truly

A. LINCOLN

"MAY I HAVE TO ANSWER FOR ROBBING NO MAN"

Response to a Delegation of Baptists

[MAY 30, 1864]

This is the draft of Lincoln's formal reply to a resolution of warm support from a delegation of Baptist missionaries.

Rev. Dr. Ide ⎫
Hon. J. R. Doolittle ⎬ Committee
& Hon. A. Hubbell ⎭

Executive Mansion,
Washington,
May 30. 1864.

In response to the preamble and resolutions of the American Baptist Home Mission Society, which you did me the honor to present, I can only thank you for thus adding to the effective and almost unanimous support which the Christian communities are so zealously giving to the country, and to liberty. Indeed it is difficult to conceive how it could be otherwise with any one professing christianity, or even having ordinary perceptions of right and wrong. To read in the Bible, as the word of God himself, that "In the sweat of *thy* face shalt thou eat bread,["] and to preach therefrom that, "In the sweat of *other mans* faces shalt thou eat bread," to my mind can scarcely be reconciled with honest sincerity. When brought to my final reckoning, may I have to answer for robbing no man of his goods; yet more tolerable even this, than for robbing one of himself, and all that was his. When, a year or two ago, those professedly holy men of the South, met in the semblance of prayer and devotion, and, in the name of Him who said "As ye would all men should do unto you, do ye even so unto them" appealed to the christian world to aid them in doing to a whole race of men, as they would have no man do unto themselves, to my thinking, they contemned and insulted God and His church, far more than did Satan when he tempted the Saviour with the Kingdoms of the earth. The devils attempt was no more false, and far less hypocritical. But let me forbear, remembering it is also written "Judge not, lest ye be judged."

"A FITTING, AND NECESSARY CONCLUSION"

Reply to the Committee Notifying President Lincoln of His Renomination, the White House

[JUNE 9, 1864]

Lincoln was renominated for president without opposition by the National Union Party—a new coalition of Republicans and prowar Democrats. Andrew Johnson, military governor of Tennessee, was nominated for vice president. This was Lincoln's reply to the delegation that traveled to the White House to inform him officially of the honor. He was the first incumbent since Martin Van Buren to be nominated to a second term and the first since Andrew Jackson—in 1836—to win reelection. Even more astonishing was the fact that in the midst of a rebellion, the election was going forward on schedule.

Gentlemen of the Committee: I will neither conceal my gratification, nor restrain the expression of my gratitude, that the Union people, through their convention, in their continued effort to save, and advance the nation, have deemed me not unworthy to remain in my present position.

I know no reason to doubt that I shall accept the nomination tendered; and yet perhaps I should not declare definitely before reading and considering what is called the Platform.

I will say now, however, I approve the declaration in favor of so amending the Constitution as to prohibit slavery throughout the nation. When the people in revolt, with a hundred days of explicit notice, that they could, within those days, resume their allegiance, without the overthrow of their institution, and that they could not so resume it afterwards, elected to stand out, such amendment of the Constitution as now proposed, became a fitting, and necessary conclusion to the final success of the Union cause. Such alone can meet and cover all cavils.

Now, the unconditional Union men, North and So
importance, and embrace it. In the joint names of Liberty
let us labor to give it legal form, and practical effect.

"THE *PEOPLE'S* BUSINESS"

Informal Remarks on the Election, the White House

[AUGUST 1864]

Hearing a "discouraging account" of his reelection prospects in New York State, Lincoln offered these trenchant comments "with grim earnestness," as recorded by artist-in-residence Francis B. Carpenter.

Well, I cannot run the political machine; I have enough on my hands without *that.* It is the *people's* business,—the election is in their hands. If they turn their backs to the fire, and get *scorched* in the rear, they'll find they have got to "*sit*" on the "blister!"

"I SHOULD DESERVE TO BE DAMNED"

Conversation with Wisconsin Politicians, the Soldiers' Home, Outside Washington

[AUGUST 1864]

By mid-1864, black Union soldiers had amply proven their bravery in the field. Apparently, however, there were still some Northern politicians who thought that compromise on emancipation might still shorten the war and save white lives. Lincoln angrily rebuked such a strategy in this conversation with former Wisconsin governor Alexander W. Randall, held at the Soldiers' Home, the President's summer residence some two miles north of Washington. The conversation was witnessed by a Wisconsin judge, who later published it in the Gray County Herald, *recalling that Lincoln spoke these words with a "gushing sympathy for those who offered their lives for their country."*

There have been men base enough to propose to me to return to slavery the black warriors of Port Hudson and Olustee [battles in Louisiana and Florida, respectively, where "colored" regiments had fought bravely—eds.] and thus win the respect of the masters they fought. Should I do so, I should deserve to be damned in time and eternity. Come what will, I will keep my faith with friend and foe. My enemies pretend I am now carrying on this war for the sole purpose of Abolition. So long as I am President, it shall be carried on for the sole purpose of restoring the Union. But no human power can subdue this rebellion without the use of the emancipation policy, and every other policy calculated to weaken the moral and physical forces of the rebellion.

Freedom has given us two hundred thousand men raised on Southern soil. It will give us more yet. Just so much it has subtracted from the enemy, and instead of alienating the South, there are now evidences of a fraternal feeling growing up between our men and the rank and file of the rebel soldiers. Let my enemies prove to the country that the destruction of slavery is not necessary to a restoration of the Union. I will abide the issue.

"KINDLY PAYING ATTENTION"

Letter to John McMahon

[AUGUST 6, 1864]

"I hope you will be kind enough to pay attention," wrote one angry citizen to the President. "White men is in class number one & black men in class number two & must be governed by white men forever." This tongue-in-cheek reply was drafted by the President, and sent out over the signature of his secretary, John G. Nicolay.

John McMahon   Washington, D.C.
Harmbrook, Bradford Co Penn.   Aug. 6. 1864

The President has received yours of yesterday, and is kindly paying attention to it. As it is my business to assist him whenever I can, I will thank you to inform me, for his use, whether you are either a white man or black one, because in either case, you can not be regarded as an entirely impartial judge. It may be that you belong to a third or fourth class of *yellow* or *red* men, in which case the impartiality of your judgment would be more apparant.

"ANY ONE OF YOUR CHILDREN MAY LOOK TO COME HERE"

Speech to the 166th Ohio Regiment, the White House

[AUGUST 22, 1864]

Lincoln made this emotional speech to a regiment of battle-weary soldiers on their way home after concluding their army service. The speech was published in the press the following day.

I suppose you are going home to see your families and friends. For the service you have done in this great struggle in which we are engaged I present you sincere thanks for myself and the country. I almost always feel inclined, when I happen to say anything to soldiers, to impress upon them in a few brief remarks the importance of success in this contest. It is not merely for to-day, but for all time to come that we should perpetuate for our children's children this great and free government, which we have enjoyed all our lives. I beg you to remember this, not merely for my sake, but for yours. I happen temporarily to occupy this big White House. I am a living witness that any one of your children may look to come here as my father's child has. It is in order that each of you may have through this free government which we have enjoyed, an open field and a fair chance for your industry, enterprise and intelligence; that you may all have equal privileges in the race of life, with all its desirable human aspirations. It is for this the struggle should be maintained, that we may not lose our birthright—not only for one, but for two or three years. The nation is worth fighting for, to secure such an inestimable jewel.

"MY DUTY TO . . . CO-OPERATE"

Memorandum on His Chances for Reelection

[AUGUST 23, 1864]

Lincoln asked the members of his cabinet to endorse, sight unseen, this memorandum pledging cooperation with the next president. It was written, he recalled later, "when as yet we had no adversary, and seemed to have no friends." With most Northern states "wild for peace," in the words of one political pundit, Lincoln's reelection seemed "an impossibility." Historians James G. Randall and Richard Nelson Current, however, contended that Lincoln never "abandoned hope," convinced that improved "military prospects" could still turn the tide in his favor.

Executive Mansion
Washington, Aug. 23, 1864.

This morning, as for some days past, it seems exceedingly probable that this Administration will not be re-elected. Then it will be my duty to so co-operate with the President elect, as to save the Union between the election and the inauguration; as he will have secured his election on such ground that he can not possibly save it afterwards.

A. LINCOLN

"THE PURPOSES OF THE ALMIGHTY ARE PERFECT"

Letter to Eliza P. Gurney

[SEPTEMBER 4, 1864]

No one is certain what prompted Lincoln to answer the wife of a prominent English Quaker more than a year after she wrote to offer her "hearty sympathy" for his "blessed purposes." But with election day looming, Lincoln may have again been pondering divine will. As Lincoln well knew from their previous meeting (see page 263), Mrs. Gurney and her fellow Quakers were antislavery but also antiwar.

                                               Executive Mansion
Eliza P. Gurney.   Washington, September 4. 1864.

My esteemed friend.

I have not forgotten—probably never shall forget—the very impressive occasion when yourself and friends visited me on a Sabbath forenoon two years ago. Nor has your kind letter, written nearly a year later, ever been forgotten. In all, it has been your purpose to strengthen my reliance on God. I am much indebted to the good christian people of the country for their constant prayers and consolations; and to no one of them, more than to yourself. The purposes of the Almighty are perfect, and must prevail, though we erring mortals may fail to accurately perceive them in advance. We hoped for a happy termination of this terrible war long before this; but God knows best, and has ruled otherwise. We shall yet acknowledge His wisdom and our own error therein. Meanwhile we must work earnestly in the best light He gives us, trusting that so working still conduces to the great ends He ordains. Surely He intends some great good to follow this mighty convulsion, which no mortal could make, and no mortal could stay.

Your people—the Friends—have had, and are having, a very great trial. On principle, and faith, opposed to both war and oppression, they can only practically oppose oppression by war. In this hard dilemma, some have chosen one horn and some the other. For those appealing to me on contentious grounds, I have done, and shall do, the best I could and can, in my own conscience, under my oath to the law. That you believe this I doubt not; and believing it, I shall still receive, for our country and myself, your earnest prayers to our Father in Heaven. Your sincere friend

A. LINCOLN.

"STRUGGLING TO MAINTAIN GOVERNMENT, NOT TO OVERTHROW IT"

From a Response to a Serenade, the White House

[OCTOBER 19, 1864]

Lincoln was serenaded by loyal Marylanders celebrating the end of slavery in their state. He acknowledged them from an upstairs White House window, and with his eleven-year-old son, Tad, holding a torch for light, read this reply, pledging to abide by the Constitution if he was defeated for reelection.

Something said by the Secretary of State in his recent speech at Auburn, has been construed by some into a threat that, if I shall be beaten at the election, I will between then and the end of my constitutional term, do what I may be able, to ruin the government.

Others regard the fact that the Chicago Convention adjourned, not *sine die,* but to meet again, if called to do so by a particular individual, as the intimation of a purpose that if their nominee shall be elected, he will at once seize control of the government. I hope the good people will permit themselves to suffer no uneasiness on either point. I am struggling to maintain government, not to overthrow it. I am struggling especially to prevent others from overthrowing it. I therefore say, that if I shall live, I shall remain President until the fourth of next March; and that whoever shall be constitutionally elected therefor in November, shall be duly installed as President on the fourth of March; and that in the interval I shall do my utmost that whoever is to hold the helm for the next voyage, shall start with the best possible chance to save the ship.

This is due to the people both on principle, and under the constitution. Their will, constitutionally expressed, is the ultimate law for all. If they should deliberately resolve to have immediate peace even at the loss of their country, and their liberty, I know not the power or the right to resist them. It is their own business, and they must do as they please with their own. I believe, however, they are still resolved to preserve their country and their liberty; and in this, in office or out of it, I am resolved to stand by them.

I may add that in this purpose to save the country and it's liberties, no classes of people seem so nearly unanimous as the soldiers in the field and the seamen afloat. Do they not have the hardest of it? Who should quail while they do not?

God bless the soldiers and seamen, with all their brave commanders.

"DISCHARGE HIM AT ONCE"

Letter to the Governor of Kentucky

[NOVEMBER 10, 1864]

On election day, November 9, Kentucky governor Thomas E. Bramlette wired Lincoln to complain that a general he described as "a loyal man and prominent citizen" had been arrested merely for opposing the President's reelection. Although so-called arrests of civilians by the military were by then not uncommon, the governor could not believe that Lincoln would "sanction this ostracizing of loyal men who honestly oppose you." This is Lincoln's reply, complete with a self-depreciating reference to his poor showing at the polls in his native Kentucky, one of only two states he had lost in the election.

Office U.S. Military Telegraph,
Gov. Bramlette   War Department,
Frankfort, Ky.   Washington, D.C., Nov. 10. 1864.

Yours of yesterday received. I can scarcely believe that Gen. Jno. B. Houston has been arrested "for no other offence than opposition to my re-election" for if that had been deemed sufficient cause of arrest, I should have heard of more than one arrest in Kentucky on election day. If however, Gen. Houston has been arrested for no other cause than opposition to my re-election Gen. Burbridge will discharge him at once. I send him a copy of this as an order to that effect.

A. LINCOLN.

"THE ELECTION WAS A NECESSITY"

Response to a Serenade, the White House

[NOVEMBER 10, 1864]

Two days after his reelection, the President read this response to a victory serenade by local Lincoln Johnson clubs from a second-floor White House window. "Not very graceful," he said of the effort later, "but I am growing old enough not to care much for the manner of doing things."

It has long been a grave question whether any government, not *too* strong for the liberties of its people, can be strong *enough* to maintain its own existence, in great emergencies.

On this point the present rebellion brought our republic to a severe test; and a presidential election occurring in regular course during the rebellion added not a little to the strain. If the loyal people, *united,* were put to the utmost of their strength by the rebellion, must they not fail when *divided,* and partially paralized, by a political war among themselves?

But the election was a necessity.

We can not have free government without elections; and if the rebellion could force us to forego, or postpone a national election, it might fairly claim to have already conquered and ruined us. The strife of the election is but human-nature practically applied to the facts of the case. What has occurred in this case, must ever recur in similar cases. Human-nature will not change. In any future great national trial, compared with the men of this, we shall have as weak, and as strong; as silly and as wise; as bad and good. Let us, therefore, study the incidents of this, as philosophy to learn wisdom from, and none of them as wrongs to be revenged.

But the election, along with its incidental, and undesirable strife, has done good too. It has demonstrated that a people's government can sustain a national election, in the midst of a great civil war. Until now it has not been known to the world that this was a possibility. It shows also how *sound,* and how *strong* we still are. It shows that, even among candidates of the same party, he who is most devoted to the Union, and most opposed to treason, can receive most of the people's votes. It shows also, to the extent yet known, that we have more men now, than we had when the war began. Gold is good in its place; but living, brave, patriotic men, are better than gold.

But the rebellion continues; and now that the election is over, may not all, having a common interest, re-unite in a common effort, to save our common country? For my own part I have striven, and shall strive to avoid placing any obstacle in the way. So long as I have been here I have not willingly planted a thorn in any man's bosom.

While I am deeply sensible to the high compliment of a re-election; and duly grateful, as I trust, to Almighty God for having directed my countrymen to a right conclusion, as I think, for their own good, it adds nothing to my satisfaction that any other man may be disappointed or pained by the result.

May I ask those who have not differed with me, to join with me, in this same spirit towards those who have?

And now, let me close by asking three hearty cheers for our brave soldiers and seamen and their gallant and skillful commanders.

"NOT THE SORT OF RELIGION UPON WHICH PEOPLE CAN GET TO HEAVEN"

Story Written for a Newspaper

[DECEMBER 6, 1864]

Lincoln wrote out this story on a piece of boxboard for Washington journalist Noah Brooks, signing his name, adding the title, and announcing: "Here is one speech of mine which has never been printed, and I think it worth printing." Brooks saw that it was published the next day in the **Chronicle.**

THE PRESIDENT'S LAST, SHORTEST, AND BEST SPEECH

On thursday of last week two ladies from Tennessee came before the President asking the release of their husbands held as prisoners of war at Johnson's Island. They were put off till friday, when they came again; and were again put off to saturday. At each of the interviews one of the ladies urged that her husband was a religious man. On saturday the President ordered the release of the prisoners, and then said to this lady "You say your husband is a religious man; tell him when you meet him, that I say I am not much of a judge of religion, but that, in my opinion, the religion that sets men to rebel and fight against their government, because, as they think, that government does not sufficiently help *some* men to eat their bread on the sweat of *other* men's faces, is not the sort of religion upon which people can get to heaven!"

A. LINCOLN.

"THE VOICE OF THE PEOPLE"

From the Annual Message to Congress

[DECEMBER 6, 1864]

This extract is from Lincoln's fourth and final annual message to Congress, which he ended by repeating his determination not to surrender emancipation to win peace. "The war will cease on the part of the government," he said simply, "whenever it shall have ceased on the part of those who began it." The New York Tribune *called the message "straightforward and business-like," but the London* Times *found "the tenour . . . decidedly warlike." In this extract, Lincoln reiterated his support for the total abolition of slavery, and again marveled at the calmness and the pro-Union outcome of the recent election.*

At the last session of Congress a proposed amendment of the Constitution abolishing slavery throughout the United States, passed the Senate, but failed for lack of the requisite two-thirds vote in the House of Representatives. Although the present is the same Congress, and nearly the same members, and without questioning the wisdom or patriotism of those who stood in opposition, I venture to recommend the reconsideration and passage of the measure at the present session. Of course the abstract question is not changed; but an intervening election shows, almost certainly, that the next Congress will pass the measure if this does not. Hence there is only a question of *time* as to when the proposed amendment will go to the States for their action. And as it is to so go, at all events, may we not agree that the sooner the better? It is not claimed that the election has imposed a duty on members to change their views or their votes, any further than, as an additional element to be considered, their judgment may be affected by it. It is the voice of the people now, for the first time, heard upon the question. In a great national crisis, like ours, unanimity of action among those seeking a common end is very desirable—almost indispensable. And yet no approach to such unanimity is attainable, unless some deference shall be paid to the will of the majority, simply because it is the will of the majority. In this case the common end is the maintenance of the Union; and, among the means to secure that end, such will, through the election, is most clearly declared in favor of such constitutional amendment.

The most reliable indication of public purpose in this country is derived through our popular elections. Judging by the recent canvass and its result, the purpose of the people, within the loyal states, to maintain the integrity of the Union, was never more firm, nor more nearly unanimous, than now. The extraordinary calmness and good order with which the millions of voters met and mingled at the polls, give strong assurance of this. Not only all those who supported the Union ticket, so called, but a great majority of the opposing party also, may be fairly claimed to entertain, and to be actuated by, the same purpose. It is an unanswerable argument to this effect, that no candidate for any office whatever, high or low, has ventured to seek votes on the avowal that he was for giving up the Union. There have been much impugning of motives, and much heated controversy as to the proper means and best mode of advancing the Union cause; but on the distinct issue of Union or no Union, the politicians have shown their instinctive knowledge that there is no diversity among the people. In affording the people the fair opportunity of showing, one to another and to the world, this firmness and unanimity of purpose, the election has been of vast value to the national cause.

"NEITHER SLAVERY NOR INVOLUNTARY SERVITUDE . . . SHALL EXIST"

Resolution Submitting to the States the 13th Amendment to the Constitution

[FEBRUARY 1, 1865]

Lincoln's signature was not legally required to send to the states for ratification this proposed constitutional amendment abolishing slavery. Lincoln signed it anyway, perhaps because he wanted his name on the document that, once and for all, would destroy the institution against which he had fought for nearly thirty years. Abolitionist pioneer William Lloyd Garrison told Lincoln, "You have done mighty work for the freedom of all mankind."

February 1, 1865

Thirty-Eighth *Congress of the United States of America;*
At the second *Session,*
Begun and held at the City of Washington, on Monday, the fifth *day*
*of December, one thousand eight hundred and sixty-*four.

A RESOLUTION

Submitting to the legislatures of the several States a proposition to amend the Constitution of the United States.

Resolved by the Senate and House of Representatives of the United States of America in Congress assembled, (two-thirds of both houses concurring), That the following article be proposed to the legislatures of the several States as an amendment to the constitution of the United States, which, when ratified by three-fourths of said Legislatures, shall be valid, to all intents and purposes, as a part of the said Constitution, namely: Article XIII. Section 1. Neither slavery nor involuntary servitude, except as a punishment for crime whereof the party shall have been duly convicted, shall exist within the United States, or any place

subject to their jurisdiction. Section 2. Congress shall have power to
enforce this article by appropriate legislation.

SCHUYLER COLFAX
Speaker of the House of Representatives.

H. HAMLIN
Vice President of the United States,
and President of the Senate.

Approved, February 1, 1865.   ABRAHAM LINCOLN

"A KING'S CURE FOR ALL THE EVILS"

Response to a Serenade, the White House

[FEBRUARY 1, 1865]

---

*Congressional passage of the 13th Amendment brought serenaders back
to the White House. In his greetings, Lincoln took particular pride in
noting that his home state of Illinois had become the first to ratify. This
is a New York newspaper report of his remarks.*

The President said he supposed the passage through Congress of the
Constitutional amendment for the abolishment of Slavery throughout
the United States, was the occasion to which he was indebted for the
honor of this call. [Applause]. The occasion was one of congratulation
to the country and to the whole world. But there is a task yet before
us—to go forward and consummate by the votes of the States that
which Congress so nobly began yesterday. [Applause and cries—"They
will do it," &c.] He had the honor to inform those present that Illinois
had already to-day done the work. [Applause.] Maryland was about
half through; but he felt proud that Illinois was a little ahead. He
thought this measure was a very fitting if not an indispensable adjunct

to the winding up of the great difficulty. He wished the reunion of all the States perfected and so effected as to remove all causes of disturbance in the future; and to attain this end it was necessary that the original disturbing cause should, if possible, be rooted out. He thought all would bear him witness that he had never shrunk from doing all that he could to eradicate Slavery by issuing an emancipation proclamation. [Applause.] But that proclamation falls far short of what the amendment will be when fully consummated. A question might be raised whether the proclamation was legally valid. It might be added that it only aided those who came into our lines and that it was inoperative as to those who did not give themselves up, or that it would have no effect upon the children of the slaves born hereafter. In fact it would be urged that it did not meet the evil. But this amendment is a King's cure for all the evils. [Applause.] It winds the whole thing up. He would repeat that it was the fitting if not indispensable adjunct to the consummation of the great game we are playing. He could not but congratulate all present, himself, the country and the whole world upon this great moral victory.

"WITH MALICE TOWARD NONE"

Second Inaugural Address

[MARCH 4, 1865]

One of Lincoln's most polished, sophisticated efforts, perhaps the greatest of all his speeches, the second inaugural address was delivered beneath overcast skies outside the U.S. Capitol. But as Lincoln spoke, the sun burst through the clouds in what the chief justice called "an auspicious omen of the dispersion of the clouds of war." Lincoln admitted, "It made my heart jump." Several days later, he said of the speech: "I expect" it will "wear as well as—perhaps better than—any thing I have ever produced; but I believe it is not immediately popular." Lincoln explained: "Men are not flattered by being shown that there has been a difference of purpose between the Almighty and them." His magnanimous epilogue to the Civil

War was typically received along party lines. The Chicago Times *called it "slip-shod" and "puerile," but the* National Intelligencer *believed the concluding words deserved "to be printed in gold." This is Lincoln's manuscript copy.*

Fellow Countrymen:

At this second appearing to take the oath of the presidential office, there is less occasion for an extended address than there was at the first. Then a statement, somewhat in detail, of a course to be pursued, seemed fitting and proper. Now, at the expiration of four years, during which public declarations have been constantly called forth on every point and phase of the great contest which still absorbs the attention, and engrosses the energies of the nation, little that is new could be presented. The progress of our arms, upon which all else chiefly depends, is as well known to the public as to myself; and it is, I trust, reasonably satisfactory and encouraging to all. With high hope for the future, no prediction in regard to it is ventured.

On the occasion corresponding to this four years ago, all thoughts were anxiously directed to an impending civil-war. All dreaded it—all sought to avert it. While the inaugeral address was being delivered from this place, devoted altogether to *saving* the Union without war, insurgent agents were in the city seeking to *destroy* it without war—seeking to dissolve the Union, and divide effects, by negotiation. Both parties deprecated war; but one of them would *make* war rather than let the nation survive; and the other would *accept* war rather than let it perish. And the war came.

One eighth of the whole population were colored slaves, not distributed generally over the Union, but localized in the Southern part of it. These slaves constituted a peculiar and powerful interest. All knew that this interest was, somehow, the cause of the war. To strengthen, perpetuate, and extend this interest was the object for which the insurgents would rend the Union, even by war; while the government claimed no right to do more than to restrict the territorial enlargement of it. Neither party expected for the war, the magnitude, or the duration, which it has already attained. Neither anticipated that the *cause* of the conflict might cease with, or even before, the conflict itself should cease. Each looked for an easier triumph, and a result less fundamental and astounding. Both read the same Bible, and pray to the same God; and each invokes His aid against the other. It may seem strange that any men should dare to ask a just God's assistance in wringing their bread from the sweat of other men's faces; but let us judge not that we be not judged [from the Bible, Matthew and Luke—eds.]. The prayers of both could not be answered; that of neither has been answered fully. The Almighty has His own purposes. "Woe unto the world because of offences! for it must needs be that offences come; but woe to that man by whom the offence cometh! [Book of Matthew—eds.]" If we shall suppose that American Slavery is one of those offences which, in the providence of God, must needs come, but which, having continued through His appointed time, He now wills to remove, and that He gives to both North and South, this terrible war, as the woe due to those by whom the offence came, shall we discern therein any departure from those divine attributes which the believers in a Living God always ascribe to Him? Fondly do we hope—fervently do we pray—that this mighty scourge of war may speedily pass away. Yet, if God wills that it continue, until all the wealth piled by the bond-man's two hundred and fifty years of unrequited toil shall be sunk, and until every drop of blood drawn with the lash, shall be paid by another drawn with the sword, as was said three thousand years ago, so still it must be said "the judgments of the Lord, are true and righteous altogether [Psalm 19—eds.]."

With malice toward none; with charity for all; with firmness in the right, as God gives us to see the right, let us strive on to finish the work we are in; to bind up the nation's wounds; to care for him who shall have borne the battle, and for his widow, and his orphan—to do all which may achieve and cherish a just, and a lasting peace, among ourselves, and with all nations.

"I HAVE ALWAYS THOUGHT THAT ALL MEN SHOULD BE FREE"

Speech to the 140th Indiana Regiment, Washington

[MARCH 17, 1865]

Lincoln made this speech from the balcony of Washington's National Hotel in tribute to a regiment that had fought for the Union in North Carolina. Among the crowd was the poet Walt Whitman. This is Lincoln's autograph draft copy of the remarks.

FELLOW CITIZENS. A few words only. I was born in Kentucky, raised in Indiana, reside in Illinois, and now here, it is my duty to care equally for the good people of all the States. I am to-day glad of seeing it in the power of an Indianana [*sic*] regiment to present this captured flag to the good governor of their state. And yet I would not wish to compliment Indiana above other states, remembering that all have done so well. There are but few aspects of this great war on which I have not already expressed my views by speaking or writing. There is one—the recent effort of our erring brethren, sometimes so-called, to employ the slaves in their armies. The great question with them has been; "will the negro fight for them?" They ought to know better than we; and doubt-less, do know better than we. I may incidentally remark, however, that having, in my life, heard many arguments,—or strings of words meant to pass for arguments,—intended to show that the negro ought to be a slave, that if he shall now really fight to keep himself a slave, it will be a far better argument why [he] should remain a slave than I have ever before heard. He, perhaps, ought to be a slave, if he desires it ardently enough to fight for it. Or, if one out of four will, for his own freedom, fight to keep the other three in slavery, he ought to be a slave for his selfish meanness. I have always thought that all men should be free; but if any should be slaves it should be first those who desire it for *themselves,* and secondly those who *desire* it for *others.* Whenever [I] hear any one, arguing for slavery I feel a strong impulse to see it tried on him personally.

There is one thing about the negroes fighting for the rebels which we can know as well [as] they can; and that is that they can not, at [the] same time fight in their armies, and stay at home and make bread for them. And this being known and remembered we can have but little concern whether they become soldiers or not. I am rather in favor of the measure; and would at any time if I could, have loaned them a vote to carry it. We have to reach the bottom of the insurgent resources; and that they employ, or seriously think of employing, the slaves as soldiers, gives us glimpses of the bottom. Therefore I am glad of what we learn on this subject.

"A RIGHTEOUS AND SPEEDY PEACE"
His Last Public Address, the White House
[APRIL 11, 1865]

Lincoln's last public speech, delivered from a White House window after his return from a triumphant visit to conquered Richmond, was business-like and detailed, a distinct anticlimax to his rhetorical zenith at the second inaugural. But as historian Don E. Fehrenbacher has pointed out, the Reconstruction address reflected Lincoln's intention to go "to work again after having finished one heavy task." It was, Fehrenbacher added, "a voice interrupted in the middle of a sentence," which may be why the New York World *thought Lincoln groped in this address "like a traveler in an unknown country without a map." But another paper found his last speech "remarkable," both "wise in sentiment" and "pervaded by the logic of the heart." It was devoted almost exclusively to defending the effort to create a free-state government in Louisiana, and was in keeping with Lincoln's inaugural pledge of "charity for all."*

We meet this evening, not in sorrow, but in gladness of heart. The evacuation of Petersburg and Richmond, and the surrender of the principal insurgent army, give hope of a righteous and speedy peace whose joyous expression can not be restrained. In the midst of this, however, He, from Whom all blessings flow, must not be forgotten. A call for a national thanksgiving is being prepared, and will be duly promulgated. Nor must those whose harder part gives us the cause of rejoicing, be overlooked. Their honors must not be parcelled out with others. I myself, was near the front, and had the high pleasure of transmitting much of the good news to you; but no part of the honor, for plan or execution, is mine. To Gen. Grant, his skilful officers, and brave men, all belongs. The gallant Navy stood ready, but was not in reach to take active part.

By these recent successes the re-inauguration of the national authority—reconstruction—which has had a large share of thought from the first, is pressed much more closely upon our attention. It is fraught with great difficulty. Unlike the case of a war between independent nations, there is no authorized organ for us to treat with. No one man has authority to give up the rebellion for any other man. We simply must begin with, and mould from, disorganized and discordant elements. Nor is it a small additional embarrassment that we, the loyal people, differ among ourselves as to the mode, manner, and means of reconstruction.

As a general rule, I abstain from reading the reports of attacks upon myself, wishing not to be provoked by that to which I can not properly offer an answer. In spite of this precaution, however, it comes to my knowledge that I am much censured for some supposed agency in setting up, and seeking to sustain, the new State Government of Louisiana. In this I have done just so much as, and no more than, the public knows. In the Annual Message of Dec. 1863 and accompanying Proclamation, I presented *a* plan of re-construction (as the phrase goes) which, I promised, if adopted by any State, should be acceptable to, and sustained by, the Executive government of the nation. I distinctly stated that this was not the only plan which might possibly be acceptable; and I also distinctly protested that the Executive claimed no right to say when, or whether members should be admitted to seats in Congress from such States. This plan was, in advance, submitted to the then Cabinet, and distinctly approved by every member of it. One of them suggested that I should then, and in that connection, apply the Emancipation Proclamation to the theretofore excepted parts of Virginia and Louisiana; that I should drop the suggestion about apprenticeship for freed-people, and that I should omit the protest against my own power, in regard to the admission of members to Congress; but even he approved every part and parcel of the plan which has since been employed or touched by the action of Louisiana. The new constitution of Louisiana, declaring emancipation for the whole State, practically applies the Proclamation to the part previously excepted. It does not adopt apprenticeship for freed-people; and it is silent, as it could not well be otherwise, about the admission of members to Congress. So that, as it applies to Louisiana, every member of the Cabinet fully approved the plan. The Message went to Congress, and I received many commendations of the plan, written and verbal; and not a single objection to it, from any professed emancipationist, came to my knowledge, until after the news reached Washington that the people of Louisiana had begun to move in accordance with it. From about July 1862, I had corresponded with different persons, supposed to be interested, seeking a reconstruction of a State government for Louisiana. When the Message of 1863, with the plan before mentioned, reached New-Orleans, Gen. [Nathaniel P.] Banks wrote me that he was confident the people, with his military co-operation, would reconstruct, substantially on that plan. I wrote him, and some of them to try it; they tried it, and the result is known. Such only has been my agency in getting up the Louisiana government. As to sustaining it, my promise is out, as before stated. But, as bad promises are better broken than kept, I shall treat this as a bad promise, and break it, whenever I shall be convinced that keeping it is adverse to the public interest. But I have not yet been so convinced.

I have been shown a letter on this subject, supposed to be an able one, in which the writer expresses regret that my mind has not seemed to be definitely fixed on the question whether the seceded States, so called, are in the Union or out of it. It would perhaps, add astonishment to his regret, were he to learn that since I have found professed Union men endeavoring to make that question, I have *purposely* forborne any public expression upon it. As appears to me that question has not been, nor yet is, a practically material one, and that any discussion of it, while it thus remains practically immaterial, could have no effect other than the mischievous one of dividing our friends. As yet, whatever it may hereafter become, that question is bad, as the basis of a controversy, and good for nothing at all—a merely pernicious abstraction.

We all agree that the seceded States, so called, are out of their proper practical relation with the Union; and that the sole object of the government, civil and military, in regard to those States is to again get them into that proper practical relation. I believe it is not only possible, but in fact, easier, to do this, without deciding, or even considering, whether these states have even been out of the Union, than with it. Finding themselves safely at home, it would be utterly immaterial whether they had ever been abroad. Let us all join in doing the acts necessary to restoring the proper practical relation between these states and the Union; and each forever after, innocently indulge his own opinion whether, in doing the acts, he brought the States from without, into the Union, or only gave them proper assistance, they never having been out of it.

The amount of constituency, so to to [*sic*] speak, on which the new Louisiana government rests, would be more satisfactory to all, if it contained fifty, thirty, or even twenty thousand, instead of only about twelve thousand, as it does. It is also unsatisfactory to some that the elective franchise is not given to the colored man. I would myself prefer that it were now conferred on the very intelligent, and on those who serve our cause as soldiers. Still the question is not whether the Louisiana government, as it stands, is quite all that is desirable. The question is "Will it be wiser to take it as it is, and help to improve it; or to reject, and disperse it?" "Can Louisiana be brought into proper practical relation with the Union *sooner* by *sustaining*, or by *discarding* her new State Government?"

Some twelve thousand voters in the heretofore slave-state of Louisiana have sworn allegiance to the Union, assumed to be the rightful political power of the State, held elections, organized a State government, adopted a free-state constitution, giving the benefit of public schools equally to black and white, and empowering the Legislature to confer the elective franchise upon the colored man. Their Legislature has already voted to ratify the constitutional amendment recently passed by Congress, abolishing slavery throughout the nation. These twelve thousand persons are thus fully committed to the Union, and to perpetual freedom in the state—committed to the very things, and nearly all the things the nation wants—and they ask the nations recognition, and it's assistance to make good their committal. Now, if we reject, and spurn them, we do our utmost to disorganize and disperse them. We in effect say to the white men "You are worthless, or worse—

we will neither help you, nor be helped by you." To the blacks we say "This cup of liberty which these, your old masters, hold to your lips, we will dash from you, and leave you to the chances of gathering the spilled and scattered contents in some vague and undefined when, where, and how." If this course, discouraging and paralyzing both white and black, has any tendency to bring Louisiana into proper practical relations with the Union, I have, so far, been unable to perceive it. If, on the contrary, we recognize, and sustain the new government of Louisiana the converse of all this is made true. We encourage the hearts, and nerve the arms of the twelve thousand to adhere to their work, and argue for it, and proselyte for it, and fight for it, and feed it, and grow it, and ripen it to a complete success. The colored man too, in seeing all united for him, is inspired with vigilance, and energy, and daring, to the same end. Grant that he desires the elective franchise, will he not attain it sooner by saving the already advanced steps toward it, than by running backward over them? Concede that the new government of Louisiana is only to what it should be as the egg is to the fowl, we shall sooner have the fowl by hatching the egg than by smashing it? Again, if we reject Louisiana, we also reject one vote in favor of the proposed amendment to the national constitution. To meet this proposition, it has been argued that no more than three fourths of those States which have not attempted secession are necessary to validly ratify the amendment. I do not commit myself against this, further than to say that such a ratification would be questionable, and sure to be persistently questioned; while a ratification by three fourths of all the States would be unquestioned and unquestionable.

I repeat the question. "Can Louisiana be brought into proper practical relation with the Union *sooner* by *sustaining* or by *discarding* her new State Government["]?

What has been said of Louisiana will apply generally to other States. And yet so great peculiarities pertain to each state; and such important and sudden changes occur in the same state; and withal, so new and unprecedented is the whole case, that no exclusive, and inflexible plan can safely be prescribed as to details and colatterals. Such exclusive, and inflexible plan, would surely become a new entanglement. Important principles may, and must, be inflexible.

In the present *"situation"* as the phrase goes, it may be my duty to make some new announcement to the people of the South. I am considering, and shall not fail to act, when satisfied that action will be proper.

"A Union of Hearts and Hands"
From His Last Letter, to James H. Van Alen
[APRIL 14, 1865]

The original text of this letter has never been found, nor has the note that inspired it, a plea from a New York general that Lincoln take special precautions against assassination. This reply was published in the **Sunday Morning Chronicle** *on April 23, but by then Lincoln had been dead a week—just as Van Alen had feared, the victim of an assassin.*

Washington, April 14th, 1865.

My dear Sir:

I intend to adopt the advice of my friends and use due precaution. . . . I thank you for the assurance you give me that I shall be supported by conservative men like yourself, in the efforts I may make to restore the Union, so as to make it, to use your language, a Union of hearts and hands as well as of States. Yours truly,

A. LINCOLN.

Afterword
THE ABRAHAM LINCOLN ASSOCIATION

BY FRANK J. WILLIAMS

Carl Sandburg was right when he said at the end of his oration before a joint session of the United States Congress:

> The people of many other countries take Lincoln now for their own. He belongs to them. He stands for decency, honest dealing, plain talk, and funny stories. . . . He had something they would like to see spread everywhere over the world . . . Democracy.

But why would the Abraham Lincoln Association, originally orga nized in Springfield, Illinois, for a neighborhood Lincoln's birthday party, become a major sponsor of this volume? The organization, known at first as the Lincoln Centennial Association, was begun in 1908 to celebrate the hundredth anniversary of Lincoln's birth the following February. Until 1924, its major function was to stage an annual observance on Lincoln's birthday, featuring prominent speakers giving banquet addresses.

Fortunately, the Association was reorganized to support activities of a broader nature. This was appropriate—as Lincoln no longer belonged just to the people of Springfield but to the entire world. The Association recognized its responsibility to help bring information about him to all people, not just those who lived within the precincts of Lincoln's hometown. Our sponsorship of this book, containing material from the million-word Lincoln utterance record that relates to democracy, civil liberties, and freedom, represents a recognition of this mission.

It also represents recognition of changes in our emphasis over the years. After the Association reorganized in 1924, its principal mission was to discover and make accessible unknown facts about the life of Lincoln. Beginning in 1940, with the publication of *The Abraham Lincoln Quarterly,* the Association increased its emphasis on the interpretation of the facts already accumulated and, at the same time, brought Lincoln's presidency more frequently within its examination.

This bold research program was undertaken as a result of the leadership of Springfield lawyer Logan Hay (the son of Milton Hay, who had studied law in Lincoln's office), who hoped the Association would ". . . contribute something solid and lasting to the understanding and appreciation of Lincoln's life."

An extensive publications program began with the first annual volume of the *Lincoln Centennial Association Papers.* This was followed shortly by a bulletin published regularly and written by Paul M. Angle, the first full-time, paid secretary. It was he who made the Association famous in 1928 by uncovering the fraud of the Wilma Frances Minor letters, purportedly written by and between Abraham Lincoln and Ann Rutledge. In 1929, the Lincoln Centennial Association changed its name to the Abraham Lincoln Association. Successor secretaries read like a *Who's Who* of Lincoln scholars: Benjamin P. Thomas, Harry E. Pratt, William E. Baringer, and Roy P. Basler. As a result, other important reference books became available: *Lincoln Day by Day: A Chronology, 1809–1865* (Angle and Thomas), *Lincoln's New Salem* (Thomas), *Personal Finances of Abraham Lincoln* (edited by Pratt). Then, exhausted and wrongly believing its work to be finished, the Association almost ceased to exist when *The Collected Works of Abraham Lincoln* was published in 1953. It revived to raise the financing necessary for furnishing the restored old state capitol, where Lincoln delivered his House Divided speech, and it remains active to this day in the vanguard of Lincoln studies.

Sixty-six years have elapsed since the Association inaugurated its publishing program, and sixty years have passed since the first of its special studies appeared. As this present volume attests, the work is not over. This is the only book anywhere that attempts to present in one place the documents, speeches, and writings of Lincoln relating to such a critical part of man's existence: freedom. To that end, the contribution of the Abraham Lincoln Association in publishing *The Collected Works* cannot be overemphasized, as it is the source for most of these selections expressing Lincoln's literary and democratic genius.

There are other efforts under way too. The annual *Journal of the Abraham Lincoln Association,* the successor to *The Abraham Lincoln Quarterly,* publishes, in addition to news in the Lincoln field, thought-provoking papers on various aspects of Lincoln's life. Lincoln symposia are held every February 12 in Springfield. The Association is a major sponsor of the Lincoln Legals Project, an effort to collect, collate, and publish all documents relating to the twenty-four-year law practice of Abraham Lincoln. Support of other Lincoln groups and projects is not neglected. Financial support was provided to the International Conference on Abraham Lincoln and Democracy held in Taipei, Taiwan, last year—at which this project was much discussed—and new Lincoln societies have been formed with the Association's aid.

The Association is pleased to be a part of Governor Cuomo's Lincoln on Democracy project and hopes that this book can eventually be made available everywhere in the world.

Today, citizens of America worried about their communities, as well as citizens of the world seeking freedom, search for leaders with Lincoln's qualities. He was a politician without being corrupted, calm without being lethargic, pliant without being opportunistic, tough but gentle, resolute without being arbitrary, and pious without being doctrinaire. He believed in "the ultimate justice of the people."

These characteristics, along with the country that nurtured them, are, in a real sense, the last best, hope of earth. They are heard in the words of Lincoln written in 1863: "Thanks to all. For the great Republic—for the principle it lives by and keeps alive—for man's vast future—thanks to all."

Lincoln, the Nation, and the World: A Chronology

1809–1865

The following chronicle charts not only the history of Abraham Lincoln's life but also external events that surely shaped it. It attempts to place him within the context of both national and world events, as well as the cultural and scientific breakthroughs that were at the same time enriching mid-nineteenth-century society.

Whenever possible, the chronology adapts Lincoln's own, all-too-rare words of self-description—drawn from his two pre–Civil War autobiographical sketches—to enhance descriptions of his early experiences. Unfortunately, while these "little sketches" constitute fundamental building blocks in the Lincoln story, they are seldom revealing. As prolific as he was overall—his collected speeches and letters now fill ten volumes—Lincoln never kept a personal diary of his day-to-day activities, never recorded his innermost thoughts in a personal journal. The only time he ventured to start a scrapbook, he filled it with official newspaper reprints of his debates with Stephen A. Douglas. Even most of his letters to intimate friends were rarely revealing. Familiar though he is to us, he remains always elusive, a baffling mystery, whether intentionally or not, of his own making.

There can of course be little mystery about Lincoln's enormous influence on history, but we cannot tell for certain how well informed Lincoln himself ever became about the world around him, or even precisely when he began to pay close attention to events unfolding in his own country. Save for the Mexican War, which he opposed, Lincoln's autobiographical sketches barely mentioned events outside the crisis-roiled United States. Likewise, his speeches and letters paid no more than occasional attention to global affairs.

We do know, however, that the future president was a voracious newspaper reader, especially once a new job as village postmaster exposed him regularly to the periodicals that arrived for local subscribers. Lincoln typically read them first and delivered them later. From then on, he was irresistibly drawn to public issues and, increasingly, to public service. Technological advances held some fascination for him, too; in his thirties he even sought to patent an invention of his own, a device to buoy vessels over shoals. His interest in literature, such as it was, confined itself mainly to Shakespeare, the Bible, and some Robert Burns, along with one particularly maudlin verse that he committed to memory and recited so often that he was thought by some to be its author. We are not even certain that Lincoln ever read a novel from cover to cover. As president he did borrow a Harriet Beecher Stowe book from the Library of Congress, possibly to prepare himself for a meeting with the celebrated author, but characteristically he did not ask for her famous novel, *Uncle Tom's Cabin.* Instead, he requested her *Key to Uncle Tom's Cabin,* a nonfiction sequel that purported to present "the original facts and documents upon which the story is founded."

A man who could resist the most popular and influential American fiction of his age could certainly be expected to turn a deaf ear to the products of modern European writers, artists, composers, and scientists. Not that science and culture completely eluded him. He was not completely immune to the written word, and he liked music, even if his tastes were pedestrian. He once quoted poet Alexander Pope in the unlikely setting of a Wisconsin agricultural fair. And in a lecture on discoveries and inventions he acknowledged the relationship between freedom of thought and "the consequent advancement of civilization and the arts."

With Lincoln's election to the presidency, his horizons quickly broadened, at least to the extent that the "fiery trial" of civil war permitted him to look beyond his own grueling responsibilities. Now, he would sit in the audience for operas not only by Verdi but by Weber, Mozart, and others. He attended the theater regularly, and once corresponded with a leading actor about his favorite soliloquy from *Hamlet.* He agreed to sit for painters and sculptors. He experimented with new technologies—improved weaponry, for the most part—firsthand. And by the time Dickens's own brother sent Lincoln a flattering request for his autograph in 1862, the President undoubtedly had heard of the novelist and perhaps had even glanced at one of his works. By then his wife, Mary, was eagerly stocking the White House library, armed with a $250 annual congressional appropriation which Lincoln occasionally supplemented out of his own pocket. Included in the purchases were volumes of poetry, travel books, and histories of England and Scotland. It seems likely that the President had occasion to open some of them. Just as he had done with his basic education, which came "by littles," Lincoln was learning on his own about the arts and letters.

As for his own contribution to literature, Lincoln likely undervalued it, but there is ample evidence that he understood his impact on history. Convinced that he was endeavoring to save democracy for the world, he surely sensed that whether the Civil War was won or lost, his presidency would earn him a permanent place in chronologies of world events. "We cannot escape history," he told Congress in 1862. "We . . . will be remembered in spite of ourselves . . . in honor or dishonor, to the latest generation." Once relieved of slavery, he believed, our "beloved history, and cherished memories," would be "vindicated."

Not long before his assassination, a group of Southern delegates to a peace conference urged him to emulate King Charles I of England, who, centuries earlier, had faced his own civil war. Charles had generously allowed rebels to cease hostilities, short of abject surrender. Now the Southerners wanted Lincoln to do likewise. "I do not profess to be posted in history," responded Lincoln, feigning naïveté. "All I distinctly recollect about the case of Charles I is, that he lost his head."

Lincoln did not, and the rest, as the following chronology shows, is history.

→>> <<←

Chronology

1809 ⫷⫷⟵

Lincoln   Lincoln is born on the morning of February 12 in a primitive, one-room, dirt-floor log cabin on Nolin Creek near Hodgenville, in central Kentucky. He is the second child and first son of Thomas Lincoln, carpenter and farmer (b. 1778), and Nancy Hanks Lincoln (b. ca. 1784). Thomas is able only to "bunglingly sign his own name," as his son will disparagingly put it; Nancy uses an "X" on legal documents.

The Nation   James Madison is inaugurated March 4 as the nation's fourth president; Elizabeth Seton founds Sisters of Charity; Revolutionary War philosopher Thomas Paine dies in poverty; poet Edgar Allan Poe and inventor Cyrus McCormick are born.

The World   Papal States are annexed by Napoleon. Among the world figures born this year: teacher of the blind Louis Braille, in France; novelist Nikolai Gogol, near Mirogorod, Russia; naturalist Charles Darwin (on the same day as Lincoln), in Shrewsbury, England; poet Alfred, Lord Tennyson, in Somersby, Lincolnshire; and in a comfortable home in Liverpool, William Gladstone, who would become prime minister of Britain three years after Lincoln's death.

1811 ⫷⫷⟵

Lincoln   His family relocates to a new farm, eleven miles to the north, along Knob Creek, "on the road from Beardstown, Ky. to Nashville, Tenn."

The Nation   Future president William Henry Harrison defeats Indians at Battle of Tippecanoe; Harriet Beecher Stowe, future author of *Uncle Tom's Cabin,* is born in Litchfield, Connecticut.

The World   Austria faces bankruptcy crisis; Duke of Wellington turns back the French at Fuentes de Oñoro and Albuera; King George III of England goes insane, son becomes prince regent.

1815 ≪≪←

Lincoln   At age six, he attends a so-called "ABC" school for the first time; students "blab" their lessons aloud.

The Nation   General Andrew Jackson defeats British at Battle of New Orleans, fought after Treaty of Ghent ending War of 1812 had already been signed but not yet communicated to U.S.; future women's suffrage advocate Elizabeth Cady Stanton born in Jamestown, New York.

The World   Wellington and Gebhard von Blücher crush Napoleon at Waterloo; Napoleon is exiled to St. Helena; Congress of Vienna proclaims parts of Poland a kingdom in union with Russia; Otto von Bismarck is born in Schönhausen, Germany; in England, surveyor John McAdam builds first roads of crushed stone.

1816 ≪≪←

Lincoln   The family moves again in December, this time to "an unbroken forest" on Little Pigeon Creek across the Ohio River in southwestern Indiana, "partly on account of slavery," Lincoln later recalls, but "chiefly on account of the difficulty in land titles in Kentucky." They clear woods and build a cabin. "A., though very young, was large of his age, and had an axe put into his hands at once; and from that till within his twenty-third year, he was almost constantly handling that most useful instrument. . . ."

The Nation   Indiana becomes the nineteenth state in the Union; Second Bank of U.S. is chartered; President Madison signs protective tariff legislation; James Monroe is elected the nation's fifth president.

The World   Polish patriot and American Revolutionary War hero Tadeusz Kosciuszko (Lincoln born the same day, 63 years later) spends final year of life campaigning for freedom for Poland; Gioacchino Rossini's *The Barber of Seville* debuts in Rome; Lord Byron writes third canto of "Childe Harold's Pilgrimage."

1818 ⟪⟪←

Lincoln   His mother dies at age thirty-four from "milk sickness," caused by milk from cows that had eaten poisonous snakeroot. Abraham is "kicked by a horse and apparently killed for a time," but recovers.

The Nation   Illinois becomes twenty-first state; construction begins on New York State's Erie Canal (as president, Lincoln will call the need for its expansion "obvious and unquestionable"); professional horse racing is introduced (a neighbor will later claim that as an adult, Lincoln "enjoyed the races," and "would often place a small wager").

The World   A constitution is enacted in Bavaria and Baden; Karl Marx is born in Treves, Prussia (years later he will complain that "Lincoln's Acts appear like the mean pettifogging conditions which one lawyer puts to his opposing lawyer," hastening to add: "But this does not alter their historic content. . . ."); Thomas Bowdler's "bowdlerized" Shakespeare appears, omitting sections that he insists "cannot be read aloud in a family."

1819 ⟪⟪←

Lincoln   His father, Thomas, marries Sarah Bush Johnston, a widow with three children. "She proved a good and kind mother."

The Nation   America suffers economic depression following "Panic of 1819"; Jethro Wood invents first plow made of iron; Southern territory swells as Alabama gains statehood and Spain cedes Florida to the U.S. under Adams-Onís Treaty, but Congress refuses to admit Missouri Territory as slave state (Jefferson calls this harbinger of sectional discord "a fire bell in the night"); *Savannah* makes first part-steam voyage, twenty-nine days long, across Atlantic; Walt Whitman, whose works will include eulogies to Lincoln, is born on Long Island, New York.

The World   Future queen Victoria is born in London; future prince Albert of Saxe-Coburg-Gotha is born the same year (during the Lincoln administration's severest diplomatic crisis, the *Trent* Affair, he will advise conciliation); forty-nine-year-old composer Ludwig van Beethoven goes deaf.

1820 ⫸

Lincoln   He again attends school. "A. went to A.B.C. schools by littles," he remembered. "The aggregate . . . did not amount to one year. . . . What he has in the way of education, he has picked up." Among the things he will "pick up" over the next few years: the Bible, *Pilgrim's Progress,* and Parson Mason Locke Weems's *The Life and Memorable Services of George Washington.* Later he admits: "He was never . . . inside of a college or academy building till since he had a law-license."

The Nation The Missouri Compromise is enacted, barring slavery in territories north of 36° 30' latitude; James Monroe is elected to second term as president (his 1823 Monroe Doctrine will proclaim "hands off" to foreign intervention in Americas); future women's rights leader Susan B. Anthony is born in Adams, Massachusetts.

The World   George IV becomes king of England; Portuguese citizens revolt, demanding constitutional government; Napoleon dies in exile.

1824 ⫸

Lincoln   He again attends school briefly. His first surviving written words probably date from this year: "Abraham Lincoln/his hand and pen/he will be good but/god knows When." Later he admits: "He regrets his want of education, and does what he can to supply the want."

The Nation Revolutionary War hero Marquis de Lafayette begins final tour of America; Erie Canal is completed; John Quincy Adams is elected president in contest decided in House of Representatives after four candidates fail to win electoral vote majority; in Pawtucket, Rhode Island, women workers go on strike for first time.

The World   England legalizes trade unions; Lord Byron dies at Missolonghi; Simón Bolívar is declared emperor of Peru; two French scientists prove conclusively that sperm cause fertilization; Mexico becomes a republic; Ludwig van Beethoven debuts Ninth Symphony.

1826 ⫷⫷⫷

Lincoln   His sister Sarah marries Aaron Grigsby, of whom Abraham does not particularly approve. (Years later he asks Grigsby's brother to vote for him for president "if your neighbors will let you.")

The Nation   On July 4th, America celebrates fiftieth anniversary of the Declaration of Independence—the document Lincoln will proclaim "gave liberty, not alone to the people of this country, but hope to the world"; as the nation rejoices, aged former presidents John Adams and Thomas Jefferson both die; James Fenimore Cooper advances stature of American literature with *The Last of the Mohicans*.

The World   Russia declares war on Persia; first railroad tunnel is opened on Britain's Liverpool-Manchester line.

1828 ⫷⫷⫷

Lincoln   His sister Sarah Lincoln Grigsby dies in childbirth in January. Three months later he makes his first flatboat trip down the Mississippi River to New Orleans, where he probably sees his first slave auction; during the trip, while trading cargo along the river coast, he and a colleague repulse an attack by "seven negroes with intent to kill and rob."

The Nation   Modern Democratic Party is founded; Congress passes so-called Tariff of Abomination, curtailing imports; South Carolina responds by declaring right to nullify federal laws; Andrew Jackson defeats incumbent Adams for presidency; Noah Webster publishes *American Dictionary of the English Language;* construction begins on Baltimore & Ohio, first American passenger railroad; Gilbert Stuart, America's premier portrait painter, dies.

The World   Vincent Guerrero leads liberals' revolt in Mexico; Catholic Emancipation Act is debated in England as Wellington becomes prime minister (he reluctantly supports it and it becomes law); Karl Baedeker publishes first travel guide (to Rhine region); Leo Tolstoy is born in Russia; Jules Verne is born in France; earthquake in Japan kills thirty thousand.

1830 ⫷⫷⫷

Lincoln

In March, he helps his family move from "the old homestead in Indiana" to an uncleared plot of land "at the junction of the timberland prairie" about ten miles "westerly" of Decatur, Illinois, on the north side of the Sangamon River. The family transports its possessions in ox-drawn wagons, with Lincoln leading one of the teams. He then helps his father and step-brothers build a new log cabin, and splits enough log rails to encircle ten acres for farming. Later these rails are supposedly rediscovered and displayed in public as symbols of Lincoln's rise from pioneer poverty. But he insists they are "far from being the first, or only rails ever made by A." Family is "greatly afflicted with augue [sic] and fever" during the "Winter of the Deep Snow."

The Nation

In U.S. Senate, Daniel Webster and Robert Hayne conduct memorable debate on states' rights and constitution; Joseph Smith founds Church of Jesus Christ of Latter-Day Saints (Mormons); in South Carolina a locomotive pulls a train for the first time anywhere in America; British-born reformer Fanny Wright, who shocks public by appearing on a lecture platform, helps inspire women's rights movement.

The World

William IV, the "Sailor-King," ascends British throne; revolution grips France, Charles X abdicates, and Louis Philippe emerges as "Citizen King"; in Warsaw, Polish military revolts against Russian rule; Belgium revolts and gains independence from Dutch.

1831 ⫷⫷⫷

Lincoln

His family moves again, this time to nearby Coles County, Illinois. Lincoln makes his second flatboat journey down the Mississippi to New Orleans. Afterward, Lincoln leaves his family forever and moves to the village of New Salem, a cluster of cabins near a river mill; here he lives for six years. He "rapidly made acquaintances and friends," including schoolmaster Mentor Graham, who urges him to read further, and Ann Rutledge, a tavernkeeper's daughter with whom he may have been romantically involved. Lincoln becomes a clerk "in charge of a store and Mill," and wins a now-legendary wrestling match against a local bully. He reads Shakespeare and Robert Burns. His interest in politics is kindled, and he casts his first ballot.

The Nation   Ex-president John Quincy Adams takes seat in House of Representatives, where he will serve as eloquent antislavery spokesman until death in 1848; William Lloyd Garrison launches abolitionist journal, *The Liberator;* Nat Turner's slave insurrection is suppressed—he is tried, convicted, and executed in November; first American railroad line opens.

The World   In Poland, diet declares independence from Russia, but Russian forces crush revolt with victory at Ostroleka; several thousand Poles flee, mostly to Paris, in what comes to be called the Great Emigration; Ottoman rule ends in Greece; Victor Hugo publishes *Notre Dame de Paris;* Pope Gregory XVI is elected in Rome, succeeding Pius VIII; Michael Faraday conducts experiments in electromagnetic induction.

1832 ≪←

Lincoln   "An avowed [Henry] Clay man," he is defeated in his first try for elective office as a Whig candidate for the Illinois House of Representatives, the only time he loses a direct popular vote; though he wins his home precinct 277 to 7, he finishes eighth in a field of thirteen. In the summer, he serves briefly in the Black Hawk War, and "to his own surprise" is elected captain of his volunteer company, later writing that he "has not since had any success in life which gave him so much satisfaction." Recalling his wartime service, he will later joke that he fought "a good many bloody battles with the mosquitoes." After the war, he is unsure about his future, and briefly considers a career as a blacksmith.

The Nation   President Jackson vetoes recharter of Second Bank of U.S., is reelected president four months later; South Carolina passes ominous Ordinance of Nullification, early warning of sectional crisis to come; Congress responds with compromise tariff; New England Anti-Slavery Society founded in Boston; New York City inaugurates horse-drawn trolley service; last surviving signer of Declaration of Independence dies.

The World   After prolonged political crisis, and with a hundred peers absent, England enacts Reform Bill extending franchise; Italian patriot Giuseppe Mazzini organizes secret *"Giovina Italia"* society (Young Italy), dedicated to Italian unification under republican government.

1833 ⫷⫷⫷

Lincoln	He is appointed postmaster of New Salem by the Jackson administration, a post "too insignificant, to make . . . politics an objection"; as postmaster he gets his first opportunity to read newspapers regularly. He also "studies a little." He becomes a county surveyor: "this procured bread and kept soul and body together." He enters a partnership in a New Salem "grocery," or tavern, but does nothing "but get deeper and deeper in debt," and eventually "the store winked out," saddling him with enormous obligations which take him years to repay. He supports himself by hiring out as a laborer, and boards with local families.
The Nation	Whig Party is formed, a coalition of anti-Jackson forces; Henry Clay's Compromise Tariff is adopted by Congress.
The World	Slavery is abolished in British Empire; American missionaries increase activities in China.

1834 ⫷⫷⫷

Lincoln	In his second try for elective office, he wins a seat in the state legislature with "the highest vote cast for any candidate"; he takes his seat December 1. John Todd Stuart, his future law partner, urges him to study law. Lincoln borrows books and goes "at it in good earnest," studying alone and continuing to survey "to pay board and clothing bills." He works to master William Blackstone's *Commentaries* and Joseph Chitty's *Precedents and Pleadings*.
The Nation	George Bancroft publishes first volume of milestone *History of the United States* (thirty years later, Bancroft will ask Lincoln for a handwritten copy of the Gettysburg Address, and in 1865 he will deliver and publish a major Lincoln eulogy); Cyrus McCormick patents the reaper, which will revolutionize American agriculture (twenty-one years later, Lincoln will represent McCormick competition in patent infringement case).
The World	Spanish Inquisition officially ends—some six hundred years after it began; Lafayette dies; William IV attempts to force Robert Peel ministry on Parliament, last English king to attempt imposing a government.

1835 ≪←

Lincoln   In the legislature, he works for internal improvements. On August 25, Ann Rutledge dies in New Salem at age twenty-two.

The Nation   Jackson survives first assassination attempt on U.S. president; five hundred buildings burn in New York City fire; Samuel Langhorne Clemens, future Mark Twain, is born in Florida, Missouri; James Gordon Bennett founds New York *Herald;* P. T. Barnum begins career as showman by displaying black woman he claims is 160-year-old nurse of George Washington (in 1861, Mrs. Lincoln will visit his New York City museum, but President-elect Lincoln, suspicious of Barnum's repeated pleas to join her, refuses); gold is discovered in Georgia; Indian tribes forced across Mississippi River.

The World   Emperor Ferdinand I assumes Austrian throne after death of Francis, last Holy Roman Emperor; Prime Minister Peel resigns; birth of Polish violinst Henri Wieniawski; French philosopher Victor Cousin declares *"L'art pour l'art"*—"Art for art's sake" (twenty-five years later, Lincoln has portrait painted for first time and marvels at how artist adds "a touch here and a touch there," making it "look more like me," but admits: "I do not understand it").

1836 ≪←

Lincoln   He obtains his license to practice law. Reelected to the state legislature, he finishes first among seventeen candidates. He suffers a bout of melancholia, which he comes to describe as "the hypo," short for hypochondria.

The Nation   Texas declares independence from Mexico, triggering war; "Davy" Crockett and "Jim" Bowie die defending Alamo; Martin Van Buren is elected president; Roger Brooke Taney succeeds John Marshall as chief justice (Lincoln will choose successor when Taney dies twenty-eight years later); Revolutionary War–era figures Betsy Ross, Aaron Burr, and James Madison all die; John Ericsson, future developer of Civil War ironclad gunboats, patents screw propeller.

The World   Charles Dickens serializes *The Pickwick Papers* in London; English propose a People's Charter guaranteeing universal suffrage.

1837 ⫷⫷⫷

Lincoln   In the legislature, he works to bring about the relocation of the state capital from Vandalia to Springfield. He moves there himself on April 15, 1837, the midpoint of his life; he is twenty-eight years old, and will die exactly twenty-eight years later to the day. In the legislature, he is one of two signers of a brief protest against both slavery and abolitionism (twenty-three years later, he says "his position . . . so far as it goes . . . was then the same that it is now"). He is a chief supporter of the Illinois internal improvement system and Illinois state bank. He becomes the law partner of John Todd Stuart and is admitted to the Illinois bar. After a halfhearted one-year courtship of aging, adipose Mary Owens ("*nothing* could have commenced at the size of infancy, and reached her present bulk in less than thirty-five or forty years," he jokes), she rejects *him*: "Mr. Lincoln was deficient in those little links which make up the chain of a woman's happiness," she later explains.

The Nation Panic of 1837 is triggered when New York banks suspend specie payments; abolitionist Elijah Lovejoy is murdered in Alton, Illinois, site of a future Lincoln-Douglas debate; Nathaniel Hawthorne publishes *Twice-Told Tales* (meeting Lincoln years later, author, a Democrat, will note "a great deal of native sense; no bookish cultivation; no refinement; honest at heart . . . and yet, in some sort, sly"); Samuel Morse demonstrates telegraph in New York City (years later, Lincoln will observe demonstration of Morse signaling from tower near summer White House north of Washington); future Civil War Colonel Robert Gould Shaw born in Boston (in 1863 he will be killed leading "colored" regiment of Massachusetts volunteers in attack on Battery Wagner, South Carolina).

The World   King William IV dies after seven-year rule and Victoria becomes queen of Great Britain.

1838 ⫷⫷⫷

Lincoln   He is again reelected to the state legislature, finishing with the highest vote of seven winners. He delivers an address on "The Perpetuation of Our Political Institutions" at a meeting of the Young Men's Lyceum in Springfield, preaching a "love of law and order" in wake of growing mob violence over slavery. Confiding to a friend about social life in Springfield, he calls it "a dull business," adding: "I am quite as lonesome here as ever was anywhere in my life. I have been spoken to by but one woman since I've been here, and should not have been by her if she could have avoided it."

The Nation   Transatlantic steamship service begins; future actor and Lincoln assassin John Wilkes Booth born in Maryland.

The World   Louis Daguerre demonstrates the Daguerrean process of photography (Lincoln will pose for a daguerreotype a decade later); England boasts ninety naval vessels to America's fifteen.

1839 ≪≪←

Lincoln   He is admitted to practice before the U.S. Circuit Court, and chosen a presidential elector for 1840. In Springfield, he becomes acquainted with future wife Mary Ann Todd. She, too, is Kentucky-born, but unlike Lincoln, her father is wealthy: she grew up in a grand city house, and was unusually well educated, especially for a girl—"vital, brilliant, witty," according to her niece. She is a distant cousin of Lincoln's law partner, and the sister-in-law of fellow Illinois legislator Ninian Edwards. Lincoln, Mrs. Edwards remembers, is "charmed with Mary's wit and sagacity—her will—her nature—and culture."

The Nation   Abolitionists found Liberty Party; Illinois's improvements system collapses; Samuel Morse exhibits daguerreotype in New York; Charles Goodyear discovers vulcanization, clearing way for commercial production of rubber; according to folklore, Abner Doubleday lays out first baseball field in a farmer's pasture in Cooperstown, New York.

The World   First Opium War rages between Great Britain and China; Christian VIII succeeds uncle, Ferdinand IV, as king of Denmark.

1840 ≪≪←

Lincoln   Despite opposition from her family, he becomes engaged to marry Mary Todd. He is reelected to the legislature, but with the lowest vote total in the county. He vows not to seek reelection in 1842.

The Nation   William Henry Harrison is elected first Whig president; U.S. now counts 2,800 miles of railroad to England's 1,300.

The World   Victoria marries Albert; William II succeeds father on Dutch throne; Canadians achieve North-South unification; Polish tragedienne Helen(a) Modjeska, later a noted Lady Macbeth, is born in Cracow; French socialist Pierre Proudhon declares *"La propriété, c'est le vol"*—"Property is theft."

1841 «‹‹

Lincoln   For reasons still unknown, he breaks his engagement to Mary on "fatal first of Jany." Describing himself as "the most miserable man living," he suffers a prolonged depression over the rift, missing several legislative roll calls. He ends his four-year association with Stuart and becomes the law partner of prominent attorney Stephen Logan. Returning from a trip to Louisville, he observes chained slaves being sold downriver, a sight he will recall thirteen years later as "a continual torment to me."

The Nation   A month after inauguration, William Henry Harrison becomes first president to die in office, succeeded by "His Accidency," Vice President John Tyler (twenty years later, Tyler will support secession and win election to Confederate Congress); telegraphs begin operating in U.S.; slaves seize a vessel carrying them to Louisiana and hijack it to freedom in Bahamas; first university degrees conferred on women; future Supreme Court justice Oliver Wendell Holmes, Jr., is born (as young officer during Civil War, his cry, "Get down, you fool!" will save President Lincoln from enemy gunfire at Fort Stevens).

The World   Britain proclaims rule over Hong Kong; first edition of London *Punch* appears; Scottish doctor James Braid discovers and coins word "hypnosis"; Pierre Auguste Renoir is born in Limoges, France.

1842 ≪≪←

Lincoln   Reunited with Mary Todd, he begins courting her again. They marry in her sister's Springfield home on November 4 and take up residence at noisy Globe Tavern in the heart of the city. Mary's sister calls the long-delayed marriage "quick and sudden," complaining she had only "one or two hours notice" to arrange the event. Nervous Lincoln looks "as if he were going to the slaughter," recalls his best man.

The Nation John Charles Frémont begins first expedition across Rockies (during the Civil War "the Pathfinder" will become Union general, clash with Lincoln, and briefly consider challenging him for president in 1864); first Boston-Albany railroad line opens; U.S.-Canada border fixed under Webster-Ashburton Treaty.

The World   Labor riots plague north of England; Boers establish Orange Free State; the polka takes Europe by storm.

1843 ≪≪←

Lincoln   He loses Whig nomination for Congress, but yearns for a second chance, telling one potential supporter: "If you should hear anyone say that Lincoln don't want to go to Congress . . . tell him you have reason to believe he is mistaken. The truth is, I would like to go very much." Lincoln is chosen Whig elector for the 1844 presidential race. On August 1, his first child, Robert Todd Lincoln, is born (a future secretary of war under two presidents, and the only Lincoln child to live past teenage years).

The Nation Jefferson Davis, future president of the Confederacy, begins political career as delegate to a state convention in Alabama; Andrew Johnson, later Lincoln's vice president and White House successor, is first elected to Congress; Dorothea Dix reports to Massachusetts legislature on inhumane conditions in prisons and asylums; Barnum's "Siamese Twins," Chang and Eng Bunker, marry unjoined sisters (alternating nights with each wife, they will father total of twenty-two children).

The World   William Wordsworth is named England's poet laureate; General Baldomero Espartero is driven from Spain by rebels, and thirteen-year-old Isabella II is declared queen.

1844 ≪≪

Lincoln Abraham and Mary move into the only home they will ever own, a one-and-a-half-story cottage sold by the minister who had married them, for $1,500 in cash and land. Dissolving his partnership with Logan, Lincoln starts his own practice, taking as his junior partner newly licensed William Henry Herndon (later a Lincoln biographer and champion of the Lincoln–Ann Rutledge romance story). Lincoln campaigns vigorously for his hero, Henry Clay, for president.

The Nation Democrats demand acquisition of Oregon, declaring, "Fiftyfour forty or fight!"; James Knox Polk defeats Clay for White House; Morse sends first message over new Washington-Baltimore telegraph line: "What hath God wrought."

The World German weaver Friedrich G. Keller invents wood pulp paper; Sarah Bernhardt born Rosine Bernard in Paris; weavers revolt in Silesia; YMCA founded in England; American ships gain access to five ports in China.

1845 ≪≪

Lincoln His law practice grows. He secures a promise that, under the system of rotation, the next Whig nomination to Congress will be his.

The Nation Texas is annexed, later admitted to Union; Florida becomes a state; Mexico breaks diplomatic relations with U.S.; Poe writes "The Raven"; Andrew Jackson dies at his estate near Nashville, Tennessee; Frederick Douglass, Maryland-born former slave, publishes autobiography (years later, President Lincoln will greet him in White House).

The World Spain approves new constitution; Maoris rise up against British in New Zealand; Anglo-Sikh War breaks out.

1846 ≪≪

Lincoln He probably sits for his first photograph, taken in Springfield by a former druggist who masters the Daguerrean process. His second son, Edward Baker Lincoln, is born March 10. The

Whigs nominate Lincoln for Congress, and he wins the election 6,340 to 4,829.

The Nation U.S. declares war on Mexico; Wilmot Proviso proposed, which would bar slavery in new territory acquired from Mexico (it later passes in House with Lincoln's support, but is voted down in Senate—Representative David Wilmot will become senator and wartime supporter of Lincoln); Elias Howe patents sewing machine; Smithsonian Institution organized; Mormons head west to Great Salt Lake.

The World Ireland's potato crop fails, triggering devastating famine; England repeals corn laws; after revolts break out in Galicia, Russian and Austrian troops march on, and Austria later annexes Cracow; Pope Pius IX succeeds Gregory XVI; poets Elizabeth Barrett and Robert Browning are married (Lincoln will add Mrs. Browning's collected poems to White House library in 1862).

1847 ‹‹‹

Lincoln He visits Chicago for the first time to protest Polk vetoes of internal improvement bills. He takes his seat in Congress December 6. Less than three weeks later, he offers the "Spot Resolution," suggesting the United States provoked the Mexican War; Democrats assail him as "Spotty" Lincoln (he will point out in 1860 that the war was all but over by the time he got to Congress, and that "he voted for all the supply measures . . . and for all the measures in any way favorable to the officers, soldiers, and their families . . .").

The Nation In Mexican War, General Winfield Scott wins at Vera Cruz, Cerro Gordo, Churubusco, Chapultepec, and marches triumphantly into Mexico City; Henry Ward Beecher assumes pulpit of Plymouth Congregational Church in Brooklyn, New York (from which he will invite Lincoln to speak for first time in New York thirteen years later); Frederick Douglass founds abolitionist newspaper, *North Star;* Thomas Alva Edison is born in Milan, Ohio; Alexander Graham Bell is born in Edinburgh, Scotland; Ralph Waldo Emerson publishes first volume of poetry (six years later, Lincoln probably hears Emerson speak in Springfield); Henry Wadsworth Longfellow publishes

"Evangeline" (as president, Lincoln will borrow poet's *Song of Hiawatha* from Library of Congress).

The World   Liberia becomes independent African republic; Charlotte Brontë publishes *Jane Eyre,* sister Emily brings out *Wuthering Heights;* Italian chemist Ascania Sobrero discovers nitroglycerin.

1848 ⟨⟨←

Lincoln   He delivers a speech on the House floor assailing Polk's conduct of the Mexican War; speaks for Whig White House candidate Zachary Taylor throughout Massachusetts (meeting his own future secretary of state, William H. Seward, in Boston); attends the Whig National Convention in Philadelphia as a Taylor supporter.

The Nation   Treaty of Guadalupe-Hidalgo February 2 formally ends Mexican War, with U.S. receiving what is now Texas, New Mexico, California, Utah, Nevada, Arizona, and parts of Colorado and Wyoming; gold discovered at Sutter's Mill near Coloma, California; John Quincy Adams dies—Congressman Lincoln is on House floor when "Old Man Eloquent" is stricken; Zachary Taylor becomes second and last Whig elected president; first Women's Rights convention held in Seneca Falls, New York; New York News Agency founded—later the Associated Press.

The World   Revolution and unrest grip Europe as nationalistic yearnings are fueled by unemployment, crop failures, and disease; uprisings in Paris compel Louis Philippe to abdicate; Louis Napoleon is elected French president; Metternich resigns after revolt in Vienna, followed by second and third revolutions; revolutions in Berlin, Milan, and Parma; in Rome, papal premier murdered and Pope flees; Piedmont tries to drive Austrians out of Lombardy; Czech revolt quelled by Austria; in Hungary, Lajos Kossuth leads insurrection for independence; in Frankfurt, calls heard for German unification; Karl Marx and Friedrich Engels publish pamphlet, *Communist Manifesto.*

1849 ‹‹‹‹

Lincoln He votes in the House to ban slavery from the territories and the District of Columbia. His congressional term expires, and under the one-term-only political arrangement "among whig friends," he is not offered renomination; appears for the first and only time before the Supreme Court; applies for a patent for an invention to lift heavy vessels over shallow waters. He seeks a patronage job from the Taylor administration, but despite his "active part" in the 1848 campaign is denied the post of commissioner of the Land Office. Instead, he is offered the governorship of Oregon Territory, but declines.

The Nation Thousands of prospectors head west as California gold rush is in full swing; new U.S. Department of Interior established (Lincoln votes to push bill on his fortieth birthday, February 12); Edgar Allan Poe dies; Amelia Bloomer urges radical reform of women's fashions, replacing dresses with trousers, or "bloomers."

The World Revolutions of 1848 continue, but royal forces reassert power; French take Rome and reinstate Pope, forcing Mazzini into exile; Kossuth resigns as Hungarian leader, flees into exile, imprisonment.

1850 ‹‹‹‹

Lincoln His son Eddie dies February 1 after a protracted illness. In political hibernation, Lincoln resumes his legal career, riding a four-hundred-mile judicial circuit to earn his living, practicing law, he says, "with greater earnestness than ever before." His third son, William Wallace Lincoln, is born December 21.

The Nation President Taylor dies; Millard Fillmore succeeds to presidency; Henry Clay–inspired Compromise of 1850 enacted, its passage adroitly managed by Lincoln's future opponent Stephen A. Douglas; bills guarantee California's admission to Union as free state and abolition of Washington slave trade, but toughen fugitive slave laws (President Fillmore predicts it is "final settlement" of sectional disputes); John C. Calhoun, champion of slavery and states' rights, dies; Soprano Jenny Lind, "the Swedish Nightingale," tours America, earning fortune for herself and impresario Barnum.

The World   Prussia enacts liberalized constitution; France institutes old-age insurance; Hung Hiu-tsen declares himself Chinese emperor, seizes Nanking and Shanghai; German chemist Robert W. Bunsen perfects gas burner; Alfred, Lord Tennyson becomes English poet laureate on death of Wordsworth.

1851 ≪←

Lincoln   He refuses a request to visit his dying father, instead sending word that "if we could meet now, it is doubtful whether it would not be more painful than pleasant." Thomas Lincoln dies January 17.

The Nation   The *New York Times* is founded; New York & Erie Railroad opens, world's longest at only 446 miles; Charles Sumner is named to serve out Daniel Webster's term as Massachusetts senator (during Lincoln presidency, Sumner will become close to both President and Mrs. Lincoln); Harriet Beecher Stowe's *Uncle Tom's Cabin* is serialized in *National Era;* two other important American novels also appear: Hawthorne's *The House of the Seven Gables* and Herman Melville's *Moby-Dick.*

The World   Coup d'état of Louis Napoleon in France; Jean Foucault demonstrates earth's rotation; technological marvels go on display at London Exposition; Cuba is declared independent; Verdi's *Rigoletto* opens in Venice; John Tenniel's first caricatures appear in *Punch* (in 1865, his *Britannia Sympathises with Columbia* will vivify England's regret for its four years of relentless criticism of Lincoln).

1852 ≪←

Lincoln   He eulogizes Henry Clay in Springfield. Chosen a Whig elector in the presidential race, he supports Winfield Scott, but, recognizing the "hopelessness" of the contest, does "less" in Illinois. He rents a pew at Springfield's First Presbyterian Church, but while Mary formally joins, he does not.

The Nation   Henry Clay and Daniel Webster die; Franklin Pierce defeats General Scott for presidency; Wells, Fargo & Company is founded; Stowe's *Uncle Tom's Cabin* is published in book form, selling 300,000 copies in first year alone, arousing nation with harrowing portrayal of slave life (Mrs. Stowe meets President Lincoln years later in White House); Kossuth visits America, Lincoln calling him "most worthy and distinguished representative of the cause of civil and religious liberty on the continent of Europe," future Confederate commander Robert E. Lee becomes Superintendent of West Point.

The World   Camillo Cavour becomes Piedmontese premier; Second Empire begins in France, and Louis Napoleon declares himself Emperor Napoleon III; Duke of Wellington dies; Foucault invents gyroscope.

1853 ⫷⫷⟵

Lincoln   His fourth and last son, Thomas Lincoln, is born April 4, nicknamed "Tad" by his parents. Lincoln takes both criminal and corporate cases as his law practice continues to expand.

The Nation   Commodore Matthew Perry sails squadron into Japan to negotiate treaty to open trade; U.S. obtains 45,000 acres from Mexico in Gadsden Purchase.

The World   Crimean War begins with Turkey battling Russian expansionism; Queen Victoria given chloroform during delivery of seventh child, prompting thousands of her subjects to do likewise; Verdi debuts *Il Trovatore* in Rome (Lincoln will see opera in 1862).

1854 ⫷⫷⟵

Lincoln   "Aroused" as "he had never been before" by the passage of the Kansas-Nebraska Act, he reenters the political arena to stay. He responds memorably to Senator Stephen A. Douglas, champion of Kansas-Nebraska, at a three-hour marathon address at the Springfield fairgrounds. He also speaks against the act in Bloomington and Peoria, and believes that his "speeches at once attracted a more marked attention than they ever had before." Reelected to the state legislature, he declines the seat to make himself eligible for the legislature's selection of the next U.S. senator.

The Nation   Antislavery restraints of Missouri Compromise repealed by Kansas-Nebraska Act May 22; Republican Party, comprised of Whigs and disaffected Democrats, formed July 6; free-staters and slaveholders fight each other in Kansas Territory; Henry David Thoreau publishes *Walden.*

The World   Portugal abolishes slavery in its dominions; British and French join Crimean War against Russia; allied victory at Balaklava, siege at Sebastopol; American and French steamers collide in Arctic, three hundred killed; viceroy of Egypt assassinated; Australian gold rush begins; Tennyson writes "Charge of the Light Brigade."

1855 〈〈〈

Lincoln   After coming within a handful of votes of election to the U.S. Senate February 8 in the state legislature (which then chose senators), Lincoln throws his support to another candidate, conceding defeat. He appears for the defense in the McCormick reaper case in Cincinnati, but cocounsel Edwin M. Stanton, unimpressed, blocks his participation (seven years later, Stanton will become Lincoln's secretary of war and one of his most loyal ministers).

The Nation   Walt Whitman publishes first edition of *Leaves of Grass;* railroad train crosses Mississippi for first time on first bridge to span river.

The World   Alexander II succeeds Nicholas I as tsar of Russia; Charlotte Brontë dies; Ferdinand de Lesseps wins French concession to build Suez Canal; Florence Nightingale revolutionizes battlefield nursing by demanding sanitary standards; Henry Bessemer obtains patent for improved steelmaking process.

1856 〈〈〈

Lincoln   He helps launch the Republican Party in Illinois, giving an unrecorded "lost speech" in Bloomington that reportedly mesmerizes the audience. At the first Republican National Convention in Philadelphia in June, eleven states cast a total of 110 votes for Lincoln for vice president, but he loses the nomination to William L. Dayton. He makes "over fifty speeches" for the Republican ticket. As an attorney, he successfully represents the Illinois Central Railroad in the McLean County Tax Case and charges his largest legal fee ever—$5,000—a sum equal to his typical annual earnings at the time. The family enlarges its house to a full two stories: "What a pleasant home Abe Lincoln has," one newspaper reports four years later.

The Nation   James Buchanan defeats first Republican candidate, John C. Frémont, for president; Senator Charles Sumner is viciously caned into unconsciousness on Senate floor by a Southern congressman; zealot John Brown, avenging sack of Lawrence, Kansas, by "Border Ruffians," leads "Pottawatamie Massacre" that leaves five proslavery Kansas settlers dead in May; three months later he makes brave stand against proslavery raiders from Missouri at Osawatomie.

The World   Crimean War ends; Sigmund Freud is born in Freiberg, Moravia; 13½-ton "Big Ben" is cast at an English bell foundry; Gustave Flaubert publishes *Madame Bovary*.

1857 ‹‹‹

Lincoln   He sues his own client, Illinois Central Railroad, to collect a $4,800 balance on his legal fee. He speaks repeatedly against the Dred Scott Decision. A newspaper describes him, probably for the first time, as Stephen A. Douglas's likely "successor" in the Senate. With Mary, he visits, in her words, "Niagara, Canada, New York and other points of interest"—probably a pleasure trip, marking the only time in his life Lincoln sets foot outside the United States. He successfully defends railroad interests in the "Effie Afton Case," in which a steamboat company sues for damages after its vessel is destroyed in collision with the first railroad bridge to span the Mississippi; the 9-to-3 jury deadlock is viewed as a victory for the railroad industry.

The Nation   In historic, explosive Dred Scott Decision, Taney's Supreme Court rules Negroes ineligible for U.S. citizenship, and Congress powerless to bar slave "property" from territories; financial crisis grips U.S.; *Atlantic Monthly* is founded; more violence reported in Kansas Territory.

The World   Siege of Delhi begins as Indians mutiny against British; Garibaldi forms Italian National Association to spur unification; Pasteur proves living organisms cause fermentation; National Portrait Gallery and Museum of Ornamental Art (later Victoria & Albert) open in London.

1858 ⫷⫷⤎

Lincoln   He successfully defends Duff Armstrong in a legendary murder case, using moon-phase tables in the *Farmer's Almanac* to
cast doubt on an eyewitness who claims to have seen the attack
in bright moonlight; he takes no fee. His party's "First and
only choice" for the Senate, he wins the Republican nomination in June, accepting with the House Divided speech, the
most sectional and radical of his addresses to date. In the
campaign, seeking to share a platform with the better-financed
incumbent Douglas, he settles for an enthusiastically followed
series of seven debates, before crowds as large as fifteen thousand, throughout the summer and fall. In the election, his
party wins the popular vote, but the State legislature remains
in Democratic hands; since legislatures then directly elected
senators, Lincoln's defeat is assured, but with an eye on the
future he says: "Another explosion will come."

The Nation   Dred Scott dies; National Association of Baseball Players is
formed; Minnesota gains statehood; Theodore Roosevelt is
born in New York City (he will watch Lincoln funeral from
brownstone window seven years later); Cyrus Field lays first
Atlantic cable, but it functions less than four weeks.

The World   "Young Italy" revolutionary Felice Orsini makes unsuccessful
attempt on life of Napoleon III; Victoria approves transfer to
Crown of powers of East India Company as peace is restored,
government reorganized in India; Lord Derby briefly becomes
British prime minister; Prussian king Frederick William IV
declared insane and Prince William becomes regent; Ber-
nadette Soubirous claims she sees vision of Virgin Mary in
Lourdes, France; long-standing ban on Jews is lifted, and Lio-
nel Rothschild becomes first Jew to sit in British Parliament;
Anglo-Chinese War ends with Treaty of Tientsin; expatriate
artist James A. Whistler publishes first etchings in Paris; Dickens and William Makepeace Thackeray begin five-year feud.

1859 ⫷⫷⤎

Lincoln   Douglas officially wins the legislature's vote for U.S. senator,
54 to 46. Lincoln seeks a publisher for transcripts of the debates, which he has preserved in a scrapbook. On April 16 he
writes, "I do not think myself fit for the Presidency." He sends

son Robert to Phillips Exeter Academy in New Hampshire after he fails Harvard entrance exams. He tours Ohio, Wisconsin, Iowa, Kansas Territory, delivering political speeches. Later he hints at his availability for the presidency ("I have enlisted for the permanent success of the Republican cause . . ."). Asked to supply information about his life for the newspapers, he writes an autobiographical sketch. Throughout the year, he continues his legal business.

The Nation   John Brown leads armed raid on federal arsenal at Harpers Ferry, Virginia, to incite slave insurrection, but is captured by Marines under Colonel Robert E. Lee, tried, and executed in December ("He agreed with us in thinking slavery wrong," Lincoln comments, but adds: "That cannot excuse violence, bloodshed, and treason . . ."); Oregon becomes a state; at Titusville, Pennsylvania, the first American oil well is drilled; daredevil Charles Blondin crosses Niagara Falls on tightrope (the next year, a cartoonist portrays Lincoln as a "political Blondin" trying to forge the chasm between North and South astride a rail).

The World   Darwin publishes *On the Origin of Species by Means of Natural Selection* (according to Lincoln's law partner, Lincoln regarded Darwin's works as "entirely too heavy for an ordinary mind to digest"); Dickens brings out a *A Tale of Two Cities,* George Eliot publishes *Adam Bede;* Lord Palmerston succeeds Lord Derby as British prime minister, as work begins on Suez Canal, which he opposes; Count Cavour begins campaign to unify Italy.

1860 ⋘

Lincoln   Speaking in February before fifteen hundred people at the Great Hall of Cooper Union in Manhattan, Lincoln makes a brilliant first impression on a dubious eastern audience with his address on slavery, subsequently circulated as a pamphlet. He poses for a widely reproduced, flattering photograph at the Mathew Brady Gallery in New York (Brady later insists the broadly circulated image is "the means of his election" as president). From New York, he tours New England, impressing even his son's skeptical classmates in a speech at Exeter. The Lincoln-Douglas debates are published with an introductory letter by Lincoln. In April, he defends his $200 honorarium for the Cooper Union appearance ("I took it, *and did not know it was wrong*"). Illinois pledges its delegates to Lincoln for president May 10. A week before the Republican National Convention, he admits, "The taste *is* in my mouth a little"; he does some legal work, but jokes to a fellow lawyer, "My *forte* is as a Statesman, rather than as a Prosecutor." Lincoln, who has attended national nominating conventions in the past, declines to go to Chicago for the 1860 meeting. He believes he can win by being everybody's second choice: "If I have any chance, it consists mainly in the fact that the *whole* opposition would vote for me if nominated." Though he urges backers to make no binding agreements in exchange for votes, they ignore his request. At the convention, the favorite, Seward, leads on the first ballot, but Lincoln overtakes him and is nominated after the third roll call; Hannibal Hamlin of Maine is nominated for vice president. The Democrats split: the Northern faction nominates Senator Douglas, the Southern chooses John C. Breckinridge. A fourth, Constitutional Union Party nominates John Bell. Lincoln follows tradition and declines to campaign or to "write or speak anything upon doctrinal points." He remains in Springfield, merely posing for photographers and artists, and greeting visitors. The Republican Party runs a William Henry Harrison–type "hullabaloo" campaign, short on issues, long on hoopla; the country is flooded with Lincoln pictures, banners, song sheets, and broadsides emphasizing "Honest Old Abe's" inspiring rise from rail-splitter and flatboatman. An eleven-year-old girl from upstate New York writes to suggest the candidate grow a beard ("you would look a great deal better for your face is so thin"), but Lincoln gently replies that at age fifty-one it would be affectation to do so "now." His name does not appear on the ballot in ten states, yet on November 7, attracting less than 40 percent of the popular vote (1,866,452 to 1,376,157 for Douglas, 849,781 for Breckinridge, 588,879 for Bell), he wins election with 180 electoral votes to a combined total of 123 for his three rivals. After the election he focuses on cabinet selections, and begins to grow a beard after all.

The Nation   Prince of Wales, future King Edward VII, tours America, and visit attracts as much press attention as presidential election (but when he passes through Springfield, President-elect Lincoln declines to greet him, judging the gesture improper); Pony Express service begins between Sacramento, California, and St. Joseph, Missouri; twenty thousand New England shoe workers go on strike (Lincoln gives support in preconvention speeches there); South Carolina reacts to Lincoln's election by seceding from the Union on December 20; Major Robert Anderson consolidates all federal forces in Charleston, South Carolina, at Fort Sumter, as South Carolinians demand President Buchanan abandon Charleston altogether.

The World   Dutch abolish slavery in East Indies; Decrees of 1860 revive legislative powers in France; first Italian parliament meets in Turin as Nice and Savoy are ceded to France; Garibaldi's "red shirts" take Naples and Palermo, and King Victor Emmanuel II of Sardinia invades Papal States; Garibaldi proclaims him king of all Italy; first British Open golf tournament staged; both Edgar Degas and Edouard Manet exhibit important paintings in France as Impressionist movement is under way.

1861 ⫷⫷⫷

Lincoln   He drafts his inaugural address, rents out his house, and pays a final visit to his stepmother. He fills his cabinet largely with former convention rivals: Seward (State); Salmon P. Chase (Treasury); Simon Cameron (War); Edward Bates (Attorney General); Caleb B. Smith (Interior); also Montgomery Blair (Postmaster General); and Gideon Welles (Navy). He departs his hometown the day before his fifty-second birthday with a touching farewell address which he later revises and improves aboard his train. On the long journey east to Washington, he gives countless informal talks reaffirming the sanctity of the Union and minimizing his own threat to the South. The trip ends with a much-mocked late-night secret passage through Baltimore to foil a suspected assassination plot. With troops guarding Washington, he is sworn in March 4 by Chief Justice Taney, and in his inaugural address vows a "solemn oath" to preserve the Union, telling the South: "We are not enemies . . . we must not be enemies." Lincoln elects to supply Fort Sumter in hostile Charleston, South Carolina, harbor, prompting a bombardment and the start of war April 12; he calls for 75,000 volunteers on April 19, and orders a blockade of Southern ports. He suspends habeas corpus in Maryland to thwart secession, inspiring Taney's *ex parte Merryman* decision challenging his powers; but Lincoln simply ignores the ruling. His message to a special session of Congress July 4 defines the coming struggle as "a People's contest," and asks for 400,000 additional troops. He appoints General George B. McClellan commander of the Department of the Potomac July 27. He overrides General Frémont's unauthorized proclamation of emancipation in Missouri, and removes him on October 24. Two friends die in early war action: young Zouave colonel Elmer E. Ellsworth, who is given a White House funeral, killed in Virginia on May 24; Illinois political colleague and namesake of his late son Eddie, Edward D. Baker, at a skirmish in Virginia October 21. General Scott retires and Lincoln names McClellan commander of the entire Union army November 1. He begins regularly to attend the theater in Washington, borrows books from the Library of Congress, and establishes a grueling office routine that includes *"public-opinion baths"*— open sessions crowded by office seekers and favor seekers.

The Nation   Between January 9 and 26, Mississippi, Florida, Alabama, Georgia, and Louisiana follow South Carolina out of Union; Confederate government formed in February with Jefferson Davis as president; Texas, Virginia, Arkansas, North Carolina, and Tennessee secede and join Confederacy; Robert E. Lee declines command of Union forces and heads south to offer services to Confederacy. Crittenden Compromise, seeking reinstatement of Missouri Compromise boundaries to save Union, fails; former President Tyler chairs peace convention in Washington in February (and in November is elected to Confederate Congress); Stephen A. Douglas dies at forty-eight while on tour decrying secession and Lincoln orders White House draped in black; federal arsenal and fort seized in Florida in early January; expecting easy victory in first engagement at Manassas, Virginia (Bull Run), Union troops are instead routed, dealing blow to North; in November, Union seizes Confederate envoys en route to England on British ship *Trent,* igniting diplomatic crisis that simmers until Christmastime, when, after much discussion in cabinet, Lincoln orders envoys released, a decision that may have prevented war with England; transcontinental telegraph line completed, and Pony Express service ends; Kansas becomes state.

The World   Tsar Alexander II emancipates Russian serfs; soldiers fire at crowds of demonstrators protesting Russian rule in Warsaw Massacre; parliament officially declares Italy a kingdom under Victor Emmanuel II; Italy's Count Cavour and England's Prince Albert both die; among the year's major books: Dickens's *Great Expectations,* Eliot's *Silas Marner,* and from

Russia, *The House of the Dead* by Fyodor Dostoevski; work begins on Beaux-Arts–style opera houses in Paris and Vienna.

1862 ⟪⟵

Lincoln

He names Stanton his new secretary of war on January 13. Son Willie dies at age eleven February 20 after a brief illness, sending Mary into a self-described "fiery furnace of affliction" from which she never fully recovers. Even with war raging, Lincoln signs the Homestead Act May 20, granting settlers 160 free acres for farms; the Land Grant Act, to funnel proceeds of land sales into agricultural education—the forerunner of state university systems; and measures banning slavery in the District of Columbia and the territories. During the year, he names three westerners Supreme Court justices: Noah Swayne of Ohio, Samuel Miller of Iowa, and old friend David Davis (later the executor of his estate) of Illinois. He begins annual summer residence at the Soldier's Home north of Washington, commuting to the White House daily. He writes, and on July 22 first reads to the cabinet, a draft Emancipation Proclamation, crafted as a war measure confiscating rebel property; but at Seward's urging he withholds announcement pending a Union victory so it will not seem like the government's "last *shriek,* on the retreat." After the Battle of Antietam in September, he issues the proclamation, which abolishes slavery in states still in rebellion January 1. He dismisses McClellan as general in chief March 11, though the "Little Corporal" retains command of the Army of the Potomac. In October he replaces Don Carlos Buell with General William Rosecrans as commander of the western forces. On November 5 he relieves McClellan and names General Ambrose E. Burnside commander of the Army of the Potomac. He visits the front several times. In an eloquent annual message to Congress December 1, he proposes a constitutional amendment for gradual, compensated emancipation in loyal slave states.

The Nation

McClellan's Peninsular campaign to capture Confederate capital of Richmond, Virginia, ends in failure, with part of blame directed at Lincoln for withholding some troops to guard Washington; ironclads *Monitor* and *Virginia (Merrimac)* battle at Hampton Roads, Virginia; General John Pope outmaneuvered and routed at Second Bull Run by Lee; McClellan wins bloody one-day Battle of Antietam, Maryland; new com-

mander, Ambrose Burnside, is soundly defeated at Fredericks-
burg, Virginia, in December; West Virginia splits from Virginia and gains admission to Union; in West, Ulysses S. Grant
captures Forts Henry and Donelson, issuing famous call for
"unconditional . . . surrender," wins costly victory at Shiloh,
Tennessee, in April, with staggering loss of nearly 24,000 men
on both sides; sixty-year-old Admiral David Farragut captures
New Orleans, Louisiana, in April; writer Henry David Thoreau dies; Richard J. Gatling patents ten-barrel, rapid-fire gun.

The World   Otto von Bismarck becomes president of Prussian cabinet and
foreign minister, declaring nation's problems must be fought
with "blood and iron"; Sarah Bernhardt makes debut at Comé-
die Française; attacks on Emancipation Proclamation come
from both France ("oil cast on the flames") and England ("Mr.
Lincoln will . . . excite a servile war").

1863 «««

Lincoln   His arm trembling from three hours of New Year's Day hand-
shaking, Lincoln signs the final Emancipation Proclamation
January 1, worried that future generations will think his shaky
penmanship reflected indecision: "If my name ever goes into
history, it will be because of this act." Three days later, he
rescinds General Grant's onerous order banning Jews "as a
class" from military camps in Tennessee. He names John P.
Usher the new secretary of the interior, replacing Smith. He
signs the Currency Act, creating a national banking system,
and approves the first conscription measure March 3. He
names General Joseph Hooker to succeed Burnside January 5,
replaces Hooker with General George Meade June 28, gives
Grant command in the West in September. He again makes
occasional visits to the field. Breaking routine to accept a
speaking invitation outside Washington, he travels to the site
of the Gettysburg battle triumph to deliver his most famous
presidential address ("a perfect gem; deep in feeling . . . compact in every word and comma," the Springfield, Massachusetts *Republican* comments); afterward, he comes down with
a mild case of smallpox. He names Stephen Field of California
to the Supreme Court. His party wins election tests in Pennsylvania and Ohio. On December 8, with an eye on eventual
restoration of the Union, he announces the Proclamation of

Amnesty and Reconstruction. Lincoln visits the theater ten times this year, including three performances of *Henry IV*.

The Nation   Confederate forces prevail at Chancellorsville, Virginia, but lose General "Stonewall" Jackson, who dies after accidental shooting by own troops (North and South report 30,000 dead, wounded, and missing); Union scores twin victories in July at Gettysburg, Pennsylvania, repulsing Confederate invasion of the North, and at Vicksburg, Mississippi, placing entire Mississippi River in Union hands (at Gettysburg, 51,000 casualties reported altogether); free mail service introduced within U.S.; 1,000 die in July draft riots in New York City, blacks particular victims of mobs protesting conscription; William C. Quantrill's Raiders kill 150 civilians in Kansas in August.

The World   Tsar Alexander II moves against second Polish revolution, and Polish autonomy is abolished again; civil war erupts in Afghanistan; French capture Mexico City; novelist Thackeray dies; Siemens steel process demonstrated in France; British government seizes Laird shipyards in Liverpool, where Confederate ironclads are being built (the ironclads are impounded, a blow to South).

1864 ⟨⟨←

Lincoln   In this presidential election year, Lincoln is determined that the canvass proceed as scheduled, rebellion notwithstanding—a major, often overlooked accomplishment. He poses at Brady's Washington photo gallery February 9, in a long session that yields models for the penny and the five-dollar bill. Later in the month, the press publishes a dissident Republican circular urging that Salmon P. Chase replace Lincoln on the national ticket; the episode instead coalesces support for the President, and Chase resigns from the cabinet, June 30. Lincoln meets Grant for the first time at a White House reception March 8; four days later, he promotes him to general in chief, with the rank of lieutenant general, and names William T. Sherman to succeed Grant in command of Union forces in the West. As late as May 13, influential editor Horace Greeley calls for the selection of "some other" candidate than the President. But Lincoln is renominated June 8 on the first ballot by the new National Union Party, a coalition of Republicans and War Democrats, with Andrew Johnson of Tennessee nominated for vice president as Hamlin is dumped from the ticket; the party platform endorses a constitutional amendment to abolish all slavery. Lincoln grants a New York artist six months of sittings for a painting commemorating emancipation. He names James Speed, his best friend's brother, as attorney general. He pocket vetoes the Wade-Davis Reconstruction Bill in July, judging its readmission-to-the-Union requirements too stringent. Following battlefield setbacks, Lincoln believes he will lose the election to Democrat George McClellan; he even drafts a memorandum on August 23 acknowledging the duty to cooperate with his successor, and asks the cabinet to sign it sight unseen. But battlefield successes follow, and then, in September, the President placates radicals in his own party by replacing Postmaster General Blair; William Dennison is named his successor. On November 8, Lincoln receives 55 percent (2,213,665) of the civilian vote to 45 percent (1,802,237) for McClellan, winning twenty-two of twenty-five states for 212 of 233 electoral votes. He is badly defeated only in his birthplace, Kentucky, although he wins his Springfield hometown by just 20 votes. Soldiers vote 116,887 to 33,748—78 percent—in his favor. The eleven Confederate states do not participate, but their combined 1860 electoral strength of 88 votes would not have come close to changing the '64 outcome. When Chief Justice Taney dies, Lincoln names Chase his replacement on December 6. In one two week period, he goes to the theater four times to see Edwin Booth, brother of his future assassin, play Richard III, Julius Caesar, Shylock, and Hamlet.

The Nation   Senate passes 13th Amendment abolishing slavery, in April; statehood for Nevada; Grant's bloody Wilderness campaign in Virginia ends without decisive Union success; Grant lays siege to Petersburg, Virginia, gateway to Richmond; Admiral Farragut ("Damn the torpedoes, full speed ahead!") wins at Mobile Bay, Alabama, in August; General Sherman ("war . . . is all hell") captures Atlanta September 1, begins march through Georgia to sea; Sherman takes Savannah, Georgia, in October, as Union also wins at Nashville under General George H. Thomas; 900 cavalry kill 150 Cheyenne and Arapaho Indians at Sand Creek, Colorado, Massacre; songwriter Stephen Foster dies; first Union prisoners arrive at Andersonville, Georgia, prison camp in February.

The World   Marx founds International Workingmen's Association in London; Florence becomes a capital of Italy as kingdom abandons claims to Rome; Austria and Prussia battle Denmark; Pasteur develops process to "pasteurize" wine; Tolstoy begins *War and Peace;* Austrian Archduke Maximilian is crowned emperor of Mexico, his wife Carlota empress, as French troops drive President Benito Juárez from capital.

1865 ⫷⫷

Lincoln

He meets Confederate peace commissioners at the Hampton Roads (Virginia) Conference February 3, but refuses to negotiate on emancipation, or accept armistice in place of surrender. He urges "malice toward none, charity for all" in his extraordinary second inaugural address March 4. He chooses Hugh McCulloch secretary of the treasury to succeed Fessenden. He visits Union commanders in Virginia, then enters the conquered Confederate capital of Richmond April 4. Liberated slaves greet him exuberantly, "the great deliverer meeting the delivered," in the words of one journalist. Jubilant crowds march to the White House April 10 to celebrate Lee's surrender to Grant; speaking from a window, Lincoln requests that the band play "one of the best tunes I have ever heard," one "we fairly captured" as a "lawful prize" of war—"Dixie." He makes his last speech from the White House on April 11. On Good Friday, April 14, he is fatally shot at close range from behind by John Wilkes Booth while enjoying a comedy in a Washington theater. Carried to a boardinghouse across the street, he lingers for nine hours, dying on the morning of April 15. His death inspires reverential Easter Sunday eulogies across the North, in which he is compared to Moses and Christ. A flood of portraits of "the Martyr of Liberty" are rushed into publication, evidence of a quickly burgeoning myth. After funerals in Washington and crape-bedecked cities north and west, with thousands viewing his remains, he is buried in a receiving vault in a cemetery outside Springfield, May 4.

The Nation

House passes 13th Amendment by three votes January 31; President signs and sends it to states (where it will be ratified eight months after Lincoln's death); Lee made general in chief of all Confederate forces, too late to change outcome of war; after final campaign Richmond falls and Davis flees south, later captured wearing wife's raglan, possibly to avoid detection; Lee surrenders army to Grant at Appomattox, Virginia, April 9, effectively ending Civil War; as Lincoln is attacked in

Ford's Theater, Booth coconspirator makes unsuccessful attempt on life of Seward; on the day of Lincoln's death, American flag is raised at recaptured Fort Sumter four years and three days after its bombardment signaled start of Civil War.

The World   British Prime Minister Palmerston dies; new Atlantic cable completed; Boers and Basutos battle in Orange Free State, Africa; Joseph Lister pioneers antiseptic surgery; Pasteur conquers silkworm disease; Gregor Mendel publishes laws of heredity; Lewis Carroll publishes *Alice's Adventures in Wonderland;* and London *Punch* apologizes to Lincoln in verse for four years of relentless criticism: "The Old World and the New, from sea to sea, / Utter one voice of sympathy and shame! / Sure heart, so stopped when it last beat high, / Sad life, cut short just as its triumph came."

Acknowledgments

First and foremost, gratitude must go to the representatives of the Teachers' Section of Poland's Solidarity Union, whose visit to Governor Cuomo in Albany in July 1989 inspired this undertaking. Among the delegation was Wiktor Kulerski, who has since become a major official in Poland's education ministry.

We express our thanks, too, to the American Federation of Teachers (AFT) and New York State United Teachers (NYSUT), who arranged the Albany meeting and subsequently provided key support and sound advice to the project. Particularly we thank Albert Shanker and David Dorn of the AFT, and Thomas Hobart and Herb Magidson of NYSUT. Their plan eventually to adapt the contents of this book into syllabus materials and teaching guides for Polish students and instructors at all grade levels will help ensure that Lincoln's writings will be more available and more understandable to readers in that country.

The Lincoln materials themselves were not chosen solely by the editors. They were nominated by a corps of forty-seven distinguished historians who volunteered to consider which among the more than one million known words of Lincoln deserved to be included in this first anthology of his writings on democracy. Their names and affiliations are listed elsewhere in this volume. Enough cannot be said to thank these generous scholars. Included among these honored and accomplished individuals are several Pulitzer Prize winners, a winner of the coveted Bancroft Prize, and the recipients of innumerable other awards and accolades. All were understandably preoccupied with projects of their own, yet all of them took the time to offer thoughtful, useful nominations for the book.

We thank in particular the seven distinguished scholars who not only proposed Lincoln materials but wrote introductions to the seven chronologically arranged sections that comprise the book: Gabor S. Boritt, William E. Gienapp, Charles B. Strozier, Richard Nelson Current, James M. McPherson,

Mark E. Neely, Jr., and Hans L. Trefousse—listed in the order in which their sections appear. Their biographies appear at the end of the book.

In addition, Frank J. Williams, President of the Abraham Lincoln Association (ALA) of Springfield, Illinois, acted as a surrogate father to this effort, as he does for so many Lincoln undertakings in which he believes. Early on, Frank designated Lincoln on Democracy as an official project of the Association—no small gesture, because it enabled us to commence fund-raising efforts immediately.

Others among the principal scholars must be acknowledged for additional labors that are not readily apparent in the book itself. Richard Current, for example, the dean of Lincoln scholars—who is supposed to be enjoying retirement—was pressed into service reading and rereading the material, greatly improving it with his wise comments and practiced eye for errors. Mark Neely offered detailed and much-appreciated advice on everything from illustrations to editing, all of it essential. And Gabor Boritt, in addition to reading the material, helped invigorate interest in the entire project by inviting Governor Cuomo to speak at the Gettysburg National Cemetery on November 19, 1989, the 126th anniversary of Lincoln's Gettysburg Address.

Messrs. Current, Boritt, Williams, and Neely all came to New York to advise the governor personally at the very inception of the project, at a long and valuable meeting out of which evolved the format of this book. Joining us for that session were Charles Strozier, Hans Trefousse, James McPherson, and LaWanda Cox of Hunter College, all of whom contributed to the brainstorming.

Readers of the text included Thomas F. Schwartz of the Illinois State Historical Library; Paul M. Zall, a serious scholar of Lincoln's humor; and Robert V. Bruce, the 1988 Pulitzer laureate in history. Chuck Strozier, who once studied in Poland, helped us to choose a translating team for the project. And Kyle Husfloen of Galena, Illinois, provided a revealing hometown press review of orator Lincoln in action.

In the long but speedily traveled road from idea to book, many others offered crucial support.

New York Telephone provided the initial grant, and we thank company president Frederic Salerno, along with Ted Federici, for their generosity. Further support came, as noted, from the teachers' unions, and also from the Forbes Foundation, for which we are particularly grateful to Steve Forbes, a man whose knowledge of Lincoln documents rivals that of many historians. Generous additional funding came from the Alfred Jurzykowski Foundation of New York City, the Brooklyn Union Gas Company, the New York State AFL-CIO, the Kosciuszko Foundation, the Park Tower Group, Lincoln Savings Bank, and the University at Albany Foundation.

Further support was provided by Time Warner Inc., Kadokawa Publishing Ltd., the First Albany Corporation, KeyCorp, and the New York Council for the Humanities.

We are also grateful for the early and useful support of Dr. Feliks Gross of the Polish Institute for Arts & Sciences in America, who advised us on Polish-language publication and international distribution; to Richard Lourie, Director of the Institute for Translation at the State University of New York at Stony Brook, for assembling a roster of distinguished men and women to create a Polish-language edition—among them the 1980 Nobel Prize winner in literature, Czeslaw Milosz; and to Waldemar Lipka-Chudzik, the Polish consul general at New York, who acted as our early liaison to the Polish government.

At our publishers, Cornelia & Michael Bessie Books, Mike Bessie was an enthusiastic supporter of *Lincoln on Democracy.* Our editor, Amy Gash, was a patient and supportive enthusiast, even when the manuscript she thought would come in at 350 pages slowly swelled to one nearly 50 percent larger. And Geri Thoma of the Elaine Markson Agency was an early and important believer in the project. We are particularly grateful to Willard Bunn, Jr., Chairman Emeritus of the Marine Bank of Springfield, Illinois, and his assistant, Carol Fuson, for keeping the project's fiscal affairs in order. Harry Rosenthal of our New York office performed a similar task here.

In the Executive Chamber in Albany, Dan Kinley, Assistant Secretary to the Governor for Education, helped nurture the project's early promise as a teaching tool. Gary Fryer, the governor's press secretary, provided an important reminder of the indispensable utility of an English-language edition to accompany the Polish. And Junko T. Haverlick, Director of the Governor's Office of Special Projects and Protocol, opened many international doors to us.

When this project became an official part of New York State's International Partnership Program (IPP), an initiative of our Department of Economic Development, a number of hardworking people were pressed into service transferring tens of thousands of words by Lincoln into a coherent manuscript. Amelia Varney-Kiet and Valdina Plummer assumed principal responsibility for typing the book, and they did it superbly. Vincent Lipani, Eric Scheffel, and Carol Wright served as proofreaders, making certain that as many times as the ironic error *"Untied* States" crept into the manuscript, it was discovered and promptly corrected. Special thanks go to Carol, who also managed a voluminous correspondence between the IPP office and the forty-three Lincoln scholars around the country with her customary efficiency and coolness under fire.

Also at the state's Department of Economic Development, we are grateful to Executive Deputy Commissioner Alan Sullivan, Deputy Commissioner and Counsel Lesley Douglass Webster, Deputy Commissioner for Intergovernmental Affairs Kevin O'Connor, Director of Media Services Bern Rotman, attorney Glenn Weiner, and Audio Visual Program Manager Joan Lapp. Further assistance came from staff at the State Urban Development Corporation, particularly from Lee Smith, director of the Governor's Industrial Cooperation Council, and Valerie Caproni, UDC's general counsel.

Larry Josephs provided editorial supervision, and made a tremendous contribution to the promotion of the project as well—as did all the members of our public affairs staff: Jan Levy, Brian Kell, Steve Vitoff, and Danielle Parris. We are especially grateful to State Economic Development Director Vincent Tese, who enthusiastically welcomed Lincoln on Democracy as a new IPP initiative that could help open doors to the emerging democracies in Eastern Europe. We are hopeful that *Lincoln on Democracy* will do so.

Early on in this project, Consul General Lipka-Chudzik wrote to inform us that his government viewed "the selection of A. Lincoln's works as the first, landmark publication of classic western democratic ideas to be introduced to wide circles of Polish society."

Without the help of the people and organizations we have cited, this landmark could not possibly have been accomplished. We thank them all.

—H.H.

Biographies of the Editors and Contributors

MARIO M. CUOMO was elected the fifty-second governor of New York in 1982, and reelected in 1986 by the widest margin in the state's history. The governor has devoted his administration to the themes of "jobs and justice" for all New Yorkers, and among its accomplishments have been the creation of more than one million new jobs, farsighted investments to rebuild the state's vast infrastructure, and establishment of the lowest state tax rates in twenty years. In addition, Governor Cuomo gained widespread recognition as one of this generation's great public speakers after his eloquent keynote address at the 1984 Democratic National Convention. He has since delivered two widely acclaimed addresses on Lincoln: at the Abraham Lincoln Association in Springfield, Illinois, in 1985, and at the national cemetery in Gettysburg, Pennsylvania, in 1989, in both of which he exhorted Americans to complete Lincoln's "unfinished work." The governor is the author of two books: *Forest Hills Diary: The Crisis of Low-Income Housing* (1974) and *Diaries of Mario M. Cuomo: The Campaign for Governor* (1983). He has also published *The Cuomo Commission Report: A New American Formula for a Strong Economy* (1988).

HAROLD HOLZER is the coauthor of *The Lincoln Image: Abraham Lincoln and the Popular Print* (1984), *Changing the Lincoln Image* (1985), *The Confederate Image: Prints of the Lost Cause* (1987), and *The Lincoln Family Album* (1990). He has also written two pamphlets on Lincoln and more than 150 articles in newspapers, magazines, and historical journals, and has lectured widely on the subject throughout the United States and in England. Among his awards for his Lincoln writings are the Barondess Award of the Civil War Round Table, the Diploma of Honor from Lincoln Memorial University, and the Award of Achievement from the Lincoln Group of New York. Holzer serves in the Cuomo administration as special counselor to the director of economic development. He lives in Rye, New York.

GABOR S. BORITT is Robert C. Fluhrer Distinguished Professor of Civil War Studies and Director of the Civil War Institute at Gettysburg College. In addition to coauthoring *The Lincoln Image, Changing the Lincoln Image,* and *The Confederate Image,* the Hungarian-born Boritt wrote *Lincoln and the Economics of the American Dream,* a pathfinding examination of Lincoln's views on "the right to rise," published in 1978. More recently he served as editor of *The Historian's Lincoln: Pseudohistory, Psychohistory, and History* (1988) and *The Historian's Lincoln: Rebuttals . . .* (1988). Professor Boritt lives in Gettysburg, Pennsylvania.

RICHARD NELSON CURRENT is University Distinguished Professor of History Emeritus, University of North Carolina at Greensboro. Universally acknowledged to be the dean of Lincoln scholars in America, he was awarded the prestigious Logan Hay Medal by the Abraham Lincoln Association in 1989. A former president of the Southern Historical Association, Professor Current has taught and lectured at universities and colleges throughout the world— even in Antarctica—including a term as Harmsworth Professor of American History at Oxford. He is coauthor of *Lincoln the President: Last Full Measure* (1955), winner of the Bancroft Prize. Among his eighteen other major books are *The Lincoln Nobody Knows* (1958), *Lincoln and the First Shot* (1962), and *Speaking of Abraham Lincoln: The Man and His Meaning for Our Times* (1983). Professor Current lives in South Natick, Massachusetts.

WILLIAM E. GIENAPP recently joined the faculty of Harvard University as Professor of History after eight years at the University of Wyoming in Laramie. He is the author of *The Origins of the Republican Party, 1854–1856* (1987). More recently he wrote chapters covering the years 1789 to 1877 for *Nation of Nations: A Narrative History of the United States.* Professor Gienapp is currently at work on two major efforts: *Republican Crisis,* a book on the political realignment of the 1850s, and a new biography of Abraham Lincoln. He lives in Lincoln, Massachusetts.

JAMES M. MCPHERSON is Edwards Professor of History at Princeton University. He won the Pulitzer Prize for history for his bestselling 1988 book, *Battle Cry of Freedom: The Civil War Era,* the most popular Civil War volume of our generation. Since joining the faculty of Princeton in 1962, Professor McPherson has also acted as Commonwealth Fund Lecturer in American History at the University of London, and has held a number of fellowships. His many books include *Marching Toward Freedom: The Negro in the Civil War* (1968), *The Abolitionist Legacy: From Reconstruction to the NAACP* (1976), and *Ordeal by Fire: The Civil War and Reconstruction* (1982). He is currently at work on a collection of his essays and papers on the Lincoln theme. Professor McPherson lives in Princeton, New Jersey.

MARK E. NEELY, JR. has served for more than seventeen years as Director of the Louis A. Warren Lincoln Library and Museum. He has produced a number of books, including *The Abraham Lincoln Encyclopedia* (1982). He coauthored *The Lincoln Image, Changing the Lincoln Image,* and *The Confederate Image,* and with R. Gerald McMurtry wrote *Insanity File: The Case of Mary Todd Lincoln* (1986). He has won the Barondess/Lincoln Award as well as the 1989 Fletcher Pratt Award from Chicago's Civil War Round Table. Dr. Neely is currently at work on a book about civil liberties during the Civil War, as well as *The Lincoln Family Album,* scheduled for publication this year. Dr. Neely lives in Fort Wayne, Indiana.

CHARLES B. STROZIER is Professor of History and Codirector of the Center on Violence and Human Survival at the John Jay College, City University of New York. Professor Strozier studied at Harvard and the University of Chicago, as well as in Poland. Considered this generation's leading psychobiographer of Lincoln, he wrote *Lincoln's Quest for Union: Public and Private Meanings* in 1982, and earlier was coeditor of and contributor to *The Public and the Private Lincoln: Contemporary Perspectives* (1979). He lives in Brooklyn, New York.

HANS L. TREFOUSSE is Distinguished Professor of History at Brooklyn College, where he won a Distinguished Teacher Award. Born in Germany, Professor Trefousse has also been a Guggenheim fellow, and he teaches at the Graduate Center of the City University of New York. A leading scholar on the Reconstruction era, Trefousse has published widely on the subject. His books include *The Radical Republicans* (1969), *Ben Butler: The South Called Him Beast* (1974), *Carl Schurz: A Biography* (1981), and the acclaimed new work, *Andrew Johnson: A Biography* (1989). Professor Trefousse has also written an important monograph on the Emancipation Proclamation. He lives on Staten Island, New York.

FRANK J. WILLIAMS is President of the Abraham Lincoln Association, which is currently sponsoring the effort to gather all the documents from Lincoln's twenty-four-year-long career as a lawyer, for publication in the 1990s. Previously, Mr. Williams served for more than ten years as President of the Lincoln Group of Boston. In that role he cosponsored the 1984 Brown University scholarly symposium "Abraham Lincoln and the American Political Tradition." An attorney by profession, he is also at work compiling the first definitive bibliography of published writings on Lincoln in sixty years. He lives in Hope Valley, Rhode Island.

Consulting Scholars

Forty historians and Lincoln students aided in the preparation of *Lincoln on Democracy* by joining the contributors in nominating the speeches and letters presented in this book. Following is a list of these scholars:

DWIGHT G. ANDERSON, Professor of Political Science, San Diego State University; author of *Abraham Lincoln: The Quest for Immortality* (1982).

JEAN H. BAKER, Elizabeth Todd Professor of History, Goucher College; author of *Mary Todd Lincoln: A Biography* (1987).

HERMAN BELZ, Professor of History, University of Maryland; author of *Emancipation and Equal Rights: Politics and Constitutionalism in the Civil War* (1978).

WALDO W. BRADEN, Boyd Professor of Speech Communications Emeritus, Louisiana State University; author of *Abraham Lincoln: Public Speaker* (1988).

ROBERT V. BRUCE, Professor of History Emeritus, Boston University (Pulitzer Prize winner); author of *Lincoln and the Tools of War* (1956).

LARRY E. BURGESS, Director, A. K. Smiley Public Library, Redlands, California.

STEVEN L. CARSON, Editor, *Manuscript Society News,* and former President, Lincoln Group of the District of Columbia.

LAWANDA COX, Professor of History Emeritus, Hunter College, City University of New York; author of *Lincoln and Black Freedom: A Study in Presidential Leadership* (1981).

CULLOM DAVIS, Professor of History, Sangamon State University; Director and Senior Editor of the Lincoln Legals Project.

DAVID HERBERT DONALD, Charles Warren Professor of American History and Professor of American Civilization, Harvard University (Pulitzer Prize winner); author of *Lincoln Reconsidered* (1956).

ROBERT F. ENGS, Associate Professor of History, University of Pennsylvania; author of *Freedom's First Generation: Black Hampton, Virginia, 1861–1890* (1979).

DON E. FEHRENBACHER, William Robertson Coe Professor of History and American Studies Emeritus, Stanford University (Pulitzer Prize winner); editor of *Abraham Lincoln: A Documentary Portrait* (1964).

GEORGE M. FREDRICKSON, Edgar E. Robinson Professor of United States History, Stanford University; author of *The Inner Civil War: Northern Intellectuals and the Crisis of the Union* (1965).

ARNOLD GATES, former Literary Editor, *The Lincoln Herald.*

WILLIAM HANCHETT, Professor of History Emeritus, San Diego State University; author of *The Lincoln Murder Conspiracies* (1983).

WILLIAM F. HANNA, Vice President, Lincoln Group of Boston, author of *Abraham Among the Yankees: Abraham Lincoln's 1848 Visit to Massachusetts* (1983).

DAVID HEIN, Chairman, Department of Religion, Hood College; coauthor of *Essays on Lincoln's Faith and Politics* (1983).

JAMES T. HICKEY, former Curator, Henry Horner Lincoln Collection, Illinois State Historical Library, Springfield.

HAROLD M. HYMAN, William P. Hobby Professor of History and Director, Center for the History of Leadership Institutions, Rice University; author of *Era of the Oath: Northern Loyalty Tests During the Civil War and Reconstruction* (1954).

PAUL KALLINA, former editor, *The Lincolnian,* journal of the Lincoln Group of the District of Columbia.

PHILIP B. KUNHARDT, JR., author of *A New Birth of Freedom: Lincoln at Gettysburg* (1983).

MARY ELLEN MCELLIGOTT, Editor, *Illinois Historical Journal.*

WILLIAM S. MCFEELY, Richard B. Russell Professor of American History, University of Georgia (Pulitzer Prize winner); author of *Grant: A Biography* (1981).

ABRAHAM LINCOLN MAROVITZ, U.S. District Judge, Chicago; author of many monographs on Lincoln.

HERBERT MITGANG, *New York Times* correspondent and author of the play *Mr. Lincoln* (1982).

RALPH G. NEWMAN, bibliophile, author of *Abraham Lincoln: An Autobiographical Narrative* (1974).

STEPHEN B. OATES, Paul Murray Kendall Professor of Biography, University of Massachusetts at Amherst; author of *With Malice Toward None: The Life of Abraham Lincoln* (1977).

LLOYD OSTENDORF, Historian, Dayton, Ohio; author, *Lincoln in Photographs: An Album of Every Known Pose* (1963).

GEORGE PAINTER, Historian, Lincoln Home National Historic Site, Springfield, Illinois.

GARY PLANCK, Literary Editor, *The Lincoln Herald.*

W. EMERSON RECK, author of *A. Lincoln: His Last 24 Hours* (1987).

THOMAS F. SCHWARTZ, Curator, Henry Horner Lincoln Collection, Illinois State Historical Library, Springfield.

JOHN Y. SIMON, Vice President and Executive Director, The Ulysses S. Grant Association; editor-in-chief, *Papers of Ulysses S. Grant* (1963–).

RICHARD SLOAN, President, Lincoln Group of New York.

JOSEPH E. SUPPIGER, Editor, *The Lincoln Herald.*

WAYNE C. TEMPLE, Chief Deputy Director, Illinois State Archives; author of *By Square and Compass: The Building of Lincoln's Home and Its Saga* (1984).

THOMAS REED TURNER, Professor of History and Chairman of the Department of History, Bridgewater State College; author of *Beware the People Weeping: Public Opinion and the Assassination of Abraham Lincoln* (1987).

DANIEL E. WEINBERG, proprietor, the Abraham Lincoln Book Shop, Chicago.

MAJOR L. WILSON, Professor of History at Memphis State University; author of *Space, Time, and Freedom: The Quest for Nationality and the Irrepressible Conflict, 1815–1861* (1974).

P. M. ZALL, Consultant to the Huntington Library, San Marino, California; author of *Abe Lincoln Laughing* (1984).

Index

Taylor, Zachary, 40, 55, 373, 374; A.L.
eulogy of, 46–48
Temperance movement, 28–30
10 percent plan, 305
Tennessee, 293, 322, 385; new
government, 1864, 305
Tennyson, Alfred, Lord, 358, 375, 377
territorial expansion, 148–50
territories: Douglas on slavery in, 102;
extension of slavery into, 57, 60, 61,
84–85, 106, 145, 146, 172; and
Federal authority to exclude slavery,
101, 164–65; as homes for free
whites, 59, 85; and popular
sovereignty doctrine, 98, 158, 167;
slavery excluded from, 66, 93, 103,
109–10, 127, 141, 147, 189;
Southerners and, 172. *See also* Dred
Scott decision; Kansas-Nebraska Act;
Missouri Compromise (1820)
Texas, 30–31, 34–35, 221, 287, 366, 371
Thackeray, William Makepeace, 379, 386
Thomas, Benjamin P., 352
Thomas, General George H., 387
Thompson, George, 319–20
Thoreau, Henry David, 377, 385
trade unions, 361. *See also* labor
transportation policy, 5, 141
Trefousse, Hans L.: Lincoln and
Democracy, 1863–65, essay, 301–6
Trent affair, 239, 360, 383
Trenton, New Jersey, State Senate,
speeches in, 196
Trumbull, Lyman, 107; letter to, 180
Turner, Nat, 168, 364
Tyler, John, 369, 383
tyranny, 128, 155, 193; charged against
A.L., 260, 297, and liberty, 321

Union: A.L. and, 188, 191–92, 306; and
Constitutional Union Party, 147; and
denial of Constitutional rights, 205–6;
dissolution of, 60, 80–82, 86, 106,
289; and execution of laws during
war, 204–5; Northern loyalty to, 81;
perpetuity confirmed by history,
203–4; question of whether seceded
states are in or out of, 309, 346–47;
and Reconstruction plans, 305; saving
of, xxxvii, 186, 195–97, 212, 245, 249;
saving of, A.L. reply to Greeley,
253–54; saving of, and 1864
presidential election, 337; saving of,
and A.L. commitment, 60, 74; saving
of, and Civil War, 326; saving of, and
emancipation, 319–20; saving of, and
God's Will, 255; saving of, and
Negro enlistments, 317–18; saving of,
and slavery, 57, 74–75, 253–54;

saving of, by resisting secession,
184–87; Southern friends of, 226; and
state rights, 220–21; threatened, 170,
172, 203; victory and democracy,
187; war aims (1861), 184
Union military forces, 311; A.L. speech to
Ohio Regiment (1864), 328; and
"Fighting Joe" Hooker, 275; military
arrests and desertions, 279–81; and
Negro soldiers, 288–92, 309–10,
316–18, 322, 325–26; and resignation
of Southern officers, 223; seizure of
churches and ousting of pastors, 312;
soldiers and sailors remaining with
North, 223–24; soldiers and seamen,
332, 334, 342, 343–44, 345, 387;
victories in Eastern and Western
theaters, 242–43; victory at Antietam,
255–56; victory at Gettysburg, 242,
283. *See also* Civil War; names of
battle sites; names of generals
United States: history between 1803–1853,
3–7; political freedom in, 4. *See also*
American people; American
Republic; Federal government; Union
Usher, John P., 385

Vallandigham, Clement L., 242, 277
Van Alen, General James H., letter to,
349
Van Buren, Martin, 11, 324, 366
Venezuela, xl
Vicksburg, Mississippi: fall of (July 1863),
243; lynchings, 17–18
Vicksburg, Mississippi, Battle of (1863),
283, 386
Victoria, Queen of England, xxxix, 360,
367, 369, 376
Victory Serenade, White House, A.L.
response to, 283–84
Vidal, Gore, 15
Virginia, 293, 385; ceding of territories
and slavery, 66; and John Brown's
raid, 142; and Reconstruction, 345;
reconvening of state legislature after
fall of Richmond, 305; Union defeats
in, 1862, 240
Von Schneidau, Johan Carl Frederic
Polycarpus, 53
voting rights. *See* Negro suffrage

Wade, Benjamin F., 303
Wade-Davis Bill and Manifesto, 303, 387
Wadsworth, General James S., 304; letter
to, 313
Wait, William S., letter to, 24–25
Walesa, Lech, xxvii–xxviii
Walker, Lewis E., 235
War of 1812, 359